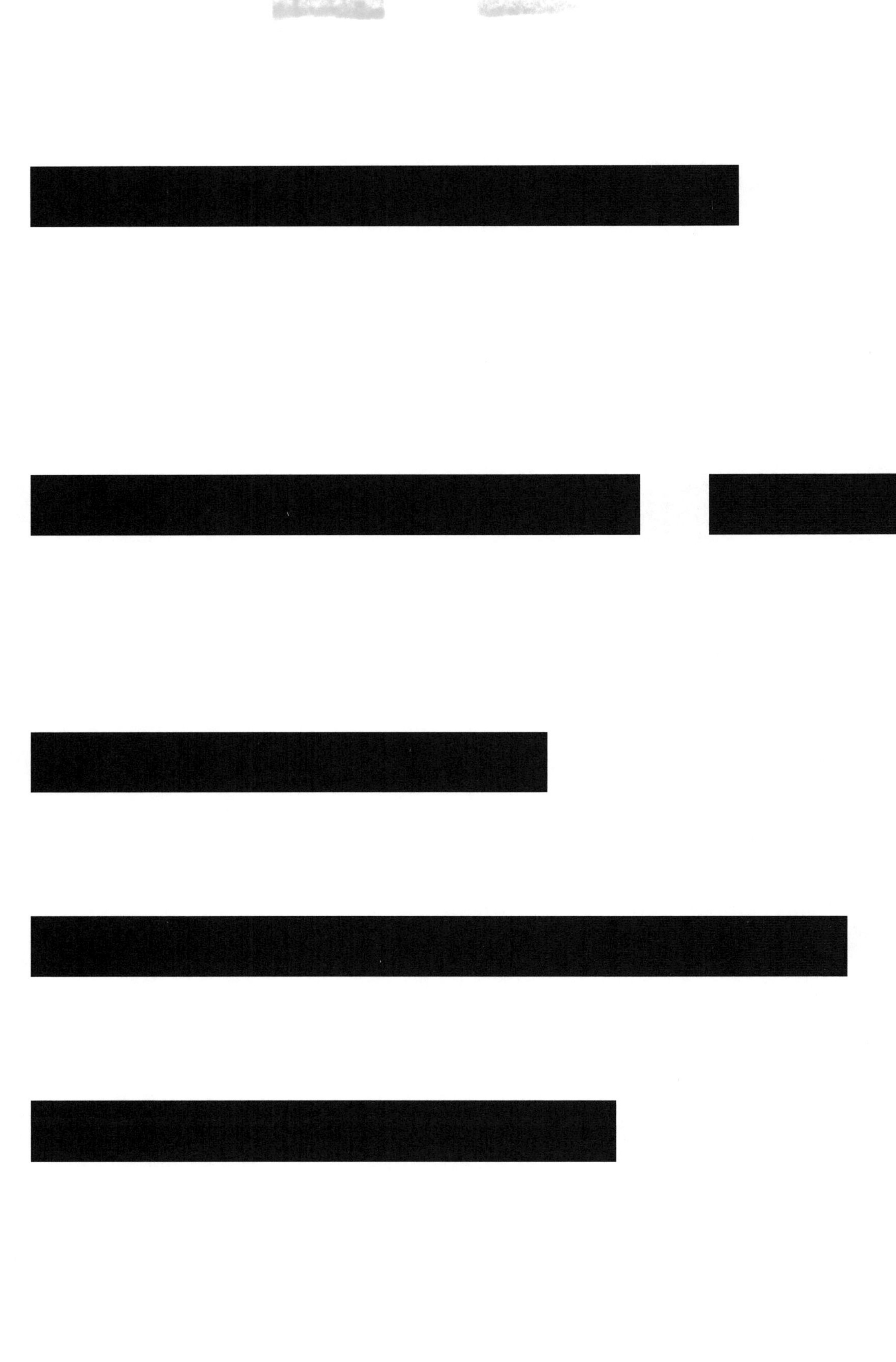

SURVEYING THE AVANT-GARDE

QUESTIONS ON MODERNISM, ART, AND THE AMERICAS IN TRANSATLANTIC MAGAZINES

LORI COLE

The Pennsylvania State University Press
University Park, Pennsylvania

Portions of this book draw from previously published essays by the author, and are adapted with permission from the original publishers.

"'Do You Believe in Angels?' and Other Inquiries: Eugene Jolas' Questionnaires for *transition* Magazine." *Cabinet*, no. 53 (Spring 2014): 13–20.

"'How Do You Imagine Latin America?' Questioning Latin American Art and Identity in Print." *Global South* 7, no. 2 (2014): 110–33.

"Madrid: Questioning the Avant-Garde." In *The Oxford Critical and Cultural History of Modernist Magazines*, vol. 3, *Europe 1880–1940*, edited by Peter Brooker, Sascha Bru, Andrew Thacker, and Christian Weikop, 369–92. Oxford: Oxford University Press, 2013. By permission of Oxford University Press.

"Reproducing the Avant-Garde: The Art of Modernist Magazines." In *The Aesthetics of Matter: Modernism, the Avant-Garde and Material Exchange*, edited by Sarah Posman, Anne Reverseau, David Ayers, Sascha Bru, and Benedikt Hjartarson, 183–94. European Avant-Garde and Modernism Studies Series 3. Berlin: Walter de Gruyter, 2013.

"*¿Qué es la vanguardia?* Ultraism Between Madrid and Buenos Aires." In *Modernidad y vanguardia: Rutas de intercambio entre España y Latinoamérica (1920–1970)*, edited by Paula Barreiro López and Fabiola Martínez Rodríguez, 127–37. Madrid: Museo Nacional Centro de Arte Reina Sofía, 2015.

"What Is the Avant-Garde? The Questionnaire as Historiography." *Journal of Art Historiography* (December 2011).

Library of Congress Cataloging-in-Publication Data

Names: Cole, Lori, 1980– author.

Title: Surveying the avant-garde : questions on modernism, art, and the Americas in transatlantic magazines / Lori Cole.

Other titles: Refiguring modernism.

Description: University Park, Pennsylvania : The Pennsylvania State University Press, [2018] | Series: Refiguring modernism | Includes bibliographical references and index.

Summary: "Examines art and literature of the Americas through the lens of the questionnaire, a genre as central as the manifesto to the history of the avant-garde. Demonstrates how modernism and the avant-garde were debated at the very moment of their development and consolidation"—Provided by publisher.

Identifiers: LCCN 2017060109 | ISBN 978027108092-5 (pbk : alk. paper)

Subjects: LCSH: Avant-garde (Aesthetics)—America—History—20th century. | Questionnaires—America—History—20th century.| Arts—America—Periodicals—History—20th century. | Nationalism and the Arts—America—History—20th century. | Modernism (Aesthetics)—America—History—20th century.

Classification: LCC BH301.A94 C65 2018 | DDC 700/.411—dc23

LC record available at https://lccn.loc.gov/2017060109

Published by
The Pennsylvania State University Press, University Park, PA 16802-1003

The Pennsylvania State University Press is a member of the Association of University Presses.

It is the policy of The Pennsylvania State University Press to use acid-free paper. Publications on uncoated stock satisfy the minimum requirements of American National Standard for Information Sciences—Permanence of Paper for Printed Library Material, ANSI Z39.48–1992.

Designed by
Jesse Kidwell

Typeset in
Bau and Arnhem

CONTENTS

1 "¿Qué es la vanguardia?," *La Gaceta Literaria* (Madrid), no. 83 (June 1, 1930): 1. Printed with the permission of Miguel de Torre Borges. Photo reproduced from the original held by the Biblioteca Nacional de España.
p. 6

2 Immanuel Kant, "Beantwortung der Frage: Was ist Aufklärung?," *Berlinische Monatsschrift* (December 1784): 481. Photo: Beinecke Rare Book and Manuscript Library, Yale University.
p. 25

3 Francis Picabia, "Que fais tu 291?," *Camera Work* (New York), no. 47 (July 1914): 72. © 2017 Artists Rights Society (ARS), New York / ADAGP, Paris. Photo: Marquand Library of Art and Archaeology, Princeton University.
p. 38

4 "¿Existe una literatura proletaria?," *Amauta* (Lima), no. 18 (October 1928): 1. © Archivo José Carlos Mariátegui / web: archivo.mariategui.org. Photo reproduced from the original held by the Department of Special Collections of the Hesburgh Libraries of the University of Notre Dame.
p. 40

5 Eduardo Abela, *Fiesta en el Batey*, 1927, oil on canvas, mounted on wood, 23 ¾ × 17 ½ in. Collection Ramón and Nercys Cernuda.
p. 59

6 "Exposición de arte nuevo," *Revista de Avance* (Havana) 1, no. 5 (May 15, 1927). Photo reproduced from the original held by the Biblioteca Nacional de España.
p. 61

ACKNOWLEDGMENTS

This book began in the library of the Reina Sofía in the summer of 2009, where Jordana Mendelson, my advisor, advocate, and friend, had directed me to read the questionnaire "What Is the Avant-Garde?," issued by *La Gaceta Literaria* in 1930. One of the respondents to the questionnaire cited a 1907 survey from *El Nuevo Mercurio* asking "What Is Modernism?" This discovery alerted me to the genealogy of the questionnaire and its widespread use, a project that culminated in this book, but whose research is certainly not exhausted.

It has been many years since that fortuitous encounter, and I want to thank everyone whose support, advice, and guidance have enabled me to pursue this project. In addition to Jordana, I would like to extend my thanks to Gabriela Basterra, who inspired me with her intellectual example and unwavering emotional support. I am grateful to Peter Nicholls for his frank and generous readings of the manuscript, and to Ara Merjian, for his early comments on the project and his ongoing friendship. I also want to acknowledge the kindness and input I received from Sylvia Molloy, Edward Sullivan, Ana Dopico, Jacques Lezra, and Emily Apter, as well as from the rest of the faculty and staff in the Comparative Literature Department at New York University, who had faith in a truly interdisciplinary endeavor. My friends from graduate school helped me as much as the faculty did, and I thank in particular Patricia López, Magalí Armillas-Tiseyra, Sage Anderson, Mar Gómez Glez, Daniel Hoffman-Schwartz, Pu Wang, Sonia Werner, Anna Krakus, and Ceci Moss for their spirit of collaboration and for their good company.

Throughout graduate school I had the opportunity to meet colleagues who became early advocates of this book and good friends. I am grateful to have participated in the Modernist Magazines NEH seminar in Tulsa, which provided me with a scholarly community and a framework for this project. I would like to thank Sean Latham, Daniel Worden, Michael Rozendal, Jeff Drouin, Eurie Dahn, and Carey Snyder for their feedback and encouragement, and to acknowledge the support of the late Bob Scholes. I want to express my particular gratitude to Gayle Rogers, who has remained available to read drafts and offer advice over the many years it took to complete this book.

As I worked on this project, the support of a Joan Tisch Teaching Fellowship at the Whitney Museum of American Art brought the questions of national identity that I explore here into focus. I am indebted to the Education Department at the Whitney, and I thank Kathryn Potts for her continued support. I am also grateful to Emily Liebert, Jennie Goldstein, Paula Burleigh, and Megan Heuer, for generously exchanging ideas with me and for their friendship. My project also benefited from the support of a Junior Research Fellowship at the Center for the History of Collecting at the Frick Collection.

My colleagues and students at Brandeis University welcomed me at an important juncture in my research, and I am especially grateful to Gannit Ankori, for her faith in me, to Jonathan Unglaub, for his support, to Lucy Kim, for her friendship, as well as to Chris Bedford, Peter Kalb, and Nancy Scott. I am fortunate to have been the recipient of the Charlotte Zysman Postdoctoral Fellowship, which allowed me to organize a symposium, whose participants expanded and enriched my understanding of magazines. In particular, I am grateful to Ann Ardis, for her generosity, and to Gwen Allen, whose pioneering work inspired me and whose advice has been invaluable. In Boston I was also lucky to meet Ruth Erickson and Tessa Paneth-Pollak, whom I thank for the community they gave me and for their friendship. Sina Najafi supported my idiosyncratic interest in questionnaires and offered a public platform for my research, for which I am very grateful, and I would like to thank Kim Conaty and the rest of the participants in the *Cabinet* series on the Magazine as a Medium for gamely discussing questionnaires, interviews, and letters to the editor with me.

I enjoyed conducting research for this project at the National Library of Spain, the Museo Reina Sofía Library, the McFarlin Library and Special Collections at the University of Tulsa, the Beinecke Rare Book and Manuscript Library at Yale University, the Fales Library at New York University, the New York Public Library, and The Museum of Modern Art Library, and I am grateful for the help I received at each institution. Early selections of my research were published in a variety of journals and edited collections, and I want to thank all of the editors and readers for their feedback, and in particular Peter Brooker, for his early support and encouragement. I also thank the libraries, estates, and heirs, in particular Betsy Jolas and Miguel de Torre Borges, who generously granted me permission to publish the images that I include here.

Throughout the course of my research I presented selections of this book at conferences hosted by the College Art Association, the Modern Language Association, the Modernist Studies Association, the Latin American Studies

Association, the American Comparative Literature Association, the Tate Modern, the Art Institute of Chicago, the CUNY Graduate Center, the Institute for Comparative Literature and Society at Columbia University, the Museo Nacional Centro de Arte Reina Sofía, the Global Modernisms Symposium at Ithaca College, and the Mandel Center for the Humanities at Brandeis University. I thank all of the organizers of these conferences, my co-panelists, and those who attended, for their interest and feedback.

My colleagues at New York University have encouraged my interdisciplinary interests and enabled me to complete this project. I would especially like to thank Sukhdev Sandhu, Nicole Pandolfo, Robin Nagle, Emma Heany, Joanna Epstein, Justin Jackson, and Patrick Vitale for being such supportive colleagues. I am grateful to the NYU Center for the Humanities for funding the Global Modernisms Group, and I want to thank Kelly Sullivan for forming this community with me, and to thank everyone who participated in our events, in particular Effie Rentzou, to whom I am grateful for championing my work. I am fortunate to have collaborated with colleagues at other institutions who have also facilitated and advanced my research, especially Bibi Obler, Chris Holmes, Jen Spitzer, Chris Bush, Tim Wientzen, Dushko Petrovich, Tatiana Flores, María del Pilar Blanco, Michele Greet, Fabiola Martínez, Vanessa Fernández, Niko Vicario, and Lily Sheehan.

I want to express my gratitude to Paul Saint-Amour, who believed in this manuscript and shepherded it through the writing and editing process at a critical moment. I am also indebted to Jonathan Eburne, the Refiguring Modernism series editor at Penn State University Press, whose remarks and insights helped buoy the project and shape my revisions. Harper Montgomery was the manuscript's first reader, and I am grateful for her invaluable feedback. I also want to thank the anonymous readers whose reports helped sharpen and clarify the aims of the book and guide my revisions. Ellie Goodman at Penn State University Press has been a thoughtful editor and great sounding board, and I thank her for her early and generous support of the project, as well as Hannah Hebert for her assistance with its completion. I also want to acknowledge the work of Ramón Urzúa-Navas, Silvia Benedetti, Tara Clayton, and Sage Anderson, whose input on translation, research, and editing has greatly improved this book.

Most importantly, I want to express my immense gratitude to my family and friends, whose love and support have sustained me and enabled my work. First, I want to thank my parents, Linda and Jeffrey Cole, for their unconditional love and for their faith in my choices. Debra Cole I thank for her imagination and spirit, through which she transmitted to me her passion for literature, and I thank Gavin Cole Beier, for his exuberant affection. I am grateful to Steven Cole, whose sensitivity, wisdom, and good humor ground me. I extend my gratitude to Roger and Emily Grimes for enthusiastically welcoming me into their family, and to Sophie Grimes, for her friendship. To my dearest friends who I consider my family, I am indebted to you, and thank in particular John Arceci, Brooks

King, Stephanie Drew, YiPei Chen-Josephson, Bina Venkataraman, Juliette Berg, Ian McAlpin, Jeremy Robbins, Aparna Wilder, Sandy Aylesworth, Jeanne Gerrity, Sarah Bickens, Matt Swagler, Kelly Berry, Lily Sutton, Ruth Graham, Rebecca Lederer, Heather Greenberg, Talia Abbott Chalew, and the entire Park Slope Family. Our lives together preceded and will outlast this research, but helped me realize it.

Finally, I dedicate this book to Tennessee Grimes, and thank him for his love and patience, for his sense of humor and sense of adventure, for his commitment to protecting my time, and for his belief in the value of my work. This effort is for him, and for our daughter, Iowa Rose Cole, whose infectious joy and curiosity propel me forward. May she never cease to question.

INTRODUCTION: QUESTIONING THE AVANT-GARDE

In 1928, in the Mexican journal *Contemporáneos*, one of its editors, Jaime Torres Bodet, wearily remarked on the abundance of questionnaires being issued in magazines internationally. He blamed this outpouring on a North American propensity for metrics, asking, "Who doesn't know that one of the most lucrative sports in North America is good statistics?"[1] Such accusations against the United States were familiar to Torres Bodet's Mexican readers. The questionnaire he skewered was "A Complete Handbook of Opinion," published by *Vanity Fair* a few months earlier, which posed the question "Are you an ancient or a modern?" to Ezra Pound, Aldous Huxley, and Sherwood Anderson, among others, and asked them to rate a list of cultural figures on a scale of zero to twenty-five. Their answers, of course, exceeded the rigid form; Pound's response includes the remark "To ask me if I am an ancient or modern appears to me almost as satisfactory as asking whether New York is west of Rapallo, or Rapallo east of New York. If I must classify myself I am perfectly willing to classify myself along with the conflict: immortal."[2] Both Torres Bodet and Pound perpetuate the questionnaire as a forum for debate while critiquing it as inadequate, demonstrating the genre's ubiquity and its resilience.

Although Torres Bodet condemns the questionnaire as emblematic of North America's compulsion to quantify culture, he nevertheless gives great weight to the survey he derides, translating it into Spanish and almost lovingly recounting its results to his Mexican readers. Even more significantly, he inserts the *Vanity Fair* questionnaire into a genealogy of the genre, identifying as its precursor an earlier poll titled "French literature as judged by current British authors." In that poll, issued by the French publication *Le Gaulois du Dimanche* in 1899, the British authors in question denounce Voltaire as being "too cosmopolitan."[3] Torres Bodet translates and transports these international debates to his

Mexican audience while detailing the physical experience of reading *Vanity Fair*, thereby demonstrating how one might be interpellated by the question and its answers. He observes,

> Upon closing the magazine—in whose pages a world of forms and dates remains intact—we compare the picture of our old preferences with the current frameless landscape in which we recognize ourselves. Seen like that, in that double mirror in which our culture looks at itself in the simultaneous reflection of yesterday and today, how we gain in volume, in a profound third dimension, that which we lose in feigned, superficial unity! One feels almost a desire to add another questionnaire to the interminable list: that of the ten famous writers that we read in 1915, whom we deemed irreplaceable, and whom, nevertheless, we ended up replacing.[4]

In reflecting on the questionnaire, Torres Bodet "recognizes himself," and uses it as an opportunity to compare his former and current preferences. Moreover, Torres Bodet writes that the experience evokes in him a "desire to add another questionnaire to the interminable list," narrating a response that other readers might have, which perhaps accounts for the era's excess of surveys. Thus, what began as a critique of a supposedly North American genre concludes as a capitulation to the form, demonstrating the questionnaire's tractability and its international reach in the 1920s, as well as its drive toward self-replication.

This example—a critic recounting a North American questionnaire in a Mexican magazine—is one of many that points to the fluidity with which such questions traveled across borders through the magazines that published them, reaching and inspiring new audiences and aiding modernism's global expansion. It also suggests how each questionnaire was situated within a vast genealogy of other questions for its writers and readers, indicating that audiences at the time were well acquainted with the form. In the same year, 1928, the editors of the Madrid-based *La Gaceta Literaria* note its pervasiveness: "The genre of the questionnaire spreads like a bad cold. Everyone feels entitled to the expectation of wit, to the cough of opinions. An essentially democratic form (a universal suffrage of newspapers and magazines), it is sometimes even amusing."[5] One French writer referred to the phenomenon as "enquêteomanie," or "questionnaire-mania."[6] An analysis of this mode of inquiry, which circulated and culled contributors internationally through its widespread reproduction in print culture, allows us to reexamine the map of modernism as it unfolded.

Questionnaires like the one considered by Torres Bodet were issued with great frequency throughout the 1920s and 1930s. In this book I analyze the genre and the ways in which it was used to define the relationship between art and national identity within the triangulation of the United States, Latin America, and Europe in the early twentieth century. Popularized in late nineteenth-century France, questionnaires were adapted by editors across the globe to suit the specific needs of their movements and magazines, signaling the genre's integration within a set of avant-garde practices. The questions issued were broad and open-ended, at once new and sometimes variations on those that preceded them. I examine a selection of such questions, including "What should American art be?," "How do you imagine Latin America?," and "Why do Americans live in Europe?" Structurally porous exercises, these surveys yielded a compendium of written responses from artists and writers, which function as privileged points of entry into debates over aesthetic and national identities at a time when ideas like "modernism" and the "avant-garde" were still in formation. Despite the genre's origins, the range of questions issued in the 1920s and 1930s point to the proliferation of literary and artistic communities beyond France, spurring anxiety that in turn fueled questionnaires such as that of *L'Intransigeant* in 1928 asking if Paris was really the "world center for art."[7]

If we look at how "modernism," "the avant-garde," and later "the contemporary" were each debated at the moment of their respective development and consolidation, particularly in relation to national concerns, we can better understand the complexity of these fields of study today. For example, in 1930 *La Gaceta Literaria* issued a questionnaire asking, "What is the avant-garde? Does the avant-garde exist? Has it ever existed? How have you understood it?"[8] (fig. 1). The reflexivity of this line of questioning suggests that the avant-garde—in this context, specifically the Spanish avant-garde—was anxious to define itself and to ensure its legacy. One respondent identifies a previous poll as the model for this questionnaire, a survey issued by *El Nuevo Mercurio* in 1907 that asked, "What is modernism? Do you think a new literary movement or new intellectual or artistic tendency exists?" This citation of an earlier survey, inserted into a questionnaire response, indicated to me that these artists and critics were self-consciously participating in a genre whose history they knew, which they were deliberately reinhabiting and perpetuating.[9] Following the lead of this respondent, I began chronicling all of the questionnaires that I encountered, many of which I compiled into an index that appears at the end of this volume. However, my findings quickly surpassed my ability to catalogue them, demonstrating the frequency and consistency with which questionnaires were issued over the course of the twentieth century, and continue to be issued today. The purpose of this book is to establish an account of the largely overlooked but persistently significant genre of the questionnaire, and to demonstrate how these questions of art and national identity informed artists' and writers' understanding of their work and their place in the world.

It is precisely the slipperiness of designations like "modernism" and "the avant-garde"—along with their accompanying cultural nuances—that necessitated the innumerable questions and answers published by magazine editors, who sought to tease out and solidify the meaning of these terms according

La Gaceta Literaria

ibérica:americana:internacional

LETRAS ARTE CIENCIA

periódico quincenal (1 y 15 de cada mes)

dirección:

E. GIMÉNEZ CABALLERO PEDRO SAINZ RODRÍGUEZ

Año IV Madrid, 1 de Junio de 1930 Núm. 83

Redacción y Administración:
PRINCIPE DE VERGARA, 42 y 44
Donde debe dirigirse toda la correspondencia
Se reciben suscripciones
en las principales librerías

30 CENTIMOS

SUSCRIPCION ANUAL....
ANUNCIOS DE TARIFA....

España y Países del Convenio postal Hispano americano.... 7,50 ptas.
Extranjero..... 10,00 —
15 cts. la línea del cuerpo 8
Pólizas de suscripción
Descuentos: trimestre, 20 %;
semestre, 15 %;
anual, 20 %

UNA ENCUESTA SENSACIONAL

¿QUÉ ES LA VANGUARDIA?

RESPUESTAS DE GREGORIO MARAÑÓN, GIMÉNEZ CABALLERO, JOSÉ BERGAMÍN, JOSÉ MORENO VILLA, ROSA CHACEL, VALENTÍN ANDRÉS ALVAREZ, JAIME IBARRA.

Palabras del doctor Marañón en el Cineclub acerca de la vanguardia y el cinematógrafo

Con mucho gusto quiero presentar los "films" biológicos de Painlevé en esta Sociedad, que nunca ha merecido como hoy llamarse de vanguardia, puesto que se pone al servicio de la Biología, esto es, del conocimiento de la vida, que es la expresión más genuina de la modernidad.

Yo confieso mi poca simpatía por la palabra *vanguardia*. Como todo lo que quiere decir mucho, se expone a encubrir el sentimiento antípoda. El hombre es todavía un animal lo suficientemente débil para que sólo en raras oca-

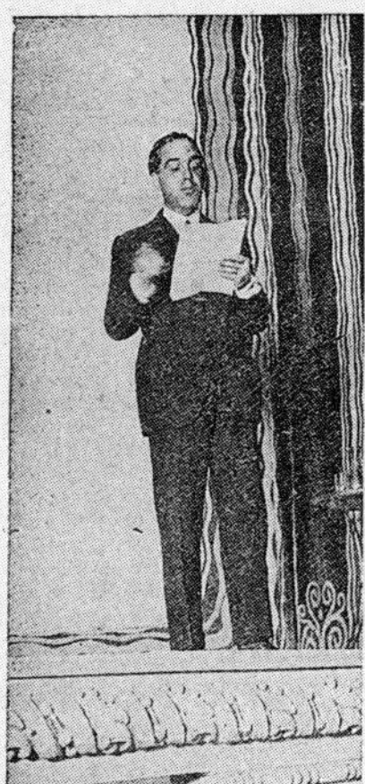

Marañón en el Cineclub.   (Foto C. I. A P.)

siones le sea permitido ser sincero; y tiene que ingeniarse para revestir de apariencias contrarias todo lo que es y no debía ser; todo lo que quisiera ser sin haberlo conseguido.

La mayoría de los actos sociales no son más que la expresión de este juego, tan arraigado en el alma humana, que se cumple con la naturalidad de los instintos; como que en realidad es una forma del instinto; y del instinto más rudimentario: el de la conservación. Fijémonos sólo en dos formas esenciales de la vida del hombre: el traje y el lenguaje.

El traje, que primitivamente obedecía a la necesidad de defenderse de las agresiones del

(Continúa en la página 3.)

Justificación

Hace tiempo que flotaba esta encuesta en el ambiente literario español. Hace tiempo, porque el concepto "vanguardia", en lugar de apagarse tras las primeras manifestaciones de un arte en las bocas ajenas, que, muchas veces—la mayoría—, lo piensan y lo dicen sin sentido de la adecuación.

Hoy, a todo lo que extraña, lo que choca, se le ha dado en llamar, por sistema y sin conocimiento, "vanguardia". Pero también no a lo que extraña o choca, sino a lo que no consigue una realidad artística y, en ocasiones, política.

Hubo un momento—no creo que hoy se haya prolongado, ni siquiera que su nombre subsista, aunque sí su recuerdo—, un momento todavía no lejano en nuestra vida literaria, en que la determinada palabra y su contenido abrigaron a un grupo de valores nacientes que traían nuevo brío y, sobre todo, sinceridad admirable en el deseo—ahora, logrado—de combatir y mudar las viejas fórmulas y los modos decadentes.

¿A unos—de los componentes de ese grupo—se les colocaba con oficiosidad indebida la palabra? ¿Otros la merecían? ¿Estaban orgullosos de ella?

El problema de entonces era distinto del de hoy. Sin que la conjunción de aquellos escritores pudiera llevarse a cabo por las relaciones de estilo o de dirección de unos y otros. Si se realizaba por el común afán renovador. Desde aquel momento ese sentido de la renovación ha venido sorprendiendo, cuando no confundiendo, a un público que sólo sabe en tales casos y fenómenos sorprenderse o confundirse. A un público que todo lo que no entiende (conste que no me refiero a los hombres de pensamiento a quienes, alejados, no interesa la cuestión, o después de haber meditado sobre ello combaten la tendencia o tendencias) lo califica de "vanguardismo", y que no suelta la palabra sólo para desvirtuar, día tras día, su contenido.

¿Existe la "vanguardia"? ¿Ha existido? No soy yo quien debe contestar. Son aquellos va-

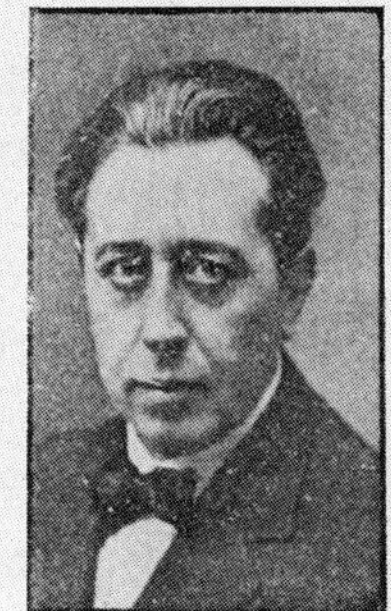

Miguel Pérez Ferrero

lores iniciales—ya estos valores reales—los que despejarán las incógnitas.

Yo, únicamente, venía estimando que era necesario establecer la encuesta. Fijar los conceptos

MIGUEL PEREZ FERRERO

CUATRO PREGUNTAS FIJAS

1.ª ¿EXISTE O HA EXISTIDO LA VANGUARDIA?
2.ª ¿CÓMO LA HA ENTENDIDO USTED?
3.ª A SU JUICIO, ¿QUÉ POSTULADOS LITERARIOS PRESENTA O PRESENTÓ EN SU DIA?
4.ª ¿CÓMO LA JUZGÓ Y LA JUZGA AHORA DESDE SU PUNTO DE VISTA POLITICO?

Las respuestas ocuparán varios números sucesivos.

E. GIMÉNEZ CABALLERO

1.—En el mundo literario, del arte y de las letras, ha existido. Ya no existe. El momento actual es la llegada de todas las retaguardias. De los reservistas. En España sólo queda el sector específicamente político, donde la vanguardia faudcia, juventud, subversión) puede aún actuar.

2, 3 y 4.—Lo que ahora pudiera decir a estas preguntas ya lo expliqué en largo ensayo publicado por *Cosmópolis* (septiembre 1929). A lo que añado: La *vanguardia* fué un término bélico, nacido de la gran guerra. Primero adoptó un aire subvertedor, irracional, libertario. (Dadaísmo, futurismo, maximalismo, cubismo... Todos los ismos). Después un aire constructor, ordenador. (Tomismo, clasicismo, bolchevismo, fascismo, gongorismo... Todos los demás ismos.)

Hoy: lo literario del primer grupo fecunda el movimiento llamado *superrealista*, príncipe heredero de la vanguardia demoledora.

En política, la vanguardia del grupo segundo (el disciplinador) se injerta en el fenómeno juvenil de "lo universitario", de "lo estudiante". *Misticismo irracional*, por un lado. *Disciplina federada*, por otro. Esos *cabos* son el fin de "la vanguardia" y el principio de un nuevo movimiento de "adelantados".

Todo lo demás, basura. *Reservismo.* Jóvenes españoles: ojo con todos los reservistas del país. ¡Alerta a todas las madureces emplastadas!

JOSÉ BERGAMÍN

1).—La noción de vanguardia supone una estrategia más o menos bélica, de aplicación inadecuada a todo movimiento literario o artístico. Además, por su extensión misma, rechaza, lógicamente, por incomprensivas, las aproximaciones genéricas y diferencias específicas que deberían definirla. Me parece, por tanto, respecto al arte literario y poético, una noción incongruente, impertinente.

EN ESTE NUMERO COLABORAN: Gregorio Marañón, Eugenio d'Ors, Dr. Saul Mézan, Rocasolano, Balcells, De Benito, Torres López, García Valdecasas, Gómez Piñán, Recaséns Siches, José Bergamín, Giménez Caballero, José Moreno Villa, Rosa Chacel, Valentín Andrés Alvarez, Sebastiá Gasch, Pérez Ferrero, Rafael Marquina, Jaime Ibarra, Salazar Chapela, Antonio Porras, Quintiliano Saldaña, Adolphe Falgairolle, P. Mazzei, L. Amado Herrero, Agustín Espinosa, Gil Benumeya, Jorge Rubio González, L. Gómez Mesa, E. Domingo, J. López Nuño y Jenaro Artiles.

GABRIEL MIRO HA MUERTO

El ilustre y malogrado Gabriel Miró, muerto en Madrid el 27 de mayo, a las nueve y media de la noche, y de cuya capital figura literaria nos ocuparemos en nuestro próximo número.

Fig. 1 "¿Qué es la vanguardia?," *La Gaceta Literaria* (Madrid), no. 83 (June 1, 1930): 1.

to the inclination of an editorial platform, a national tradition, or an artistic movement. As early as 1913 the Spanish writer Manuel Machado wrote, "What is modernism? You may ask me. And indeed you yourself are a little at fault that I cannot satisfactorily explain it. A word of purely common origin, formed by the astonishment of the majority before the latest novelties, the word modernism means something different to each person who utters it."[10] Inquiries on modernism and the avant-garde were issued regularly across Europe and the Americas in the 1920s and 1930s, and many featured locally specific inflections of these terms. For instance, an inquiry in *Lampadario* issued in Quito in 1931 included a question on the "importance of nativism in the international avant-garde."[11] This insertion of nativism into a discussion of the avant-garde shifts attention away from a European version of the "international" to highlight regional differences, demonstrating how such magazines' assessments of these concepts can enrich our understanding of the period today.

A productive tension between what is considered modernist versus avant-garde is embodied by the material itself. The reach of the questionnaire—its capacity to solidify the concerns of communities across borders as well as its manifestations in different geographies and languages—suggests that notions of modernism and the avant-garde have always been unstable and under construction. This book addresses the desire of each individual writer, artist, editor, and magazine to participate in the debates of their era, offering a model for understanding the period that is both transnational and local. The numerous questions posed about time, obsolescence, and periodization suggest that the questionnaire can be a tool for exploring the ways in which "modernism," "the avant-garde," and "the contemporary," have been framed and deployed throughout history.

Other questions, such as "What should American art be?," emphasize the contributions of writers and artists from the Americas to a broader modernist network. The geographic axes of interaction that I foreground—between Latin America, North America, Spain, and France—reorient the dominant map of modernism to include Latin America and Spain, which are often studied independently from the other regions. North Americans and Latin Americans were participating in similar canon-building enterprises; they frequently jockeyed for cultural position in relation to each other and to Europeans. For Latin Americans, the assertion of cultural autonomy was part of a broader anticolonial struggle. I do not purport to cover questionnaires issued across the globe, but rather focus on a selection of transatlantic avant-garde questionnaires in order to demonstrate how these print communities were at once independent and deeply interdependent. This push and pull between the local and the global was exemplified by the questionnaire.

The Questionnaire and the Manifesto

The questionnaire is a genre essential to the international avant-garde, enabling local artistic and literary communities to conceptualize themselves relationally. While manifestos have long been considered foundational to the development of the avant-garde, I argue that the questionnaire was as central as the manifesto to forming, announcing, and recounting the history of the avant-garde. The manifesto and the questionnaire both worked to articulate collective identifications in print. However, unlike the manifesto, which carries a singular message boldly oriented toward the future, the questionnaire is often retroactive and contains a plurality of responses, destabilizing the unified voice of the manifesto and producing a polyvalent portrait of a community. A manifesto is also predicated on a contradiction; that is, it proclaims a platform that its author has yet to enact, while a questionnaire allows respondents to operate in a reflective mode to address the anxieties underlying their group formation.

This give and take between the bold claims of the manifesto and the more open-ended, ambivalent form of the questionnaire characterized print culture in the 1920s and 1930s. Consideration of the questionnaire can thus radically alter our approach to analyzing the manifesto. The two forms have a dynamic, interdependent relationship. I argue that the questionnaire, more inclusive and multivocal than the manifesto, offers a critical record of the avant-garde and serves as a key tool for its analysis. By reconsidering the historical avant-garde through the lens of the questionnaire, I hope to defamiliarize the manifesto and to offer the questionnaire as generating an alternative, self-reflexive historiography of the period. Moreover, because of its protracted use, the questionnaire allows us to rethink the period through a genre that provides continuity, rather than rupture, with our own aesthetic debates.

The Magazine

Questionnaires emerged in response to the formal logic of periodicals, which have been increasingly recognized for their importance to the modern period. All now-canonical modernists published in magazines, such as James Joyce, who serialized *Ulysses* in the *Little Review* from 1918 to 1920, and Picasso, whose artwork circulated in magazines internationally (including *transition*, *Camera Work*, and *Revista de Avance*). Many modernist artists and writers, such as Jorge Luis Borges, Ezra Pound, Alfred Stieglitz, and José Carlos Mariátegui, were themselves editors, eager to shape the direction of their own communities. Magazines are also material objects that necessitate visual analysis, and they have been crucial to writing the history of Latin American art in particular. But magazines can be elusive objects of study: they are ephemeral and sometimes difficult to access, and when they are digitized it is hard to grasp their materiality; it is impossible to master the print run of most magazines (the *Crisis*,

for example, began publication in 1910 and is still in print today); it is over-
whelming to try to gauge the significance of every artist and writer included in
a publication, many of whom are lost to history; and cumulatively, a group of
magazines comprises an enormous body of unwieldy scholarship. Magazines
have been published in every language since the origin of print, and one cannot
approach the study of magazines with any claim to totality. Similarly, the
questionnaires that I track proliferate, and while I have compiled a number of
them at the end of the book, the list continues to grow and multiply, resisting
comprehensive assessment.

My aim in this book is to underscore that the magazine as a medium is
constitutive of modernism, and to demonstrate how the questionnaire offers an
entryway into analyzing the magazine and its role in the history of literature and
art. The questionnaire itself is a kind of microcosm of the magazine wherein artists and writers appear side by side, and where their disparate ideas are united,
if only momentarily, by their shared investment in a magazine's platform. Analyzing questionnaires allows us to examine the central concerns of magazines,
and also to make sense of the magazine as a medium; its flexibility, internationalism, and persistence as a form are indeed the reasons why it remains home to
the questionnaire today.

The Americas

The magazine takes on even greater importance as a vehicle for disseminating
art, literature, and criticism in cultures without established institutions to support the arts, like those in the Americas in the early twentieth century. While the
point of departure for this project was the questionnaire, my research led me to
some looming central questions: How was art and literature of the Americas being defined in the early twentieth century? What was its relationship to Europe?
What was its role in the increasingly global culture of the time? Many of the
questionnaires that I encountered echoed these themes, such as "What should
American art be?" and "Why do Americans live in Europe?" As a result, the
Americas became the prevailing context for making sense of the questionnaire
as a genre, and for analyzing how it operated both locally and transnationally. If
I had focused instead on the questionnaire's early history in France, or exclusively on a specific medium (painting, for instance, which always seems to be in
crisis), or on the contemporary moment (which, like the avant-garde, is contested), different concerns would have arisen and structured the book to different
ends. However, due to my primary focus on Spanish- and English-language
questionnaires from the 1920s and 1930s, the Americas emerged as an inescapable, central, and ascendant object of interest and inquiry for artists and writers
across the regions in question.

One of my primary claims is that while North America and Latin America
can by no means be conflated, they were both considered possible heirs to
Europe: the North because of its increasing financial might and the promise of

its immigrant populations, and the South because of a problematic portrayal of its perceived revitalizing purity and future potential. Communities across the region capitalized on these positions to launch, define, and claim new artistic canons. I analyze North American and Latin American print communities relationally, as many of these magazines, editors, and contributors were in conversation with each other and with European artists and writers. Furthermore, many of those involved with these magazines also traveled and lived abroad, and I scrutinize the questions and answers that their shifting cultural status—and their magazines' itinerant locations—generated.

Indeed, one of the primary aims of this project has been to examine the national self-fashioning of writers and artists from across the Americas, as well as from Europe, and to underscore their dialogue in print. While many magazines—and questionnaires—worked to communicate a version of "America" that could compete with the cultural achievements of Europe, they reflected a transatlantic route of travel undertaken by editors and contributors themselves, as figures like the Cuban artist Eduardo Abela, for example, responded to a questionnaire issued by a Latin American magazine from Paris. By drawing attention to these artists' and writers' networks of travel and exchange, I emphasize that any attempt to forge a national canon was inevitably already influenced by multiple transnational points of contact. Yet such regional or national canon formation was clearly the goal of many of the North American and Latin American magazines that I study; this tension between nationalism and internationalism is voiced through the questions that they issue.

The magazines and protagonists that I consider illustrate these transatlantic entanglements. Eugene Jolas, editor of the expatriate magazine *transition*, had his work included in the Paris-based Latin American journal *Imán*, while Carpentier, who helped edit both the Cuban *Revista de Avance* and *Imán*, had writing published in *transition*. These editors also read and poached from each other's publications. Jolas, for instance, wrote to his wife Maria in 1936 from New York to ask her to send him every copy that they had of *Revista de Avance* and the Peruvian magazine *Amauta* in their home in France, because "they contain a good many texts and documents that we need for *transition*."[12] This request came years after the Latin American magazines in question had folded, but the publications remained vital to the transatlantic transmission of texts and ideas. Similar cross-periodical conversations emerged in the review sections of magazines, which sometimes included reviews of questionnaires.

These exchanges suggest an expansive model of the avant-garde, wherein the relations between artists and writers and their sites of production comprise a dynamic network that defies monolithic or nationalistic characterization. Many North Americans and Latin Americans wrote for and founded magazines abroad, even as such transnational axes—relations between Spain and Latin America, France and the Americas, or the United States and Latin America—were precisely the formations that they called into question in their surveys.

Moreover, many Latin American magazines announced their anticolonial resistance to U.S. and Spanish forces, even as they showcased cutting-edge culture from those places in their magazines. Similarly, North American magazines published European art and literature in translation as a paradoxical means of bolstering nationally specific institutions. Such tensions repeatedly surfaced in questionnaires.

Scholars have long recognized that modernism was a global phenomenon; questionnaires from the period offer insights into how such globalism operated. They invited artists and writers to assert their regional or national identities within a convention of the international avant-garde. While formulations like "American" or "Latin American" art and literature—or even "Cuban" or "Argentine" art and literature—might seem like broad strokes, these are the frameworks that artists and writers themselves invoked to situate themselves in the world. In turn, questions of national, temporal, or artistic concern were often repurposed and recirculated. For instance, "What should American art be?" or "What is the avant-garde?" were asked in various ways throughout the 1920s and 1930s, generating a vast archive through which we can track the construction of "American art" and the "avant-garde" as they were in formation.

Art and Literature

The assertion of cultural power in the Americas occurred via multiple platforms, including magazines, art and literature, and rhetoric. First, magazines were cultural institutions that helped form and facilitate the development of literature and art in the Americas, and often had their own publishing imprints and exhibition programs. The magazine *Revista de Avance*, for instance, mounted the first exhibition of avant-garde art in Havana. Second, these communities supported artists and writers who were eager to articulate their version of "American" art in their work. Visual artists often represented specific sites throughout the Americas, as in the case of artists such as Stuart Davis, hailed by *transition* as an "American painter"; Eduardo Abela, who depicted Cuban people and landscapes; and Norah Borges, who featured the architecture of Buenos Aires in her woodcuts. Writers, in their poetry, prose, and criticism, demonstrated the potential of an enriched English, as in the case of Gertrude Stein and writers in the *transition* circle, or a "universal" Latin American literature, as alluded to by Carpentier. Lastly, I am concerned with the discourse surrounding North American and Latin American art and literature, to which the questionnaire provides access. The question of what constituted "American art" gave meaning to these other institutional and cultural pursuits, united as they were in a shared effort to identify, create, and disseminate a new kind of avant-garde.

As a result, this book necessarily gives equal importance to art and literature, two fields of inquiry that are inextricable in the study of the magazine. The magazine is itself a hybrid literary-visual object, containing both art and literature; it is at once a vehicle for texts and a materially designed artifact featuring small-scale exhibitions. Magazines offer us archives or records of works by now-canonical artists and writers as they were presented in their earliest incarnations, as well as insights into changing cultural tastes. Collaborating across media and borders to produce and contribute to magazines, artists and writers also responded to questionnaires about the movements and periods to which they belonged. Questionnaires, like manifestos, touched on ideas central to artistic and literary movements alike. Accordingly, I examine how magazines functioned as sites of display for visual art as well as vehicles for literature and translation, including the translation of questionnaires. Throughout the twentieth and into the twenty-first century, editors persist in issuing questions on the nature of theory, poetry, and visual art, suggesting the genre's continued relevance to both literature and art history today, and its ongoing capacity to encapsulate pressing political and aesthetic debates.

In my first chapter I offer a detailed overview and exploratory genealogy of the genre of the questionnaire, attending to its relationship to the manifesto and to its multiple historical and international uses. I offer a prehistory of the form before examining the prevalence of the *enquête* in late nineteenth-century France, and touching on a number of aspects of the questionnaire: its relationship to the magazine as a commercial and art object, its uneasy interface with social science, its strange assertion of both certainty and doubt, and its playful, political, and artistic iterations. I also reflect on the charged nomenclature present in these questionnaires, addressing how artists and writers of the period viewed themselves and their place in the Americas.

The focus of my second chapter is the Cuban magazine *Revista de Avance*, whose 1928 questionnaire "What Should American Art Be?" reinforced its aims to articulate and consolidate a Latin American avant-garde. *Revista de Avance* was founded in 1927 by a group of writers advocating for Cuban cultural and economic independence. The magazine launched and promoted the first exhibition of avant-garde art in Havana in 1927 and reproduced the same work in print, creating a kind of portable museum and positioning the magazine as a purveyor of cutting-edge art. *Revista de Avance*'s goal of forging a proprietary avant-garde was underscored by its 1928 questionnaire. Respondents to "What Should American Art Be?" sought to assert an autochthonous artistic identity that could compete with, and perhaps displace, art from North America and especially that of Europe.

Revista de Avance shared many ambitions and contributors with the magazines that I examine in the third chapter, in which I explore transatlantic relations between Paris—here a stand-in for Europe and often seen as the center of artistic production—and the Americas, as evidenced by two journals edited in Paris: *transition*, an American publication, and *Imán*, a Latin American magazine. I look at how translation, a touchstone for international

literary transmission, served varied and sometimes contradictory functions
for these journals. The editors of *transition* hoped that the translation of foreign-language European work into English would spur a distinctly American
avant-garde, as well as an enriched and elastic relationship to language. *Imán*,
which translated European and American texts into Spanish for its readership,
tested out how Hispanophone integration with the international might look in
print, while prodding its European contributors for their views on Latin America. Questions such as "Why do Americans live in Europe?" and "How do you
imagine Latin America?" gave voice, shape, and meaning to these magazines'
principal concerns with language and its capacity for cultural transmission.

The question "What is the avant-garde?" structures my fourth chapter,
which considers the contested literary relationship between Spain and Latin
America in the 1920s. Magazines from across these regions perceived themselves as outside of the dominant avant-garde, and they vied for cultural
prominence, often confronting a colonialist dynamic. The poetic movement
Ultraism exemplifies this tension, as it originated in Spain and was transported
to Argentina. Argentine writers claimed the movement as their own in their
questionnaire responses, while the Spanish avant-garde similarly highlighted
Ultraism as foundational in its questionnaires. Both Spanish and Argentine
writers answer the chapter's central question in light of their own national
interests, which are revisited in a series of print-cultural debates over the transatlantic relationship between Spain and Latin America and its colonial legacy.

In my fifth and final chapter I consider the reverberations of these transatlantic tensions through the conceit of "contemporary unrest," as announced
by the French magazine *Cahiers de l'Étoile* in an international survey of 1930.
This questionnaire adds the term "contemporary" to those under interrogation.
It gathered responses from major literary and artistic figures from around the
world, including F. T. Marinetti, John Dos Passos, Jean Toomer, Guillermo
de Torre, Juan Marinello, and José Carlos Mariátegui, suggesting that this
periodizing framework could help forge an international cultural network.
After outlining how such figures addressed "contemporary unrest" through
local lenses, I then consider the shifting significance of the "contemporary"
and the questionnaire as a form throughout the twentieth and into the
twenty-first century, particularly in the context of artistic and academic debates.
The examples I offer indicate that the questionnaire remains a valuable means
of positioning oneself in relation to one's peers, and a meaningful tool for tracking and critiquing one's historical moment.

While questions have regularly been posed on artistic and national identity
as well as periodization, magazines themselves have also been the subject of
inquiry. My conclusion considers the close relationship between the magazine
as a medium and the questionnaire, noting the genre's capacity to interrogate the formation of communities in print. I analyze three questionnaires on
magazines issued at different historical moments—1924, 1976, and 2006—

to demonstrate the questionnaire's inextricability from its vehicle. My appendix offers a supplement to the book, allowing readers to see the ubiquity of the questionnaire phenomenon and to observe the persistence of certain shared concerns.

I want to emphasize from the outset that the questionnaire is an ever-expanding topic of study. At first glance, perhaps, the questionnaire might seem a marginal, bureaucratic, or banal form; yet as a genre it has been fundamental to the modern period, and remains a vital mode of inquiry today. No single book can comprehensively analyze the entirety of the genre, nor its importance to modern and contemporary art and literature. My book is therefore a proposition, a point of departure for future studies that expand and build upon these principal claims. The questionnaire also continues to vibrantly shape the field of contemporary art, as current art magazines issue surveys at a rapid pace. I invite scholars of contemporary art to contribute to the growing appendix, and to fashion a theory of the contemporary questionnaire with a better sense of its rich history.

My book raises many of the same questions that are featured in the surveys I analyze. In response, it proposes some alternative approaches to conceptualizing the modernist period, namely an expansion beyond the primacy of the manifesto to consider the interrogatory energies of the questionnaire, an adjustment in focus from Anglo-American production to the hemispheric relationship between the Americas, as well as toward the transnational pull between the Americas and Europe. A study of the questionnaire introduces doubt and ambivalence as potential structuring devices for the field of global modernism. By putting pressure on terms like "modernism," "the avant-garde," and "the contemporary," this book demonstrates how such nomenclature has always been unstable and contested, and reveals the questionnaire to be a medium through which we might examine and make sense of these designations. It also destabilizes the idea of "American art," a term that is called into question in the surveys I consider. Ultimately, the multiplicity of voices raised in response to questionnaires show how writers, artists, and editors themselves engaged in the aesthetic debates that informed and propelled their work.

Questionnaires enabled artists and writers to assess a movement and to position themselves within it. The questions, too—"What is the avant-garde?," "How do you imagine Latin America?," and "What should American art be?"—are telling, as they reframe anxieties as assertions by claiming "the avant-garde," "Latin America," or "American art" as categories to be reckoned with at a moment when artists and writers across the Americas and Europe were expanding, reorienting, and reconstituting the map of modernism. By reanimating these questionnaires, we can reconsider the concerns that they raise and determine the extent to which they persist in shaping our own understanding of the avant-garde.

1. DEFINING THE **QUESTIONNAIRE**

"What should American art be? What should the attitude of American artists
toward European art be?" The Cuban magazine *Revista de Avance* presented
these questions to its contributors in 1928.[1] In the context of the question
"*¿Qué debe ser el arte americano?*," the designation "American" signifies "Latin
American" and served to articulate a collective identity in opposition to those of
North America and Europe. In the same year, the Paris-based expatriate magazine *transition* polled its European writers, asking, "How are the influences of
the United States manifesting themselves upon Europe?" The magazine then
surveyed its North American contributors, inquiring, "Why do Americans live
in Europe?"[2] These questionnaires, posed in the same year across the Atlantic,
demonstrate both how avant-garde publications grappled with the concept of
"America," particularly in relation to Europe, and also how the questionnaire
became a site for negotiating these aesthetic and national identities. The
questionnaire was a rhetorical strategy, enabling artists and writers to situate
themselves in conversation with international movements while simultaneously
forging local artistic platforms. By tracking the genre of the questionnaire and
its uses in the early twentieth century, we can trace how print communities
across the Atlantic defined the Americas in relation to international forces.

To start, what is a questionnaire? Also known as surveys, symposia, or
inquiries, questionnaires are issued by magazine editors to their contributors,
prompting them to reflect on a set of concerns regarding a periodical or group's
identity. These are broad, open-ended questions, such as "What is modernism?," "Why do you write?," and "Where is painting going?" The responses
are compiled and published in subsequent issues of the magazine, marking
a self-reflexive circuit that links editor, contributor, and reader to ideas
that form the basis of the magazine's mission. A decidedly international

phenomenon, such questions were issued in multiple languages to contributors across geographic boundaries. While it is an overdetermined form, accessible only to those who are asked to participate by the editors, rather than a truly democratic exercise, the questionnaire does interpellate the reader, inviting them to imagine their own stake in a larger discourse. Many questionnaires also sparked letters to the editor, allowing readers to continue debates initiated by the original set of questions.

Magazines were appealing forums for such exchanges because they enabled dispersed groups of artists and writers to collaborate across borders. However, such geographic dispersion also generated anxiety about the contributors' collective purpose. How could artists and writers across vast geographies convey a sense of belonging to a common artistic or political project? Questionnaires addressed this anxiety by providing a space for individuals to insert themselves into broader community formations in print. Through questionnaires, artists and writers could position themselves and their work in relation—or in opposition—to their far-flung peers.

Surveys were also a means by which magazines and their contributors could adapt or repudiate international trends, allowing cultural producers in the Americas and elsewhere to situate themselves vis-à-vis European movements. Indebted to French publications for popularizing the questionnaire in the late nineteenth century, magazines in places like Spain and the Americas quickly adopted the genre, articulating their cultural positions in an international mode. Indeed, *because* the genre was so widespread in France, it became a means by which Spanish, North American, and Latin American publications could insert themselves into an international dialogue about what it meant to be "modern." Taken together, questionnaires and their responses yield an alternative historiography of modernism: a self-reflexive history of art and literature as told by its key players, who, in the early twentieth century, were developing increasingly expansive notions of artistic and national identity in their work and in print.

Transnational Periodical Studies

By privileging the genre of the questionnaire, I am centralizing the role of the periodical in the development of modernism. A portable, ephemeral technology that laid the groundwork for subsequent cultural networks, the magazine is a space of display, a vehicle for literary distribution, and a site for collaboration across media. As objects of transit and transmission, magazines also foster contact between writers and artists of different nationalities, serving as hinges between the multiple locations of modernism. Typically held and read by individuals, magazines model a kind of simultaneous consumption and mass reading ritual analogous to that of the newspaper, similarly inviting readers to recognize themselves as part of a likeminded community.[3] The questionnaire format underscores this sense of investment, as it allows readers to speculate on their own responses to questions on topics central to a magazine's identity.

Moreover, the questionnaire echoes the function and format of the magazine itself, as responses are juxtaposed to form a collage of disparate viewpoints, united by a shared commitment to a larger project or movement.

The goal of many artistic communities in the early twentieth century was to establish an avant-garde identity with international currency, an effort abetted and circulated by magazines. Reflecting on the 1920s two decades later, Alejo Carpentier lists the magazines imported from across Spain and Latin America, that galvanized their Cuban readers. He writes, "It was the time of the 'avant-garde,' of far-fetched metaphors, of magazines, necessarily titled *Espiral*, *Proa*, *Vértice*, *Hélice*, etc. Moreover, all the youth of the continent suffered in those years from the same fever."[4] By translating and publishing examples of avant-garde material being produced elsewhere, magazines inspired, challenged, or affirmed the work of their own contributors, providing a set of peers or rivals against which they could assert their own artistic platforms. This rivalry is legible in the relational formation of questions issued by North American and Latin American magazines vis-à-vis Europe. Indeed, the simultaneity of exchange facilitated by magazines prompted anxieties regarding artistic canons and national identities evident in questionnaires issued throughout the 1920s and 1930s.

Magazines supplemented, and sometimes launched, the careers of nearly all modernist writers and artists, providing them with a venue—and often a paycheck—for their work. In the early twentieth century, eighty percent of writers published their first work in magazines.[5] As Ezra Pound remarks in his essay "Small Magazines," written in 1930, "The history of contemporary letters has, to a very manifest extent, been written in such magazines."[6] Similarly, magazines serve as records of the highly fruitful and experimental period of modern and avant-garde art, giving rise to what curator Leah Dickerman calls "an emergent modern exhibition culture."[7] "Within the art world specifically," Dickerman writes, "the idea of a transnational avant-garde was fostered by the rampant proliferation of journals."[8] Such journals were helmed by figures who served to connect these transnational communities, such as Alfred Stieglitz, Eugene Jolas, José Ortega y Gasset, Guillermo de Torre, and Alejo Carpentier. Rapid transmission of avant-garde production was enabled by an international periodical network, which these artists, writers, and editors helped to shape.

The centrality of magazines to the development of the avant-garde across the globe has increasingly been a focus of scholarship. Known as "periodical studies," this field has generated reflections on the material conditions, design, and visual and editorial content of both commercial and coterie publications.[9] In 1995 Sean Latham and Robert Scholes founded the Modernist Journals Project to digitize magazines such as *Scribner's*, the *Crisis*, and *Camera Work*, so as to make them accessible to a broader audience.[10] Similarly, Andrew Thacker and Peter Brooker initiated a Modernist Magazines website in 2006, operated out of the University of Sussex, and have launched a series of encyclopedic edited collections on the topic.[11] In their introduction to the first volume, they assert that "periodicals functioned as points of reference, debate, and transmission at the heart of an internally variegated and often internationally connected counter-cultural sphere."[12]

By analyzing questionnaires we can take stock of this internationally connected network, paying particular attention to the discrepancies it made visible. To do so, this book integrates Hispanophone production into the map of modernism and emphasizes the magazine's function as a vehicle of expression for authors and artists alike. Many scholars have studied foreign-language magazines in their national contexts, and art historians, particularly those working in the Latin American or postwar contexts, have produced groundbreaking scholarship on magazines.[13] However, due to linguistic and disciplinary constraints, such work often remains studied within national literary traditions, while art-historical analyses of the magazine as a medium rarely reach literary audiences invested in periodicals, and vice versa. This book synthesizes scholarship being produced in these multiple fields through a focus on the questionnaire. The questionnaire, much like the manifesto, is a genre that invites transnational literary and art historical analysis, and it provides access to the formation and contestation of national canons in the modern period.

Modernism and the Avant-Garde

Surveys issued in the 1920s and 1930s responded to the effects of modernization both locally and internationally, allowing us to determine what constituted "modernity" and "modernism" for artists and writers of the time. Such questions counter what Mary Louise Pratt calls a "diffusionist notion of modernity," which assumes a center that transmits culture belatedly to a periphery, and instead support the "global and relational account of modernity," which she champions.[14] Inquiries that called relations between Europe and the Americas into question—such as "How Do You Imagine Latin America?" and "Why Do Americans Live in Europe?— indicate that editors, artists, and writers were acutely aware of their transatlantic positions. Laura Doyle and Laura Winkiel call this "self-consciousness about positionality" characteristic of modernism. An "aesthetic self-awareness," they argue, "expresses a *geocultural* consciousness—a sense of speaking from the outside or inside or both at once, of orienting toward and away from the metropole, of existing somewhere between belonging and dispersion."[15] This "aesthetic self-awareness," as well as a heightened attention to one's geocultural position, was codified in questionnaires. As such, questionnaires offer insight into the consolidation of literary and artistic communities within an incipient global modernism.

I want to underscore the simultaneity and interconnectivity of debates over modern art and identity that occurred internationally through questionnaires. However, I also recognize that the magazines I consider were necessarily the product of particular political, economic, and cultural conditions. Notably, many of the conditions that led to the rise of aestheticism and the subsequent movements that Peter Bürger addresses in his landmark 1974 study *Theory of the Avant-Garde* were specific to a European economic and cultural climate. Bürger reads the development of the historical avant-garde as a reaction to aestheticism's separation of art and praxis, but unlike in Europe, Latin American art in the late nineteenth century was not yet independent from the state.[16] As a result, even in the early twentieth century, the artistic communities that I examine in sites like Cuba and Argentina were not concerned with attacking art as an institution; they worked to construct literary and artistic canons rather than to refute or undermine them.

In late nineteenth-century Latin America there were few, if any, literary or artistic institutions that were autonomous from the state, nor were there significant audiences for art and literature. In 1890 literacy rates in England and France were in the ninetieth percentile, which sustained many large-circulation newspapers. In Brazil in 1920, by contrast, 75 percent of the population was illiterate, and, until 1930, the average print run of a novel was only one thousand copies.[17] Consequently, Latin American writers had to expand and legitimize their profession and to establish markets for their work. Although in the early twentieth century Latin American literature shifted from a state-sponsored endeavor to an independent practice, even amid nascent modernization, Latin American artists and writers still lacked robust markets and institutions compared to their European peers.[18] As the critic Néstor García Canclini writes,

> At the end of the nineteenth century and beginning of the twentieth [modernization] was driven by the progressive oligarchy, alphabetization, and Europeanized intellectuals; between the 1920s and 1930s by the expansion of capitalism, the democratizing ascent of the middle classes and liberalism, the contribution of immigrants, and the massive spread of schools, the press, and the radio . . . but these movements could not fulfill the operations of European modernity. They did not form autonomous markets for each artistic field, nor did they achieve an extensive professionalization of artists and writers, or an economic development capable of sustaining efforts at experimental renewal and cultural democratization.[19]

Different rates of literacy, urbanization, and economic growth prevented markets and audiences for Latin American cultural production from rivaling those in Europe. Even as late as 1979 Alejo Carpentier noted the discrepancy in readership in Europe versus Latin America, riffing on a questionnaire issued by the Surrealist magazine *Littérature* and other magazines. As he observes, "For whom do you write? This is periodically asked in the tone of a questionnaire by certain literary magazines in Europe. And the European writer designates, as an answer, the sector of the public *that he himself has chosen as a recipient of his work.* But this question, 'For whom do you write?,' is inconceivable in Latin America, where the writer, in almost all of the countries of the continent, can only respond: 'I write for whoever can read.'"[20] Such disparities gave rise to questionnaires that investigated Latin America's relationship to Europe while also asserting national and regional identities so as to develop stronger local cultural institutions.

Many Latin Americans sought European markets for their work because of these uneven cultural conditions, and magazines enabled a rich cultural exchange between the two regions in the modern period. Furthermore, due to a range of political and personal factors, intermediaries such as Jorge Luis Borges, Alejo Carpentier, and Elvira de Alvear lived abroad, while many Europeans, such as Guillermo de Torre and Robert Desnos, turned their attention to Latin American cultural production. *Imán*'s questionnaire "How Do You Imagine Latin America?," which was addressed primarily to European Surrealists in Paris, elucidates some of the longing for recognition that undergirded the transatlantic exchange between Latin America and Europe at this time.

However, Latin America comprises a vast geographic terrain containing varied experiences of colonialism, urbanism, and cultural development; as García Canclini notes, "neither modernization nor modernism developed in the same way in all the countries of the continent."[21] Perhaps the desire to establish an *arte americano* or other cultural designations codified in questionnaires emerged in response to this sense of dispersion. This heterogeneous context generated a set of Latin American avant-gardes that, according to Vicky Unruh, consisted of "contentious encounters manifesting the changing alliances that accompany shifting economic, social, and political conditions."[22] She observes that most Latin American avant-garde manifestos opposed "social and artistic conventions and traditions in general," along with "romanticism, symbolism, and/or elements of Spanish American *modernismo*, [and] particular elements of European vanguardism."[23] Unruh distinguishes between the *modernismo* of Rúben Darío and the subsequent activities of the Latin American *vanguardia*, which aligned more closely with the historical avant-garde and with modernism in Europe and North America, while showcasing autochthonous elements.[24]

Modernismo, a poetic movement originated by Rubén Darío, predated the Anglo-American term "modernism," lasting from roughly 1888 to 1920. This movement greatly influenced literary developments in Latin America and Spain and helped facilitate the subsequent cultural exchanges that I examine in this book.[25] As literary historian Alejandro Mejías-López maintains, it was through *modernismo* that Latin Americans participated in and shaped international artistic discourse, as it allowed them to "become a force to contend with in the transnational market of symbolic goods, to occupy a position in the transnational literary field, and to attain cultural authority, freeing Spanish America from what Henry James called 'the burden of Europe.'"[26] With this newfound cultural authority, editors and critics took stock of the generation of writers and artists that came after *modernismo*, assessing their position in the global literary marketplace.

The subsequent generation of Latin American artists and writers, known as the *vanguardia*, took for granted the connectivity with Europe that the *modernistas* had facilitated.[27] However, many felt that Latin America had yet to assert itself on a world stage. To do so, the *vanguardia* hoped to define and enact a new idea of "Latin American art" that had international currency. Thus, while the debates over Latin American art and identity that I discuss in this book are indebted to the legacy of *modernismo*—which launched Latin America into an aesthetic interchange with Europe in the late nineteenth century— most of them concern the "avant-garde" or *vanguardia*. In addition to aligning with a Hispanophone trajectory, the designation "avant-garde" emphasizes the radical impulse behind the questionnaire, linking it to the manifesto and the self-reflexive discourse that the two forms embody.[28]

Originally a French military term, by 1910 the definition of "avant-garde" had evolved to include "pioneers or innovators in any art."[29] Many scholars have continued to emphasize its military origins. For instance, Raymond Williams argues, "The avant-garde, aggressive from the beginning, saw itself as the breakthrough to the future: its members were not the bearers of a progress already repetitiously defined, but the militants of a creativity which would revive and liberate humanity."[30] Matei Calinescu similarly relates the avant-garde to a "struggle for futurity" with militaristic and utopian implications.[31] Such revolutionary fervor, fueled by programmatic texts printed in the magazines that I consider, underscores the political stakes of artistic projects. It is perhaps because of the alignment of the avant-garde with futurity that manifestos have been privileged over questionnaires, which are more often retrospective in scope. Yet questionnaires effectively encapsulate the struggles and conflicts that such movements faced in order to assert their aesthetic positions.

Critics have long oscillated between invocations of the "avant-garde" and "modernism."[32] To address the ambivalent usage of such terminology, I turn to the writers and artists who structured the discourse of the era. In fact, these terms—"modern," "modernism," "avant-garde," and later "contemporary"—are precisely those that are interrogated by questionnaires, as artists, writers, and editors sought to make sense of their own historical formations. Inquiries on modernism and the avant-garde proliferated, as evidenced *La Gaceta Literaria* asking, "What is the avant-garde?" in 1930 in Madrid and the Ecuadorean magazine *Lampadario* asking the same question the following year, among many other examples.[33] Even the term "contemporary" was called into question, as in the 1930 survey on "contemporary unrest" that I examine in chapter 5. Consequently, we can track writers' and artists' own assessments of such terminology by analyzing the questions and answers that they generate.

Toward a Genealogy of the Questionnaire

While the questionnaire was ubiquitous in the early twentieth century, facilitated by the growth of print culture and an increasingly globalized public sphere, the impulse to openly debate aesthetic agendas is deeply rooted in artistic and literary history. The genre of the questionnaire can be traced as far back as the Italian Renaissance, wherein *paragoni*, or "comparisons of the arts," were issued on the relative merits of painting and sculpture. For instance, in 1546 Benedetto Varchi sent a *paragone* to sculptors such as Michelangelo and painters such as Bronzino, who replied with letters that Varchi then compiled and published in 1549 as *Due Lezzioni*.[34] Leatrice Mendelsohn, in her study on Varchi's *Due Lezzioni*, argues that the *paragone* is a mode of philosophical inquiry, emerging from the scholastic *disputatio* and most closely resembling the apology or defense of poetry.[35] Tellingly, the *paragone* was borne of literary culture, art history, and rhetorical theory. Indebted to these concomitant modes of address, the *paragone* served as an important medium for debate.

As the *paragone* gave way to the questionnaire, these debates were sometimes philosophical in nature. Long before questionnaires were issued on modernism, the avant-garde, and the contemporary, Kant received a questionnaire from the *Berlin Monthly* asking, "What Is Enlightenment?," suggesting that the form was used to periodize from its inception (fig. 2). In 1784 Kant published his response, calling for "freedom to make public use of one's reason in all matters."[36] Foucault seized upon Kant's text in 1984 to trace the implications of his approach to the Enlightenment for modernity and postmodernity. Foucault concludes that Kant's response offers a model for relating to one's time. He writes, "Thinking back on Kant's text, I wonder whether we may not envisage modernity rather as an attitude than as a period of history. And by 'attitude,' I mean a mode of relating to contemporary reality."[37] Foucault then calls to "reactivate" this "attitude toward contemporary reality" as a means of critiquing one's historical formation, an approach that also provides a framework for theorizing the questionnaire.

Foucault historicizes the genre by writing, "Today when a periodical asks its readers a question, it does so in order to collect opinions on some subject about which everyone has an opinion already; there is not much likelihood of learning anything new. In the eighteenth century, editors preferred to question the public on problems that did not yet have solutions. I don't know whether or not that practice was more effective; it was unquestionably more entertaining."[38] Foucault praises the open-ended nature of the questionnaire. Moreover, Foucault sees in Kant's response an opening to a "permanent critique of our historical era." Foucault clarifies this position, referring to the text as "a reflection by Kant on the contemporary status of his own enterprise . . . a particular analysis of the specific moment at which he is writing and because of which he is writing."[39] According to this logic, the questionnaire offers a forum in which to consider the stakes of one's own enterprise at a moment when it is still unfixed

Berlinische Monatsschrift.

1784.

Zwölftes Stük. December.

I.

Beantwortung der Frage:
Was ist Aufklärung?
(S. Decemb. 1783. S. 516.)

Aufklärung ist der Ausgang des Menschen aus seiner selbst verschuldeten Unmündigkeit. Unmündigkeit ist das Unvermögen, sich seines Verstandes ohne Leitung eines anderen zu bedienen. Selbstverschuldet ist diese Unmündigkeit, wenn die Ursache derselben nicht am Mangel des Verstandes, sondern der Entschließung und des Muthes liegt, sich seiner ohne Leitung eines andern zu bedienen. Sapere aude! Habe Muth dich deines eigenen Verstandes zu bedienen! ist also der Wahlspruch der Aufklärung.

Faulheit und Feigheit sind die Ursachen, warum ein so großer Theil der Menschen, nachdem sie die Natur längst von fremder Leitung frei gesprochen

B. Monatsschr, IV, B, 6, St.   Hh   (na-in history. The timely and capacious nature of the genre allows for such critique, synthesizing the philosophical inclination to question with an invitation to self-reflection.

It is the flexible nature of the questionnaire and its capacity to facilitate debate about issues that are still unfolding that lead it to generate such rich artistic and literary archives. As the adoption and propagation of the form proceeded, there were other precursors to the modern questionnaire. Very different in tone and intent, a formal predecessor was the parlor game that came to be affiliated with Proust, who published his answers as "Salon Confidences Written by Marcel" in an 1892 article in *La Revue Illustrée*, thus inscribing the gesture in print culture.[40] (Recently *Vanity Fair* transformed this set of questions into an online interactive game, wherein one can fill out one's own answers to Proust's questionnaire and see how they compare to those written by celebrities.)[41] While the questionnaire Proust participated in is more of a personal quiz, a means of assessing oneself more than one's era, it did popularize the genre, particularly through its quick, witty format. In turn, the modern questionnaire married aesthetic debate with this playful form.

Author and artist interviews constitute another significant precursor to the questionnaire, and a closely aligned mode of writing. Arising out of an instinct similar to the *paragone*—that is, to hear from artists directly— literary interviews were featured in French publications in the 1880s. Jules Huret conducted many of these early interviews, and soon started to present them as questionnaires to his subjects. For instance, in 1891 he published the survey "Inquiry on Literary Evolution," of writers such as Émile Zola and Stéphane Mallarmé for *L'Écho de Paris*, and he went on the following year to issue "Inquiry into the Social Question of Europe." While the results of these polls were originally printed in magazines such as *L'Écho de Paris* or excerpted in newspapers like *Le Figaro*, they were also subsequently compiled as books, demonstrating their wide appeal and commercial potential.[42]

Growing in popularity and scope in the late nineteenth and early twentieth century, *enquêtes* became a regular feature of French publications. Many were issued on literature, such as "How Do You Define Poetry?," printed in 1923 in *La Muse Française*, and "Une enquête franco-allemande," published in 1895 in the *Mercure de France*, on the relative merits of French and German liter-ature.[43] Some foregrounded visual culture as their primary concern, such as the "Questionnaire on the Utility of Art" published in *Le Buccin* in 1919, or an *enquête* issued by Charles Morice for the *Mercure de France* in 1905 that includ-ed questions such as "Is Impressionism finished? Can it renew itself?" and "What opinion do you have of Cézanne?"[44] *Enquêtes* of this era, according to the cultural historian Venita Datta, professionalized writers by inserting them into broader collectives and by providing a public platform for their ideas. "Marking the emergence of a new intellectual generation," Datta writes, *enquêtes* "gave young writers the opportunity to establish a dialogue with their elders, who were also polled."[45] These questionnaires helped expand a writer's audience and authority. While such French *enquêtes* have been tracked by scholars such as Datta, the subsequent international proliferation of the genre has not received the same scholarly attention.

The questionnaire was soon adopted by print publications internationally, many of which based their surveys on these early French examples, just as many publications, such as the *London Mercury* and *El Nuevo Mercurio*, modeled themselves on the *Mercure de France*. The questionnaire became a tool by which magazines communicated their ideological and aesthetic concerns to audiences. Some inquiries were political in nature, such as the 1926 "Negro in Art" symposium issued in the *Crisis*, the magazine of the National Association for the Advancement of Colored People, founded by W. E. B. Du Bois in 1910. This questionnaire asked prominent thinkers such as Langston Hughes, Countee Cullen, and Carl Van Vechten to express their positions on the portrayal of race and its implications for artistic, social, and political progress.[46] As the genre gained traction, magazines also began producing more playful questionnaires, such as the *Little Review*'s open-ended survey of 1929 that culminated with the question "Why do you go on living?"[47] The range of inquiries that were issued in the 1920s and 1930s attests to the malleability of the genre.

Avant-Garde Questionnaire vs. Social Science Survey

Concomitant with the avant-garde questionnaire, the social science survey is also linked to the rise of modernity, when it was first pioneered by Francis Galton in the late nineteenth century. While Auguste Comte and John Stuart Mill also referred to surveys in the nineteenth century, Charles Booth's landmark sociological study *The Life and Labour of the People of London* (1899–1903) was the first significant work to be produced based on data collected from surveys.[48] In America, the social science survey was used to assess questions of race and immigration in turn-of-the-century studies such as Jane Addams's *Hull House Papers* (1895), DuBois's *The Philadelphia Negro* (1899), and the Russell Sage Foundation's *Pittsburgh Survey* (1907–8).[49] Social science surveys were distributed using a variety of methods, including magazines, but unlike the questionnaires that I examine, such surveys were tools that gathered statistical information from samples of the population in order to obtain objective results. Although the avant-garde questionnaire became a prominent means of collective self-assessment at the same time as the social science survey, the genre I consider here is ultimately a literary device rather than an analytical tool.[50]

Responses to avant-garde questionnaires were not aggregated or positioned as scientific discoveries, but rather offered to the public as literary reflections. Matthew Josephson, a writer involved with *transition* and other magazines of the era, sums up the distinction between the two forms of inquiry succinctly, noting that "although they may have been somewhat diverting, [questionnaires] could scarcely lay claim to having made any scientific approach to the subjects they treated."[51] The impulse to question and tabulate responses may imply a desire for statistical quantification, but the avant-garde questionnaire ultimately works against the survey's data-driven logic to parody empiricism. *transition* encapsulates this position toward sociology in its manifesto "Revolution of the Word," announcing, "We are not concerned with the propagation of sociological ideas, except to emancipate the creative elements from the present ideology."[52]

By usurping aspects of social science for artistic purposes, the avant-garde could at once harness and destabilize its authority. The Surrealists, for instance, often invoked the trappings of social science; they set up a Central Bureau for Surrealist Research, "open daily from 4:30 to 6:30," as announced in *La révolution surréaliste*, their magazine, which was itself modeled on the conservative science journal *La nature*.[53] These seemingly parodic gestures, including the Surrealists' use of the questionnaire, worked in service of their aesthetic aims. In the magazine *Minotaure*, for example, André Breton and Paul Éluard issued a questionnaire asking, "What was the most important encounter of your life? To what extent does or did this encounter give you the impression of chance? Of necessity?"[54] This questionnaire emphasizes chance encounters and the role of the subconscious in aesthetics, reinscribing these ideas as central to the group's identity. Yet the questionnaire in this context produces unquantifiable results, suggesting that the Surrealists playfully subverted the genre even as they took it seriously as a means of self-assessment. (Note that this is just one example of the numerous questionnaires issued by the Surrealists.)[55] It was the questionnaire's proximity to social scientific discourse that enabled artists and writers to appropriate the language of bureaucracy that was gaining momentum internationally.

Even as bureaucratic language was satirized or undermined by the avant-garde, it lent authority to the aesthetic agendas of specific movements and magazines. Indeed, the prescribed form of the questionnaire structured the anxieties that propelled it, as in the case of the *Chapbook*'s 1922 questionnaire asking, "Do you think there is any chance of verse being eventually displaced by prose, as narrative poetry apparently is being by the novel, and ballads already have been by newspaper reports?" This questionnaire uses the very language that it fears is displacing poetry—that is, prose—to ensure poetry's legacy. As was its intention, the questionnaire received reassuring responses, such as "Yes I think poetry is necessary."[56] Questionnaires were appealing because they provided a formula that contributors and readers recognized, at once engaging in, mocking, and usurping social scientific discourse to bolster aesthetic platforms.

Manifestos and Questionnaires

Like the questionnaire, the manifesto was an essential mode of writing for historical avant-gardes: it elucidated their aspirations, garnered support for their ideas, and outlined their aesthetic strategies. Paradoxically, a manifesto at once breaks with the past and gestures toward history, allowing writers to position themselves in an avant-garde trajectory even as they announce their ideological departure from it. Manifestos often inaugurated magazines, declaring their bold artistic programs and plans for the future, while questionnaires, by contrast, allowed editors and contributors to reflect on and amend such claims, opening up a site for debate, doubt, and ambivalence. Together, the manifesto and the questionnaire worked to consolidate communities in print and to articulate their common concerns. The history and theory of the manifesto thus provides a road map for an analysis of the questionnaire, its most closely related print-cultural form. In turn, a theory of the manifesto must also take the questionnaire into account.

The manifesto has long been considered one of the defining genres of modernism and the avant-garde, but its usage dates back several centuries. Originally a formal pronouncement issued by state authorities, the manifesto soon became a tool by which dissenting groups could subvert dominant political discourse. Minority political factions first repurposed the manifesto in seventeenth-century England during the Pamphlet Wars, as Janet Lyon outlines.[57] According to Lyon, early manifestos rebuked narratives of progress, challenging the gradualist agenda of political modernity. With the rise of print culture in the eighteenth century, manifestos continued to propagate alternative political ideologies, drawing attention to the unfulfilled promises of post-Enlightenment Europe.[58]

By the nineteenth century the manifesto was recognized as a mode of political dissent, with a distinctive formula and an authoritative voice. The culmination of this evolution was Marx and Engels's transformational *Manifesto of the Communist Party*, published in London in 1848. Engels describes this manifesto in his preface as a "complete theoretical and practical party program" intended to clarify his and Marx's views to both their supporters and their opponents.[59] By cultivating an audience with shared grievances and a common enemy, and by assuming an instructive and commanding tone, the manifesto aided in organizing the party and articulating its goals, while also strengthening the authority of the manifesto as a form. In his analysis of the genre, Martin Puchner identifies the *Communist Manifesto* as the oppositional political text that served as a model for the artistic avant-garde, most notably the 1909 *Futurist Manifesto*.[60]

However, throughout the nineteenth century, prior to the Futurists' appropriation of the manifesto, tracts and prefaces resembling proto-manifestos began to accompany art and literature.[61] For instance, Romantic poets used prefaces, counterintuitively, to explain to the public their decision to retreat from society into nature. William Wordsworth denies that his "Preface to Lyrical Ballads," from 1800 was "a systematic defense of the theory, upon which the poems were written," but treats it as such.[62] Aestheticists added prefaces to their work to assert the autonomy of art. In his 1835 preface to *Mademoiselle de Maupin*, Théophile Gautier claims "the useless alone is truly beautiful."[63] Oscar Wilde also valorizes the aesthetic and celebrates the power of the artist in his 1891 preface to *The Picture of Dorian Gray*. Similarly, in his conclusion to *The Renaissance* in 1868, Walter Pater announces the value of "poetic passion, the desire of beauty, the love of art for its own sake."[64] The Symbolists also lauded art's self-referential qualities. In his *Symbolist Manifesto* of 1886, the poet Jean Moréas writes that reality consists of "appearances destined to represent to the senses their esoteric affinities with primordial Ideas."[65] Although it predates the hyperbolic avant-garde writings typically affiliated with the form, the *Symbolist Manifesto*, according to Puchner, anticipated how "schools would rely on manifestos to denounce their predecessors and competitors for the purpose of rewriting the history of art."[66]

Literary prologues were similarly prevalent in Latin America in the nineteenth century, representing what Julio Ramos calls a "metadiscourse," an emergent literature in which poets established their authority within a limited, burgeoning autonomous sphere.[67] For instance, after encountering Parnassianism and Symbolism, Rubén Darío pionneered *modernismo*, a mode of poetic production characterized by sensual, mystical imagery that he showcased in his first book of poetry, *Azul* (1888). Darío outlined his aesthetic vision in his second collection of poems, *Prosas Profanas* (1896). In a prologue entitled "Preliminary Words," he writes that "insinuating voices . . . solicit that which, in good conscience, I have not believed fruitful nor opportune: a manifesto."[68] Throughout the text, Darío at once assimilates and dismisses the conventions of the manifesto, acknowledging the contradictions inherent in writing something prescriptive about artistic freedom. Like the European tracts, such prefaces served as literary precursors to avant-garde manifestos.

Starting with the *Futurist Manifesto* in 1909, the genre became a crucial means of defining and disseminating avant-garde movements. At once a programmatic tool and a vehicle for artistic experimentation, the manifesto reveals a tension between its formal qualities and its content. Seeking to define, organize, and defend art movements, the manifesto as a form belies the innovative spirit and artistic aims of many avant-gardes; yet the complexity of avant-garde artistic production necessitated the manifesto to theorize and clarify such practices to the public. As the critic Ronald Vroon notes, "The greater the distance [the avant-garde] placed between themselves and the literary tradition, the more they needed a verbal instrument for explaining, defending and propagandizing their views."[69] Some movements reconciled these contradictions by deploying brash or aggressive literary devices, thereby enacting their avant-garde platforms. Such gestures include wild typography, as in the Vorticists' *Blast* (1914–15), which uses bold, capitalized text to "blast" and "bless" at will, while others feature excessive letters for emphasis, as in Carlo Carrá's *The Painting of Sounds, Noises, and Smells* (1913), in which he announces the Futurists' desire for "1. Reds, rrrreds, the rrrrrreddest rrrrrreds that shouuuuuuut."[70] Other manifestos lure readers in through anecdotes, dialogues, prose poems, or bullet points, as in Theo van Doesburg's *Manifesto I of De Stijl* (1918), in which he enumerates a list of his positions. Such formal techniques can be playful, but they also place the manifesto writer in a position of authority: one who airs the grievances of a collective and offers a strident proposal for change.

Unlike those who respond to a questionnaire armed with their own agenda and interests, a manifesto writer operates as an individual theoretician within a movement, one who assumes the voice of a collective and the role of both spokesperson and participant. For instance, Kazimir Malevich asserts the origin of his authority as follows: "Under Suprematism I understand the supremacy of pure feeling in creative art."[71] Others, to avoid serving as a proxy for a group, write in the third person plural—"We, rayonists and futurists"[72]— phrasing demands accordingly, as Salvador Dalí, Lluís Montanyà, and Sebastià Gasch proclaim, "WE DENOUNCE" in their 1928 *Yellow Manifesto*.[73] Regardless, manifesto writers typically cite supporters to demonstrate the force of their convictions, and to persuade readers to identify with their positions.[74]

As public texts typically printed in newspapers or magazines, manifestos explicitly seek and address an audience. In some cases, the audience is rendered exclusive, as in Walter Gropius's "Manifesto of the Bauhaus" (1919), wherein he calls on "Architects, painters, sculptors" to "all return to crafts!"[75] Other manifestos provoke the audience, sometimes setting themselves up antagonistically against a foil, such as the bourgeoisie or those who cling to the artistic traditions of the past, a tactic used by Tristan Tzara in his "Dada Manifesto" (1918). While in some cases "shocking the recipient becomes the dominant principle of artistic intent," as Bürger writes, such a gesture can also foreground the group's critical faculties and create an alternative set of values to the one that it vigorously opposes.[76]

Manifestos also tend to denounce or displace the movements that precede them, as when the Futurists distance themselves from the Cubists by declaring, "We Futurists combat the Cézannesque objectivism of color, just as we reject his classical objectivity of form."[77] Pierre Bourdieu argues that movements establish themselves by highlighting their differences from earlier cultural producers, which means "creating a new position beyond the positions presently occupied, ahead of them, in the avant-garde."[78] In his 1928 *Cannibalist Manifesto*, Oswald de Andrade playfully reclaims derogatory stereotypes about Brazil, thereby performing how he will assimilate and remake European culture through autochthonous means.[79] Such maneuvers allow manifesto writers to deflect or overcome their precursors. Through the manifesto, artists and writers can situate their work in an avant-garde lineage while differentiating themselves from their predecessors.

As a foundational document, the manifesto typically inaugurates magazines. By contrast, the questionnaire is more often a historicizing tool, enabling artists and writers to reflect on the ideas that unite, and sometimes divide, their print communities. In this way, the manifesto and the questionnaire can be read as bookends, marking the temporality of avant-garde projects. Both the manifesto and questionnaire are meta-editorial contributions to publications and conspicuous sites of reflection. Both are also written genres that retain a sense of orality, performing a conversational style. However, unlike a manifesto, whose signatories align with a single polemical text, the questionnaire produces a patchwork of responses, offering a composite portrait of a community. Containing a plurality of voices, the questionnaire destabilizes the unified front of the manifesto. Questionnaire responses, linked through juxtaposition, also generate a disjointed reading experience. Yet it is precisely *because* questionnaires offer a venue for disagreement, represented by multiple, distinct subject positions, that they deepen our understanding of the aesthetic debates that shaped the twentieth century.

Indeed, the bravado of a manifesto can obscure the underlying anxiety that propels it, while questionnaires crystallize and directly confront such anxieties, addressing gaps in the exalted rhetoric of the avant-garde. For example, a manifesto and questionnaire were printed in 1924 in consecutive issues of the Argentine magazine *Martín Fierro*. The manifesto announces a "new sensibility," while the questionnaire asks, "Do you believe in the existence of an Argentine sensibility?"[80] The questionnaire centralizes the national, which was elided in the manifesto. Questionnaires often clarify the apprehensions and ambitions that are subsumed by the brashness of the manifesto. In this way, the two forms jointly constitute a history of modernism, as told by its protagonists.

In the early twentieth century, the invocation of either genre signaled participation in the international avant-garde. Some magazines, such as *Blast*, featured only manifestos, and Pound, one of the journal's editors, though he responded to many of them, made his disdain for the questionnaire known in his response to one issued by the *Left Review* in 1937, on the Spanish Civil War, announcing, "Questionnaire an escape mechanism for young fools who are too cowardly to think; too lazy to investigate the nature of money."[81] However, other manifesto writers embraced the questionnaire. In 1909 F. T. Marinetti reprinted his 1905 *International Survey on Free Verse* alongside his *Futurist Manifesto*, thereby reinforcing the connection between the two forms.[82] Some magazines were so short-lived that they issued *either* a manifesto or a questionnaire. While *Blast* is an example of the former, *Imán* embodies the latter. *Imán*'s one and only issue in 1931 included the survey "How Do You Imagine Latin America?," posed to European Surrealists. More often than not, however, both manifestos and questionnaires were simply a commonplace of small magazines, defining and refining a movement or editorial agenda.

Like manifestos, questionnaires were also tools with which magazines or movements competed according to the logic of the market. Raymond Williams calls avant-garde groups "competitively self-promoting" and derides the manifesto as a form of "self-advertising."[83] Questionnaires could similarly advance a magazine's commercial function, as they might stoke or respond to controversy, which could in turn create or expand a market for the publication. For instance, in response to the deliberately provocative question "Who Is the Greatest Painter in Mexico?," printed in *El Universal Ilustrado* in Mexico City in 1922, Diego Rivera declares that *he* is.[84]

Such questionnaires benefited editors and contributors alike. For editors, this potentially controversial material—which enabled them to stake a claim in significant aesthetic debates—was obtained at little or no cost and often filled several issues of the magazine. The quantity of respondents underscored the abundance of viewpoints being presented while also enumerating a list of artists and writers invested in the publication, which was sometimes supplemented by photographs of the contributors as well.[85] The most prominent names of respondents and the most provocative questions were often highlighted for publicity purposes, as in the case of *transition*'s 1928 questionnaire "Inquiry Among European Writers into the Spirit of America," wherein the magazine claimed to contain "what Europe thinks of the U.S." Gorham Munson, a writer and editor involved with *Secession*, the *Modernist*, and the *Gargoyle*, corroborated such commercial benefits, arguing that "little magazines should revel in polemics. Writers with 'names' will contribute, without payment, to little magazines if controversy is sharp enough and interesting enough to draw them in or if the little magazine, having acquired a prestige of its own, will print the work of the 'names' which is too unconventional for the big periodicals."[86] These kinds of assessments emboldened editors, spurring further questionnaires.

Answering a questionnaire was also appealing from a writer's point of view. Participants were often published alongside more established authors or artists, and they could voice their opinions on various topics that concerned them and their work. More than a low-stakes contribution to a magazine, a questionnaire offered a platform for contributors to position themselves in relation to a magazine's editorial mission. "What Should American Art Be?," for example, identifies and affirms the cultural authority and legitimacy of this category, as corroborated by nearly all of the respondents. Similarly, "Do You Believe in the Existence of an Argentine Sensibility?" instantiates an "Argentine sensibility" through the act of asking.[87] Questionnaires allowed editors to assert an ideological agenda with which its contributors were eager to engage.

While some questionnaires conjured a collective into being, others pointed to the dissipation of a community. "What Is 291?" was issued in 1914 by Alfred Stieglitz in his magazine *Camera Work* when it and his gallery, known by its address simply as "291," were losing focus and support. For Stieglitz, the questionnaire was a strategy used to forestall the dissolution of his community and to reassert its significance. In his introduction to the questionnaire, Stieglitz demurs:

"What is 291?" Do I know? No one thus far had told the world. No one thus far had suggested its real meaning in *Camera Work*, and so again it flashed upon me to ask myself "What is 291?" I would like to know. How find out? Why not let the people tell me what it is to them. And in telling me, perhaps they will tell each other. Some say 'tis I. *I know it is not I.* What is it? And then and there I decided that a Number of *Camera Work* should be devoted to this question.[88]

Stieglitz has "the people tell me what 291 is to them," claiming, "It is not I." His coy posturing reveals his stake in the survey's responses, demonstrating how editors are often the real protagonists of such debates. Similarly, respondents often use questionnaires as sites to showcase their own work. Alberto Giacometti submitted a drawing to *Commune* in response to its 1935 questionnaire asking, "Where Is Painting Going?," and Ramón Gómez de la Serna replied with a playful dialogue to "What Is the Avant-Garde?," thereby enacting their positions through their creative interventions.[89]

Whether initiating or shoring up a group, the questionnaire affirms the importance of the community it polls. Sometimes this proclamation of significance is the sole result of the exercise, since the questionnaire might not accomplish its purported goals. Summarizing the results of the *Revista de Avance* questionnaire, for instance, one of the magazine's editors, Francisco Ichaso, laments the "bias of our findings."[90] Similarly, in response to a letter published in *transition*, Eugene Jolas admits, "the answer[s] to my two questionnaires were in many ways disappointing."[91] An editor's protest of bias or disappointment is part of the posturing inherent to the genre, much like Stieglitz's dramatization of the origins of his question. While editors like Ichaso and Jolas may characterize the responses they receive as inadequate, the questionnaire still offers prestige and publicity for magazine, editor, and contributor alike.

Some respondents also critique the genre, even as they participate in it. For example, in his contribution to *transition*'s 1928 questionnaire "Inquiry Among European Writers into the Spirit of America," the French historian Bernard Faÿ writes, "I never respond to literary inquiries for they seem to me to be one of the vainest intellectual fads of modern times"—and then he goes on to respond at length.[92] (The irony of responding to a questionnaire by announcing that he would *never* respond to a questionnaire is heightened by the fact that a European is angrily writing about his disdain for America in an American publication based in Europe.) However, many of those polled also chose *not* to respond to questionnaires; their refusals were sometimes printed, as in the case of Djuna Barnes, who is represented by the following response in the *Little Review* in 1929: "I am sorry but the list of questions does not interest me to answer. Nor have I that respect for the public."[93] Even parodic questionnaires were being published at the time, such as the Argentine magazine *Campana de Palo*'s 1926

poll "What, in Your Opinion, Is the Worst Book of the Year?"[94] The magazine
wrote replies in the style of well-known authors like Borges, and had each of
them nominate a novel published by the magazine, so that the questionnaire
served as a kind of publicity stunt. Such a backlash against the questionnaire—even from those participating in it—indicates how familiar critics and
audiences were with the genre in the modern period.

In some instances, readers responded angrily to questionnaires, even
though they were not officially polled. In reaction to *transition*'s surveys, Waverly
Louis Root, an American who wrote for the Paris edition of the *Chicago Tribune*
and *transition*, penned a furious "Open Letter to the Editor" railing against the
two questionnaires: "The self-conscious artist makes me sick. . . . This business
of asking him to indulge in soul-searching in answer to questionnaires only
aggravates a vicious habit particular to the breed. . . . I am against encouraging
him to make any more exposition of himself than is necessary." After attacking
artistic self-assessment in general, Root goes on to condemn the content of
transition's questionnaires specifically. He writes, "Just consider the literary
cakewalk which has been the result of your two questionnaires. With one or two
exceptions you have a collection of insincere egotistic strutting statements. . . .
Seriously now, what do you expect a person to answer when you ask him what
vision he has of himself in relation to the twentieth century?"[95]
For Root, questionnaires can produce nothing but "egoistic strutting,"
since they require the already "self-conscious artist" to further reflect on him
or herself.

Although Jolas concedes that the questionnaires did not produce the kinds
of results he had sought, he does defend them, arguing in response to Root that
the surveys "served to elucidate the chaos of certain ideas and I feel convinced
now that in spite of the objective inadequacy of certain replies, we have come
nearer to clarity today."[96] Regardless of the answers received, for Jolas, the
questionnaires helped clarify *transition*'s platform. Certainly, Root's criticisms
are applicable to many questionnaires, as they are often obscurely written and
difficult to answer. Generating flamboyant answers at times, they are usually
more concerned with articulating a magazine's aspirations than with soliciting
clear responses. Reactions like Root's are reminders that although the form can
seem utopian, the questionnaire could also yield frustration or disappointment
for editors, respondents, and readers.

Magazines also printed dissenting responses to their questionnaires.
In reply to "What Is 291?," issued by *Camera Work*, Edward Steichen, Stieglitz's
former colleague and fellow artist, who helped launch the gallery, repudiates
the exercise in strong terms, writing, "I resent this inquiry . . . as being impertinent, egoistic and previous."[97] Steichen goes on to characterize 291 as stuck in
an irrecoverable past, and he attacks the questionnaire as an attempt to "permanently establish its value." Although Steichen suggests that the questionnaire
must be "simply the result of 291's finding itself with nothing better to do," he

nevertheless contributes a lengthy response that is published in its entirety.[98] Stieglitz thus co-opts the negative response, even as he provides Steichen with a forum in which to voice his dissent.

Sometimes such criticism was folded into the editorial framing of the survey. In the case of the questionnaire on "contemporary unrest," issued by *Cahiers de l'Étoile* in 1930, the editors anticipated backlash, noting, "Some of the people to whom the questionnaire was sent reproached us as it is customary to do." These detractors, according to the editors, complained that the questionnaire was "undertaken only to secure publicity; that we had found a pretext to interview famous people; or to [have people] provide us with interesting texts for free; and the most serious charge was this: our text was biased, our questions were asked so as to cause favorable responses to our own theories." Such allegations were warranted, as questionnaires often *did* garner publicity for a magazine, solicit responses from well-known artists and writers at little or no cost, and affirm the magazine's own platform. However, the editors also note that many participants took the questions seriously, as evidenced by the quantity of replies. "It went around the world and inspired hundreds of responses in journals and magazines," they declare.[99]

Despite any deficit in the questions asked or answers received, questionnaires perform a community-building function by inviting contributors to identify their investment in a shared project, and to recast their aesthetic contributions according to this larger vision. As the critic Faith Binckes writes, "Composite textual forms can construct, or even impose, collective identity."[100] For example, a questionnaire titled "Who Are We? What Are We Like?" issued in 1929 in the San Juan–based magazine *Índice* asked its contributors "Is there an unmistakably and authentically Puerto Rican way of being?"[101] In this instance, Puerto Rican identity is naturalized through its formulation in a questionnaire, much as the categories of "American art" or an "Argentine sensibility" were similarly instantiated in the form of questions. Responses to these questions generate a rich historical archive, yet they are not as polished or legible as other collections, such as anthologies, and they include negative, often contradictory entries.[102] As such, they more closely resemble Ezra Pound's definition of an "active periodical," which he considers "something different from an anthology collected after the fact [which] does not enter active contemporary life as effectively as the review that definitely, even with foolhardiness, asserts its hope and ambition."[103] Much like the magazines in which they appear, questionnaires and their responses are part of an active and ongoing conversation. Magazines aim to remain present and engaged; the questionnaire allows them to publicly reflect on their purpose as they continue to evolve.

Art and Artists in Print

Questionnaires are among the few outlets available to artists to publicly reflect on their visual production in writing and to relate their work to that of their peers. However, it is important to note the discrepancy in their position from that of writers, for whom a questionnaire response could be an extension of their practice. Possibly because the questionnaire represents a departure from artists' primary means of expression, many of their responses are visually striking, such as Francis Picabia's enigmatic reply to "What Is 291?" in *Camera Work* (fig. 3). Picabia's contribution reads like a poetic text, syncopated with thick black lines.[104] These dark pen strokes later punctuate the covers of the magazine *291*, with which Picabia was involved, implying continuity between the two print projects.

Magazines like *Camera Work* and *291* contained high-quality reproductions of artwork, demonstrating how the periodical is often itself a collectible object featuring small-scale exhibitions. Printed in *Camera Work* were "mezzotint photogravures, duogravures, one-color halftones, duplex halftones, four-color halftones, and collotypes," by photographers such as Paul Strand, Edward Steichen, and Berenice Abbott, along with reproductions of artwork by artists like Picasso, Matisse, and John Marin.[105] Magazines also often serve as proxies for physical art venues, allowing distant readers to see artwork to which they might not otherwise have access. *Camera Work*, for instance, enabled a wide audience to experience its exhibitions through installation shots, and thus to feel connected to a physical location—in its case, the gallery 291. The *Little Review* similarly brought together European and American avant-gardes through its magazine and accompanying gallery, which featured work by artists such as Man Ray and Fernand Léger. Sometimes the magazine functioned as an exhibition catalogue, as it did for the *Machine-Age Exposition* mounted by the *Little Review* in 1927.[106] Other publications, such as the Spanish *Ultra*, offered opportunities for display on paper that compensated for a lack of exhibition space for avant-garde art in Madrid at the time. As Guillermo de Torre, who helped shape *Ultra*, claims, "the magazine is a vitrine and a poster." Still others functioned as sites for unrealized installations, as in the case of Marcel Duchamp's *Fountain* from 1917; rejected by the Society of Independent Artists, it was instead featured in the *Blind Man*, a magazine edited by Duchamp along with Henri-Pierre Roché and Beatrice Wood.[107] Published with the title *The Exhibit Refused by the Independents*, Stieglitz's photograph of Duchamp's *Fountain* places the work on a pedestal in front of Marsden Hartley's 1913 painting *The Warriors*, thereby elevating its status as art.

The magazine's supplemental or compensatory function as an exhibition space was particularly important in locations that lacked established art institutions. While galleries like 291, begun in 1905, were founded in the early part of the twentieth century, modern art museums in North America were not established until later: the Museum of Modern Art was founded in 1929, the Whitney in 1931, and the San Francisco Museum of Modern Art in 1935. Modern art museums in Latin America came later still: 1948 in Brazil, 1956 in Argentina, and 1964 in Mexico City.[108] As a result, in the early twentieth century magazines

QUE FAIS TU 291?

J'y sème dit 291 mon coeur est une source au caractère difficile elle se surmène un poète lui en a donne le livret revêtu de la forme humaine ▬

291 arrange ses cheveux sur son front ▬ Mais impossible de prendre feu et l'âme est gonflée de vie qui remplit toutes les heures d'un soleil ses yeux ses oreilles prédisent une intelligence c'est pourquoi on ne lui apprit ni métier ni art mais il trouvera sa place dans l'enchaînement sublime ▬

Deux âmes et le ciel dans cette ville bruyante elles trouvent moyen de s'unir parmi cette rumeur de commerce scene mystique ▬ Pour moi je crois que la fenêtre s'ouvre jusqu'a la perspective tout près de l'embouchure proximite de la mer ▬ Insousience des choses matérielles ▬ La vérité mais sans polémique ▬ Il faut voir en lui une proclamation sans affirmation nuée matinale c'est l'unique terrain devant l'univers qui refusera de voir la valeur de son enseignement ▬ Le conservateur "vive la France" "vive la Guerre" le temps de fumer une cigarette ▬ J'ai répondu que je refusais toute discussion ▬

291 c'est un grand pas de fait qui commence et qui finit d'inépuisable abondance accoudés a la fenêtre des catéchumènes ▬ Si clairvoyant et scrupuleux èvènement sensationel généreux pour sa clientèle qui se coudoie pressée dans cet espace restreint ▬ Comprenons bien la pensée de 291 voilà un façon nouvelle de concevoir la vie il aime son métier je suis content de te voir ▬ Son prestige montera rapidement jusqu'aux marches du trône et les services télégraphiques et téléphoniques ont été interrompus en maints endroits ▬ C'est pourquoi il fait de la musique et sa musique est un source inépuisable ▬ Le conservateur si tu me rapportes je te donnerai ▬ Il ne le connait pas il est bon c'est un Dieu je l'aime ▬

St. Cloud 17 Juillet 1914.   FRANCIS PICABIA

WHAT DOEST THOU, 291?

There do I sow says 291; my heart is a spring of fastidious disposition; 291 overworks itself; a poet has written the book and has clad it in human form.

291 arranges the locks on its forehead—but the flames cannot scorch it; its soul is filled with a life that fills each hour with sunshine; its eyes, its ears announce an intelligence; that is why it has been taught neither craft nor art, but it will find its place in the sublime sequence.

Two souls and the sky in this clamorous city; they manage to unite in the midst of the commercial uproar; a mystical communion. For my part, I believe the window opens to the perspective close to the proximate intermingling of the sea—indifference to concrete matter—truth without polemics. We must see in him a proclamation devoid of affirmation, morning dew; 'tis the only place in the Universe which will refuse to see the value of his teaching. The conservative "Vive la France." "Vive la Guerre;" time to smoke a cigarette. I answered that I refused to discuss. 291 is a big step forward which begins and which ends from inexhaustible abundance, leaning on its elbows at the window of the catechumens. Clear sighted and scrupulous, a sensational event, generous towards his patrons who elbow one another hurriedly in these small quarters. Let us get a good understanding of the spirit of 291; here is a new way to conceive life; he enjoys his work; I am glad to see thee. His prestige will ascend rapidly the steps of the throne and telegraphic and telephonic communications have been interrupted in many places—that is why he is a musician and his music is an inexhaustible spring—the conservative "if thou bringest to me I will give to thee." He knows him not; he is good; he is a God; I love him.

St. Cloud, July 17, 1914.   FRANCIS PICABIA

72

Fig. 3 Francis Picabia, "Que fais tu 291?," *Camera Work* (New York), no. 47 (July 1914): 72.

operated as sites for the display and circulation of new art. For example, *La Pluma*, in Uruguay, featured artwork in a regularly recurring section titled Exhibition. Because magazines showcased and shored up national canons, particularly in the Americas, they were apt sites for questioning what form "American art" might take. Artists actively reflected on the aesthetic and historical formations in which they lived and worked, as corroborated by their frequent participation in questionnaires.

Circulating Art and Literature of the Americas

The questionnaire embodies the collaboration that magazines facilitated, transmitting avant-garde art and literature to larger, and often foreign, readerships. Moreover, questionnaires themselves were often translated between national print contexts. For instance, in 1928 the Peruvian magazine *Amauta*, edited by the Marxist intellectual José Carlos Mariátegui, translated and reprinted a questionnaire by Henri Barbusse that had been issued in the French communist magazine *Monde* a month earlier, asking, "Does a proletarian literature exist? Do you believe in the existence of an art and literature expressive of the aspirations of the working class?"[109] (fig. 4). *Amauta* also translated the questionnaire's responses, received from André Breton in France, Waldo Frank in the United States, and Miguel de Unamuno in Spain. Others, like *Camera Work*, published questionnaire responses in the original languages in which they were received—in its case, German, French, and Spanish—as well as in English translation.[110] Such internationalism was made possible by print culture; through translation, publications could gather distant contributors and repurpose their ideas in new cultural contexts.

It was through translation in magazines that avant-gardes were distributed internationally. For example, Futurism gained traction in the Hispanophone world when Rubén Darío summarized and translated sections of Marinetti's "Founding Manifesto of Futurism" (1909) for Argentine readers in *La Nación*, and Ramón Gómez de la Serna translated it for Spanish audiences in *Prometeo*.[111] Marius de Zayas, a Mexican artist and critic, conducted an interview with Picasso in 1911, and wrote an article based on their conversations, which he translated and published in *Camera Work*.[112] Other intermediaries similarly transported avant-gardes to new national contexts through their writing. The Spanish poet and critic Guillermo de Torre reported on Expressionism, Dadaism, and Surrealism for Spanish journals such as *Grecia, Cosmópolis, Reflector, Ultra*, and *Alfar*. The poet William Carlos Williams edited an issue of the magazine *Others* devoted to Latin American poetry in translation in 1916, and he translated a story by the Guatemalan writer Rafael Arévalo Mártinez for the *Little Review* in 1918.[113] Williams's work reached Latin America too, as *Revista de Avance* translated a quotation by Williams from the magazine *Blues*: "The important thing is that a new magazine must be broadly open to experiment."[114] This transnational dissemination of art and ideas in magazines

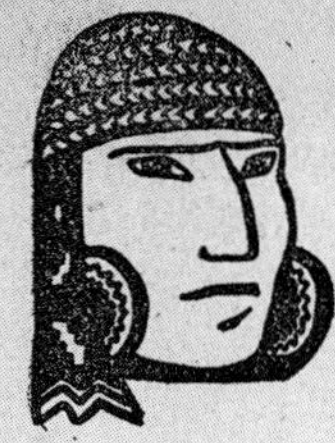

AMAUTA

18

LIMA   OCTUBRE   1928

¿EXISTE UNA LITERATURA PROLETARIA?

"Monde", el interesante hebdomadario dirigido por Henri Barbusse, ha a-
bierto esta encuesta, promoviendo un debate que encontrará, seguramente, largo y fuerte eco en las revistas literarias, artísticas y políticas. Del No. 16 de
"Monde" (8 de Septiembre) traducimos para nuestros lectores las primeras respuestas, omitiendo sólo la de Paul Souday, crítico de "Le Temps" de París, quien
no opina como artista, ni como político, ni como filósofo, sino como crítico ilustre, viejo, pedante y un poco zonzo. Hacemos gracia a nuestros lectores de esta opinión fastidiosa y acatarrada y los invitamos a seguir la encuesta en los
números venideros de "Monde". Los puntos de vista de "Amauta" sobre la
cuestión están ya, en parte, expresados. Pero los ilustraremos y completaremos
en este debate. Que estas páginas sirvan, en tanto, a la iniciación del lector.

1º.—¿Crée Ud., que la producción artística y literaria sea un
fenómeno puramente individual?   ¿No piensa Ud. que pueda y de-
ba ser el reflejo de las grandes corrientes que determinan la evolución
económica y social de la humanidad?

2º.—¿Crée Ud. en la existencia de una literatura y de un arte
expresivos de las aspiraciones de la clase obrera? ¿Cuáles son, según
Ud., sus principales representantes?

ANDRE BRETON:

1.—Seguramente, la producción artística y literaria es como todo fenómeno intelectual, en el sentido de que no podría a su respecto plantearse otro problema que el de la **soberanía del pensamiento**.
Es decir que es imposible responder a vuestra primera pregunta afirmativa o negativamente y que la sola actitud filosófica en semejante
caso consiste en hacer valer "la contradicción" (que existe) entre el
carácter del pensamiento humano que nosotros nos representamos como absoluto y la realidad de este pensamiento en una muchedumbre
de seres humanos individuales de pensamiento limitado; hay ahí una
contradicción que no puede ser resuelta sino en el progreso indefini-
do, en la serie al menos prácticamente infinita de las generaciones hu-
manas sucesivas.   En este sentido el pensamiento humano posee la
soberanía y no la posée; y su capacidad de conocer es tan ilimitada

Fig. 4 "¿Existe una literatura proletaria?," *Amauta* (Lima), no. 18 (October 1928): 1. © Archivo José
Carlos Mariátegui / web: archivo.mariategui.org.

created a feedback loop that sometimes took the form of polemics, often posed through questionnaires, revealing how different audiences represented, poached, or countered international cultural developments in relation to their own projects.

Such cultural exchange occurred at a time when communities across the Americas were developing visual and literary identities that they displayed and distributed through periodicals. In the early twentieth century the definition of what constituted "American" culture was very much in flux; terms such as "Pan-American," "Hispanic American," "Inter-American," "South American," "Native American," and "Indo-American" were used to describe a range of identities and relationships. The writers and editors whom I translate throughout this project themselves toggle between the designations "suramérica," "América Latina," "Hispanoamérica," and "América." For the sake of clarity, unless the term "America" or "American" is in quotes, I am using it to refer to the United States. I otherwise use the term Latin America, because it is the convention of the scholarly field. However, part of the purpose of these questionnaires— and of this book—is to highlight the ambiguity of what constitutes "America," for North Americans, Latin Americans, and Europeans alike. Interrogating the concept of the Americas in its various iterations, these print communities demonstrate the multiple ways such identifications have been called into question.

It is important to note that these terms have contested histories. For instance, the term "Pan-American" was originally used by Simón Bolívar in his "Jamaica Letter" of 1815 to signify pan-Latin American unity, but was then co-opted by the United States for ideological and commercial reasons.[115] Similarly, the name "Latin America" emerged from France in 1862 to advance the interests of Napoleon III.[116] Pablo Rojas Paz, an editor of *Proa*, acknowledges the insufficiency of all of these labels in his response to the "meridian debate" in 1927, writing, "Many have concocted long, terrible names for us— North America invented Pan American; France came up with Latin American; Spain created the term Hispanic American. Each of these names, though thinly disguised as an overture to harmonious relations, is actually an expression of its creator's frustrated imperialist designs."[117] Yet the reason editors such as Rojas Paz and others continued to think about the region comprehensively, despite the ideological burden of nomenclature, was precisely to assert autonomy in the face of U.S. and European interests. As art historian Mari Carmen Ramírez notes, "to acknowledge the existence of an art of continental versus national or local projection is equivalent to recognizing the unfettered right of this art—as well as the peoples it represents—to express themselves on their own terms."[118] Thus, while the appellations "America" and "Latin America" have always been politically charged, part of what these questionnaires seek to do is to claim, define, and pin down their usage, a task often fraught with contradictions.

Many magazine editors tried to position "American art" as heir to European culture; however, these editors' views as to what constituted "America," and by extension "American art," differed greatly. Stieglitz, for instance, was focused on cultivating an artistic community in the United States. When Stieglitz founded *Camera Work* in 1903, the concept of American art was not yet established as a category for artists, collectors, or museums, and part of his project was to build institutions to define and sustain this output. He held shows like *Younger American Painters* in 1910 and *Seven Americans* in 1925, marketed exhibitions toward the "American public," and called his gallery An American Place in 1929.[119] After the 1913 Armory show, Picabia corroborated Stieglitz's optimism for America by stating, "France is almost outplayed. It is in America that I believe that the theories of The New Art will hold most tenaciously."[120] Stieglitz capitalized on such statements, issuing the questionnaire "What Is 291?" the following year in part to solicit responses about the centrality of his magazine and gallery to the development of an American avant-garde. Marsden Hartley, replying to the questionnaire from Berlin, reflected, "When I think of what America has been with '291,' I am thinking how strange it would have been without it. . . . There is nothing anywhere—not in Europe even—that is the equivalent of it."[121] Stieglitz deployed testimonials like Hartley's to position his community the site where new art could find a receptive audience.

Although Stieglitz primarily sought to foster art in the United States, he had some admirers from Latin America. Writing about her encounter with Stieglitz at An American Place in 1931, Victoria Ocampo, the Argentine editor of the Buenos Aires–based magazine *Sur* (1931–70), muses on the expansiveness of what constitutes "America" in relation to Europe, marveling at the name of Stieglitz's gallery: "Yes, indeed, a haven of refuge for those few men and women who suffer in the desert atmosphere of America, because they bear still within them Europe, and they suffer from the musty atmosphere of Europe, because they already bear within them America. Exiles of Europe in America, exiles of America in Europe. I understood then that even *I belong there*, as the Yankees put it. This nostalgia is the nostalgia of a group identical in all the continent."[122] The version of America that Stieglitz presented in relation to Europe at his gallery resonated with an Argentine who spent time abroad, suggesting a kinship "in all the continent."

Ocampo, who describes Stieglitz's gallery as a refuge for restless "Americans," was encouraged by another inter-American traveler, Waldo Frank, to meet Stieglitz. Frank contributed to *Camera Work* as well as writing the books *Our America* (1919), which was celebrated by many Latin Americans for its critique of North American materialism, and later *The Re-discovery of America* (1929), which championed a spiritual synthesis between the Americas.[123] Frank subsequently went on a lecture tour to Mexico, Brazil, Chile, Peru, Argentina, Uruguay, Bolivia, Colombia, and Cuba.[124] Frank's pan-American-ism was embraced by many Latin American editors and writers. In an issue of

Revista de Avance dedicated to Frank, editor Félix Lizaso wrote, "Men like Waldo Frank . . . through the uprightness of their word and the greatness of their art, tell the dissenters in their country the measure of our tragedy and force them to say *their word* to South America."[125] Frank responded by writing an "open letter" to *Revista de Avance* in support of its editors' ongoing struggle for cultural and political independence.[126]

Like Frank, other North American writers shared a vision for a more expansive notion of the Americas. Eugene Jolas, the editor of *transition*, declared, "The intellectual frontiers of America do not exist for us, and we are as much interested in the wonders brought by esthetic explorers from Mexico, the West-Indies, South America, and our own Southern and South-Western past, as in the synthetic atmosphere of industrial activism."[127] According to Jolas, "America" had porous borders and could synthesize disparate elements from across the hemisphere, which would position it to eventually displace Europe as a dominant cultural force. Other North American magazines similarly looked to Latin America as a source of cultural vitality. For example, in response to a 1927 questionnaire issued by the *New Masses*, provocatively titled "Are Artists People?," the critic Edwin Seaver argued, "The last American culture was that of the Mayas."[128] The issue's cover features a woodcut by Rufino Tamayo, a Mexican artist who spent time in the United States, underscoring the fluidity of cultural production between the hemispheres.

Some Latin Americans also expressed enthusiasm for a joint art of the Americas. As Diego Rivera writes in his coauthored booklet *Portrait of America* of 1934, "I have always maintained that art in America, if some day it can be said to come into being, will be the product of a fusion between the marvelous indigenous art which derives from the immemorial depths of time in the center and south of the continent . . . and that of the industrial worker of the north."[129] However, more typically, Latin American magazines such as *Revista de Avance* or *Imán*, although they included U.S. contributors, sought to differentiate Latin America from the United States. For instance, in response to the questionnaire "What Should American Art Be?," the Venezuelan historian and poet Rufino Blanco Fombona clarifies, "we are not talking about the Yankees," while one of the magazine's editors maintains that "Yankee imperialism" is a "common enemy" uniting Latin Americans.[130] The genre of the questionnaire was a strategy by which both North Americans and Latin Americans defined and differentiated their work, even as magazines modeled how art and literature of the Americas might be integrated with international culture.

Questionnaires provided a platform for self-representation, a forum for these artists and writers to establish local avant-garde movements in conversation with the international. By generating a compilation of multiple, ambivalent viewpoints, questionnaires such as "What Should American Art Be?," "How Do You Imagine Latin America?," and "Why Do Americans Live in Europe?" showcase the many national and aesthetic positions that the term "America" implied.

These questionnaires impelled writers, editors, and readers alike to characterize the place of the Americas in the transatlantic imaginary and to determine
their own identifications accordingly.

2. PICTURING **LATIN AMERICA**

The questionnaire issued by *Revista de Avance* in 1928 asking, "What should American art be? What should the attitude of American artists toward European art be?" puts pressure on the designation *arte americano* in ways that were characteristic of the period, as magazines across the Americas sought to displace European dominance by developing, defining, and defending an idea of "American art." Publishing a broad array of literature, criticism, and visual art, *Revista de Avance* hoped to forge a coalition of Latin American artists and writers to jointly assert cultural and political autonomy from Europe and the United States. However, two of the artists receiving the questionnaire responded from abroad; Carlos Enríquez and Eduardo Abela—both of whom had been featured in the magazine's groundbreaking *Expocisión de Arte Nuevo* (Exhibition of New Art) the previous year—wrote in from New York and Paris respectively, demonstrating how any question of "American art" was imbricated in a triangulation of relationships between North America, Latin America, and Europe. Efforts to distinguish a uniquely "American art" resulted precisely from these conditions, which gave urgency to the desire for an independent Latin American cultural sphere.

Like other magazines across the Americas, *Revista de Avance* introduced audiences to both local and international literature and art while strengthening its aesthetic and ideological ties. The Cuban intellectuals who founded *Revista de Avance* were indelibly marked by the national fight for independence— and inspired by the poet and revolutionary José Martí—to seize and define their country's cultural and political identity. Launched by Juan Marinello, Jorge Mañach, Martí Casanovas, Francisco Ichaso, and Alejo Carpentier in 1927, *Revista de Avance* was intended to be the mouthpiece of "Minorism," a group formed in 1923 in support of Cuban independence, Latin American solidarity, and artistic innovation. Alejo Carpentier, a founding editor of the magazine, described the Minorists' interests in "recent forms in art, Afro-Cuban music, [and] literary nationalism."[1] The editors were also involved in the annual salons and exhibitions held at the Asociación de Pintores y Escultores (Association of Painters and Sculptors), including a 1923 conference on art and architecture organized by editor Jorge Mañach. Such activities led to the *Exhibition of New Art*, held at the Association of Painters and Sculptors in 1927, which *Revista de Avance* mounted, sponsored, and promoted. The magazine featured the artists' work in its pages along with reviews of the show, thus enacting a version of what "American art" should be, before issuing its questionnaire in 1928.

Throughout its print run, *Revista de Avance* communicated its vision for "American art" both visually and rhetorically. In many ways, the relational nature of its questionnaire arose directly from the pages of the magazine, which featured work by international writers and artists such as Ezra Pound, Salvador Dalí, André Gide, John Dos Passos, and Alice Neel, who were printed alongside Cubans Félix Lizaso, Eduardo Abela, and Víctor Manuel as well as other Latin Americans such as Pablo Palacio, Diego Rivera, Norah Borges, and Horacio Quiroga. *Revista de Avance* was also connected to a network of magazines across Latin America, including *Amauta* in Peru and *Repertorio Americano* in Costa Rica, with which it shared contributors. Because of these relationships, as well as Cuba's geopolitical position, *Revista de Avance*'s editors were poised to respond to outside influences, but were also wary of being co-opted for the agenda of another country or region. The magazine tested its nexus of transnational relationships through its questionnaire, seeking support from its community of contributors to champion an *arte americano* for international distribution.

The Political and Artistic Climate in Cuba

Embedded in the question of what "American art" should be in relation to Europe—and, as many respondents took it, to the United States as well—was a history of political resistance on the part of the writers and artists involved in *Revista de Avance*. The drive toward Cuban cultural independence was inextricable from the country's struggle for political autonomy. The first push for independence resulted in the Ten Years' War (1868–78), which led to the establishment of the Cuban Revolutionary Party in 1892 by Martí, who then died in battle during the Independence War (1895–98). The involvement of the United States in this war constituted an act of aggression against Spain, leading to the Spanish-American War, which culminated in the Treaty of Paris. Signed in December 1898, this treaty made Cuba a semisovereign republic, but the United States retained the right to intervene in Cuban affairs.[2] The result of these policies, as well as the Platt Amendment, passed in 1901, was that the United States built military bases in Cuba and controlled large tracts of its land; the United States also staged a military intervention in Cuba that lasted from 1906 to 1909. Exacerbating such foreign intervention, the effects of World War I inflated the price of sugar until 1920, causing widespread financial hardship for Cuban citizens and public institutions, including universities and newspapers. Cubans also battled internal corruption, first under Alfredo Zayas (1921–25) and then during the even more repressive reign of Gerardo Machado (1925–33), prompting intellectuals to initiate political and aesthetic forms of resistance against Spain, the United States, and their own government.

Because of his political push for independence as well as his influential writing, Martí was lauded as the primary inspiration for the Cuban avant-garde. In his now canonical essay "Nuestra América" (Our America, 1891), Martí eloquently stirs Latin American cultural pride, urging his readers to band together to resist imperialism, racism, and tyranny. Martí's masterful text cemented his influence on the ensuing generation of writers, particularly since he centralizes their purpose: "Trenches of ideas are worth more than trenches of stone. A cloud of ideas is a thing no armored prow can smash though. A vital idea set ablaze before the world at the right moment can, like the mystic banner of the last judgment, stop a fleet of battleships." By proclaiming the necessity of a "vital idea" in such vivid, martial language, Martí privileges the role of the intellectual in combatting imperialism. Likewise, Martí hails artistic creation in the broadest terms as necessary to secure an independent future: "They understand that there is too much imitation, and that salvation lies in creating. Create is this generation's password." By assigning his audience the task of creating "trenches of ideas," he provided the spiritual basis for the mission of *Revista de Avance*, that is, to develop an authentically "American" culture.[3]

For Martí, such a cultural movement would reflect the diverse heritages of all Latin Americans. Martí describes Latin America's racial, religious, and ethnic makeup as follows: "Our feet upon a rosary, our heads white, and our bodies a motley of Indian and *criollo* we boldly entered the community of nations." In "Nuestra América," embracing racial diversity is deemed crucial in the fight for independence. Martí decries the impulse to emulate European or North American trends, criticizing those who return from other countries and try to govern Latin American nations with ideas received abroad. Instead, he argues, Latin Americans must develop their own institutions and leaders. "No Yankee or European book could furnish the key to the Hispanoamerican enigma," he writes. Such distinctions are echoed in the *Revista de Avance* questionnaire and its responses, which similarly eschew imitation and express a desire for the kind of cultural authority and unity described by Martí.[4]

Martí's vision, in conjunction with other influences, spurred the subsequent generation's quest for cultural independence. Also informing the development of Cuban culture and politics was another landmark text, José Enrique Rodó's treatise on Latin American identity, *Ariel* (1900), as well as, more broadly, the Mexican Revolution (1910), the Russian Revolution (1917), and the university reform movement stemming from Córdoba, Argentina, in 1918, which advocated for free, egalitarian education that would be autonomous from the state.[5] In addition to Martí's politically engaged poetry, that of Julián de Casal modeled an aestheticist path, two traditions that *Revista de Avance* sought to reconcile.[6]

Those writers and artists shaped by the wars of independence, the U.S. military presence in Cuba, and the poetics of Martí and Casal became known as the Generation of 1910. Many of them went on to publish in *Revista de Avance*, as did the subsequent generation, known as the Generation of 1923. The earlier group included Enrique José Varona, José Antonio González Lanuza, and José Antonio Ramos. They initiated the "Conference Society" in 1910, which offered lectures on cultural issues and some of its members founded the magazine *Cuba Contemporánea* (1913–27). The magazine was created to serve as "the expression of the first republican generation" and was open to "all orientations of the modern spirit."[7] Through such activities, this group of writers forged alternative cultural and political institutions and worked to confront government corruption.

The subsequent generation, the Generation of 1923, came together through an act of resistance that became known as the "Protest of the Thirteen," coalescing into a political program whose sensibility informed *Revista de Avance*. On March 18, 1923, a group of thirteen artists and writers gathered at the Academia de Ciencias, where the justice minister from Zayas's presidency, Erasmo Regueiferos Bodet, was slated to speak. Regueiferos was involved in the fraudulent purchase of the Santa Clara Convent in Old Havana, from which the government was poised to profit. Taking Regueiferos as a symbol of rampant political corruption, the writer and activist Rubén Martínez Villena interrupted the proceedings, announcing "that he and his colleagues were leaving the room in protest against public dishonesty, there represented by Mr. Regueiferos."[8] The protest was publicized in major newspapers across the country, including the prominent *Heraldo de Cuba*, earning the group notoriety. A day later they signed a declaration called "The Protest of the Thirteen," characterizing their walkout as a "civic act of protest" intended to "demonstrate the nonconformity of youth, whom we represent," and called for adherents who similarly felt "indignant against those who mistreat the Republic." Urging supporters to "react vigorously and somehow punish criminal rulers," the protestors aligned with youth, patriotism, and political resistance.[9]

As they gathered followers, the protesters became known as the "Grupo Minorista" (Minorist Group) and came to include journalists, artists, lawyers, poets, and musicians. Four years later, on May 7, 1927, the Grupo Minorista wrote a "Declaration" advocating for political reform and aesthetic innovation, which they published in three magazines: *Social*, *Carteles*, and *Revista de Avance*.[10] In this document they critique the "false values" of the Cuban government as well as its "subjugation to foreign demands." They rally for "new forms of government," education reform, academic freedom, Latin American unity, for "the economic independence of Cuba and against Yankee imperialism."

Despite their name, they claim to represent "a majority group, in the sense of constituting the spokesperson, platform, and index of the majority of people." Advocating for "new art in its diverse manifestations," the Minorists describe themselves as "a group of intellectual workers (writers, painters, musicians, sculptors)."[11]

Intent on reinvigorating art and literature, the Grupo Minorista broke with *Cuba Contemporánea*, favoring instead the illustrated monthly magazine *Social* (1916–33), and several of its members later founded *Revista de Avance* (1927–30).[12] Because *Revista de Avance* was established the year *Cuba Contemporánea* folded, it was seen at once as a continuation of *Cuba Contemporánea* (and, by extension, the Generation of 1910) and also as a decisive break with it. Francisco Ichaso, an editor of *Revista de Avance*, describes the differences between *Cuba Contemporánea* and *Revista de Avance* as follows: "*Cuba Contemporánea* was a magazine of serious format, of long, careful, intelligent articles; it was a dense, circumspect, gray magazine, like most of the men who made it and read it. *Revista de Avance* was light in format and had short pieces, whose style was mischievous, arbitrary, iconoclastic. It was the literary and artistic organ of a generation determined to energetically review the past generation's work and to bring to Cuban life a different slant."[13] Aligning with the Generation of 1923 and the Minorists, *Revista de Avance* departed from *Cuba Contemporánea* in tone, content, and format. However, it continued to share many contributors with *Social*, including Juan Marinello, José Zacarías Tallet, Alejo Carpentier, and Fernando Ortiz, as the two magazines retained a similar cultural sensibility and anti-imperialist stance.[14]

Galvanized by the activities of the Grupo Minorista and magazines such as *Social*, those who worked on *Revista de Avance* were also impelled by the ever-worsening political situation. Between 1911 and 1927 North American involvement in the Cuban economy expanded, and by 1927 U.S. investments in Cuba reached 1,014 million dollars.[15] The local political situation also worsened. The dictator Gerardo Machado rose to power in 1925; by decreeing a *prórroga de poderes* in 1927, he stayed in power until 1933, violently squashing student protests and censoring publications. Machado gave U.S. industries commercial protections and reduced tariffs, so that by 1925 "U.S. firms owned a quarter of the arable land in Cuba, and U.S. financial credits and loans to Cuba controlled the value of the peso along with the island's banking system."[16] As a result, Cubans struggled to establish local political parties and institutions. Some that were formed in 1923 despite these restrictions included the Junta for National Renovation, organized by the anthropologist Fernando Ortiz to petition the government to enact labor, health, law, and education reform, as well as the University of Havana Student Federation and the First Congress of Cuban Students, both founded by the student activist Julio Antonio Mella to advocate for improved education, an end to government corruption, and Cuban independence.[17]

In reaction to these rapidly changing political conditions, the Grupo Minorista dissolved in 1928. In June 1929 Emilio Roig de Leuchsenring, the literary
editor for *Social*, officially declared the end of the group in an article for the
magazine, reflecting that in five years they had produced "admirable revolutionary work of purification and of literary, artistic, and socio-political renewal . . .
work that has not yet been equaled or surpassed before or since in our country
by any literary or artistic group."[18] He credits the Minorists with advancing the
struggle for political and artistic independence. Although they disbanded due to
infighting, many of the members of the group would continue to collaborate on
Revista de Avance and other literary and political projects.

Throughout the existence of the Grupo Minorista, its members contributed
to magazines across Latin America, introducing audiences to Cuban thought
and building relationships with writers whom *Revista de Avance* would later
call upon to help define *arte americano*. For instance, in 1925 Minorists Félix
Lizaso and José Fernández de Castro published the essay "Modern Poetry in
Cuba" in *Proa*, a magazine founded by Jorge Luis Borges and other writers in
Buenos Aires. The essay articulates the goals and even the title of what would
become *Revista de Avance*. They describe their search for a "beyond"—much as
Borges, in his writing for *Proa*, and the Ultraists in Spain did—asserting, "The
young are expected to go beyond [*más allá*], in the perennial revolution, which
any advancement [*avance*] entails; they are expected to astonish the stragglers
and to move them in ways unknown, even to those who accompany them."[19] The
"avance" that would become the magazine's name is here situated in relation to
aesthetic innovations across the Spanish-speaking world, notably the Ultraist
search for the *más alla*.

In the same essay the authors underscore Latin America's collective "fight
for political independence and the constant struggle with the Spanish mentality, reproduced over the last century, and in different parts of our America."[20]
By referring to "nuestra América" the authors cite their beloved precursor
Martí, and also voice their opposition to an imperialist "Spanish mentality" in
solidarity with other Latin American countries. Throughout, the two authors
hail their influences as border-crossing modernist poets and *cronistas*—Martí,
Casal, Mexican writer Manuel Gutiérrez Nájera, and Nicaraguan poet Rubén
Darío—thus situating the Cuban struggle for independence within a larger
Latin American literary framework. They conclude by announcing the birth of
a new Cuban aesthetic: "For the first time in Cuba, a generation of remarkably
young poets expresses itself with its own identity and defined direction."[21] This
sense of optimism about their project, coupled with the political and literary experiences of the group, formed the basis of a new publication, *Revista de Avance*.

Founding *Revista de Avance*

Founded in 1927 by editors Juan Marinello, Jorge Mañach, Martí Casanovas,
Francisco Ichaso, and Alejo Carpentier, *Revista de Avance* expanded on the work

of the Minorists in the spheres of literature, art, and politics. It consisted of fifty bimonthly issues published between March 16, 1927, and September 30, 1930, with a circulation of approximately three thousand copies. By 1930 it was 10.5 × 7.75 inches in size, staple-bound, and typically ran about thirty pages. The title of the magazine changed yearly; covers were boldly and colorfully titled "1927" or "1928," with the name *revista de avance* stamped in lowercase letters underneath.[22] The two names jointly implied the magazine's impulse toward change. As the editors announce in the first issue, "We want movement, change, advancement, even in the magazine's name! And we want absolute independence—even from time!"[23] This orientation toward the future is reflected in the titles of avant-garde magazines throughout Latin America. As Gilberto Mendonça Teles and Klaus Müller-Bergh explain, titles like *Revista de Avance*, *Proa*, *Vértice*, and *Hélice* "presuppose a single concept of the avant-garde . . . collectively suggesting the sense of that which is at the forefront, that which is the sharpest, most visible, and most dynamic."[24] Through its forward-looking name and attitude, *Revista de Avance* announced its connection to the project of the avant-garde.

The magazine was born of political resistance, and its history was punctuated by additional confrontations between its editors and the government. Carpentier was among the sixty-four people incarcerated in the cárcel de Prado in Havana on July 9, 1927, for having signed the "anti-imperialist and pro-democratic manifesto." He was jailed for seven months, and upon his release he left the country for Paris.[25] (I detail Carpentier's involvement in print culture abroad and his role as a transnational intermediary in chapter 3.) Carpentier continued to write for a variety of Cuban publications while in Paris, but José Zacarías Tallet (who, incidentally, was jailed alongside Carpentier) replaced him on the editorial staff of *Revista de Avance* starting with the second issue, and thus Carpentier was not involved with the questionnaire. Similarly, Casanovas was accused of being a communist and was subsequently jailed and exiled, and Félix Lizaso took over for him on the magazine's eleventh issue.[26] Clearly committed to political struggles in Cuba, *Revista de Avance* also expressed support for those occurring in Puerto Rico, Mexico, and the Dominican Republic; it printed commentary on uprisings in Nicaragua and Mexico, and covered the political situation in Russia. The editors' involvement with the Protest of the Thirteen and the Grupo Minorista, among other forms of resistance, legitimated the magazine's calls for political reform and ensured it an audience of likeminded supporters.

Revista de Avance brought its political concerns into conversation with the arts, stating that the publication "is intended to be, exclusively, a cultural magazine . . . with all [of] the diverse ideological concerns that this purpose implies."[27] Culling contributors from across Latin America, *Revista de Avance* published Peruvian editor and Marxist intellectual José Carlos Mariátegui, Mexican *estridentista* Manuel Maples Arce, Argentine writer Leopoldo

Lugones, Peruvian poet César Vallejo, and Guatemalan novelist Miguel Ángel
Asturias. This range of material demonstrates the editors' knowledge of Hispanophone literary developments and their commitment to promoting Latin
American writing. In the same issue in which the questionnaire appears, the
editors state, "A longing for solidarity—that is, ultimately, a comprehensive
understanding—animates the intellectual politics of young Americans today (at
least this one). We have already begun to feel ashamed that we all know Europe
better than we know ourselves."[28]

Indeed, the magazine's ambivalence toward Europe—particularly Spain—
was evidenced in its relationship to Spanish authors and journals. *Revista de
Avance* featured Generation of '98 writer Miguel de Unamuno, Generation of '27
poet Federico García Lorca, philosopher, critic, and editor José Ortega y Gasset,
and many from the *Gaceta Literaria* community, including Rámon Gómez de la
Serna.[29] The editors also responded to the controversial "meridian debate" that
Guillermo de Torre initiated in *La Gaceta Literaria* about Spain's intellectual
claim to Latin America.[30] The magazine was intent on foregrounding Cuban
artistic achievements in relation to those of Spain. In 1928 the Cuban writer
Raúl Roa García writes in *Revista de Avance*, "Before the Ultraists, Martí, new
poet."[31] (Ultraism, which I address in chapter 4, was a Spanish poetic movement
transported to Latin America.) Conversely, Félix Lizaso, an editor of *Revista de
Avance*, wrote for *La Gaceta Literaria*, as did many other contributors, asserting
Cuba's cultural importance to a Spanish audience.[32] For instance, in the Cuban
novelist Lino Novas Calvo's two-part series for *La Gaceta Literaria* entitled "Cuba
literaria" (1931), he announces, "All of us young Cuban writers are children of
Revista de Avance," emphasizing the magazine's centrality to a Cuban literary
genealogy while introducing it to Spanish readers.[33] *Revista de Avance* thus featured Spanish literature while still asserting a national cultural agenda.

Revista de Avance also showcased cutting-edge developments in art and
literature from around the world. It featured foreign material in Spanish
translation by theorists such as Bertrand Russell, Oswald Spengler, and Carl
Jung; experimental French writers such as André Gide and Blaise Cendrars; and
Americans such as Ezra Pound, John Dos Passos, Countee Cullen, Langston
Hughes, Waldo Frank, and Sherwood Anderson, many of whom Francine Masiello identifies as "dissident writers . . . who might voice opposition to colonialist
expansion."[34] Such juxtapositions created a conversation between writers from
Cuba and elsewhere. Similarly, the magazine displayed visual art from across
Europe and the Americas. It reproduced images by European avant-garde
artists, including Picasso, Matisse, Max Ernst, George Grosz, and Salvador Dalí,
as well as the American artist Henry Glintenkamp, known for his drawings for
the socialist periodical the *Masses*, the Guatemalan-born Carlos Mérida, the Argentine artist Norah Borges, and Mexican artists such as José Clemente Orozco
and Diego Rivera. For instance, an early issue of the magazine printed details
of Rivera's frescos for the Ministry of Education in Mexico City, which depict

indigenous children engaging in everyday activities in Rivera's flattened, figurative style.[35] By publishing such work alongside that of Cuban artists and writers, *Revista de Avance* sought to inform its audience about international artistic and literary movements while cultivating and showcasing *cubanidad*. Describing these goals, Mendonça Teles and Müller-Bergh argue that the magazine engaged in "the reflexive, self-analytical desire to determine autochthonous national idiosyncrasies and [to see] how they fit into Latin American and universal reality."[36]

Revista de Avance was most prominently a platform for the new generation of Cuban artists, such as Eduardo Abela, Carlos Enríquez, Antonio Gattorno, and Víctor Manuel. One issue, for example, contained a supplement devoted to the Spanish-born Cuban artist Jaime Valls, featuring *El Son* (1927), a crisp line drawing of a circle of five musicians with exaggerated black features, whose bodies lean into their instruments in the shared rhythm of the *son*, a musical style characterized by Afro-Cuban percussion.[37] *Revista de Avance* also informed its readers about avant-garde music, covering international luminaries such as Bela Bartok and Arnold Schoenberg, as well as local composers such as Amadeo Roldán and Alejandro García Caturla.[38] The magazine championed Afro-Cuban art and literature, publishing the *poesía negra* of Ramón Guirao and Emilio Ballagas, Afro-Cuban writings by Nicolas Guillén, Carpentier, and Tallet, reflections on Afro-Cuban music by Roldán and García Caturla, as well as drawings, like that of Valls, of Afro-Cuban subjects. Some of these artists and writers exoticized blackness even as they made it visible, a strategy of self-differentiation that helped market their work abroad.[39] In this and other ways, the magazine's position on race was contradictory.[40] Nevertheless, *Revista de Avance* hoped to identify uniquely Cuban—and, by extension, Latin American—cultural attributes. *Poesía negra*, for instance, was part of what the editors termed their "search for the autochthonous."[41] This "search for indigenous strains," Francine Masiello argues, led the magazine's editors "to propose a set of wide alliances that would link Cubans to other Latin Americans in search of a common past."[42]

The magazine outlined these goals in its editorials. In its first manifesto-like statement, "Al llevar el ancla" (Raising the anchor), the five founding editors (Carpentier, Casanovas, Ichaso, Mañach, and Marinello) describe the magazine as a boat with martial intentions, echoing the rhetoric of magazines such as the Argentine *Proa* (Prow). Full of allusions to the sea, wind, and fish, the essay proposes the metaphor of the editors aboard a ship (the magazine), sailing forward and refusing to surrender to their adversaries. To follow their line of thought, the seas ahead might be rough, but the editors will manage to navigate them: "For, even if it sounds a little emphatic, this ship sails with a certain heroic spirit, willing to sink, like many others, if adverse wind blows, but refusing in advance any pathetic tow lines. In the end, the crew is scarce and all of us, somehow or other, know how to swim."[43] The editors position themselves as skillful helmsmen, capable of confronting the challenges that face their aesthetic project. They also assert their alertness to the international: "Our little antenna [is] ready for whatever messages of other lands and seas we can intercept along our course. We will decipher them, and may even dare to answer them."[44] With this declaration, the editors playfully stake out their platform and solicit likeminded readers to join their cause.

Jorge Mañach expanded on the magazine's aesthetic program—and its nautical metaphor—in a series of interrelated articles in *Revista de Avance*'s first three issues. In "Vanguardismo," published in the first issue, Mañach writes, "It seems high time to sharpen the word 'avant-garde' with a kind of militant *-ism*. Because, when fundamentally considered, every *-ism* is like a prow which unites, strengthens, and tunes the timbers of a social sailboat."[45] This boat will not only sail into the winds of change, as suggested by the opening editorial, but will also spawn a new movement, according to Mañach. Mañach invokes the original militaristic inflection of the term "avant-garde," defining it as "the militant in-carnation of an attitude that was originally vague and unfocused, [and now] has managed to enlist hordes of passionate followers and to spur an expanded state of consciousness."[46] Through this series of articles, Mañach reinforced *Revista de Avance*'s mission and its commitment to the avant-garde.

Self-consciously inserting itself into an international avant-garde through such texts, *Revista de Avance* also demonstrated its capacity to synthesize and critique printed material from across the Americas and Europe. Its book review section had an almost pedagogical function: "It is certainly not necessary to comment extensively here on distant literary markets," the editors write in the opening of the Foreign Letters section, "but it is worth briefly drawing atten-tion to them, to stimulate *criollo* curiosity."[47] In this way, the editors educated their audience as they crafted local taste. They similarly reviewed magazines from Europe, such as Marinetti's *La Città Futura*, as well as Latin American publications: *Amauta* in Peru, *Martín Fierro* in Argentina, *Repertorio Americano* in Costa Rica, and the Mexican magazines *Contemporáneos*, *Forma*, *La Batal-la*, *Mástiles*, *Circunvalación*, and *Norte*. In a single issue from 1929, *Revista de Avance* mentioned the North American magazines *Blues*, *transition*, the *Hound and Horn*, and the *Dial*. Introducing *Blues* to Cuban audiences, *Revista de Avance* also critiqued the magazine, concluding that it displayed an "experimental and reactive energy, even if at times it is too accommodating of Joyce's dangerous springboard."[48] Playfully brusque in tone, these reviews established the editors of *Revista de Avance* as incisive readers and critics of international periodicals. To a similar end, the last section of every magazine, "Index Barbarorum," was devoted to tracking linguistic misuse, where the "errors and abuses of language committed by careless writers or speakers were prosecuted."[49] These sections indicate how *Revista de Avance* bolstered its aesthetic platform while cannily maneuvering within a complex network of both local and foreign cultural production.

Revista de Avance also emerged from and engendered a vast periodical network within Cuba. For example, Carpentier, Mañach, Tallet, and Marinello assisted with *Venezuela Libre: Órgano revolucionario latinoamericano* (1921–25), which shared their interest in forging Latin American unity, while Tallet and other contributors worked on *América Libre: Revista revolucionaria americana* (1927) to advance political and educational reform.[50] There were several Minorist-affiliated magazines as well, including the short-lived *Los minoristas* and the *Revista del Grupo Minorista de Matanzas*, both from 1927. *Revista de Avance* was also in dialogue with the Cuban magazines *Atuei* (1927–28), *Juventud* (1923–25), *Revista de La Habana* (1930), *Grafos* (1932–38), *Mediodía* (1936–39), and *Revista de Oriente* (1928). As early as the second issue of *Revista de Avance*, the magazine announced its indebtedness to other periodicals in Cuba: "Certain cultural tasks cannot be improvised: they need the prior labor of digging and pruning, the first fertilizer. Such work has been carried out in Cuba, in recent years, by some diligent publications, whose judgment would be capricious and unjust to ignore within the very task of civilizing refinement that we have taken upon ourselves."[51] The editors acknowledge that their work emerged out of a larger periodical culture, and also hope to demonstrate their solidarity with other publications, declaring, "The fundamental aim of those intentions is the same as ours. Their paths are parallel. If we sail in different ships, it is because we understand that here it takes a whole spirited fleet of efforts going along the same course."[52] Through their extended nautical metaphor, the editors maintain that *Revista de Avance* would rather promote itself alongside these other periodicals than compete with them.

Like most small magazines, *Revista de Avance* relied on subscriptions to fund its production and accompanying cultural activities. In the magazine's third issue, the editors made an impassioned plea to subscribers: "To friends of '1927': Because our work is completely disinterested, even onerous, we unscrupulously exhort those that until now have been reading '1927' with pleasure and approval to adhere as subscribers to our magazine, thus contributing to our enterprise in the most effective manner: economic strength."[53] The editors report back in the next issue that over two hundred people responded to the call, and were thus named "founding subscribers."[54] Such support covered some of the costs of publication and *Revista de Avance*'s other cultural endeavors.

More than just a magazine, *Revista de Avance* served as a cultural nexus for an emergent Cuban avant-garde. It held art exhibitions, such as the *Exhibition of New Art*, started a publishing house called Las ediciones de la revista de avance, and promoted Cuban concerts.[55] Many of the group's writers also participated in the annual salons and exhibitions held at the Association of Painters and Sculptors as well at the Asociación del Club Cubano de Bellas Artes (Association of the Cuban Club of Fine Arts).[56] The impulse to construct and promote a uniquely Cuban culture within a broader Latin American context was legible in all of the work of *Revista de Avance*, particularly in its art exhibition and subsequent questionnaire.

Exposición de Arte Nuevo

Revista de Avance worked tirelessly to advocate for the visual arts in Cuba, both through its reproduction of artwork in the pages of the magazine and by staging the first exhibition of avant-garde art in the nation. The *Exhibition of New Art* opened at the Association of Painters and Sculptors on May 7, 1927, and ran through May 31, 1927. It included the work of Cuban artists Eduardo Abela, Rafael Blanco, Gabriel Castaño, Antonio Gattorno, Marcelo Pogolotti, Carlos Enríquez, and Víctor Manuel, among others, as well as the American artist Alice Neel (then the wife of Carlos Enríquez) and the Latvian-born Adja Yunkers.[57] Some of these artists had signed the Declaration of the Grupo Minorista, and many had their work featured in previous issues of *Revista de Avance.* Despite its inclusion of two foreign artists, the exhibition was accompanied by a manifesto, published in the magazine, which proclaimed the group "artists of the new generation, who . . . fight to incorporate our art into the great undertakings of our time without neglecting . . . its essential Cubanism."[58] *Revista de Avance* organized and promoted the *Exhibition of New Art* and its accompanying symposia, reproduced images of artwork from the exhibition, and published reviews of the show, clearly aiming to galvanize and institute a national avant-garde.

As in other parts of Latin America, there were few opportunities for artists in Cuba in the early twentieth century. As Néstor García Canclini explains, "The first phase of Latin American modernism was stimulated by artists and writers returning to their home countries after a time in Europe. It was not as much the direct, transplanted, influence of the European avant-garde that awoke the desire for modernization in Latin American visual arts but rather the questions raised by Latin Americans themselves as to how to make their international experience relevant to developing societies."[59] Such a trajectory played out in Cuba as well. To counter the conservative approach of the San Alejandro Academy, the reigning art school in Cuba, many Cuban artists traveled to Paris to immerse themselves in the latest tendencies in avant-garde art. In Paris these artists worked alongside artists from around the world and were involved in movements such as Fauvism, Cubism, and Expressionism.[60] The Association of Painters and Sculptors, founded in Havana in 1915 by the artist Federico Edelman Pintó as an alternative to the academic model, was the primary venue for these artists' work in Cuba and held the *Exhibition of New Art.*[61]

The artists in the exhibition were part of the *vanguardia*, a nonaffiliated group of Latin American artists working in a variety of cities and styles from roughly 1916 through the 1930s, who sought to create new visual vocabularies in which to express their experiences at home and abroad. Across Latin America, *vanguardia* artists aimed to refashion art's public function and to refocus its energies by addressing the region's past civilizations and its African and

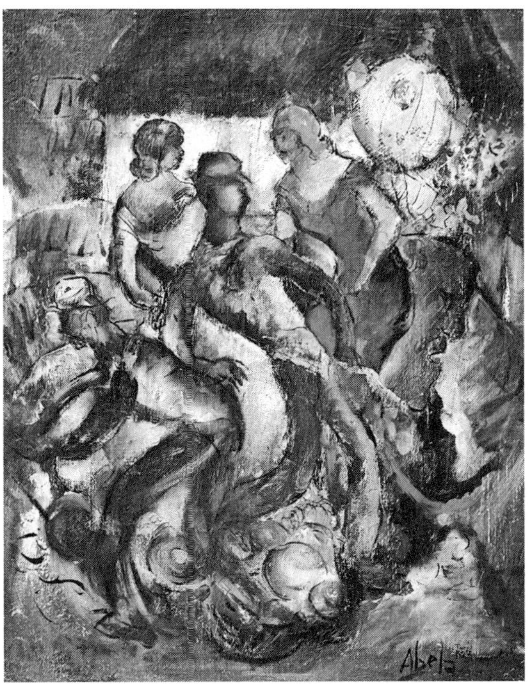

Fig. 5 Eduardo Abela, *Fiesta en el Batey*, 1927, oil on canvas, mounted on wood, 23 ¾ × 17 ½ in. Collection Ramón and Nercys Cernuda.

indigenous populations.[62] This impulse led to artistic developments such as Mexican Muralism, *indigenismo* in the Andean countries, and *antropofagia* in Brazil, among other avant-garde iterations.[63] As such varied movements suggest, there can be no single or homogeneous category of Latin American art. Latin America encompasses both urban and rural terrain, Spanish-, Portuguese-, and French-speaking populations, as well as locally divergent native traditions and wide-ranging political, social, and economic histories. Art from across Latin America was at once regionally specific and made in conversation with artistic production throughout the continent as well as in relation to that of Europe, the United States, and elsewhere. Despite such diversity, the term "Latin American art" had international currency and a rhetorical force that jointly advanced various countries' disparate movements and interests.

In the case of Cuba, *vanguardia* artists such as Eduardo Abela, Antonio Gattorno, and Víctor Manuel reconciled avant-garde ideas gleaned from Europe with Cuban-specific themes. Their works typically featured Cuban music and landscapes, and often centralized female figures, as in Abela's painting *Fiesta en el Batey* (1927; fig. 5). In this piece, the exaggerated movements of dancing bodies are inextricable from the trees, forming a mass of bright colors and swirling lines. One woman daubed in red stands out, echoing a flickering lantern alongside her. Through an expressionistic handling of paint, Abela showcases at once the vegetation and the rhythms of the *batey*, or sugar mill settlement. In the more static *Mujeres junto al río* (Women by the river, 1927), Gattorno elongates and distorts his female figures, seeming to equate the women with the leaves, hills, and sky against which they are placed. Víctor Manuel similarly flattens his female subjects against the backdrop of a landscape, as in his undated *Dos mujeres y paisaje* (Two women and landscape), providing the viewer with a more closely cropped and intimate pose, as the women lean on a windowsill that frames the painting.[64] Notably, these Cuban artists' paintings retain the centrality of the figure, unlike the work of many concomitant European avant-garde artists. They also often depict rural life, which signaled Cuba's fight for independence and may have also hinted at the oppression of the Zayas and Machado regimes.[65] While the combination of autochthonous subject matter and European technique could sometimes tend toward self-exotification, the Cuban avant-garde synthesized such heterogeneous elements to develop a national aesthetic.[66]

Several of the works featured in the *Exhibition of New Art* were reproduced in the pages of the magazine. In a double-page spread, for example, the editors present two figurative paintings, by Antonio Gattorno and Luis López Méndez, alongside a pair of cityscapes by Marcelo Pogolotti and L. Romero Arciaga (fig. 6). While the artists' styles differ, the two figurative paintings foreground racialized bodies, depicted against rolling hills in the case of Gattorno and lush tropical vegetation in that of López Méndez. Pogolotti and Arciaga both juxtapose the built environment with the natural one. Whether considered individually or together, these paintings offer a stylized representation of the nation—composed of its people, landscapes, and cityscapes—all notably executed with either expressionistic or abstract techniques, signaling a vision for a new Cuban avant-garde.

The rhetoric accompanying these images celebrated the artwork as part of a burgeoning national movement. The text printed alongside them describes the exhibition as the first to "embrace, exclusively, the artistic avant-garde." "After this exhibition, one can already speak of something current and militant about . . . avant-garde art in Cuba," the editors announce, noting that "what was until now a hazy premonition, is [finally] a reality."[67] The editors also describe themselves as both "participants and initiators of this first collective exhibition of new art . . . the first of its kind to be celebrated in Havana," explicitly linking the exhibition's name, patronage, and animating forces to the magazine.[68] In a manifesto-like essay published in the same issue, editor Martí Casanovas situates the artists' work and the exhibition in the narrative of change established by the magazine, writing, "We fully condemn and negate the art of the nineteenth century. . . . The highest aspiration of our young artists is to forget all that has existed, all the museums they have visited, all the pyrotechnics of past art.

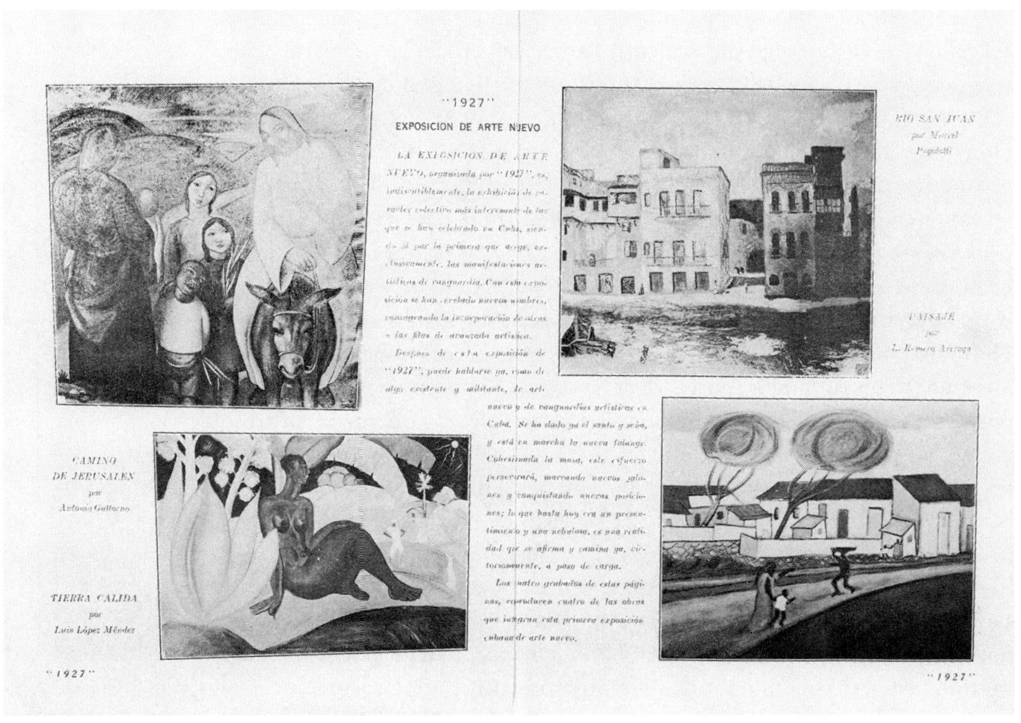

Fig. 6 "Exposición de arte nuevo," *Revista de Avance* (Havana) 1, no. 5 (May 15, 1927).

We are trying to start anew."[69] Casanovas argues that the artists in the exhibition (and by extension, the magazine) are definitively breaking with the past. Building on the achievements of the *Exhibition of New Art*, *Revista de Avance* continued to emphatically proclaim the importance of an *arte americano*, and posed it formally as a category in a questionnaire the following year.

Questioning Latin American Art

In September 1928 the journal published "Indagación: ¿Qué debe ser el arte americano?" The editors explain that they preferred the term *indagación* (inquiry) to *encuesta* (questionnaire) because the former "has not yet been perverted by bad company: it is innocent of that malice of means and of filling up, of frivolous sliminess with which journalism has corrupted questionnaires, almost always cajoling idlers."[70] Such ambivalence about the questionnaire was common throughout the 1920s, prompting an abundance of editorial justifications. Despite their rhetorical distaste for the questionnaire, the editors of *Revista de Avance* still inscribed their aspirations for Latin American art into a genre that marked their participation in the international avant-garde.

Printed under the heading "What should American art be?," the inquiry
asks, "Do you believe that the work of an American artist should reveal American concerns? Do you believe that 'Americanness' is a matter of perspective,
content, or medium? Do you believe that there might be characteristics common to the art of all of the countries in our America? What should the attitude
of American artists toward European art be?"[71] (fig. 7). "We invite replies from
any American with a considered opinion," the editors note. "For obvious reasons, please make the answers as brief as possible."[72] Many of the seventeen
responses received were nevertheless quite lengthy, and they were published
in the magazine's subsequent twelve issues, marking a full year of debate.
The questionnaire invited writers and artists from across Cuba and Latin
America to confront their shared anxieties about Latin America's cultural
position as well as their collective ambitions to elevate Latin American art to
greater prominence.

Through the use of the phrase "our America" in the questionnaire, the
editors explicitly align with a discourse of Latin American solidarity stemming
from Martí's 1891 essay. It is important to differentiate this notion of "America"
from North America, a distinction underscored by several emphatic responses.
The Venezuelan historian and poet Rufino Blanco Fombona insists "we are
not talking about the Yankees."[73] Raúl Roa, a lawyer, activist, and politician,
cautions artists to maintain "an eminently critical attitude" so as to avoid being
an "intellectual colony of Europe, as we already are economically to the United
States."[74] The Mexican writer Jaime Torres Bodet distinguishes between an
americanidad of the spirit and one of the machine. Torres Bodet celebrates
Latin American specificity as an antidote to "living undefined, letting oneself
be swept up in the tide of European fashions and preferences . . . an easy and
perfectly tropical way of being *marginal.*"[75] But he recognizes the challenges of
this position, writing, "Of course, how can one demand to see real specificity in
art and literature in today's Latin American republics when everything seems to
be conspiring against it: the speed of international communications, the rapid
penetration of the most exotic cultures, and the increased weakening of the
colonial tradition, a small, hazy refuge for the Americanness of the spirit, that
the other—the Americanness of the machine—is hurrying to devour."[76] Torres
Bodet argues that in a modernized, interconnected world, artists need to work
harder to perpetuate autochthonous culture, to stave off both "the tide of European fashions" and "the Americanness of the machine." Paradoxically, Torres
Bodet uses "international communications"—that is, a questionnaire issued in
a border-crossing magazine—to define and disseminate his positions.

In addition to their wariness of the United States, many respondents also
distinguish Latin American art from that of Europe and its influence. According
to Eduardo Áviles Ramírez, a Nicaraguan poet residing in Cuba, "the American
artist must exalt the classical forms of Indian art" as a way of "escaping vile
servitude to Europe" and create "human art" in the face of the trend toward

directrices

U N A E N C U E S T A

Tras el epígrafe, que ho de fulminar su sentido, preferimos llamarla una indagación. Y no porque sea más castizo, sino porque esta otra palabra no ha sido aún pervertida por las malas compañías: está inocente de esa malicia de recurso y de relleno, de esa frívola untuosidad en que el periodismo ha enviciado a las encuestas, sonsacadoras esquineras casi siempre.

No queremos reclutar lectores ni agenciarnos atención. Buscamos la exploración del problema subterráneo más hondo sobre el cual se mueve hoy la conciencia artística americana. Y hemos querido minar esa hondura sin luz con cuatro preguntas que nos parecen rectas y verticales —hacia la misma entraña del asunto:

¿ Qué debe ser el arte americano ?

1a.—¿ Cree usted que la obra del artista americano debe revelar una preocupación americana ?

2a.—¿ Cree usted que la americanidad es cuestión de óptica, de contenido o de vehículo ?

3a.—¿ Cree usted en la posibilidad de caracteres comunes al arte de todos los países de nuestra América ?

4a.—¿ Cuál debe ser la actitud del artista americano ante lo europeo ?

Invitamos a que contesten cuantos americanos tengan algo meditado que decir. Sólo rogamos, por razones obvias, que las respuestas sean lo más enjutas posible.

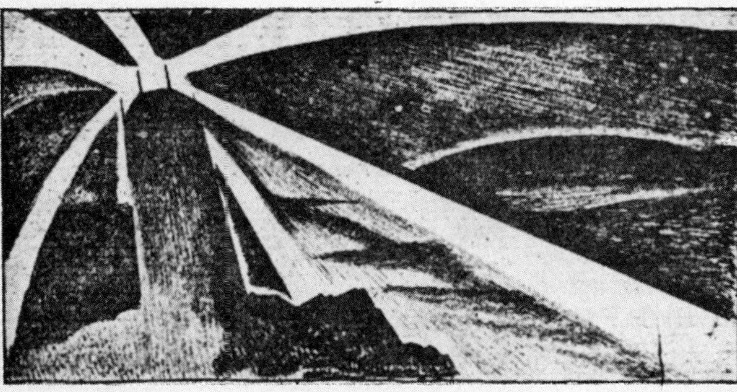

235

Fig. 7 Los Cinco, "Directrices: Una encuesta," *Revista de Avance* (Havana) 2, no. 26 (September 15, 1928): 235.

"dehumanization" in art, as identified by Ortega y Gasset.[77] The painter Eduardo Abela situates Latin American art as the fertile future of a decaying Europe, writing, "European art, properly speaking, old and weary of itself, has sought transfusions to keep it strong. . . . American art is a life that arises against a life that has already been."[78] The Uruguayan critic and folklorist Ildefonso Pereda Valdés also positions Europe in the past, maintaining that the American artist ought to treat the European with "a respectful admiration, as if we were in front of a museum where everything has already been made and nothing new could be expected from it," and cautions that "respect does not mean submission: to admire is not to imitate."[79] This disdain for imitation can be found in many of the responses, as the contributors aim to assert Latin American cultural autonomy.

Other respondents acknowledge the influence of European art, or see it as a point of departure for Latin American production. The painter Carlos Enríquez insists that art from "Primitivism to Surrealism is a common language of the true artist" and that "the only intelligent attitude . . . is understanding and the exchange of ideas."[80] Such an exchange of ideas might even help distinguish one's artistic identity, the novelist Luis Felipe Rodríguez argues. "Let us embrace that which is European," he writes, "as a strong, old discipline [against which] to affirm that which is ours."[81] José Antonio Ramos, a Cuban writer, takes this reasoning even further, arguing that many Latin Americans found success *because* of Europe; he cites Rubén Darío and Diego Rivera as examples, and observes the lack of support for the arts in Latin America.[82] Latin America, he argues, because of its economic and linguistic disadvantages, depends on Europe and the United States to inspire and sustain its artists. "Our language is a dying language," he proclaims. "Today's world thinks and works in English." He also offers a counterpoint to the other responses by suggesting that Europe is a fitting destination in which to absorb culture: "Europe is a museum, an excellent workshop. Why not use it too?" Although he laments Latin America's uneven economic, linguistic, and cultural position, Antonio Ramos ends his response with a call for invention: "Let's write, paint, sculpt, create music: the only possible metaphysics, to create! And tirelessly."[83]

After a year of printing such long, impassioned, and sometimes contradictory responses, *Revista de Avance* editor Francisco Ichaso wrote his own reflection on the questionnaire and its results. He remained ambivalent about the genre, acknowledging the "bias of our findings," and pointed out that many of those solicited chose not to respond, since the questionnaire's ubiquity had led some writers to be wary of it. As Ichaso explains, "The questionnaire is a journalistic genre that has few supporters in informed sectors. As with interviews and competitions, it has fallen to the same level of contempt. Almost every writer who believes he 'has arrived' begins, cautiously, by not responding to questionnaires, by not giving interviews, and by not going to competitions."[84] Whatever the limitations of the genre, Ichaso defends the magazine's choice to issue the questionnaire. He argues that it is a site wherein those of "agile spirit" can maneuver through what might be perceived as a rigid formula: "We're actually a little unfair to questionnaires. Like any other form, they try to invite a group of writers to rethink certain topics. Rigid? The questionnaire is only rigid for those dogmatic spirits who believe that the truth can only be found in the 'yes, father; no, father' of catechisms."[85] He even celebrates the act of questioning as fundamental to artistic creation, suggesting, "perhaps the only thing that we can do before the enigmas of the world is formulate questions."[86] Ichaso further validates the exercise by citing the response of Torres Bodet, who had proclaimed that "he who has not formulated, in the court of his own conscience, this interrogation of transcendental responsibilities, lives—in artistic matters at least—a provisional, more or less borrowed life."[87] For Ichaso, the questionnaire fulfilled its purpose because it "gathered a dozen collaborators on an issue," which collectively demonstrated a "unanimous desire to present our spiritual profile to the world with lines as distinctive as our geography."[88]

The goal of the questionnaire, according to Ichaso, was not simply to reach the contributors whose responses filled the journal, but rather to inspire a wider audience to reckon with the concept of "American art." This is the true measure of the questionnaire's reach, he argues: "If our questionnaire has created or recreated the problem of American art for more than one man on the continent; if, apart from those responses given as publicity, more than one reader of '1929' [*Revista de Avance*] has answered the questions with curious earnestness, then our purpose was fulfilled."[89] Ichaso lauds the inquiry for "creating or recreating the problem of American art" for its readers. Ichaso also applauds the respondents for transforming what he admits were somewhat simple, reductive questions into serious aesthetic debate. For instance, Ichaso concedes that the first question, "Do you think the work of an American artist should reveal American concerns?," needs to be true in order for the remaining questions to be meaningful. He notes "that this preoccupation must exist or not is what's important . . . the ethical or political corollary of what our attitude should be to that which is European [is] secondary."[90] Basically, if the first question was not answered in the affirmative, it could derail the entire exercise. However, Ichaso explains that many participants—he points to Torres Bodet and Raúl Maestri specifically—"come to the same conclusion by different paths," demonstrating the expansiveness of the genre despite its seeming rigidity. According to Ichaso, these respondents ultimately determined that "the American concern in the work of an American artist is not problematic; it's compulsory, inescapable."[91] By reframing the first question as necessarily true in their responses, the questionnaire's contributors validated the editors' instincts.

However, by then asking what Latin America's relationship should be in relation to Europe, *Revista de Avance* implicitly acknowledged the continent's anxiety about its transatlantic position. Ichaso maintains that Europe is interested in Latin American artistic production, writing, "France, Italy, Spain are

perched on their Atlantic balconies, their ears alert to murmurs from the West,
eager to capture our message."[92] Yet in a contradictory gesture, Ichaso also be-
moans the fact that Latin Americans require validation from Europeans, noting,
"It is fairly sad for our artistic dignity that it is the European artists and critics
themselves who have to be the ones to remind us of our duty not to continue to
be subsidiaries of Europe."[93] The scholar Vicky Unruh explains the problem as
follows: "The Americanist component of Latin America's vanguardist activity
was also always ironically intertwined with European expectations of an imagined New World."[94] Managing such expectations put Latin American artists,
many of whom had spent time in Europe, in a difficult position. Echoing Martí's
warning against imitation, Ichaso decries the "European mold that we learn
in the academy, the university, and the book" for precluding "the spontaneous
that's within us."[95] Moreover, "Europe cannot look at us with respect while we
live, spiritually, under its tutelage," Ichaso writes. Autonomy is required, partially to attract European interest, he suggests. Ichaso continues, "It's doubtful that
Europe feels great interest in listening to itself over and over again through the
resounding echo of its voice in our mountains." He thus calls for spontaneous,
autochthonous artistic gestures to counteract Europe, but also to attract its
attention. In this way, Ichaso recreates the struggles of many of the respondents
to the questionnaire, who seem eager to carve out a space for uniquely Latin
American art, but one that still retains a relationship to Europe.

Ichaso, and by extension *Revista de Avance*, was faced with the task of
articulating an artistic identity that was not in some way a reflection of Europe.
The scholar George Yúdice describes this as Latin America's double bind in
relation to Europe, arguing that Latin Americans were poised to either "be
modern like the Europeans" or to resort to "a primitivism . . . which the Europeans themselves have called for in order to regenerate a supposedly decaying
civilization."[96] Ichaso wrestles with this problematic position, adopting Abela's
metaphor of offering "transfusions" to a Europe in decline: "The danger is
not in generously giving our blood for the urgent transfusions that a limping
old world already requires, but in becoming too interested in the injection of
the drug of cosmopolitanism, whether it comes from the West or the North."
Instead of the threat of primitivism or exotification, Ichaso warns against an
excessive interest in Europe and North America. "We are . . . a little addicted to
cosmopolitanism," he laments, citing Paris and New York as particular problems.[97] Through such statements, Ichaso situates North America and Europe as
antagonists, which prevent an authentic artistic culture from emerging in Latin
America. Ichaso goes so far as to refer to "Yankee imperialism" as a "common
enemy" uniting Latin Americans. He writes, "The peoples living South of the
Rio Grande must adopt a common continental attitude before such problems
as Yankee imperialism—our common enemy—the question of *mestizaje*—be
it from the mixture of the indigenous or black races with the Spanish, Italian,
or the Chinese—and also with respect to the European or North American

interpretations, which are generally defective due to a lack of knowledge or excessive greed. This attitude would be advisable as much for Americans from the Antilles as for those from Tierra del Fuego."[98] Ichaso advocates for a united Latin America that can respond to its unique racial composition so as to combat U.S. imperialism and counter misinformation about the region disseminated by Europeans and North Americans.

Elaborating on this "common continental attitude," Ichaso calls for "an art of the people" that is not superficial or trite. He cautions, "We must beware . . . of confusing 'essential Americanness' with that sort of external, picturesque *criollismo*, which is practiced throughout America."[99] Instead of turning to the folkloric, the American artist has a duty to "interpret the soul of America, which is in its mountains, valleys, rivers, in its men, its customs, traditions, and songs." While such artistic responses to geography may be specific to an individual country, Ichaso argues that art across the continent is nevertheless united by "bonds stronger than language, race, geography and history," because Latin Americans share a "marvelous equality before destiny."[100] This lofty rhetoric does not clearly indicate what such art might look like in practice, but it does inspire a shared sense of purpose. As for Latin America's position in relation to Europe and the United States, Ichaso concludes by quoting Martí: "We must make our republics part of the world, but our republics must remain our foundation."[101]

The Legacy of *Revista de Avance*

For Ichaso, the writers who responded to the inquiry formed "a mosaic of differences," but nevertheless succeeded in "highlighting the shared American vein."[102] Such a statement stakes a claim for "American art" that can encompass variation while simultaneously addressing a collective experience. By asking, "What should American art be?," the editors of *Revista de Avance* worked to build such a coalition. Throughout its print run, the magazine continued to advocate for art, music, and writing that reflected Cuba and Latin America's complex racial and cultural heritages, and to publish work by North American, Spanish, and French writers and artists, offering a snapshot of the avant-garde both at home and abroad. The editors also continued to fight for autonomous political and cultural institutions in Cuba.

Emerging out of political upheaval, *Revista de Avance* collapsed in tandem with another government confrontation. The last issue came out on September 30, 1930, coinciding with a bloody government-student clash wherein the student Rafael Trejo was killed. The editors suspended publication in solidarity with the student movement and in protest of increased government censorship and repression.[103] This tragedy was not the only political impetus behind the end of *Revista de Avance*. In 1930 editor Juan Marinello was accused of inciting a student rebellion and was subsequently imprisoned. Moreover, by 1931, many of the editors had splintered into different political factions.[104] However, *Revista de Avance*'s editors did continue to advocate for educational reform, expanding women's rights, and the for repeal of the Platt Amendment, which occurred in 1934. Writing about the magazine's contributions in 1937, Marinello even credits the journal with sparking the 1933 revolution that overthrew Machado.[105]

The political and cultural landscape out of which *Revista de Avance* emerged generated a robust print culture that persisted after it folded. After the Spanish poet Juan Ramón Jiménez visited Cuba in 1936, his aestheticist inclinations were reflected in magazines such as *Espuela de Plata* (1939–41), *Nadie Parecía* (1942–44), and *Orígenes* (1944–56), the last of which was seen as a response to the work of *Revista de Avance*.[106] Many of those involved with *Revista de Avance* also continued to contribute to a variety of Cuban publications.[107] For instance, Carpentier, who had written for *La Discusión* (1922–23) and *El Diario de la Marina* (1927–28) before founding *Revista de Avance*, wrote for magazines such as *Social* (1924–33) and *Carteles* (1923–40) while in Paris, in addition to his work for *Imán*, which I discuss in chapter 3.[108] Much like *Revista de Avance*, these magazines disseminated Cuban literature and art, as well as offering their readers examples of work from across Latin America and abroad.

Revista de Avance's efforts were also part of a broader push to develop new cultural institutions in Cuba. The Lyceum, a women's organization, was founded in 1928 by Berta Arocena and Renée Méndez Capote to hold art exhibitions, readings, and conferences. It launched with an exhibition of Cuban avant-garde art, whose opening was covered by *Revista de Avance*, and later held one-person shows for Abela, Gattorno, Pogolotti, as well as other artists who had been featured in the *Exhibition of New Art*.[109] Abela also founded the Estudio Libre (Free Studio) in 1936. Although it only lasted five months, the studio was extremely influential, both academically and artistically, and served as a tuition-free art school that cultivated a national avant-garde.[110] The work of this avant-garde also reached wider audiences. For example, in 1944 an exhibition was held at the Museum of Modern Art in New York titled *Modern Cuban Painters*. Remarking on Cuba's *vanguardia* in his catalogue essay for the show, Alfred Barr Jr., the museum's director, describes *Revista de Avance* as foundational to the artists on view. "The writers of the new *Revista de Avance*, especially Jorge Mañach and Juan Marinello, came valiantly to the support of the young painters," Barr writes; "the new movement was underway."[111]

In his own reflections on *Revista de Avance* from 1944, editor Jorge Mañach also celebrates the magazine as a catalyst for change. Mañach writes that the editors had wanted "to react—stridently, heretically, and even with insolence— against the inertia of tradition, against mental and moral attitudes of the time, and against their corresponding modes of expression."[112] Hoping to transform the country's political and artistic climate, *Revista de Avance* questioned, and worked to reform, Cuba's cultural and political institutions. By initiating a debate about what "American art should be" in relation to international forces, *Revista de Avance* invited attention to Latin America's European, African, colonial, imported, and native heritages, and sought a commitment to building its cultural future. As *Revista de Avance* editor Félix Lizaso observed in 1961, "Magazines, when they fit into a particular historical moment of art or ideas, come to be a reflection of the cultural period in which they are bound to live and serve to illuminate or even revive it."[113] Providing a lens through which to read this turbulent period in Cuban history, *Revista de Avance* demonstrates the capacity of a magazine to report on and to embody its political and cultural moment, foregrounded in this case by the magazine's 1928 questionnaire.

Latin American Art Abroad

Revista de Avance was part of a larger network of periodicals that interrogated various incarnations of "American art" in relation to Europe. The same year that *Revista de Avance* asked, "What should American art be? What should the attitude of American artists toward European art be?," the expatriate magazine *transition* polled both its North American and European contributors about their relationship to America. In addition to their shared interest in questioning "America" and its relationship to Europe, *Revista de Avance* reviewed *transition* in 1929, calling it a "bold laboratory for English-speaking émigrés in Paris"; *transition*, in turn, published *Revista de Avance* contributors such as Alejo Carpentier and the Mexican poet Alfonso Reyes.[114] Three years later, in 1931, the Paris-based Latin American magazine *Imán* posed the inverse of the questions issued by *Revista de Avance*, asking European Surrealists such as Georges Bataille, Philippe Soupault, and Michel Leiris, "How do you imagine Latin America? What will its position be in relation to Europe?" Carpentier, who had edited *Revista de Avance* before fleeing Cuba for Paris, collaborated with the Argentine editor Elvira de Alvear to publish *Imán*, which also included a text by *transition* editor Eugene Jolas and shared many of its contributors. As I consider *transition* and *Imán*'s questionnaires in the subsequent chapter, the question of what "American art" should be persists, as does *Revista de Avance*'s approach to concerns that all three magazines addressed.

Revista de Avance wanted to establish a category of Latin American art within an international framework dominated by European cultural advancements and encroaching U.S. power. While *transition* was an American magazine and *Imán* Latin American, both aimed to assert a place for literature and art of the Americas on the world stage. Unlike *Revista de Avance*, whose location in Havana was crucial to its identity, these two magazines built their communities in Paris and worked to facilitate transatlantic collaboration through translation. While *Revista de Avance* used its questionnaire to instantiate a category of "American art," *Imán*, more in line with *transition*, sought to map out what the contours of the relationship between Europe and the Americas looked like; in fact, its questionnaire was a way of assessing Europe's *lack* of knowledge about Latin America. Nevertheless, the fluidity with which these periodicals shared contributors and editors underscores their common goals: building national canons,

forming outlets for artistic and literary expression from the Americas, introducing readers to both local and foreign material, and transmitting such work
internationally. While all three magazines probed the relationship between
Europe and the Americas through the genre of the questionnaire, their surveys
vacillate in their desire for autonomy or recognition from Europe. Read alongside each other, these questionnaires offer insight into how such magazines
at once created cultural platforms and closely examined their own geopolitical
positions in order to determine the potential for "American" art and literature
in an international context.

3. TRANSLATING THE AMERICAS

America is "a country the right age to have been born in and the wrong age to live in," Gertrude Stein wrote in 1928 in response to a questionnaire issued by *transition*, a North American magazine based in Paris. In consecutive issues in 1928, *transition* asked its European writers, "How are the influences of the United States manifesting themselves upon Europe?" and polled its American contributors, including Stein, asking, "Why do Americans live in Europe?" Three years later, in 1931, *Imán*, a Latin American magazine also based in Paris, issued a variation on the same set of questions to many of the same Europeans: "How do you imagine Latin America? What will its position be in relation to Europe?" As magazines from the Americas both located abroad, *transition* and *Imán* tested their own transatlantic positions through such questionnaires. Artists and writers from across the Americas moved to Paris in the 1920s, producing art and literature far from their home countries. Some, like Stein, chose a life of expatriatism in order to estrange and heighten their relationship to English, while others, like the Cuban writer Alejo Carpentier, who helped edit *Revista de Avance* and *Imán*, resettled due to political exigencies. Regardless of their motives for moving abroad, these artists' and writers' newfound location and the allegiances that they formed there provoked questions about their relationships to their homelands. The viewpoints of these expatriates and exiles were inscribed in the kind of work that they produced in Paris, and articulated more fully through their responses to questionnaires.

    Imán, edited by Latin Americans and printed in Spanish in Paris, and *transition*, an English-language expatriate publication, both explored what constituted "America" in terms of translation. Each journal translated texts by Franz Kafka, Hans Arp, and other Europeans into either Spanish or English. As a result of their location in Paris and their commitment to translation, these magazines were curious to know how European writers perceived the Americas, and in turn what place "American" writing had abroad. In many ways, their questionnaires sought to ratify their experiences as expatriate publications. Unlike *Revista de Avance*, which displayed and championed Latin American visual art, *Imán* was primarily a literary magazine (though it had plans to include art in future issues).[1] While *transition* did prominently feature artists from across Europe and the Americas, it too was concerned with literary translation. In this chapter I explore how the Americas were constructed through the rhetoric of translation in *transition* and *Imán*, and how these magazines' translations, at once cultural and linguistic, each sought to produce a version of America that would inherit the cultural legacy of Europe. Such a comparison traces a transatlantic route between Europe—particularly Paris—and the Americas, following the itinerary of the editors, contributors, and readers of each publication.

Eugene Jolas, the editor of *transition*, was raised between the United States and Europe. Trilingual in English, French, and German, Jolas sought a new form of transnational communication. He writes, "I dreamed a new language, a super-tongue for intercontinental expression. . . . I felt that the great Atlantic community to which I belonged demanded an Atlantic language."[2] Jolas used *transition* to develop and test out this Atlantic language. In 1929, a year after issuing the two questionnaires, *transition* published its "Revolution of the Word" proclamation. This text announces, "The revolution of the English language is an accomplished fact," thus experimenting with the potential of English to be the "Atlantic language" that Jolas had envisioned.[3] However, in 1933 the magazine stopped translating all of its submissions into English clearly struggling to determine which linguistic model best suited its purposes. Jolas sought to reinvigorate English-language writing through examples of European work, and conversely to introduce material from America to European audiences. Yet his notion of what constituted America was expansive, and he imagined English could be infused with the multiple languages that immigrants brought to the United States.

The editor of *Imán*, Elvira de Alvear, showcased Spanish-language writing abroad and translated North American and European material into Spanish. She ran a literary salon in Paris that brought together Latin American and European writers, including Robert Desnos, Vicente Huidobro, Miguel Ángel Asturias, and James Joyce. *Imán* shared many contributors with *transition* and even published an essay by Jolas, translated into Spanish, while Alejo Carpentier, who worked as the editorial secretary of *Imán*, had an essay published in *transition*. Carpentier also published in the dissident Surrealist publications *Bifur* and *Documents* while in Paris, and likely drew on his friendships with Georges Bataille, Robert Desnos, and Michel Leiris to issue them the questionnaire "How Do You Imagine Latin America?" Carpentier also transported the questionnaire back to Latin America through an essay he wrote for the Cuban magazine *Carteles*, wherein he summarizes the survey and calls upon Latin

Americans to "mobilize our energies to translate America with the most intensity possible."[4] Carpentier implies that translation, not only linguistic but also cultural, was the means by which Latin American art and literature would gain an international audience.

Both *transition* and *Imán* hoped that their work would advance greater transatlantic understanding, even as they unmasked tensions between Europe and the Americas through their questionnaires. For Jolas, this reckoning would culminate in an "Atlantic language," a utopian form of transatlantic communication. For *Imán*, an improved transatlantic relationship would help catalyze and distribute Latin American literature, thereby undermining Europeans' exotification of the region. Both publications worked to establish a place for the Americas in the transatlantic imaginary through the material that they published and the questions that they issued. Through translation, these magazines modeled for their readers how art and literature of the Americas might be integrated with international culture.

Latin American Print Culture in Paris

Artists and writers from across the Americas looked to Paris as a model for urban artistic experience and as a site for creative expression. As scholar Marcy Schwartz explains, "The modernist turn toward Paris, from the Spanish American *modernista* movement beginning in the late nineteenth century to the North American 'Lost Generation' of the 1920s and 1930s, is emblematic of the Americas' search for cultural identification outside the newer nations' colonial roots."[5] Ironically, for Latin Americans, France provided a way of eliding Spain and its colonial dominance. Paris also beckoned to artists and writers because it offered an international community of likeminded peers and institutions that would support and display their work. Such resources enabled them to create a professional space—that is, to build an audience and a market—for their intellectual output, a space largely unavailable to them in Latin America.[6] These opportunities were made possible for Latin Americans through grants issued by their governments, particularly after World War I.[7] Also, key cultural intermediaries who traveled to Paris from the late nineteenth century through World War I established a foundation for the following generation of painters, poets, and writers who flocked to the city in the 1920s.

Most notably, Rubén Darío worked abroad as a *cronista* and journalist, as did many Latin American poets at the time. Darío chronicled his experiences in Paris, including his visit to the 1900 World's Fair, for *La Nación* in Argentina.[8] Darío also founded the magazine *Mundial* (1911–14) in Paris. As the critic Jaime Hanneken observes, *Mundial* enacted an important reversal: "Instead of reproducing Parisian culture in local publishing centers (primarily Buenos Aires and Mexico City), Darío promise[d] to produce Latin American culture in the metropolis."[9] Other Latin American magazines provided a similar function. The writer and diplomat Francisco García Calderón's *Revista de América* (1912–14), for example, also published Spanish-language material in Paris. Such magazines had a twofold function: they enabled authors to generate work in their native language for their peers, and also introduced French audiences to Latin American writing.

Modernistas like Darío laid the groundwork for subsequent generations of writers to forge careers in Paris. Two outlets for such writing were the French journals *La Revue Argentine* (1934–45) and *La Revue de l'Amérique Latine* (1922–32), which, unlike the earlier examples, translated and published Latin American writing in French. The *Revue de l'Amérique Latine*, for instance, printed the work of André Gide alongside Argentine writer Leopoldo Lugones, Mexican poet Alfonso Reyes, and Spanish poet Ramón Gómez de la Serna. Furthermore, the publication reviewed Latin American magazines for French audiences, including *Repertorio Americano* from Costa Rica and *Cuba Contemporánea*, thus reinforcing links between the transnational print communities to which many Latin American writers belonged. Summarizing its mission, the editors of *La Revue de l'Amérique Latine* assert that the magazine "publishes the work of French, Hispano-American and Brazilian writers, scholars, and politicians, on Latin America and its relations with France; provides translations of novels, stories, news, poems, and essays by Latin American writers; its numerous and various chronicles summarize the intellectual, artistic, economic, and social life of the entire Latin American continent."[10] Such outlets brought Hispanophone writers into contact with their European counterparts in print.

However, some magazines based in Latin America did not approve of those in Paris. For instance, the Argentine magazine *Nosotros* condemned Leopoldo Lugones's magazine *La Revue Sud-Américaine*, a text-heavy journal consisting of seven issues, all printed in 1914, which featured treatises on pan-Americanism, chronicles, and reviews of magazines from across Europe, written in French. The editors of *Nosotros* remark, "We are not interested in the success of these Argentine enterprises that look to conquer Paris with a few pages of printed paper. We will conquer Paris and Europe in due time when we deserve it—in the course of one or one hundred years—and in order to deserve it, we really need to work, materially, morally, and intellectually on our own soil, and not pass ourselves off over there disguised as French."[11] Skeptical of the enthusiasm for Latin American print culture abroad, the editors of *Nosotros* argue that Latin American writers needed to strengthen local institutions rather than look toward France for validation (a common refrain in questionnaire responses at the time).[12]

Visual artists also found communities and venues to display their work abroad, as several institutions in Paris exhibited Latin American artists. The Galerie Zak (1923–39) regularly showed work by Latin Americans, including solo exhibitions for the Uruguayan painter Joaquín Torres-García as well as the Cuban painter Eduardo Abela, both held in 1928. Alejo Carpentier reviewed Abela's show in an essay he published in *Social*, thereby transporting Abela's success abroad back to Cuba (Carpentier also wrote about the Cuban artists Marcelo Pogolotti and Carlos Enríquez, who likewise spent time in Paris, for *Social*).[13] Such dispatches conveyed the rising status of Latin Americans' work in Paris to audiences back home.

With large numbers of Latin Americans living in Paris, galleries were able to organize panregional exhibitions that would have proved challenging in the artists' home countries. As art historian Michele Greet observes, Paris was the location for the first survey show of Latin American art, held in 1924 at the Musée Galliéra. Jointly organized by the Maison de l'Amérique Latin (Latin American House) and L'Académie Internationale des Beaux-Arts (International Academy of Fine Arts), the show featured the work of forty-two Latin American artists who lived in Paris, including Argentine Xul Solar, Ecuadorean Camilo Egas, and Uruguayan Pedro Figari.[14] Similarly, in April 1930 Torres-García organized the *Première Exposition du Groupe Latino-Americain de Paris* (First exhibition of the Latin American group) at the Galerie Zak, exhibiting work by twenty-one artists, including Eduardo Abela, Diego Rivera, and José Clemente Orozco. In many ways, Torres-García created a "Latin American group" simply through the exhibition's title.[15] Such opportunities indicate why Latin American artists moved to Paris, demonstrating the strength of the institutional support for their work and the professional networks that they formed there.

In addition to increased opportunities for Latin American writers and artists in Paris, the city bolstered their cultural authority. As Marcy Schwartz writes, "To escape the role of the provincial, struggling writer at home, the Latin American intellectual came to Paris to be transformed into a citizen of the world who had transcended geographic and cultural boundaries."[16] This cosmopolitan ideal, paradoxically, contributed to the consolidation of a Latin American artistic identity. The Brazilian intellectual Pedro Luis Osorio, for instance, suggested that Paris was "the capital of Latin America" in a speech he gave launching the Maison de L'Amérique Latine.[17] Indeed, Paris was the site from which a significant portion of Latin American modernist and avant-garde production was developed, launched, and disseminated in the late nineteenth and early twentieth century. Paris also offered Latin Americans a place from which to produce culture free from the encroaching threat of U.S. imperialism. By joining the "world republic of letters"—as Pascale Casanova terms it—emanating from Paris, Latin Americans developed an acute sense of their position in an international literary and artistic economy.[18] Questions about the relationship between Europe and the Americas inevitably followed.

Paris's popularity with Latin American artists and writers created a sizable Hispanophone community in the city, which Elvira de Alvear helped to support through her salon and through *Imán*. She welcomed into her home many of the writers who went on to contribute to *Imán*, such as Latin Americans Arturo Uslar Pietri and Carlos Enríquez, Spaniards Rafael Alberti and Manuel Altolaguirre, as well as the French writers Léon-Paul Fargue and Benjamin Fondane.[19] *Imán*'s editorial secretary, Carpentier, collaborated with De Alvear and with the Surrealists whom he met through Desnos. Carpentier signed the pamphlet *Un cadavre*, contesting Breton's authority as the "pope" of Surrealism, and wrote for the magazines *Bifur* (1929–31), edited by Georges Ribemont-Dessaignes, and *Documents* (1929–30), edited by Georges Bataille, which both displayed significant interest in the Americas.[20] Although many magazines of the era included writers from across Europe and the Americas, periodicals such as *Imán* and *transition* wanted to make these transatlantic relationships explicit and to determine the nature of Europe's relationship to U.S. and Latin American culture.

Expatriate Print Culture and the Lost Generation

Paris held a similar cultural attraction for North Americans; yet those coming from the United States had the additional boon of a very strong dollar in postwar Europe. Paris's four English-language newspapers also appealed to American expatriates, ensuring that at least some writers would be able to find work abroad. As an experienced (and trilingual) reporter, Eugene Jolas was able to secure a position at the Paris edition of the *Chicago Tribune.* He spearheaded the column Rambles Through Literary Paris, for which he interviewed cultural figures such as Claire and Ivan Goll, Philippe Soupault, and André Breton, who would all later contribute to *transition*.[21] In his column Jolas extols the virtues of Paris as a global cultural center, writing, "Paris today is doubtless the cerebral crucible of the world. Nowhere does the visitor from America face such a plethora of ideas, revolutionary concepts, boldly destructive philosophies, ferociously new aesthetic principles."[22] The effects of Paris on the writers of the so-called Lost Generation—Ernest Hemingway, Malcolm Cowley, and John Dos Passos, among others—are well documented, as well as on the work of American artists working in Paris in the 1920s such as Man Ray, Berenice Abbott, and Alexander Calder.[23] However, relatively little attention has been paid to the questionnaires such as those issued by *transition*, which provided a forum for some of these artists and writers to reflect on their decision to live abroad and its effect on their work.

The magazine's two questionnaires on America's relationship to Europe tapped into a larger interest in Americans abroad. The *Tribune* ran a column from 1925 to 1930 called " We're in Paris Because . . . , " asking expatriates why they lived in Paris. In his response the painter Marsden Hartley claims, "Paris furnishes the least resistance, probably, for the artist than any other city in the world."[24] The African American writer Jessie Fauset is quoted as saying, "So I am in Paris where nobody cares—not even Americans, it seems—whether an artist is white, black, or yellow."[25] These answers suggest that Paris is more diverse, welcoming, and receptive to artistic innovation than America.[26] Ford Madox Ford—the British writer and editor who ran the literary column for the *Tribune* prior to Jolas and edited the *transatlantic review* (1924–25)—writes in *Vanity*

Fair in 1927, "The reason why large numbers of American artists live in Europe is almost entirely economic. They are very badly paid; they can live in Paris for almost nothing."[27] The *Tribune* also offered some of its own explanations for the wave of expatriatism in articles such as "Thirst for Booze and for Liberty Sends Americans Abroad" and "Why Americans Leave Home and Settle Down Permanently in Europe."[28] Alex Small, the author of these articles, cites "the desire to be part of a deracinated, cosmopolitan society" as another reason why Americans moved to Paris, a claim that Jolas explicitly probes in his questionnaires.[29]

Jolas's involvement with the *Tribune* only strengthened and validated his investment in America's relationship with Europe. In his column he asks, "What does modern France think of American letters?" Perhaps willing it to be true, he concludes, "France is watching the work of our young men with intense interest," predicting that soon "French artists will seek their inspiration in America."[30] America's economic ascendancy brought it and its cultural output newfound attention in Europe, which inspired Jolas to develop a platform to present American writing to European audiences. In one of his early columns Jolas goes so far as to proclaim, "To build an intellectual bridge between our Continent and France has always been the dream of many men on both sides of the Atlantic," thus justifying his vision for *transition*.[31] *transition* and *Imán* were in certain ways representative of the larger expatriate print culture in Paris out of which they emerged. What distinguishes their projects from others at the time is their emphasis on translation—both linguistic and cultural—and their desire to elevate the status of the Americas internationally; their questionnaires served to test these positions.

Eugene Jolas and *transition*

Encouraged by his experiences at the *Tribune* and the increasing popularity of American literary modernism, Eugene Jolas founded *transition* with Elliot Paul in 1927 in Paris, in order to publish experimental English-language work and to promote European innovations in translation.[32] Calling the magazine "an international quarterly for creative experiment," Jolas and Paul offered "American writers an opportunity to express themselves freely," and "to the writers of all other countries" they "extend[ed] an invitation to appear, side by side, in a language Americans can read and understand."[33] From its inception, *transition* was committed to linguistic and formal experimentation and was predicated upon translation. An early advertisement for the magazine announces: "The entire contents of the review will be in English with the work of contemporary writers of all countries given in translation. "[34] For Jolas, the rise of American modernism also demonstrated a market for avant-garde European literature. As he explains, "It is quite natural that the new interest in American literature should stimulate a curiosity about the literature of other lands. Languages are badly taught, in the United States, and geographic isolation makes it still more

difficult to follow contemporaneous European literature."[35] Jolas capitalized on
Americans' interest in recent literature and translated European material in the
hope of fostering more experimental writing in America.[36]

As an effect of his trilingual upbringing, Jolas focused his editorial efforts
on the capacity of language to transcend cultural and geographic boundaries.
Born in 1894 in Union Hill, New Jersey, to parents from the Rhine borderland
between France and Germany, Jolas would live and work between Europe and
America all of his life.[37] Jolas recalls that when in Europe he "daydreamed America" and in America he "felt the emotional pull of the European world," and thus
found himself "pendulating between two continents."[38] This geographic pull
was accompanied by linguistic shifts. For Jolas, "Language became a neurosis.
I used three of the basic world languages in conversation, in poetry and in my
newspaper work. I was never able to decide which of them I preferred. An almost
inextricable chaos ensued, and sometimes I sought a facile escape by intermingling all three."[39] Jolas was steeped in competing languages and torn between
poetry and reportage. His solution was to combine these multiple discourses,
and to thus transform them all. He found English capacious enough to withstand the mixing of languages and modes of writing, as it seemed to absorb the
multiple languages of America's immigrant populations. Jolas's commitment
to exploring linguistic elasticity and to the development of an expanded English
came to dominate *transition.*

Jolas moved to Paris in 1923 with the aim of starting a magazine. Reflecting on *transition* in 1949, he explains, "I had at the time, and I have still, an
almost mystic concept of an ideal America, and I wanted to make of *transition* a
continuous manifestation of this concept."[40] Jolas thought it best to explore this
idealized notion of America from afar, concluding that distance better suited
his project, as did a European context: "I wanted to build a laboratory of my own
in which I could tackle my personal language problems without having to consider an exclusively American audience. We soon reached the conclusion that
such a review could only be issued from the vantage point of Paris. My ambition
was to build a bridge between Europe and America, and particularly, to make
known to America the new aesthetic currents in Europe."[41] From Paris Jolas
could update Americans on European developments and fill what Jolas saw
as a gap in the literary world: European respect for American culture. In one
of his columns he laments, "The one thing almost every European writer
expresses about American art and letters is skepticism. . . . The real America
they do not know."[42]

transition also emerged out of a broader market for little magazines in
Paris. At the *Tribune* Jolas had access to many French- and English-language
publications of the era, and in particular he cites *La Revue Rhenane*, *La Revue de
Paris*, and *Le Journale Littéraire* as "indispensible to the student of intellectual
currents in Europe."[43] Jolas also reviewed American and European magazines
for his column, including the *Little Review* (1914–29), which he describes as

an "ultra-modern exponent of American art," and the *transatlantic review*, which he claims was "one of the most virile and important documents of present-day art."[44] Such magazines, along with *This Quarter* (1925–32), served as models for Jolas.[45]

Translation was Jolas's strategy for expanding the cultural horizons of American readers. He settled on this approach because "lately Americans have shown unmistakable signs of artistic awakening" and "a small group of intelligent readers has developed."[46] Americans could glean the latest avant-garde tendencies in Europe by reading *transition*, and conversely, Europeans could gather a wider audience than was otherwise attainable in their own languages, results that Jolas hoped "should be mutually helpful and inspiring."[47] Jolas defines and then flatters this transnational audience, writing, "Although art and literature are, in many quarters, growing more definitely racial and national in coloring and texture, their appeal is becoming distinctly international. The reader is coming into his own."[48] Courting this more internationally-inclined and open-minded reader, *transition* saw itself as a vehicle for transcontinental understanding; the audience was imagined as a "group of friends, united by a common appreciation of the beautiful."[49] *transition* also solicited readers through posters provocatively announcing that the magazine contained "What the French Think of American Writing."[50] Other advertisements included quotations from sources like the *New York Times* that derided the publication as "hopelessly muddled and unintelligible."[51] These inclusions strengthened *transition*'s image as an alternative to mainstream publications, suggesting that its readers were discerning, sophisticated, and in-the-know.[52]

Jolas lived up to his transatlantic ambitions by publishing some of the most significant work of his era. Primarily known for publishing and defending James Joyce's "Work in Progress," which became *Finnegans Wake*, *transition* also published for the first time in English translation Kafka's *Metamorphosis*, the opening of Breton's *Nadja*, selections from Alfred Döblin's *Berlin Alexanderplatz*, and extracts from Raymond Roussel's *Impressions of Africa*. Jolas, his wife Maria, and a "team of translators" translated the foreign-language material for the magazine from French, German, Russian, Serbian, Czech, Hungarian, Italian, Polish, Spanish, Swedish, and Yiddish.[53] As a result, the work of Pedro Salinas, Michel Leiris, Hugo Ball, F. T. Marinetti, Henri Michaux, Raymond Queneau, Robert Desnos, Tristan Tzara, Rainer Maria Rilke, and many other European avant-garde innovators was made available to English-speaking audiences. *transition* similarly promoted notable American literature. It published Hemingway's "Hills Like White Elephants," selections from Hart Crane's *The Bridge*, and work by William Carlos Williams, Henry Miller, Djuna Barnes, Charles Henri Ford, Gertrude Stein, and Anaïs Nin, demonstrating Jolas's editorial ability to cull the strongest writing of his day.

Adorning the magazine's covers and sleek interior pages was artwork by Europeans and Americans, including Alberto Giacometti, Hans Arp, Kurt

Schwitters, Pablo Picasso, Giorgio de Chirico, Paul Klee, Fernand Léger, Joan Miró, Diego Rivera, and Max Ernst, along with photography by Tina Modotti, Man Ray, Edward Weston, and László Moholy-Nagy. Stuart Davis's painting *Hôtel de France*, made in Paris in 1928, aptly became the cover of the issue aimed at North Americans abroad (fig. 8). Resembling a flattened stage set, the painting depicts a Parisian street populated only by a lamp, kiosk, hydrant, and loosely outlined buildings, suggesting an idealized Paris as seen by a foreigner. (It was reprinted entirely in red, as *transition* rendered its cover art monochromatic for a number of issues). Four other paintings by Davis are reproduced inside the magazine alongside an article by Elliot Paul, who hails Davis as an exemplary "American painter."[54] Throughout the magazine's lifespan, over five hundred artists and writers contributed to *transition*; about half were from the United States, while the others hailed from France, Germany, Great Britain, and, to a lesser extent, Eastern Europe, Sweden, Russia, Italy, Spain, Latin America, and Canada.[55]

To foreground the journal's wide geographic range, Jolas originally contemplated calling it "Bridge" or "Continents." In the end, Jolas was inspired by Edward Muir's collection of essays titled *Transition*, published by the Woolfs' Hogarth Press in 1926, and thought this term would be "best to symbolize the epoch."[56] He explains that "I insisted, however, that it be printed with a lowercase *t*. As an old newspaperman, I knew that the critics would give it a howling reception, and anyway it was the fashion among many continental 'little magazines' of the day."[57] The magazine initially had a text-heavy cover, with its name printed in gold on a deep red background. As it continued publication, *transition* grew in size and added colorful covers featuring work by artists, such as Davis, along with a slew of subtitles, including "The Revolution of the Word" and "An International Quarterly for Creative Experiment." Published until 1938, *transition* often exceeded two hundred pages, sometimes filling close to four hundred.

As was the case with most small magazines, *transition* was not profitable, and its location in Paris added further financial strain. First, it paid its writers in francs, which Jolas notes "becomes almost ludicrous when changed into dollars."[58] Second, Jolas acknowledges that while it was cheaper to publish in Europe, it was difficult to find printers and proofreaders who could read English. Finally, despite being produced in Europe, the magazine still had to contend with American censors, since it was distributed through bookstores in Paris, London, New York, Boston, Chicago, Detroit, Los Angeles, Minneapolis, and Philadelphia. While it was bankrolled largely by Maria Jolas's family money, *transition* eventually went into debt. As a result, it became quarterly in April 1928 and was suspended from 1930 to 1932. Then, from 1932 to 1938 it was published in Holland to keep costs down. Still, the magazine had a circulation of approximately four thousand copies in the United States, France, and Great Britain, including one thousand American subscribers.[59]

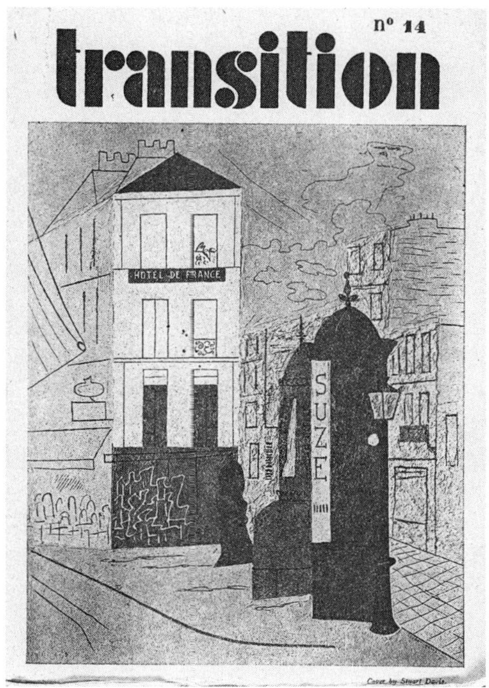

Fig. 8 Stuart Davis, *Hôtel de France*, cover of *transition* (Paris), no. 14 (Fall 1928). Art © Estate of Stuart Davis / Licensed by VAGA, New York, N.Y.

The main agent and distributor for *transition* in Paris was the English-language bookshop Shakespeare and Company, run by Sylvia Beach, who made the crucial introduction between Joyce and Jolas in 1924.[60] From its inception in April 1927 through March 1928, *transition* regularly published excerpts of Joyce's "Work in Progress" in each issue of the magazine, as well as many accompanying critical texts. In fact, the very first issue of the magazine opens with Joyce, identifying *transition* with what would become *Finnegans Wake* and cementing its legacy as a purveyor of Joyce's late, difficult work.[61] Joyce had already established his literary reputation with *Ulysses*, first serialized in the *Little Review* from 1918–20 and published in full in 1922, but *transition* launched the careers of some of Joyce's commentators. As the critic John Pilling maintains, Samuel Beckett's collaboration with *transition* was "the point at which, for all practical purposes, Beckett's writing career may be said to have begun."[62] Between 1929 and 1938 Beckett published eight pieces in *transition*, including "Dante . . . Bruno . . . Vico . . . Joyce," wherein Beckett argues that Joyce collapses form and content: "Here form *is* content, content *is* form. You complain that this stuff is not written in English. It is not written at all. It is not to be read—or rather it is not only to be read. It is to be looked at and listened to. His writing is not *about* something; *it is that something itself.*"[63] Beckett points to the radicality of Joyce's linguistic practice, which would influence *transition*'s aesthetic as it evolved. "Work in Progress" came to shape other contributions to the publication and, eventually, its editorial policy, inspiring the "Revolution of the Word" manifesto and other pronouncements that Jolas issued on the power of the writer to reinvent language.

In addition to Joyce, Gertrude Stein was a draw for audiences of *transition*, and she too became a boon to the magazine's reputation. Samuel Putnam notes that in the magazine's early days "Stein and Joyce were the two big thrills that *transition* had to offer its transatlantic customers."[64] They were so popular that in November 1927 the editors revised their call for submissions, noting that "imitations of James Joyce and Gertrude Stein are automatically rejected."[65] Between 1927 and 1932, *transition* published a dozen texts by Gertrude Stein, among them "An Elucidation," *Tender Buttons*, and *Four Saints in Three Acts*.[66] Stein, like Joyce, experimented with English as an elastic medium, and explanatory essays often accompanied her work as well.[67] Although the relationship between Stein and *transition* was mutually beneficial, Stein took umbrage at being compared to Joyce, or worse, overshadowed by him in the magazine.[68] Elliot Paul, the magazine's first coeditor, soothed Stein's notorious ego. When Paul was replaced, the magazine's relationship with Stein soured, culminating in a negative portrayal of the *transition* circle in Stein's 1933 *Autobiography of Alice B. Toklas*.[69] In it, she goes so far as to link the magazine's demise to her lack of interest in it: "Transition grew more bulky. At Gertrude Stein's request transition reprinted 'Tender Buttons,' printed a bibliography of all her work up to date and later printed her opera, 'Four Saints.' For these printings Gertrude Stein was very grateful. In the last numbers of transition nothing of hers appeared. Transition died."[70] These and many other remarks ended Stein's previously cordial relationship with the Jolases and led them to print the "Testimony Against Gertrude Stein" in 1935, a fifteen-page supplement to *transition* that included detailed, angry retorts from Matisse, Tzara, Braque, and others to their portrayals in Stein's *Autobiography*. ("Miss Stein understood nothing of what went on around her," Braque fumes in his contribution.)[71] However, Stein did ultimately publicize the Jolases and the magazine by including them in what became a popular book; as critic Craig Monk points out, Stein cites the people she is indebted to, even as she condemns them. She "seeks to distance herself from her contemporaries, and yet the texts work . . . by contextualizing her achievement within that of the very people whom she hopes to deny," Monk observes.[72] Despite their eventual fallout, Stein embedded herself in the history of *transition* in a way that buoyed both her career and the reputation of the magazine.

transition also notably introduced American audiences to Surrealism. Jolas boasted that *transition* made Surrealism "known to the Anglo-American world" by being "the first review to present Surrealist poems, texts, dreams, etc. in

English; the first non-French review to reproduce photos of Surrealist and abstract objects and paintings."[73] The magazine published translations of texts by André Breton, Paul Éluard, and Robert Desnos, as well as art by Giorgio de Chirico, Yves Tanguy, Man Ray, and Max Ernst. *transition* also printed a manifesto called "Hands Off Love" in 1927 in support of Charlie Chaplin, signed by members of the Surrealist group as well as the magazine's editors.[74] "For a non-surrealist publication *transition* probably did more over a longer period to make the movement understandable to England and America than any other magazine," the critic Douglas McMillan observes.[75] *transition*'s editorials also echoed Surrealist language with proclamations such as "only the dream is essential."[76]

In sum, *transition* was purposefully heterogeneous, presenting a diverse selection of genres and movements. In his memoir, Malcolm Cowley describes the mélange contained in *transition* as "good writing of most types and bad writing of all. Angry, sophisticated, high-spirited, tired, primitive, expressionist, objective, subjective, incoherent, flat, it included everything that seemed new; rhapsodies to the machine were printed side by side with poems of escape from the machine, while Functionalism, Surrealism, and Gertrude Stein all nudged one another."[77] Jolas called the magazine "a more or less eclectic organ."[78] Throughout its print run, *transition* reaffirmed its interest in facilitating transatlantic exchange and encouraging linguistic experimentation through statements like those issued in 1928 that the magazine would "work for a revaluation of the spirit in its intercontinental relations" and "destroy the traditions of language and... welcome its decomposition."[79] *transition*'s eclecticism allowed it to fulfill its disparate goals, that is, to showcase a wide swath of European and American culture while expanding its readers' linguistic horizons.

Imán: Latin America Abroad

Compared to *transition*, *Imán* was much shorter lived and lesser known. Elvira de Alvear, however, was enmeshed in a literary network that gave her access to prominent writers from Europe and the Americas whom she invited to publish in the magazine's sole issue, which even included a text by Eugene Jolas. Like Jolas, Elvira de Alvear pursued *Imán* alongside her own writing. Hailing from a wealthy Argentine family, De Alvear is best known for her relationship with Borges; she allegedly gave him selections of Joyce's "Work in Progress," perhaps culled from *transition*, and he penned an eponymous poem for her after her death in 1959.[80] Borges helped advocate for her literary career as well, writing the prologue to her 1934 book of poems *Reposo*. In it he praises her treatment of "circumstantial details" and the work's "incomparable authenticity," while offering a beautifully digressive treatise on poetic construction.[81] The front book flap of *Reposo* indicates that De Alvear had two additional projects in preparation, a novel called "Visión de la pampa" and a play called "Orestes."[82]

De Alvear moved to Paris by 1929 and left by some accounts as early as 1931, by others as late as 1937 (*Imán* was published on April 30, 1931).[83] She purportedly lived in a lavish apartment until her family fortune was decimated by the effects of the 1929 stock market crash, which drove her to return to Buenos Aires. In Norah Borges's pencil-drawn portrait of Elvira de Alvear from 1927, she has a wide face, thin lips, and a large, heavy-lidded stare, a gaze which matches a photo she signed to Jorge Luis Borges "with admiration and friendship" in 1938. Beyond these details, historical records of her life are scant, and she is often eclipsed by comparisons to Victoria Ocampo, another Argentine woman of means who started the magazine *Sur* in 1931, just a few months after *Imán*. For example, a 1932 review in the French journal *Les Nouvelles Littéraires* briefly describes the "luxurious Argentine magazine *Imán*" and its relationship to French poets, citing its questionnaire and highlighting the response of Georges Ribemont-Dessaignes in particular, who writes that poetry is almost a "natural language for Hispano-Americans." However, the remainder of the article is devoted to *Sur* and features a photo of Ocampo.[84] Unlike its short-lived predecessor, *Sur* lasted for more than fifty years (1931–92), and some critics position *Imán* as its prototype or precursor.[85] The two magazines shared other connections as well. Benjamin Fondane, a contributor to *Imán*, had been invited by Ocampo to Buenos Aires to give a series of lectures. On the boat trip back, he supposedly composed the poem *Ulises*, extracts of which were published in *Imán*.[86]

As a self-consciously transatlantic magazine, *Imán* included texts by North Americans, Latin Americans, and Europeans alike, all in Spanish. The first and only issue featured poetry, criticism, and fiction by Xul Solar, Jaime Torres Bodet, Vicente Huidobro, Henri Michaux, Franz Kafka, Hans Arp, and John Dos Passos, an eclectic group in terms of style, but all important writers of the day. The magazine's Latin American contributors hailed from Uruguay, Chile, Mexico, Argentina, Cuba, Venezuela, and Guatemala, but most had convened in Paris. Multiple translators were employed by the magazine, translating writing from French, German, Italian, Russian, and English into Spanish. Some translators also had their work published in the magazine, such as Miguel Ángel Asturias. *Imán* foregrounded the act of translation by printing Léon-Paul Fargue's contribution, which was the first in the magazine after the opening editorial, in its original French alongside its Spanish translation, by Asturias. The only other contribution that was printed in a language other than Spanish was Alfred Kreymborg's response to the questionnaire, which consisted of ten brief poems written in English. *Imán*'s single issue was printed in four editions of differing qualities of paper and sold in bookstores in Buenos Aires, Paris, and Madrid; it offered subscription rates for France, Spain, Argentina, and "other American countries," indicating its intention to continue publication. The issue also claimed "rights of reproduction and translation reserved for all countries," demonstrating its far-reaching aspirations.[87] *Imán* was a hefty 250 bound pages, a one-inch-thick object. The magazine was intended to be published every three months, before the economic crisis caused Argentina to pass a law against the export of capital, depleting De Alvear's financial resources.[88]

The magazine shared many connections with *transition* and *Revista de Avance*. Carlos Enríquez, a painter featured in *Revista de Avance* who was living in Paris at the time, translated John Dos Passos's essay for *Imán*, and Adja Yunkers, another artist included in *Revista de Avance*, translated Walter Mehring's questionnaire response from its original German.[89] *Imán* published a story by Jolas, while *transition* published Carpentier's "Cuban Magic"—one of his early Afro-Cuban texts—in its June 1930 issue, translated from French into English. It also seems more than a coincidence that *Imán* translated Kafka's "The Judgment" into Spanish after it was translated by Jolas and his wife Maria into English and published in *transition* three years earlier.[90] Carpentier translated the work of Robert Desnos, another *transition* contributor, whom he had met in Cuba in March 1928, when Desnos had traveled to Havana for the VII Congreso de la Prensa Latina as a correspondent for the Argentine newspaper *La Razón*. Carpentier showed him around the city, and when Desnos returned to France later that year he gave his official travel papers to Carpentier so that the latter could flee Machado's repressive government; Carpentier sailed to Paris on the ship *España* under the name Robert Desnos.[91] Desnos published an essay titled "Lautréamont" in *Imán*, which Carpentier translated into Spanish. In it, Desnos pays homage to the Comte de Lautréamont, the Surrealist forebear and idol, who was born in Montevideo and studied in France in the second half of the nineteenth century (many cite Lautréamont in their questionnaire responses). Desnos also wrote about his experience in Cuba for *Documents*, as an introduction to an essay by Carpentier.[92] Through Desnos, Carpentier met many of the Surrealists he subsequently polled in *Imán*'s questionnaire.

Beyond Carpentier's relationships, *Imán* had other connections to the Surrealist circle in Paris. As a patron of the arts, De Alvear was an early collector of Alberto Giacommeti's sculpture. In 1929 she bought *Gazing Head* (1928–29), a piece that launched the artist into the Surrealist circle in Paris, garnering attention in *Documents* later that year.[93] *Imán* also pays homage to Surrealism through its title. "Magnet" suggests at once the magnetic pull between the north and the south poles and also *Les Champs Magnétiques*, published by André Breton and Philippe Soupault in 1920 and considered a prototype for Surrealist automatic writing.[94] De Alvear explains in her opening editorial that *Imán* had not been "planned with ideas subject to a religious dogma, nor will [it] strictly manifest a local character," but rather that the magazine would offer "a quick glance at tendencies and movements," which likely included Surrealism, and would "consult the general contemporary spirit." Extending the metaphor of the magnet, De Alvear claims that *Imán* will "centralize north and south as its title indicates, and will attract all individuals capable of producing energy, and . . . will gather them all in its magnetic field." She indicates her intention to feature photography, poetry, psychology, and travel chronicles in the magazine. Lofty, manifesto-like aspirations conclude the text, namely that *Imán* will "discover the cause of our anxieties and our aspirations," will "keep the documentation of its time," and "will be a starting point that will define the current generation."[95]

Declaring the magazine's geographic alliances, De Alvear asserts, "*Imán* is by and for limitless borders—we will be pan-national." However, she writes that the magazine will retain "its Argentine accent," emphasizing the magazine's Latin American allegiance even though it was published abroad.[96] Underscoring this position, Léon-Paul Fargue, a friend of De Alvear's, includes a Chateaubriand epigraph in his article "De una pluma a un imán" (From pen to magnet): "Providence tied, so to speak, the feet of each man to his native soil with an invincible magnet."[97] Printed in both Spanish and French on opposite pages, the text describes the magnet—and thus the magazine—in detail, serving as another kind of opening statement. Fargue continues the metaphor of the magnet and praises the magazine: "*Imán*, like everything magnetized, will read the thoughts of the world, will see and hear beyond spaces. Through tunnels, active or inert, through mines and farmlands, through systems and literatures, it will discover the presence of great geniuses, awaken the dead, attract the living." He also attributes the magazine to its editor De Alvear, writing, "I have just found in Argentina the most powerful artificial magnet that I know. It will guide Latin America to the compass; Elvira de Alvear has the rudder in her small, firm hand."[98] By describing the magazine as both a magnet and compass, Fargue's tribute reinforces *Imán*'s relationship to the avant-garde magazines of its day, which similarly invoked metaphors of orientation and travel.

Imán's cover features a line-drawn map of Latin America, thickly outlined in gray, with thinner tributaries fanning out across the continent. Encased in a gray arch, along with the magazine's name in bold and a list of contributors below, the cover's design clearly aligns the magazine with Latin America (fig. 9). To further explore its geographic allegiances, *Imán* issued a kind of complementary questionnaire to the ones circulated by *Revista de Avance* and *transition*, asking European Surrealists such as Bataille and Leiris "How do you imagine Latin America?" *transition* similarly inquired how Europeans were reacting to the influence of the United States. Such surveys drew responses that aired the "anxieties and aspirations," as De Alvear writes, that Europeans were projecting onto the Americas.

transition: "Inquiry Among European Writers into the Spirit of America"

Imán hoped to draw international attention to Latin American literature and tested out its transatlantic position through its questionnaire. *transition* also relied on the genre to promote and clarify its ambitions. The magazine announced its interest in questionnaires as early as its second issue: "During the

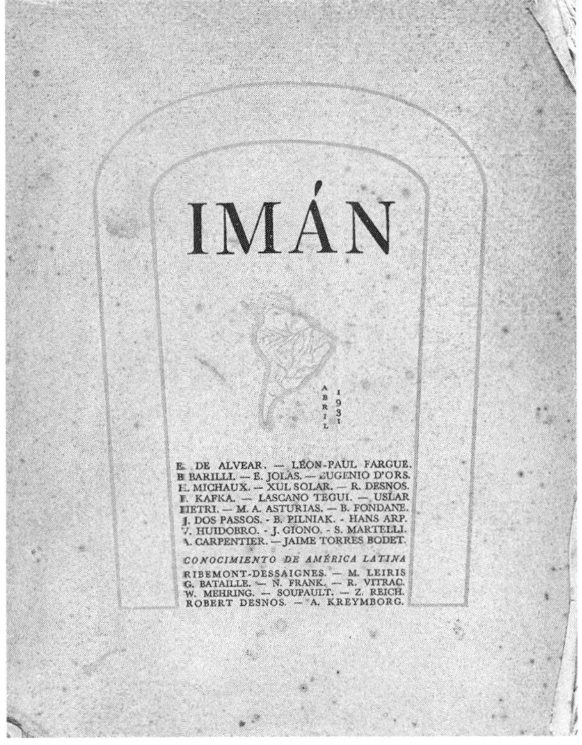

Fig. 9 Cover of *Imán* (Paris), no. 1 (April 1931). © Fundación Alejo Carpentier.

current year *transition* will conduct *enquêtes* among the artists and writers of several countries concerning the effect of one national culture upon another."[99] Prior to issuing them in 1928, the magazine began publishing primarily American work, explaining, "While *transition* will continue to regard itself as a link between Europe and America, and while it will continue to publish translations of important European work, the emphasis in the future will be placed on American contributions, as we feel that our intensified inquiry into international writing is, for the moment, at a standstill, and would yield no great results, if continued."[100] This shift in emphasis from foreign-language material to American writing likely sparked the questionnaires printed in the two subsequent issues of *transition*, which perhaps sought to validate this new direction.

In the summer and fall of 1928 *transition* issued companion questionnaires on America's relationship to Europe. The first, "Inquiry Among European Writers into the Spirit of America," provoked incendiary responses from European artists and writers about the burgeoning influence of the United States (fig. 10). Contributors such as Tristan Tzara and Benjamin Péret were so incensed about American ascendancy that, Jolas remarks, "the violence of the answers received

INQUIRY AMONG EUROPEAN WRITERS
INTO THE SPIRIT OF AMERICA

" Americanize yourselves " —
Lenine on his death-bed to   his friends.

Next to Russia, the United States is today the most important problem among the nations of the world. The new conception of life and the accelerated rhythm of its pragmatic manifestations are slowly, but surely, being felt in the old world. Some European travelers to the North-American continent assert that America represents today the essence of the Occidental spirit, i. e. an impulsion towards a new culture and a new mode of living, while others denounce what they conceive to be a danger of intellectual mechanisation that results from that spirit.

In order to crystallize these ideas, I have asked a number of European writers the following questions :
1. How, in your opinion, are the influences of the United States manifesting themselves upon Europe and in Europe ?
2. Are you for or against those influences ?
The violence of the answers received makes any commentary on my part, for the moment, superfluous.

EUGENE JOLAS

Fig. 10 "Inquiry Among European Writers into the Spirit of America," *transition* (Paris), no. 13 (Summer 1928): 248.

makes any commentary on my part, for the moment, superfluous."[101] Its correlating survey, "Why Do Americans Live in Europe?," prompted writers such as Gertrude Stein and Robert McAlmon to consider the effects of dislocation on their literary sensibilities. The two questionnaires not only roused strong feelings about Europe's relationship to America, but also helped market the magazine, as Jolas gleefully reports: "As I expected, the critics on both sides of the ocean pounced on the inquiry and soon there was a terrific exchange of verbal blows."[102] Such provocative questionnaires boosted the magazine's editorial platform and its notoriety.

Larger in format than previous issues, the summer 1928 edition was also the first to feature the subtitle "An International Quarterly for Creative Experiment," and was also designated the "American Number." It opened with a photograph of Joyce, taken by Berenice Abbott, opposite his "Work in Progress," and also featured Stein's "Descriptions of Literature," William Carlos Williams's "Improvisations," and several Man Ray photographs, reproduced on glossy paper. The questionnaire "Inquiry Among European Writers into the Spirit of America" was thus situated among a selection of predominantly American art and writing, as if demonstrating the influence about which it polled its contributors. *transition* was designed to explore the reciprocal effects of American and European cultural production on one another; yet its anxieties about this mission surface in the formulation of its two questionnaires.

The editors signaled their apprehension about the United States and its cultural position prior to publishing either questionnaire. In the March 1928 issue of the magazine Jolas and Paul assert, "The problem of the United States hovers like a huge cloud over the rest of the world."[103] Europe needed an heir, the editors argue, a position that both Russia and America were vying to occupy: "America, together with Russia, has most definitely the soil where a new civilization may possibly flower to a synthesis of the forces that have left Europe." The editors privilege America over Russia as the site for this future; however, they deem America "a country that has destroyed the immense heritage of Europe and is now clumsily playing with the instruments it has created."[104] In grave need of direction, the editors hoped that through the example of innovative European poetry and prose, Americans could learn to emulate, and thus better preserve and even enhance, European culture.[105] The magazine's concerns about America and its cultural effects surely informed the framing of its first questionnaire.

In his preface to "Inquiry Among European Writers into the Spirit of America," Jolas continues to pit Europe against the United States and Russia. "Next to Russia," Jolas writes, "the United States is today the most important problem among the nations of the world."[106] To underscore this connection, Jolas includes an epigraph from Lenin on his deathbed, saying to his friends, "Americanize yourselves." As for what America embodies, Europeans might recognize the "new conception of life" put forth by the United States, Jolas writes, since the "accelerated rhythm of its pragmatic manifestations" is already "being felt in the old world."[107] He then sets up two divergent views of America, explaining, "Some European travelers to the North-American continent assert that America represents today the essence of the Occidental spirit, i.e. an impulsion towards a new culture and a new mode of living, while others denounce what they conceive to be a danger of intellectual mechanization that results from that spirit."[108] Here Jolas reveals his own ambivalence toward the United States; America might offer a "new culture and new mode of living," but he also recognizes the "danger of mechanization" that such a culture could yield.

Jolas does not wholly celebrate America's newfound status, but rather tests out his own uncertainty, writing, "In order to crystallize these ideas, I have asked a number of European writers the following questions." The questions include "How, in your opinion, are the influences of the United States manifesting themselves upon Europe and in Europe? Are you for or against those influences?" While Jolas innocently offers the questionnaire as a means of exploring "modern American literature and ideology," these questions sparked vociferous responses from the Europeans polled, who almost uniformly depict America as overly mechanized, although some suggest that American speed and optimism were the way of the future.[109] The French historian Bernard Faÿ captures this ambivalence in his response, maintaining, "What the majority of Europeans mean by the United States is a sort of amorous and heavenly dream, mixed with hate, jealousy and suspicion, but nevertheless an interrupted dream . . . and as such it dominates us and exercises upon us a most profound influence."[110] The questionnaire elicited such conflicting reactions; in many ways, Faÿ's answer is symptomatic of his fellow Europeans' equivocal attitude toward America, one characterized at once by longing and disdain.

Many, of course, were simply outraged by increasing American dominance. Benjamin Péret, an editor of *La Révolution surréaliste*, writes that the influence of the United States is manifesting itself upon Europe "through the most emphatic garbage, the ignoble sense of money, the indigence of ideas, the savage hypocrisy in morals, and altogether through a loathsome swinishness pushed to the point of paroxysm."[111] This litany of complaints about what America represented was consistent across the responses. Charges against America included "false individualism, proud mediocrity, childish glorification of its limits erected in dogmas," according to the artist René Lalou. The playwright Roger Vitrac accuses America of being "a practical, popularizing, utilitarian nation."[112] Others filed more specific grievances. According to Tristan Tzara, America lauds "the glorification of work," which he calls the "shame of our age" and a "stupid ideology."[113] The poet Gottfried Benn simply writes, "I am against Americanism," which the critic Régis Michaud describes as "gratuitous affirmation [and] silly optimism."[114] Such condemnations of America filled the magazine.

Much of this despair and indignation originated from the prevailing belief in Europe's inevitable demise. "We now find ourselves on the decline," the poet Ivan Goll laments, imploring, "Americans, leave us alone! Let us die our death!"[115] However, others suggest that America could reinvigorate Europe. For instance, the novelist Marcel Brion writes that "America has taught us to love whatever is young, and new. . . . The beauty of an ice-box, an auto, a vacuum cleaner," arguing that from such material gains "ideas are born."[116] According to the artist Georges Hugnet, American literature may even come to positively influence European culture; Hugnet advances *transition*'s platform by writing, "It is quite regrettable that a state of mind and an achievement such as Gertrude Stein's should not be more known in France."[117]

Regardless of their positions, many respondents agreed that America prompted European self-reflection, much like the questionnaire itself. For instance, Philippe Soupault proclaims, "The United States forces and aids Europe in unifying itself."[118] Similarly, the Swiss writer Max Rychner finds America a useful foil for Europe: "Before the phenomenon of America the unity of Europe becomes a fact."[119] Vladimir Lindin concludes that the two regions require "reciprocal fertilization," and Theo van Doesburg suggests that "in their synthesis [they] can make possible a new civilization."[120] The writer Henry Poulaille even implores *transition* to increase America's visibility, corroborating the magazine's mission by urging, "It is up to you to help the United States bring out the essential qualities of her civilization. A review like your own, but publishing only Americans, would do excellent work, and would teach us many things. Our civilization needs airing, it needs more contact with life."[121] Such responses affirmed *transition*'s aim to aesthetically transform the United States, without contradicting the other respondents' gripes about American materialism.

For his part, Jolas agreed with many of the sentiments put forth in the responses, which reinforced both his positions and those of the magazine. He too was fearful of America's potentially negative influence. In 1927 he writes in *transition*, "America, swollen with mercantilism, content with its mediocrity, is influencing the world more and more. It creates a caricature of optimism and persecutes every genuine attempt to give voice to the deeper beauty of life, to discover the eternal and changeless magic of things."[122] For Jolas, the stakes of American power were also aesthetic, as he considered America's worst qualities to be linked to literary trends like social realism, which he deplored.[123] Jolas believed America to be the aesthetic future, but he argued that Europe should serve as a model for it, to help counteract its inclination toward mechanization. If America was threatening to the Europeans that Jolas polled, Latin America was a region mired in fantasy for many of the same respondents, whom Elvira de Alvear surveyed three years later in *Imán*'s questionnaire.

Imán: "Knowledge of Latin America"

transition showcased Europeans' strong feelings about the United States through its questionnaire. By contrast, *Imán*'s questionnaire "Conocimiento de América Latina" (Knowledge of Latin America) hoped to bring attention to a region lesser known to Europeans.[124] *Imán*'s questionnaire polled many of the same figures called upon by Jolas, asking, "How do you imagine Latin America? What will its position be in relation to Europe? What are, in your opinion, its fundamental problems?"[125] *Imán*'s inquiry was in some ways a complement to the one issued by *Revista de Avance*, which asked Latin Americans what the relationship should be between American and European art. Taken together, all three questionnaires speak to a larger cultural anxiety about Europe's diminishing position in the world and, in turn, the ascendancy of the Americas. However, while the United States was derided as materialistic and industrial, but feared as a financial threat, Latin America was at once denigrated and celebrated for being exotic, spiritually rich, and the potential future of Europe. As a result, *Imán*'s 1931 survey served as a counterpoint to those issued in *Revista de Avance* and *transition*, reinforcing and upending some of the positions taken in response to their questionnaires.

In her opening editorial statement, De Alvear explains her motivations for assessing Latin America's place in the transatlantic imaginary. She begins by justifying the magazine's location in Paris: "'Knowledge of Latin America' is a questionnaire prepared by *Imán* for the young literati residing in Paris, which officially represents the most intense artistic movement."[126] De Alvear then toggles between her European and Latin American audiences, claiming, "It is true that Latin America is a continent that encloses a poetic enigma; but in its exterior form it is already more than a hope," suggesting that Parisian literary circles might begin to grasp Latin America. She also voices her aspiration for the Europeans polled to actually visit her native city: "One must dream of a time no longer limited by distances, a time when we can freely circulate through all countries, and see gathered one day in Buenos Aires these authors who wanted to collaborate with *Imán* on 'Knowledge of Latin America.'"[127]

Despite the name of the questionnaire, most of the respondents knew little about Latin America; many describe Latin America in vague, utopian, and exotic terms. As Michel Leiris admits, "I know almost nothing about Latin America," except that "Isidore Ducasse [the Comte de Lautréamont] was born in Montevideo," a fact also cited by Philippe Soupault and Roger Vitrac.[128] Many also repeat the refrain of European decline, echoing those polled in *Revista de Avance* and *transition.* "Europe is dying gently, stammering, drooling, boastful," Soupault declares in his answer. As a result of Europe's imminent demise, he argues, Latin America has a "duty to determine what will be its true destiny" and should "demand complete autonomy."[129] Despite his push for Latin American autonomy, Soupault's assessment can be seen as a common gloss on European decadence rather than a detailed analysis of Latin America. The German author Walter Mehring muses, "What will the last Europeans be like? Will they not be exhibited . . . one day in a museum in Montevideo?"[130] Many saw Latin America as Europe's counterpart and future, serving to revitalize a culture in decline.

In his response Georges Ribemont-Dessaignes acknowledges that Europeans retain a colonialist perspective, calling theirs "the old entrenched civilization that judges until everything leads to itself."[131] He also points to their tendency to reduce Latin America to its luxury goods, raw materials, and exports: "[Europeans] have other knowledge of Latin America in which economic factors combine with picturesque elements: Brazilian coffee, alligator skins with which they make cute little shoes and nice car interiors, large Mexican sombreros, postage stamps that serve to balance the budgets of the indigent over there, armies in which everyone is an officer, condensed beef or smoked meat, ranches, ant hills, cigars, cacti, guano, and phosphate, and a few other things."[132] Ribemont-Dessaignes suggests that Europeans have a purely economic, exotified notion of Latin America, viewing it as an extension of their colonial conquests and global trade routes, along with the desires that these inspired.[133] Similarly, Robert Desnos acknowledges the tendency to romanticize Latin America. "For its knowledge of a hot sun and different constellations than ours, Latin America turned out to be an easy target for exoticism and speculation," he writes. (Although Desnos had traveled to Cuba and therefore had firsthand experience of the region.) Desnos also fears "the proximity of the capitalist danger of the United States," and signals his concern for "the destiny of the proletariat" accordingly.[134]

Other responses similarly highlight the threat that the United States posed to Europeans and Latin Americans alike. While Leiris acknowledges that "Europe only has a very vague notion of the continent," he considers it "the historic mission of Latin America to counterbalance the rationalist influence of the United States in the world."[135] For these authors, Latin America compensated for European decadence, and could also help counteract the increasing power of the United States. The film critic Nino Frank sympathized with Latin America's prolonged resistance to U.S. imperialism, noting that Latin America's "life is a continual struggle against the invasion of the United States."[136] He admits that he cannot imagine places like Rio de Janeiro, Buenos Aires, Mexico City, Montevideo, or Bogotá, but speculates that after Russia destroys Europe, Latin America would continue European traditions. When that happened, Frank asserts, "there would only remain a new world in the face of the old bourgeois civilization: Latin America."[137] (Note that the threat of Russia is raised again, as it was in *transition*.) Once again, Latin America is read through the lens of Europe's fears—particularly of the United States and Russia—rather than as a real place. As Ribemont-Dessaignes points out, Europeans may have taken an interest in the United States because of its economic importance, but "of Latin America Europe knows [only] its tangos."

One of the respondents polled was actually from the United States, and his contribution was published in its original English, likely because it was a set of ten poems. The American poet and editor Alfred Kreymborg's submission, titled "Ten Preludes," begins by focusing on Spain before shifting attention to the Americas and concludes with an enigmatic tribute to pan-Americanism. The verses concerning Spain—titled "Cervantes," "Unamuno," and "Picasso"—laud Spanish literature and art. Next, the poems underscore a shift in power through brief lines on "South America," which announce, "Spain lost a new world" but assert that its "tongue" and "soul" "spread fire," ostensibly through its colonial ventures. In the poem "Mexico," Kreymborg addresses the uneasy status of the term "America," writing, "The United States / are America— /we claim the name is ours," and continues, "and farther south the Aztec and the Spanish soil / flowers." Despite this claim to the name "America," Kreymborg strikes an alliance with Latin America by challenging Europe's "discovery" of the Americas. He concludes with the lines "two old Americas / search one truth."[138] Taken in sum, the verses celebrate the rise of the Americas.

While several responses focus on Europe or the United States rather than on Latin America itself, authors like Soupault nevertheless underscore what *Imán* and *Revista de Avance* jointly sought: for Latin America to assert its independence from Europe. "What I want to emphasize is that Latin America has got to stop turning to the European continent, which still retains in its eyes an incomprehensible prestige," Soupault writes.[139] For Soupault, the rest of the world was corrupt or inadequate, and "there remains, at least, for us, one hope: South America."[140] Georges Bataille also sees Latin America as the continent that will release the "impulses of an ample and prodigious human greatness."[141] Perhaps these grand hopes are naively placed in a region little understood by writers like Soupault and Bataille; nevertheless these writers show a marked interest in—and respect for—Latin America. Their responses bolster the efforts of *Imán* and magazines similarly aiming to disseminate Latin American literature and art abroad. Ribemont-Dessaignes voices the frustration felt by many of the respondents, asking, "For what should we hope so that Latin America can be more than a series of luxury goods in the eyes of Europe? . . . What would it take for Europe to know Latin America, finally, as it should?"[142] Such questions are at the heart of the magazine, which sought to introduce the varied cultural richness of Latin America to European audiences, even as it simultaneously translated and exported the work of Europeans to Hispanophone readers. However, as Ribemont-Dessaignes concedes, "for Latin America—still such a young continent—we are reduced to speculations about the future."[143] Much as the responses to *transition*'s poll revealed Europeans' fears of the United States, most of the sentiments articulated in response to *Imán*'s questionnaire were not based on actual experiences with Latin America but rather reflected ideas of what Latin America signified for Europe, and offered "speculations about the future."

"Why Do Americans Live in Europe?"

transition and *Imán* each surveyed Europeans to assess their knowledge of the Americas. It is clear from their answers that the United States was seen as a threatening force opposed by many Europeans—and, as evidenced by the responses to *Revista de Avance*'s survey, by many Latin Americans as well. Jolas aspired to shape the future of American literature, and he was eager to demonstrate its potential to Europeans. Many American writers lived and worked in Paris, and after his initial poll Jolas turned to his American contributors to survey them on their relationship to Europe. Jolas also wanted to affirm their commitment to experimental aesthetics.[144] Moreover, the "Inquiry Among European Writers into the Spirit of America" had generated great publicity for the magazine through its incendiary questions and outraged responses, as Jolas reports to Stein: "No. 13 has been getting reams of publicity in America and Europe, everybody wants to tell us what to do."[145] All of these factors—Jolas's support for innovative American literature, the large presence of Americans in Paris, and the success of the previous inquiry—led Jolas to issue a companion questionnaire in the fall of 1928 aimed at Americans abroad.

The magazine asked its American writers why they lived outside of the United States, how they perceived America's relationship to Europe, and how they saw their work in relation to their home country. Jolas first reached out to contributors in August 1928, writing, "We have all come to Europe impelled by some motive of the heart and mind. *transition* would like to present the crystallization of your ideas on the subject"[146] (fig. 11). In its lead-in to the questionnaire, the magazine notes that it had asked "a number of Americans living in Europe to write brief stories of themselves— their autobiographies of the mind, self-examinations, confessions, conceived from the standpoint of deracination."[147] (The term "deracination" was commonly used at the time to refer to the condition of someone who lacked ties with any country.) Mirroring its questionnaire, the issue was divided into two sections: "America" and "Other Countries." Even the magazine's copyright emphasized this editorial division, reading, "In the United States and in all other countries."[148] The questionnaire was printed under the heading "Why Do Americans Live in Europe?" The questionnaire asked, "Why do you prefer to live outside America? How do you envisage the spiritual future of America in the face of a dying Europe and in the face of a Russia that is adopting the American economic vision? What is your feeling about the revolutionary spirit of your age, as expressed, for instance, in such movements as communism, surrealism, anarchism? What particular vision do you have of yourself in relation to twentieth century reality?"[149] (fig. 12). Such questions position America as the potential future of a "dying Europe" and as central to "twentieth century reality," reiterating some of the anxieties that fueled the previous questionnaire.

Most respondents do not reject their American heritage, although they all agree that Paris provided a more affordable and liberating artistic climate than the United States. Many cite Prohibition and the strong dollar as reasons for moving abroad. The critic Kathleen Cannell offers a purely financial explanation: "I do not prefer to live outside America. I would prefer to live in America if I

TRANSITION

40, RUE FABERT
PARIS (7E)

EUGENE JOLAS, EDITOR
ROBERT SAGE, ASSOCIATE EDITOR

August 25- 1928

Dear, Miss Stein-

We are asking a number of Americans living in Europe to write us brief stories of themselves - their autobiographies of the mind, self-examinations, confessions, conceived from the standpoint of deracination. We have all come to Europe impelled by some motive of the heart and mind.

TRANSITION would like to present the crystallization of your ideas on this subject. In order to elicit these fundamental conceptions, we are asking you the following questions :

1.- Why do you prefer to live outside America ?

2.- How do you envisage the spiritual future of America in the face of a dying Europe and in the face of a Russia that is adopting the American economic vision ?

3.- What is your feeling about the revolutionary spirit of your age, as expressed, for instance, in such movements as communism, surrealism, anarchism ?

4.- What particular vision do you have of yourself in relation to twentieth century reality ?

The answers to these questions may be written in any form desired. May we ask you to put as much of yourself into your reply as possible ? We should like to have answers not exceeding 1,500 words by September 15, at the latest.

Very truly yours

Eugene Jolas
Robert Sage

Fig. 11 Eugene Jolas and Robert Sage, letter to Gertrude Stein, August 25, 1928.

WHY DO AMERICANS LIVE
IN EUROPE ?

> *Transition has asked a number of Americans living in Europe to write brief stories of themselves — their autobiographies of the mind, self-examinations, confessions, conceived from the standpoint of deracination.*
>
> *The following questions were asked :*
>
> *1. — Why do you prefer to live outside America ?*
>
> *2. — How do you envisage the spiritual future of America in the face of a dying Europe and in the face of a Russia that is adopting the American economic vision ?*
>
> *3. — What is your feeling about the revolutionary spirit of your age, as expressed, for instance, in such movements as communism, surrealism, anarchism ?*
>
> *4. — What particular vision do you have of yourself in relation to twentieth century reality ?*

GERTRUDE STEIN

The United States is just now the oldest country in the world, there always is an oldest country and she is it, it is she who is the mother of the twentieth century civilisation. She began to feel herself as it just after the Civil War. And so it is a country the right age to have been born in and the wrong age to live in.

She is the mother of modern civilisation and one wants to have been born in the country that has attained and live in the countries that are attaining or going to be attaining. This is perfectly natural if you only look at facts as they are. America is now early Victorian very early Victorian, she is a rich and well nourished home but not a place to work. Your

Fig. 12 "Why Do Americans Live in Europe?," *transition* (Paris), no. 14 (Fall 1928): 97.

could make enough money to do so."[150] The poet Harry Crosby creates a playful list of reasons why he lives in Europe that includes "I love flagons of wine."[151] In a later issue of *transition* William Carlos Williams also cites alcohol as a reason for Americans to move to Paris: "American artists go to France and . . . in France, they find themselves, they drink and they are awakened, shocked to realize what they are, amazed, loosed—as, in fact, they on their part shock and arouse the tenderest sentiments of astonishment and tolerance among the French."[152] Of course, alcohol was not the only draw that Paris had for American artists and writers. The journalist H. Wolf Kaufman asserts, "I first conceived the notion to leave America because I was dissatisfied with existing conditions. I didn't like the grade of books the bookshops were selling."[153] As Sylvia Beach observes in her memoir, "prohibitions and suppressions were not entirely to blame for the flight of these wild birds from America. The presence in Paris of Joyce and Pound and Picasso and Stravinsky . . . had a great deal to do with it."[154] Practical desires—money, alcohol, books—coexisted with artistic motivations for living and working abroad.

While the questionnaire asked writers to position themselves in relation to "Europe," it primarily addressed writers and artists in Paris. Indeed, Jolas later referred to this questionnaire as "Why do Americans live in France?"[155] The writer Harold J. Salemson defines Paris in his response as "the center of the world." He explains, "very selfishly, that is why I live abroad: to benefit personally by these advantages."[156] Robert McAlmon also distinguishes between France and Europe in his answer, maintaining, "I prefer Europe if you mean France, to America because there is less interference with private life here. . . . If by Europe you mean England, Italy, or Germany, I think America an exciting, stimulating, imaginative country with the fresh imagination of youth and ignorance."[157] The "Europe" invoked by the questionnaire was surely Paris. While the previous questionnaire respondents hailed from various European countries, they too were gathered in Paris, which served as a staging ground for the cultural exchange that Jolas envisioned.

Beyond fixating on their location in Paris, many of the respondents situated themselves within a "generation" or "age," as they were invited to do by Jolas' line of questioning. In her response the journalist Leigh Hoffman asserts, "I am of this age but not one of it. That is why I left America."[158] The feeling of not belonging to one's "age," as opposed to a specific place, permeates the responses. Gertrude Stein writes that America is "a country the right age to have been born in and the wrong age to live in."[159] She goes on to say that America "is a well-nourished home but not a place to work. Your parents' home is never a place to work it is a nice place to be brought up in." Stein describes America as "the wrong age to live in," yet she also defines the United States as "the mother of the twentieth century civilization." Stein inserts herself into this framework, declaring, "A country this the oldest and therefore the most important country in the world quite naturally produces the creators, and so naturally it is I an

American who was and is thinking in writing was born in America and lives in Paris. This has been and probably will be the history of the world."[160] Through such cryptic hyperbole, Stein naturalizes America's position as "the most important country in the world" and her own role as a creator. Stein solipsistically conflates her experience with that of her country, validating her biography as her literary destiny.

Stein elaborated on why Paris was the site for her literary career in subsequent texts. "Paris was where the twentieth century was," she declares in *Paris, France* (1940), echoing Jolas's question about "twentieth century reality."[161] In a 1936 lecture Stein similarly refers to Paris as the home where she lived half her life, "not the half that made me but the half in which I made what I made," suggesting that America "made her" but that Paris enabled her self-actualization. Stein claimed that living in a foreign language spurred her to break down English into its component parts and to revitalize it. Paris gave her "a special language to write" because English differed from "the language that was spoken."[162] Living in France estranged Stein from English, allowing her to reinvent it in a kind of self-imposed linguistic isolation. She narrates this inward turn in *Paris, France*: "Everybody who writes is interested in living inside themselves in order to tell what is inside themselves. That is why writers have to have two countries, the one where they belong and the one in which they live really. The second one is romantic, it is separate from themselves, it is not real but it is really there."[163] By separating herself from the place where she chose to live, Stein could better recreate English, America, and herself in her writing. Living in Paris was thus essential to Stein's literary aspirations.

Other respondents similarly maintained that living in Paris provided a productive distance from home that facilitated their creative output. The photographer Berenice Abbott writes, "The very complex nature of America is, if possible, better understood from a distance than at close range."[164] Many were also conscious of their precarious status as artists and foregrounded artistic freedom in their responses. The composer George Antheil, for instance, claims he did not even realize that he was part of an expatriate community until receiving this questionnaire: "I was astonished to think that I was probably an exile, but it is undoubtedly true."[165] Antheil moved abroad to develop an audience for his work, because "musically it is impossible to live in America."[166] Like the Europeans surveyed, many contributors similarly denounced America as utilitarian and materialistic. The writer Emily Holmes Coleman describes America as "the enemy of the artist, of the man who cannot produce something tangible when the five o'clock whistle blows."[167] Some even seem to suggest that their European education allowed them to produce better art and literature, thereby securing their country's artistic future.

Jolas encouraged the respondents to write an "autobiography of the mind," and many would go on to do so explicitly in memoirs of the era. This self-reflection often involved ruminating on the United States from a distance. As

Matthew Josephson notes in his memoir, writing in the collective third person plural, "in self-imposed 'exile,' we thought and wrote a good deal about the United States. We felt that we loved it—at a distance—and that Paris was our 'second country.'"[168] One of the foremost chroniclers of his generation, Malcolm Cowley, similarly reflects, "We had come three thousand miles in search of Europe and had found America, in a vision half-remembered, half-falsified and romanced."[169] Hemingway corroborates this sentiment, writing in *A Moveable Feast*, "Maybe away from Paris I could write about Paris as in Paris I could write about Michigan."[170] For all of these writers, distance from America enabled them to better depict their homeland. In his poem "American Letter," published in the *Bookman* in 1929, Archibald MacLeish frames this position as a question: "How can a wise man have two countries?" He responds with the refrain "It is a strange thing to be an American" and continues:, "this is our land, this is our people, / This that is neither a land nor a race."[171] MacLeish echoes the feelings of dislocation voiced by the questionnaire respondents, as they too struggled to articulate what America meant to them from afar.

Reflections on exile, expatriatism, deracination, and cosmopolitanism pervade the literature of the period. The questionnaire provided an opportunity for writers to position themselves within the matrix of these self-identifications. Walter Lowenfels, a journalist and poet, writes in response to the questionnaire, "Cosmopolitanism enjoys the advantages and cultures of all nations and improves through them the national culture, incorporating in it what other nations have discovered."[172] In his memoir, Samuel Putnam declares, "I have no desire to be a *déraciné*. Not after inspecting from close up our local 'exile' colony. I don't think I could ever be one; but I shall live and die a cosmopolitan."[173] Conversely, Robert McAlmon suggests that these identities could all be encompassed by the designation "American," writing, "I never felt myself an expatriate or anything but an American, although not through excess of patriotism. My country is much too polyglot of race, type, and variety of faith, political and otherwise, for me to discover exactly to which qualities one would have to remain loyal in order to be a hundred percent American. I had left America because of events and had never been, and am not now, romantic about Europe."[174] Jolas's questionnaire gathered together the conflicting sentiments and identifications of many Americans abroad, which dominated other accounts of the era as well.

As for Jolas, he later wrote "I belonged everywhere and nowhere and I was forever homesick for other shores."[175] Jolas's writings evince a stirring sense of displacement; the critic Gerald Kennedy calls this the feeling of the "ungrounded self," a condition that "exposes a radical uncertainty about one's relation to 'home' and to the self one has been."[176] Many American writers in Paris similarly felt that they belonged nowhere, as evidenced by proclamations such as that of Henry Miller in his 1934 *Tropic of Cancer*: "I'm not an American any more, nor a New Yorker, and even less a European, or a Parisian. I haven't any allegiance, any responsibilities, any hatreds, any worries, any prejudices, any passion. I'm neither for nor against. I'm neutral."[177] This "neutral," ungrounded position could also be a point of departure for creative expression.

Edward Said, who famously theorized the effects of exile, describes how its accompanying sense of loss could expand one's worldview. Said distinguishes between exile and expatriatism, writing that "expatriates may share in the solitude and estrangement of exile, but they do not suffer under its rigid proscriptions."[178] Jolas also found the term "exiles" inappropriate for this group of writers; it was "an appellation I always thought ludicrous."[179] Nevertheless, both the conditions of exile and expatriatism offer a position of productive distance, yielding what Said called a "plurality of vision." For Said, this "plurality of vision gives rise to an awareness of simultaneous dimensions," wherein "both the new and old environments are vivid, actual, occurring together contrapuntally."[180] A "nomadic, decentered, contrapuntal" position, as Said called it, could offer an enriched perspective on home. In his response to the questionnaire, the journalist Lansing Warren describes Americans as nomadic: "The restlessness among Americans cannot be considered as a force for deracination when it is recalled that Americans, as nearly as they can be grouped as a people, must be regarded as nomadic."[181] A variation on this "nomadic, decentered, contrapuntal" vision was what Stein tried to channel into her relationship to English and Jolas to concretize in *transition*.

From Paris to Havana: Translating Latin America

While *Imán* did not reciprocally poll its Latin American contributors as *transition* did, its questionnaire was nonetheless transferred to a Latin American context by Alejo Carpentier, who wrote about it for the Cuban magazine *Carteles* in June 1931. In his article "América ante la joven literatura Europea" (America put before young European writers), Carpentier announces the results of an "extremely interesting questionnaire," hailing the respondents as "ten authentic representatives of contemporary European literature" who had enough distance from Latin America to "express themselves freely"[182] (fig. 13). The Europeans surveyed, he notes, responded with "generosity and enthusiasm" and sometimes adopted "a frankly anti-European attitude."[183] Carpentier summarized the results of the survey and then used it as an opportunity to reflect on the relationship between Europe and Latin America more broadly.

Carpentier's article provided a counterbalance to the *Imán* questionnaire, much in the same way as *transition*'s second survey gave Americans an opportunity to address their relationship to Europe. In it he laments that "in Latin America, enthusiasm for European things has given rise to a certain spirit of imitation, which has had the deplorable consequence of delaying our vernacular expressions for many years."[184] Decrying imitation was a common refrain in the *Revista de Avance* responses too. However, Carpentier was writing from Paris, and he anticipated the following rebuttal: "[But] how . . . can you, who have spent several years studying and identifying the new musical, pictorial, and

AMÉRICA ANTE LA JOVEN LITERATURA EUROPEA

POR ALEJO CARPENTIER

UNA nueva revista literaria, redactada en nuestro idioma y editada en París, *Imán,*—publicación dirigida por Elvira de Alvear, y de la que soy Jefe de Redacción,—ofrece en su primer número los resultados de una encuesta interesantísima. Diez auténticos representantes de la literatura europea viviente exponen en ella sus ideas acerca de la América Latina; diez jóvenes escritores—entre los cuales algunos ya gloriosos, como G. Ribemont Dessaignes y Philippe Soupault—lo bastante alejados de nuestro continente para poderse expresar con toda libertad, sin partidarismos, ni aspiraciones a que los inviten a ofrecer una jira de conferencias en tierras de ultramar.

"¿Cómo se imaginan ustedes a América Latina?" se les ha preguntado: "¿cuál habrá de ser su posición ante Europa, ¿cuáles son, a su juicio, sus problemas fundamentales?"... Y estos intelectuales han respondido con una generosidad y un entusiasmo que no hubiéramos podido esperar de escritores más viejos... Es porque los franceses de las nuevas generaciones van dejando de ser—como los definía antaño un gran novelista ruso—"unos señores que se creen nacidos para hacer las delicias de la humanidad..."

Lo más curioso es que, una vez situados ante nuestro continente, estos escritores adoptan, en su mayoría, una actitud francamente antieuropea. Philippe Soupault, el más radical de todos, llega a hacer afirmaciones tan categóricas como éstas: "Soy de los que no temen afirmar que el espectáculo ofrecido por Europa, actualmente, es el de una decadencia. Por mis escritos, mis palabras, mis gestos, me esfuerzo en señalar esa muerte, por lo demás bastante ignominiosa, que merece esta península inútil, y de prepararle un bello entierro. Europa agoniza suavemente, tartamudeando, babeando, fanfarroneando, Amén... Pero Europa es una moribunda afectada por una enfermedad contagiosa. Los continentes que aceptaron con más o menos agrado, el tocar su lepra, el tragarse el microbio llamado "civilización europea", admirablemente caracterizada por una burguesía triunfante, tendrán ardua tarea que emprender si quieren verse librados de este mal... Lo que debe afirmarse con fuerza es que América Latina debe dejar de volverse hacia el continente europeo, que conserva,

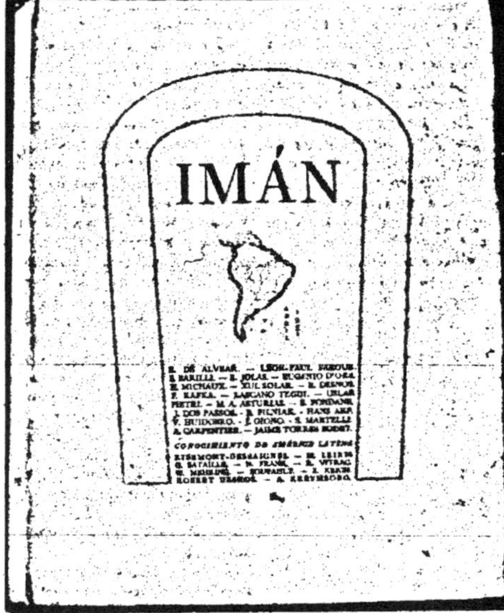

Facsímil del primer número de la nueva revista "Imán", que Carpentier glosa en su crónica

ante sus ojos, un prestigio incomprensible. Tiene el deber de precisar cuál habrá de ser su verdadero destino; está hoy bastante segura de sí misma para exigir una completa autonomía..."

Nino Frank, afirma que "América Latina puede tener entre sus manos el porvenir del mundo, su rejuvenecimiento y su opulencia, aunque su vida es una lucha contínua contra la invasión de los Estados Unidos... Siempre vencida (o casi), explotada, martirizada, deja ver al mundo, sin embargo, lo que puede ser su fuerza, cuando, de tiempo en tiempo, arranca a su modorra un breve sobresalto de energía... Sin duda, el clima, esa vegetación, esa vida aún tan sorprendentemente patriarcal, hacen que se soporte todo con una indiferencia singular, y que los hombres se vuelvan amorosamente hacia la vieja Europa de los señores Poincaré, Lloyd George y Hindenburg...

Pero Río de Janeiro, Buenos Aires, México, Montevideo, Bogotá, son ciudades que no logramos imaginar tales y como son. Sólo pensamos en New York o en Berlín. Y si algún día el experimento de la U. R. S. S. llegara a ser destruído por las fuerzas de la reacción, sólo quedaría un mundo nuevo frente a la vieja civilización burguesa: América Latina..."

Y Nino Frank termina su texto, con esta frase encantadora: "...Y no puede uno librarse de un continente así, como de una avispa".

Definiendo netamente su ideología política, Robert Desnos se sitúa en el plano marxista: "Tengo la certidumbre — afirma — que esta efervescente tierra virgen y fértil, será el teatro de acontecimientos formidables en la evolución del estado social del mundo... Pero importa ante todo que la evolución social de América Latina se lleve a cabo en el plano social. Lo que nos interesa en las conmociones de ese continente, no es saber que un general ha sido fusilado por orden de otro general; que la "libertad" ha sido hallada una vez más por un partido, al derribar otro partido, que, a su vez, salvará la *libertad* en la próxima ocasión. Lo que nos interesa es el destino del cortador de caña cubano, del sembrador de café del Brasil y de sus trabajadores, del peón de ganadería argentino, del minero peruano, del viticultor chileno. En cuatro palabras: el destino del proletariado... En la época actual, época en que todo el poder del capitalismo es debido a una larga experiencia social, a una técnica apropiada, a planos inflexiblemente realizados, es importante que el proletariado latinoamericano no se deje vencer por esa ciencia, por el capital al servicio del cual labora, quiéralo o no... Menos frases, menos lirismo. Si tales factores forman parte del medio, si son útiles y hasta necesarios durante los días de acción, es, sin embargo, indispensable desterrarlos de los programas. Los movimientos futuros deben ser movimientos de clases, y no movimientos de minorías, animadas por las mejores intenciones, pero exentas de todos los sufrimientos que hacen nacer el choque entre individuos... El estado futuro de las clases trabajadoras de América Latina, nos interesa más que el incendio de tal o cual palacio, el nombre de tal o cual cabecilla revolucionario, los bellos hechos de tal o cual héroe..."

Walter Mehring, joven escritor alemán, hace una humorística alusión, en su texto, a la decadencia de Europa: "Antes de la guerra —escribe—nos mostraban en una exhibición berlinesa, dos extraños seres, con narices en forma de pico

(Continúa en la pág. 31)

literary values of old Europe, [take such a position]?" Carpentier argues that European art and literature can be mined for methods to help one create work for an international audience. "In art," Carpentier writes, "the realization of a work has as much importance as its primary material." Some Latin American writers have strong material but do not communicate it in such a way that would facilitate translation, Carpentier argues, whereas he faults much European writing for its excellent technique and paltry source material. Instead, as if responding to both the *Revista de Avance* and *Imán* questionnaires himself, Carpentier maintains that Latin Americans must learn from, rather than imitate, European art: "It is necessary that young Americans thoroughly know the representative values of modern European art and literature . . . not in order to undertake the contemptible labor of imitation . . . [but] to discover constructive methods suitable to translate our Latin American thoughts and sensibilities with greater force."[185] By studying European writing for its techniques, Latin Americans could better showcase their compelling source material, and thereby "translate Latin American thoughts and sensibilities" accordingly.

Such an approach, Carpentier suggests, would help generate interest in Latin American literature abroad. Carpentier identifies as a Latin American writer, despite living in exile, and declares, "all of my texts published in Paris and Berlin are nourished by *criollo* essences."[186] He then calls upon Latin Americans to "mobilize our energies to translate America with the most intensity possible."[187] Carpentier does so to build a market for Latin American literature. He asserts, "it is not enough to say 'we are breaking with Europe,' to begin to offer genuinely representative expressions of a Latin American sensibility."[188] His emphasis is at once on autochthonous creation and its translation and distribution. As a result, this Latin American art and literature would be true to the continent, but also have currency abroad. He cites Ricardo Güiraldes, Diego Rivera, Heitor Villa-Lobos, and Mariano de Azuela as some of the figures already countering the "spirit of imitation"—and attracting wider audiences—through their work.

Carpentier also adds his own writing to this list. He maintains, "My novels similarly cannot be separated from our island—as you can judge from the fragments of them, *Écue-Yamba-O*, published in the first issue of *Imán*."[189] Carpentier's Afro-Cuban novel *Écue Yamba-O*, a selection of which was featured in *Imán,* dramatizes the religious syncretism of Cuba's rural black population. This formally experimental work was published alongside Kafka's "The Judgment," Miguel Ángel Asturias's "En la tiniebla del Cañaveral," two poems by Hans Arp, and an essay by John Dos Passos on theater. In this way, *Imán* demonstrated how Latin American literature might be integrated with that of Europe and North America, serving as a test case for the kind of cultural translation that Carpentier describes.

Imán was deeply invested in linguistic translation, as evidenced by its translation of writers like Kafka and John Dos Passos into Spanish, published alongside Latin American authors such as Huidobro and Asturias. Carpentier also encouraged the production of Latin American work for international distribution—to boost the status of Latin American literature abroad and to provide Europeans with a better understanding of the region. Similarly, Jolas believed that by translating foreign-language work into English, American writers might enrich their own writing and generate literature ready for international export. Beyond translation, Jolas sought a mutual language or poetics with which Europeans and Americans could communicate. In his memoir Jolas identifies this aspiration as "a new language, a super-tongue for intercontinental expression . . . an Atlantic language."[190] Stein and other questionnaire respondents' reflections on language and displacement reinforced Jolas's own linguistic goals for *transition.*

In June 1929, the year after the magazine issued its two questionnaires, *transition* published its "Revolution of the Word" proclamation, which declares, "The revolution of the English language is an accomplished fact."[191] Its signatories empower writers to reimagine language beyond its typical usage. They decry those "short stories, novels, poems and plays still under the hegemony of the banal word."[192] The treatise concludes, "the plain reader be damned," a significant shift away from the magazine's opening editorial, which declared, "the reader is coming into his own."[193] Perhaps because the magazine no longer needed to solicit or flatter an audience, it could now afford to adopt the oppositional stance typical of a manifesto. The "Revolution of the Word" proclamation can be seen as the result of Jolas's linguistic ruminations, which had preoccupied *transition* since the magazine's inception.

Jolas had long argued in the pages of *transition* that traditional language was inadequate to represent the modern world because it did not acknowledge the multiplicity of lexicons that shaped a writer, nor did it adequately express a writer's subconscious. In 1928 Jolas argues in favor of giving words "new and violent associations" that would eradicate the "purely descriptive" and thus extend "our joy in hearing and reading."[194] In his essay "Super-Occident," published a few months after the manifesto, Jolas describes his struggle to enrich language as a problem of global proportions; he asserts, "the reality of the *universal word* is still being neglected. Never has a revolution been more imperative. We need the twentieth century word. We need the word of movement, the word expressive of the great new forces around us."[195] *transition* records the evolution of Jolas's thinking about language, which he saw as a quest for words and texts that reflected the modern world, an imperative articulated in the "Revolution of the Word" manifesto, but that persisted beyond its publication.

One can also trace the effects of Joyce's experiments on the "Revolution of the Word." Just prior to printing the manifesto, Jolas published "The Revolution of Language and James Joyce" in *transition*, lauding Joyce's use of English, which, "because of its universality, seems particularly fitted for a rebirth along the lines Mr. Joyce envisaged."[196] He then describes how Joyce "creates a verbal dreamland of abstraction that may well be the language of the future."[197] Jolas also mentions other *transition* contributors who played with language, praising Leiris's experimental glossaries and commending Stein. Thus, the delay in writing a manifesto—notably, *after* issuing several questionnaires—may have stemmed from the fact that the magazine's platform emerged out of its writers' contributions, rather than the reverse.

The "Revolution of the Word" experiments with English's potential to serve as a language for "intercontinental expression." Reaffirming the choice of English in 1932, Jolas links it to his aspirations for America: "The American language, for instance, boldly disregards inherited diction. Its speech is far removed from polite literary expression. This astonishingly vital organism may well become the basis for the sociological evolution of the English language."[198] Jolas celebrates *American* English in particular: "I called it the Atlantic, or Crucible, language, for it was the result of the interracial synthesis that was going on in the United States, Latin America and Canada. It was American English, with an Anglo-Saxon basis, plus many grammatical and lexical additions from more than a hundred tongues . . . an intercontinental idiom used by millions of neo-Americans, an idiom that is the result of the ceaseless migrations of peoples of all races and tongues."[199] Identifying as one of these "neo-Americans," Jolas sees a language of "migration" as the language of the future—an English imbued with the various dialects culled from America's diverse immigrant populations. Notably, Jolas also cites Latin America as crucial to forming this "intercontinental idiom." Elsewhere he muses on the immigrant languages of New York; he saw Manhattan as a "whirling cauldron of the new vocabulary."[200] Even in Jolas's story for *Imán*, "Documento," the protagonist speculates that "new names, the names of nickel and aluminum," will be used "to designate the creations of the future."[201] For Jolas, America's permeable borders and its openness to immigrant cultures and languages elevate the future potential of English.[202]

Jolas's belief in the mosaic-like quality of American English and its prospect as an "Atlantic language" reveal his utopian aspirations for language, literature, and the magazine. As Marjorie Perloff argues, for Jolas, this visionary new language was "designed to bring together diverse peoples, to erase borders between the European nations, to produce a large cosmopolitan and international consciousness."[203] While Perloff underscores the internationalist ambitions of such a language, the critic David Bennett condemns Jolas's model, calling it a "suppression of the heterogeneous, oppositional languages or discourses in which the distinctive experiences of social groups, classes, nations, races, or sexes might remain interpretable," a particular danger during the increasingly fascist 1930s.[204] Despite Jolas's protests that *transition*'s revolution of language was more formal than political, his search for a singular language waned with the rise of fascism, particularly Nazism, which usurped and warped language to suit its purposes. Although he championed English in particular, Jolas's celebration of linguistic pluralism was meant to preserve rather than erase difference.[205]

Counteracting the magazine's promotion of English as a possible "Atlantic language," in February 1933 *transition* stopped translating all of its submissions into English and instead published French and German work in its original language. Jolas explains this decision in an editorial: "With this issue, transition enters upon a new policy of tri-lingual publication. The crisis of language is now going on in every part of the Occident. It seems, therefore, essential to retain the linguistic creative material intact, and to present constructive work, as much as possible, in the original."[206] Jolas shifts away from primarily presenting works in English in order to demonstrate the "crisis of language," likely spurred by political events, and to preserve linguistic difference. With the rise of fascism, a policy of monolingualism began to seem dangerous rather than utopian.

However, Jolas had long struggled to determine *transition*'s relationship to translation. The decision of whether or not to translate submissions had plagued the magazine as early as March 1928, when Jolas and Paul describe the "inadequacy" of their translations, "although we always attempted to do full justice to the original."[207] The magazine also tested out a different translation policy in November 1929, when it included three untranslated French texts. Jolas outlines his reasons for leaving the work in its original language: "We are departing from our usual practice of giving foreign authors in translation, because in three French contributions that appear exclusively in this number—Roger Vitrac, Robert Desnos and Jacques Prévet—the language itself is of intrinsic interest and would lose by translation."[208] Jolas presumed that these texts would serve as examples to writers in all languages. As he explains, "We do not doubt that *transition* readers will be glad to have an opportunity of looking into the experimental work which is being done in the greatest of romance languages."[209] The magazine worried that its policy of translating all foreign-language material into English conflicted with its aim to inspire linguistic experimentation. Although Jolas called *transition* "an adventure in language," such anxieties about how to enact his linguistic ideals spurred many of the questionnaires that he issued.[210]

While many of *transition*'s contributors strove to reinvigorate language, this shared project took radically different forms. Joyce's reinvention of English in "Work in Progress" is clearly distinct from Hugo Ball's sound poetry or Jolas's own multilingual poetics. In 1932 Jolas inaugurated a section of the magazine entitled Laboratory of the Word, in which he and his associate editors compiled lists of words to be retired from active service, and a Revolution of the Word Dictionary, offering readers new words culled from contemporary slang, Dadaist poems, Joyce's prose, and excerpts from the dreams of *transi-*

tion's contributors.[211] However, how can one codify an evolving language of the future? The need to invest its platform with authority in many ways contradicted the magazine's emphasis on a fluid and elastic relationship to language. Jolas fought to define a "revolution" of language, and to determine how it could best be accomplished. In 1933 he renamed the "Revolution of the Word" "The Revolution of Language," which he described as "an attitude which regards modern language as inadequate for the expression of the changing background of the world, and which posits the necessity of a radical revision of its communicative and symbolical functions."[212] Whether revolutionizing the individual word or language at large, Jolas and many of the magazine's contributors showcased their ongoing attempts to reinvent language, an experiment registered in the magazine's evolving translation policies.

Latin American Literature in Europe

Much like the Americans responding to *transition*'s questionnaire, Carpentier found his distance from Cuba productive. In Paris he introduced European audiences to Latin American literature, politics, and culture through his writing, and conversely transmitted the latest developments in Europe back to Cuban readers in articles for magazines like *Social* and *Carteles*. Carpentier had long been interested in identifying a Latin American canon, as evidenced by his involvement in *Revista de Avance*, and he continued to mull over its characteristics after moving to Paris. As Klaus Müller-Bergh explains, "the painful artistic questions about what is characteristically American in literature, the singularity of America, as much as the preoccupation with a 'nationalist labor in art' posed by these fundamental questions . . . followed Alejo Carpentier to Paris."[213] *Revista de Avance*'s central question—What should American art be?—informed much of Carpentier's writing abroad. For instance, in 1929 Carpentier contributed an article to *Social* on the Brazilian composer Heitor Villa-Lobos in which he asks, "To what extent should we 'europeanize' ourselves? Is Americanism a question of form or sensibility?" He also describes the "arduous task of creating a universal American art."[214] This quest to create an art that is at once "American" and "universal" echoes Jolas's goal of creating "an intercontinental idiom" based on English. While *Revista de Avance* focused on defining and disseminating an *arte americano*, Carpentier wanted to make such art and literature legible to a larger, primarily European, audience, as he outlined in his *Carteles* essay on *Imán*'s questionnaire. Carpentier's desire to "translate America with the most intensity possible" fueled much of his literary and critical work during his time in Europe.

However, Carpentier also recognized the pitfalls of such translation. *Imán*'s questionnaire, for instance, demonstrated Europeans' tendency to exotify Latin America. While Carpentier did offer Afro-Cuban perspectives to European magazines, thereby "translating" Latin America for audiences abroad, he recalls the hazards of this task in an essay he published in *Carteles* in 1929. In it Carpentier laments, "Continually, in the editing of new magazines, I am asked: 'Translate Latin American things, reveal to us your values, seek out popular poetry by Indians, guajiras and blacks; give us woodcuts, tell us what it is like over there.'"[215] Carpentier clearly recognizes the primitivist impulse behind such requests. In much of his writing on Latin America for Europe, and conversely his dispatches to *Social* and *Carteles* on Paris, he struggles to make sense of his role as "translator" of an "exotic culture" abroad. As one critic notes, "While Carpentier turns an ethnographic eye on Paris in his writings for a Cuban audience published in *Social* and *Carteles*, conversely he adopts an ethnographic perspective with respect to Cuba for his European readers in *Documents*, *Bifur*, and '¡Ecué-Yamba-O!'"[216] Although he replicated some of these primitivist inclinations in his own work, Carpentier ultimately advocated for a Latin American literature that did not cater to Europeans' stereotypes about the region, a position he outlined in his literary and art criticism.

Carpentier took his role as cultural intermediary and translator seriously, aiming to create and advocate for what he deemed universally legible and exportable Latin American works of literature. In 1931, a few months after *Imán* came out, Carpentier published the essay "The Cardinal Points of the Latin American Novel" in French for the Paris-based magazine *Le Cahier*, thereby "translating" Latin America for French audiences in a way that debunked stereotypes about the region.[217] In the essay, Carpentier acknowledges that the Latin American novel was formed only in the last century, but argues that this position "gives us the terribly complex spectacle of an original civilization in formation, one that recovers the time it lost in burning stages, one whose spirit proceeds in leaps, as dangerous as they are unexpected."[218] Much as in the invocation of an *arte americano*, Carpentier strengthens the category of Latin American literature by identifying and promoting it. He declares, "the South American novel is the outcome of a series of attempts, of struggles intensely oriented towards the search for a continental sensibility."[219]

First Carpentier contends with the vastness and diversity of Latin America. He acknowledges that it "is difficult to explain to a European reader," skeptical of the "possibility of a shared sensibility" in such varied terrain, what constitutes a "Latin American" novel.[220] Despite the incommensurability of Latin American nations, Carpentier asserts that "for us South Americans, there exists, outside of local problems, a certain spiritual state in the guise of thousands of diverse forms, from the ravaged coasts of the Tierra del Fuego to the Rio Grande, to the deserts of Arizona."[221] Carpentier argues that this force uniting the region is transmissible in its literature, thus corroborating *Revista de Avance*'s questionnaire and echoing some of its language. This sensibility derives from the region's language, literature, geography, and politics, and also, notably, from a shared interest in Europe. He writes that countries across Latin America "speak a single language, conduct the same expansions and the same excesses, as much in poetry as in politics, as much in the construction of a city as in enthu-

siasm for a French literary movement."[222] In his *Carteles* essay Carpentier had
anticipated criticism for not focusing exclusively on local production; here, writing for European audiences, he openly acknowledges Latin America's interest in
Europe, and even cites it as a common attribute.

The delay in forming a Latin American literary tradition, according to
Carpentier, was due to colonialism. In the "civilizing" colonial period, Jesuit
"educators of the Indians" prohibited many kinds of literature, he explains, and
thus the "first manifestations of a South American literature appeared in the
days following the independence wars."[223] Carpentier cites the oppression of
intellectuals, whom he says were seen as threatening to the state and describes
the "wave of illiterate dictators successively invading . . . American republics."
He notes that it is "easy to comprehend that, under these circumstances, Latin
American literature had not developed in a regular way. For a century, nearly all
intellectuals of this continent knew prison, exile, and, in Guatemala and Venezuela, even torture and death."[224] Carpentier himself knew this reality all too
well, having been imprisoned by the Machado regime in Cuba.

For Carpentier, Latin American literature began in the nineteenth century.
He identifies two approaches from this period: nationalist writing, such as that
of José Hernández; and writing that could be described as cosmopolitan, exemplified by Rubén Darío, who "voluntarily confronted—without fearing at times
ridiculous imitation—the influence of France." This latter type, he notes, turned
to French literature to overcome the colonizing interests of Spain. Such writers
"surprised Spain with the novelty of their language . . . by turning to France, they
made us forget the Royal Academy of the Spanish Language; in the School of
Paris, they learned to soften their language and to enrich their meter. . . . Liberated from their Castilian tutelage, they were to poetic expression what [José de]
San Martín was to the history of their continent. After them, all boldness in em-
ploying neologisms, or Latin American idioms, or local terminology created out
of expressive need was permitted."[225] It was this shift away from Spain, by way
of France, that paradoxically freed Latin American writers to generate their own
literature. Carpentier describes such authors as "looking proudly at themselves,
the atmosphere of their countries, 'their America,'" he declares, in homage to
Martí. This framework—"our America"—gives "an air of family to all Americans
of the south," whether they are of "Indian, Spanish, or black" origin, he states.
Invoking Martí, Carpentier suggests that the racial diversity of Latin America is a
hallmark of its identity.[226]

The true achievement of the Latin American novel would be measured by
its reach, Carpentier argues, especially with respect to European audiences,
whom he is courting and educating in his article. As he explains, "But it is today
when we can set out a South American novel of universal inclination, which can
withstand the test of translation and is capable of seducing a good European
reader with its power and significance."[227] This feat of *translatability* is the true
test of Latin American literature for Carpentier: work that can "seduce a good

European reader." Carpentier calls books of this kind the "cardinal points" of Latin American literature. By way of example he lists several titles, including Argentine Ricardo Güiraldes's *Don Segundo Sombra*, Columbian José Eustasio Rivera's *La vorágine*, Venezuelan Rómulo Gallegos's *Doña Bárbara*, Venezuelan Arturo Uslar Pietri's *Las lanzas coloradas* (selections of which were included in *Imán*), and Mexican Mariano Azuela's *Los de abajo.* Given such work, Carpentier concludes, "without a doubt, it won't take long for the Latin American novel to occupy the place it deserves in world literature."[228] Calling for the creation of "a Latin American novel of universal inclination" that would "occupy the place it deserves in world literature," this essay celebrates writing that manifests its Latin American origins but still emphasizes its translatability for international readers. By publishing his text in French in *Le Cahier*, Carpentier demonstrates that he is already a part of the literary culture to which he introduces foreign elements, and is already creating a market for the Latin American literature for which he advocates.

Through such essays, Carpentier conjured a place for Latin American literature in a French context. Yet he also tried to draw Europeans' attention to the specificities of Latin American politics, and in particular to the horrors of the Machado regime in Cuba. He incited his friends in Surrealist circles in Paris to action, and then reported those efforts back to Cuban audiences. In a 1933 essay in *Carteles*, "Homenage a nuestros amigos de Paris" (Homage to our friends in Paris), Carpentier lauds the work of Georges Ribemont-Dessaignes and Robert Desnos, who published a special issue of *La Nouvelle Revue Française* dedicated to Cuba. Ribemont-Dessaignes also published a two-part report on the Machado regime in the magazine *Voilà*, transferring photographs from *Carteles* to a French context.[229] Desnos, for his part, helped publish the pamphlet *La Terreur à Cuba* (Terror in Cuba), which also featured a drawing by the Cuban artist Carlos Enríquez.[230] Carpentier declares that he is pleased to "cite the names of these allies in the pages of a Cuban magazine," whose work is in stark contrast to the "millions and millions of Europeans" for whom "America is the continent of tango, tobacco, and hair gel," echoing Ribemont-Dessaignes's lament in *Imán*.[231]

Carpentier was not the sole representative of the Antilles in the Surrealist group in Paris advocating for his country's literary and political independence. The Martinican students who launched the manifesto and eponymous magazine *Légitime défense* also lived and worked in Paris in the early 1930s.[232] Those living in Paris at the time were faced with *L'Exposition coloniale internationale de Paris* (The international colonial exposition of Paris), held from May 6 to November 15, 1931, as well as the joint Surrealist and communist counterexhibition *La Verité sur les Colonies* (The truth about the colonies), mounted to contest the colonialist and dehumanizing aspects of the Exposition.[233] Thus, despite the often primitivist inclinations behind Surrealism's interest in Africa and the Caribbean, the group's commitments to those regions did have real political consequences. As the critic Timothy Brennan writes, "the active participation of Caribbean intellectuals resident in Europe, as well as the later travel of several of surrealism's members (Desnos, Leiris, Mabille, Breton) to the Caribbean, transformed surrealism from within."[234] This "transformation of Surrealism from within" reverberated in Carpentier's own writing. He returned to Havana in 1939 and wrote the groundbreaking essay "The Marvelous Real in America" in 1949 as the preface to his novel *The Kingdom of This World*. This text and others suggest what he later described in an interview: that although Surrealism originated in France, "in America, Surrealism turns out to be quotidian, current, habitual; it beats and breathes in the heart of the home, in the simplest flowering of a mushroom."[235] Carpentier's work demonstrates the reciprocal influence of Europe and the Americas and its lasting effects. This relationship was interrogated by questionnaires like those issued in *Imán* and *transition*, which sought to promote the kind of linguistic and cultural translations that were being carried out by their contributors.

transition in the 1930s

transition worked to garner support for Americans and their writing in Europe. However, by the early 1930s many expatriates had left Paris.[236] Perhaps for that reason, compounded by the logistical difficulties of putting out a magazine, in June 1930 *transition* decided to go on hiatus (it resumed again in March 1932 and ended publication in 1938).[237] Jolas justifies this gesture aesthetically: "The transitional period of literature appears to be drawing to a close. But our experimental action, I feel sure, will constitute an impulsion and a basis on which to construct for some time to come."[238] The magazine's relationship with Stein waned in the wake of *The Autobiography of Alice B. Toklas*, and its relationship with the Surrealists also soured. In 1933 Jolas wrote, "The impulse for the revolution of the word owes its genesis to such precursors as Arthur Rimbaud, James Joyce, the Futurists, the early Zurich Dadaists, certain experiments of Gertrude Stein, and Léon-Paul Fargue. It owes nothing to Surrealism."[239] Despite this elision of Surrealism, in 1938 Jolas boasted of having "introduced the texts of the then emergent school of Surrealism, a full decade before London and New York became aware of it."[240] Regardless of its reasons, throughout the 1930s *transition* lost focus and support, and altered the direction of its activities.

However, *transition* continued to rely on the questionnaire as a mode of inquiry throughout the 1930s. The genre enabled Jolas to affirm process, individuality, and open-endedness, which he continued to champion. A fear of collectivism in art and politics plagued Jolas, and became an urgent question with the rise of fascism in Europe. In 1932 he issued a survey on the fate of individualists under collective regimes (that also questioned the status of metaphysics in the age of science); responses came from a range of artists and writers from across Europe and the Americas, including H. L. Mencken, David Siqueiros, Richard Huelsenbeck, Carl Jung, and Martin Buber.[241] Jolas also conducted his ongoing search for revolutionary language through the questionnaire. In

1935 *transition* issued an "Inquiry About the Malady of Language," which asked, "Do you believe that, in the present world-crisis, the Revolution of Language is necessary in order to hasten the reintegration of the human personality? Do you envisage this possibility through a readaptation of existing words, or do you favor a revolutionary creation of new words?"[242] Jolas also used the genre to explore his interest in the relationship between language and the unconscious, putting forth an "Inquiry into the Spirit and Language of Night" in 1938, the final year of the magazine, which received responses from Sherwood Anderson, Malcolm Cowley, T. S. Eliot, and Ernest Hemingway.[243] Despite the increasingly opaque and outlandish terminology that Jolas invoked in his questionnaires (one included the question "Do you believe in angels?"), by 1938 *transition* had achieved such notoriety—bolstered by its celebrity authors—that its questionnaires garnered press from New York to Buenos Aires.[244]

As many Americans left Paris, eventually so did *transition*. In 1932 the magazine announced that henceforth it would be published in Holland by the Dutch Servire Press. Jolas himself traveled back to America for extended periods of time in the late 1930s. Those Americans who returned to the United States began reflecting on their time in Paris in their writing, incorporating their experiences into autobiographies and memoirs. Many of these memoirs, which continued to be published into the 1960s, revisited topics that came up in *transition*'s 1928 questionnaires on the relationship between America and Europe. The magazine had posed its questions to writers while they were still forming their literary personas in Paris, before they retroactively framed their experiences in their own narratives. In memoirs or loosely veiled fictional accounts, Gertrude Stein, Ernest Hemingway, Samuel Putnam, Elliot Paul, Sylvia Beach, Robert McAlmon, Kay Boyle, Matthew Josephson, and Malcolm Cowley all reinforced the idea of a generational formation, presenting their experiences as representative of their cohort. By writing about their lives in Europe, Putnam suggests Americans engaged in self-reflection, which took "the form of a certain self-questioning, a certain stock-taking, that could not in the nature of things be limited to the self but involved an attempt to strike the balance-sheet of a decade and a generation; it involved the entire question of expatriation and cosmopolitanism and the meaning of Americanism."[245] A version of this "self-questioning" about "the meaning of Americanism" had already occurred in response to *transition*'s questionnaires. Through the exercise, Jolas enabled writers and artists to assess themselves and their relationship to their peers while they still lived abroad.

For many American writers in Paris, the questionnaire provided them with an initial outlet for this kind of reckoning. As Matthew Josephson writes in his memoir of the era, "One does not know finally where one's generation begins or where it ends, nor whether it was 'lost' or found. However, one's memories, as subjective testimony, may furnish useful evidence about the movement of ideas in a certain time."[246] As "subjective testimony," the responses solicited by *transition* competed with and complemented these writers' autobiographical accounts of their experiences in Paris during the 1920s. In his reflections on the era, Cowley assigns magazines a central role, describing his generation as one in "transition from values already fixed to values that had to be created. Its members began by writing magazines with names like *transition*, *Broom* (to make a clean sweep of it), *1924*, *This Quarter* (existing in the pure present), *S4N*, *Secession*."[247] Cowley goes on to identify *transition* as "the last and the biggest of the little magazines published by the exiles."[248] Here Cowley links a generation obsessed with "the idea of salvation by exile" with the print culture that supported it.[249] While part of the impulse to document their experiences abroad came from the desire to frame the reception of their work, this generation's autobiographical inclination also further entrenched Paris as a creative capital. Many writers conflated the city with their literary production, positioning Paris, as critic Donald Pizer writes, "as a phase in the history of their inner lives and the inner lives of their characters."[250] The question as to why Americans lived in Europe was thus intimately entwined with these authors' literary self-fashioning.

Jolas had thought about issuing a follow-up questionnaire to the one from 1928, in order to determine why so many Americans *left* Paris. Jolas feared that the expatriate community that had conducted literary experiments abroad would return to America and succumb to social realism and other movements that he opposed. The following questions were included in Jolas's papers as "Suggestions about French enquête" (fig. 14), addressed to Americans who had once lived abroad but had since returned to the United States:

> At what period and for how long did you live in France? Why did you go there in the first place? Do you regret now having spent those years far from your own country? What, among the things that first attracted you to life in France, do you still hold to be essential features of intelligent living? What was your chief criticism of the French way of life? What did you most admire about it? Did you make any real friends among French people? Do you feel that your stay in France marked your creative work? If so, how? Have you any word for your French friends today? (optional question)

Building on his 1928 questionnaire, Jolas asks writers to describe the texture of their lives abroad and the influence of Europe—specifically France—on their literary output. The names listed below these questions as its intended recipients include "Kay Boyle, McLeish [sic], Hemingway, Calder, E. Paul, Mary Colum, Harold Stern, Malcolm Cowley, Josephson, Jo. Davidson, J. P. Bishop, C. Paulding, Henry Miller, Wilson (?), Universitaires? Scientifiques?" The questionnaire most likely dates to the late 1930s or 1940s.[251] (Jolas returned to America from 1939 to 1944, and died in Paris in 1952.)

Suggestions about French enquête .

1. At what period and for how long did you live in France ?

2. Why did you go there int he first place ?

3. Do you regret now having spent those years far from your own country ?

4. What , among the things that first attracted you to life in France , do
   you still hold to be essential features of intelligent living ?

5. What was your chief criticism of the French way of life ?

6. What did you most admire about it ?

7 . Did you make any real friends among French people ?

8 . Dod you feel that your stay in France marked your creative work ? If so,
   how ?

9. Have you any word for your French friends to-day ? (optional question)

Kay Boyle
McLeish
Hemingway
Calder
E. Paul
Mary Colum
Harold Stern
Malcolm Cowley
Josephson
Jo.Davidson
J.P.Bishop
C.Paulding
Henry Miller
Wilson (?)

Universitaires ?
Scientifiques ?

Fig. 14 Eugene Jolas, "Suggestions about French enquête." (n.d.).

Jolas himself had received a questionnaire about the "exile's return" in 1948 from the *American Quarterly*, a magazine based at the University of Minnesota. Questions included "What, in your opinion, are the reasons why so many expatriates have returned to, as well as why so many Europeans have taken residence in, the United States? Every society offers the artist raw material. What, in your opinion, is the nature or character of this material in the United States? What use, if any, have you made of such materials? What kinds of encouragement or discouragement, spiritually or economically, does the United States offer the artist?"[252] By 1948 the devastation of World War II had prompted not only Americans but also Europeans to flee places like Paris for refuge abroad. Yet the *American Quarterly*'s questions also highlight the connections between displacement and artistic production that Jolas had wrestled with his entire career and sought to address in *transition.*

Reviewed across the world, *transition* was, according to Jolas, "being discussed, criticized, vilified, admired. From England, Ireland, the United States, South Africa, India, Australia came reactions of every shade of opinion."[253] *transition*'s influence can also be measured by how many magazines took up its polemics. In 1929 the *Modern Quarterly* in Baltimore challenged Jolas to a debate over the "Revolution of the Word."[254] In 1939 *Poetry* reviewed *transition*'s questionnaires, alongside those issued by a range of international magazines.[255] The painter Robert Motherwell, writing to Jolas in 1947 to ask permission to reprint essays from the magazine for his Dada anthology, asserts that *transition* "remains for many of us the most important magazine ever edited by an American."[256] Yet despite *transition*'s international reach and lasting influence, the magazine became increasingly difficult to publish, particularly in the political climate of the 1930s, and it folded in 1938. As Jolas explains, "The last issue appeared in May, 1938. By then the inevitable approach of World War II made it no longer possible to concentrate on abstract laboratory problems, or to daydream about new forms in art and language."[257]

The Collapse of *Imán*

transition lasted over a decade; conversely, *Imán* ended almost instantly, as Elvira de Alvear's fortunes changed. "She had everything and gradually / Everything slipped away from her," Borges wrote on the occasion of her death in 1959.[258] The first issue of *Imán* indicated that a subscriber would receive four issues a year. However, shortly after the first issue was published, De Alvear's finances sank and she returned to Argentina, abandoning her apartment, salon, magazine, and professional circle in Paris. In his poem Borges alludes to both her literary gifts and the devastation of her family fortune. She had already begun to prepare for the second issue of *Imán* at the time of her financial collapse, offering insight into the editorial direction she had hoped the magazine would take.

The second issue was meant to feature poems from Pablo Neruda's book *Residencia en la tierra* (Residence on earth), which he had finished in 1931.

Rafael Alberti, a Spanish poet living in Paris, had placed some of Neruda's poems in the Spanish magazine *Revista de Occidente* and continued to advocate for his work. As Alberti writes in his memoir, "Living in Paris in 1931, I still kept trying to have the *Residencia* poems published. An Argentinian lady, Elvira de Alvear, agreed to finance and carry out the project. I obtained from Elvira the promise of a cash advance." (Neruda did not receive this advance, apparently meant to be five thousand francs, nor was the work published.)[259] In a letter from September 1931 Neruda describes his version of the events, noting that Alberti had explained

> that the book is in Paris, that some girl named Alvear, or De Alvear, has
> it, who puts out a magazine in Paris. That some of my poems are going
> to be published there (the magazine is called *Imán*, if it exists, which I
> doubt), that she will send me a check, and then a contract for the pub-
> lication of my book. This *Imán* [magnet] does not attract me, but what
> the hell. The worst part is that I've never heard of this magazine, nor has
> this girl written to me. . . . It makes you want to drink whiskey for three
> months.[260]

This letter implies that De Alvear had hoped to publish the book in its entirety, along with excerpts of select poems in *Imán*, although she had no direct contact with Neruda, who clearly doubted her intentions (and the existence of the magazine). Neruda claims that he had sent "the whole manuscript to a wealthy Argentine patron, Elvira de Alvear . . . but she lost it." According to critic Jason Wilson, Alejo Carpentier denied this version of events, saying that "he had asked for the manuscript from Paris, could not publish it as the magazine had gone bust thanks to the great Wall Street Crash and then [he] sent it to José Bergamín in Madrid who published it."[261] Regardless, it seems clear that Neruda would have been featured in the magazine, had it lasted. In addition to the Neruda poems, the second number of *Imán* was slated to include fragments from a book on André Gide and work by Rafael Alberti himself.[262] Unfortunately, the magazine lasted only one issue and De Alvear returned to Buenos Aires. Carpentier continued to live and write in Paris until 1939, when he returned to Cuba.

Translating the Transatlantic

Throughout his stay in Paris, Carpentier's analysis of European culture and its potential to serve as a model for an invigorated "American" literature closely mirrored Jolas's aims for *transition*. Jolas placed great hope in the future of America because of what he saw as its permeability to outside influences. He writes in 1929, "We have tried to bring together the significant international forces in the creative field, although always remaining fundamentally American in spirit."[263] Buoyed by his knowledge of French and German, and of the

European avant-garde, Jolas sought to transform American literature through exposure to European experimentation. Carpentier shared the hope that Latin Americans would borrow from Europe, particularly on the level of technique. To create a Latin American literary tradition, as the critic Alexis Márquez Rodríguez notes, Carpentier argued that it was "indispensable to start by getting to know and test out formal aspects of more advanced art and literature, so that, once these techniques had been mastered, the search and creation of their own techniques could be undertaken."[264] For Carpentier (and for Jolas, to a lesser extent), this "more advanced" tradition was French literature. While Carpentier "severely critiqued the imitation that was made of French models in Latin America," he did advocate for the study of European literature as a way of catalyzing Latin American innovation.[265] Jolas aspired to a similar outcome in *transition*, hoping that European literature in translation would encourage American writers to revitalize their language and their own writing.

Both *transition* and *Imán* contributed to the debate over what constituted "America" through their use of translation, publishing texts in either Spanish or English to disseminate international literature abroad and to spur the development of more robust literary cultures in the Americas. Through such translations they hoped to foster greater transatlantic understanding, even as they exposed tensions between Europe and the Americas through their questionnaires. Despite its interest in English, *transition* remained open to linguistic and artistic experimentation. Similarly, *Imán* intended to be pan-national. It countered and contextualized the responses to "How Do You Imagine Latin America?" by showcasing Latin American literature alongside that of Europe. Both Jolas and De Alvear presented an array of work from Europe and the Americas while galvanizing readers to assert their own literature's place in the world.

While the surveys issued by *transition* and *Imán* inscribe the Americas in a French context, questions about art and national canons in Europe and the Americas were even more contentious in a transatlantic Hispanophone context. For instance, a 1927 essay by the Spanish writer Guillermo de Torre declared Madrid the "intellectual meridian" of Latin America, a claim that was immediately challenged by magazines across the region.[266] Carpentier responded to the polemic in the Cuban magazine *Diario de la Marina,* commenting, "Today America tends to move farther away from Europe when it calmly focuses its creative energies. . . . America has to, therefore, look for meridians in itself, if it wants any meridian at all." For Carpentier, the "intellectual meridian" of Latin America was Latin America itself, yet he repeatedly asserted that European literature could serve as a model on the level of technique. As he explains in this text, "It seems to me that never in America has one turned to French literature for anything more than to find solutions to certain problems of *métier* [craft], which hold interest for anyone who attempts to translate nuances of the new spirit."[267] Thus, even before fleeing Cuba for Paris, Carpentier encouraged Latin Americans to "translate nuances of the new spirit," a position he continued to uphold; namely, for writers to look to France for lessons in craft, but to turn to Latin America itself as the source of creative expression.

Carpentier argued that every literature needed its own tradition, which he considered to be still in formation in Latin America. By contrast, Borges declares in his essay "The Argentine Writer and Tradition," "I believe that our tradition is the whole of Western culture."[268] While Carpentier asserts, "all of my texts published in Paris and Berlin are nourished by *criollo* essences," Borges, conversely, positions European culture as part of Latin America already. Borges writes in his magazine *Proa* in 1924, "The high culture that until now has been the exclusive patrimony of Europe and the few Americas that had drunk of it, begins to represent itself, in a miraculous way, as an essential product of our civilization," thus identifying "high culture" as a byproduct of the "*criollo* essences" to which Carpentier refers.[269] In the next chapter I explore how Spain and Latin America each fought to assert their place in an international avant-garde. Tensions erupted in the form of questionnaires and print-cultural debates about the transatlantic reach of national canons, leading to conflicts such as the "meridian debate" and pronouncements by Borges and others that claimed aspects of European culture as part of Latin America, challenging a colonialist dynamic and underscoring the political stakes of questions on art and national identity.

4. FORMING **NATIONAL CANONS**

In 1930 the Madrid-based magazine *La Gaceta Literaria* asked, "What is the avant-garde? Does the avant-garde exist? Has it ever existed? How would you characterize it?"[1] Many responses focused specifically on the Spanish avant-garde, citing the importance of Ultraism, a poetic movement founded in 1918. However, by the time *La Gaceta Literaria* published its questionnaire, Ultraism had already experienced an afterlife in Argentina. In 1923 the Argentine magazine *Nosotros* put forth a questionnaire titled "Our Survey on the New Literary Generation," whose respondents similarly referred to Ultraism as critical to the development of their own national avant-garde. These two questionnaires, issued across the Atlantic, each historicized the central role Ultraism played in spurring nationally specific aesthetic innovations, leading to the Generation of '27 in Spain and the "new literary generation" in Argentina. It was indeed the close ties between these transatlantic communities that necessitated the use of questionnaires to assert the significance of their own national canons.

Like the questionnaires posed by *Revista de Avance* and *Imán*, those issued in Argentina sought to displace European influence, particularly that of Spain and its colonial legacy. Spain, on the other hand, tried to insert itself into a more prominent position in both Europe and Latin America. In fact, in 1927 the Spanish poet and editor Guillermo de Torre claimed Latin American cultural production as an extension of that of Spain in his essay "Madrid, meridiano intelectual de hispanoamérica" (Madrid, intellectual meridian of Hispanic America). Literary magazines throughout Latin America refuted the article, which also incited further questionnaires. Such debates were part of a sustained conversation between Spain and Argentina, whose competing claims to Ultraism and other forms of cultural patrimony surfaced as writers and artists across the Atlantic worked to consolidate their national avant-gardes in print.

La Gaceta Literaria: Surveying the Field

"A Sensational Poll: What Is the Avant-Garde?" asked writers and artists to define the avant-garde and to determine its literary and political significance. Those who contextualized the term nationally in their responses had to contend with Spain's unique historical trajectory.[2] Spain was considered both within and on the margins of Europe, leaving artists and writers feeling caught between "calls for modernization and Europeanization (seen as the only path to civilization) and a staunchly narcissistic defense of isolationism and traditionalism (seen as the only way to maintain a distinct national identity)."[3] During World War I, Spain's neutrality shielded it from many of the hardships associated with the war, but the country nevertheless suffered a postwar economic crisis, leading to massive strikes, a rise in the cost of living, and increased social unrest. Following World War I, some of Spain's intellectuals were persecuted under the dictatorship of Miguel Primo de Rivera (1923–30) or fled to live in exile abroad. The 1930 questionnaire historicized a moment just before the highly polarized years of the Second Republic. Such upheaval resulted in divided loyalties that were legible in the activities of the avant-garde.

Aesthetically, the Spanish avant-garde could be traced back to the Generation of '98, followed by Ultraism, before culminating in the work of the Generation of '27. Spurred by Spain's defeat in the 1898 Spanish-American War to reconsider their nation's place in the world, the writers who became known as the Generation of '98 worked to establish a distinctly Spanish intellectual spirit.[4] Yet Spain also served as a space of cultural interchange for artists from Latin America; *modernismo*, the poetic movement initiated by the Nicaraguan poet Rubén Darío, along with the work of the Generation of '98, paved the way for Ultraism's experiments in poetry and print culture. Ultraism, itself culled from European aesthetic innovations, in turn aided the development of the Generation of '27, a heterogeneous group of writers, poets, playwrights, and artists working roughly between 1923 and 1930 whose literary and artistic experimentation lasted until 1936, when the outbreak of the Spanish Civil War curtailed much of its aesthetic production. The questionnaire created an opportunity for contributors to historicize and affirm Spain's place in an international avant-garde.

By posing the question "What is the avant-garde?" and by collecting and printing its responses, *La Gaceta Literaria* located itself at the center of these histories. *La Gaceta Literaria*'s mottos were "Iberian. American. International" and "Literature. Art. Science." The magazine did not focus on a specific region or genre, but rather included voices from across the Iberian Peninsula and abroad, without adopting a fixed aesthetic or political program. Referring to *La Gaceta Literaria*'s linguistic policy, which invited contributors from across Spain to write in their local languages, philosopher and leading critic José Ortega y Gasset writes in its first issue that the journal would be "supranational" and "open, even linguistically."[5] Its editors reflected the divided political allegiances of the Spanish avant-garde. Ernesto Giménez Caballero founded *La Gaceta Literaria* in 1927; a prominent supporter of the avant-garde, by 1930 he had already begun to champion Spanish fascism. Guillermo de Torre, who served as the magazine's secretary, was a poet and critic who left Spain in the late 1930s due to political repression.[6] Because *La Gaceta Literaria* was shaped by Spain's linguistic, artistic, and ideological diversity, it was well positioned to survey its contributors on the complex state of the avant-garde.

Miguel Pérez Ferrero, the magazine's film critic, initiated the questionnaire. He argued that the question "What is the avant-garde?" had been "floating . . . in the Spanish literary environment" for some time, but that the term was applied thoughtlessly to "everything that surprises, that shocks."[7] To interrogate its use and meaning, he posed the following questions: "What is the avant-garde? Does the avant-garde exist? Has it ever existed? How have you understood it? What literary tenets characterize it? How can it be judged, from your political viewpoint?"[8] Published in subsequent issues, the responses corroborate the slipperiness of the term "avant-garde" and many reinforce a national claim to it. Some imagine the avant-garde as a series of movements in the recent past; others see it as a posture of rebellion.[9] Several of those surveyed argue that the "avant-garde" is indefinable, characterizing an aesthetic approach rather than a particular platform. For example, to the poet José Bergamín, the avant-garde seems "an incongruous notion, impertinent, indefinite." This position is echoed by the writer Melchor Fernández Almagro, who views the avant-garde as "purely and simply a mood, an attitude."[10] While some considered the avant-garde apolitical, others believed that it valorized anti-bourgeois subversion. Giménez Caballero argued that the avant-garde only existed within a political framework. "In Spain," he writes, "there remains only the specifically political sector, where the avant-garde (audacity, youth, subversion) can still act."[11] By contrast, the poet Ernestina de Champourcín put forth a more diffuse notion of the avant-garde. For her, the avant-garde was "every young person who lives intensely in their time, acting on it with elements of the future, awakening with their effort the possibilities of what's to come."[12]

Many responses also acknowledge the avant-garde lineage of the questionnaire as a genre, highlighting its aptness for such an inquiry. The writer Esteban Salazar y Chapela declares, "After the phenomenon, its theory. After the avant-garde phenomenon, this theory disguised as a questionnaire."[13] The literary critic Juan Aparicio draws attention to the similarities between the 1930 questionnaire and one that appeared in 1907 in *El Nuevo Mercurio* on *modernismo*. The 1907 poll, he notes, "also tossed out four questions, identical in their epistemological fervor, and phrased analogously."[14] That questionnaire had asked, "What is modernism?," followed by a series of more specific questions: "Do you think a new literary movement or new intellectual or artistic tendency exists? What is your idea of that which is called modernism? Who are some modernists that you like? In a word, what do you think of emerging literature, of the new direction in taste and of the immediate future of our literature?"[15] It was addressed to Spanish and Latin American writers, regardless of whether they were "young or old, conservative or revolutionary," because "modernism exists and yet at the same time no one knows exactly of what it consists."[16] Respondents to this 1907 poll included literary luminaries such as Miguel de Unamuno, who described *modernista* writers as characterized by "weakness, complacency, indecision, vagueness, and disorientation. Rarely, very rarely, do I find them impassioned. They seem to be, in general, false. I don't believe in their joy, I don't believe in their sorrow, I don't believe in their skepticism, I don't believe in their faith, I don't believe in their sins nor in their repentance, I don't believe in their sensuality."[17] By citing this survey in his response, Aparicio—and by extension, *La Gaceta Literaria*—created a trajectory for the Spanish avant-garde stemming from *modernismo* and from the Generation of '98, whose writers were polled by the earlier questionnaire.

This reference to "What Is Modernism?" reinforced the modernity of the questionnaire and gave it a Hispanophone lineage. Yet *El Nuevo Mercurio*, based in Barcelona, was edited by Enrique Gómez Carrillo, a Guatemalan living in Paris who hoped to unite Europe and the Americas. In its inaugural issue *El Nuevo Mercurio* announced that it was modeled on the *Mercure de France* and that its goal was to "establish a fraternal tie between Spanish and Latin American intellectuals."[18] *El Nuevo Mercurio* also emulated the *Mercure de France*'s use of *enquêtes*. As Gómez Carrillo writes, "What we propose is to do an *enquête* like those done in Parisian magazines, and for it we ask each of the writers and artists that read *El Nuevo Mercurio* in Spain and America [the following questions]."[19] Likewise, in his response to the *Gaceta Literaria* questionnaire, the author Guillermo Díaz Plaja hails the questionnaires issued by the French magazine *L'Esprit Nouveau* as inspiring their Spanish counterparts. He writes, "There is, for instance, the typical avant-garde moment in Paris, which should be limited to the heroic times of *L'Esprit Nouveau*, when its questionnaires, frankly half-formed, referred to the need to burn down the Louvre."[20] He then compares the "heroic times of *L'Esprit Nouveau*" with "the avant-garde moment in Madrid . . . which should similarly be circumscribed by the explosive moment of *Ultra*."[21] Citing the journal that was the mouthpiece of Ultraism, he deigns Madrid the successor to the Parisian avant-garde, its print culture, and its questionnaires. Beyond these references to France, traces of Latin America's presence are also evident in the responses. The Mexican writer Jaime Torres Bodet participated in the questionnaire, and in his response the Spanish poet Benjamin Jarnés included an excerpt of an essay he published in the Argentine magazine *Proa*.[22] As these answers attest, *La Gaceta Literaria* was enmeshed in a web of European and Latin American alliances, suggesting the porousness of Spain's avant-garde.

Ultraism was the national avant-garde most often cited by the survey respondents. Like Guillermo Díaz Plaja, the poet and journalist Francisco Vighi refers to Ultraist periodicals in his response, suggesting that by signing manifestos and writing for *Grecia* and *Ultra*, he participated in what he terms "the prehistory of the avant-garde."[23] He claims that the Ultraist moment had passed by 1930, but praises Ramón Gómez de la Serna as a "one-man generation" and thanks Guillermo de Torre for teaching him to "say 'pioneer'" in those crucial early years.[24] The writer Valentín Andrés Álvarez also mentions de Torre's contributions in his response, hailing him as the originator of the term "avant-garde" in his sweeping 1925 study *Literaturas europea de vanguardia*, which foregrounds Ultraism.[25] De Torre and Gómez de la Serna also responded to the survey. Gómez de la Serna answers with a playful dialogue, thus enacting his role as an avant-garde innovator.[26] In his reply, De Torre celebrates Ultraism as the original Spanish avant-garde. However, through asides such as "the avant-garde (or '*nueva sensibilidad*' as they say in Argentina, or '*esprit nouveau*,' in international dialect)," De Torre also defines the avant-garde as inherently transnational or relational.[27] This internationalism is underscored by the fact that he submits his questionnaire response from Buenos Aires, where Ultraism had already been transplanted, sparking a new set of cultural debates.

Ultraism and the International Avant-Garde

A movement inspired by avant-garde tendencies circulating throughout Spain and Europe in the early twentieth century, Ultraism was energetically promoted by a dedicated group of Spanish poets, editors, and critics. Searching for a new expression for literary innovation, the Spanish writer Rafael Cansinos-Assens coined the term *ultra romántico* in 1918, the year that the movement began.[28] Using this idea as a point of departure, the movement became focused on the *ultra*, which designated "the search for a beyond, in aesthetic directions," according to critic Gloria Videla in her comprehensive analysis of Ultraism.[29] Videla even reads José Ortega y Gasset's landmark 1925 publication *La deshumanización del arte* as supporting this search for the beyond, citing his definition of the artist as one who creates "ultra objects" and thus invents a world beyond the real.[30]

While Ultraism arose out of a Spanish artistic milieu, it also responded to aesthetic experiments emanating from Italy, France, Germany, and Switzerland. The Ultraists were explicit about their desire to participate in a broader European avant-garde; in *Literaturas europea de vanguardia*, De Torre declares, "One of our essential objectives . . . is to fill the gaping distance that has always isolated Spain, which has forced her to work on her most recent literary developments extemporaneously, trailing behind the global movement."[31] De Torre further clarifies that Ultraism emerged from "the desire to be simultaneous with likeminded radical foreign movements."[32] Bringing Spain into dialogue with other avant-gardes sometimes involved incorporating aspects of these foreign movements. For instance, at an early Ultraist soirée Miguel Romero Martínez recited his Spanish translation of Marinetti's poem "A l'automobile," followed by José María Romero's reading of "Canción del aeroplano," his poem inspired by Marinetti.[33]

Ultraism embraced poetic aspirations common to the era. De Torre describes the central facets of Ultraism in his book as "lyric reintegration," the "genuine rehabilitation of the poem," and multiplying the impact of the poetic image through increased attention to metaphor, adjective, and rhythm.[34] De Torre called to "eradicate punctuation" and enumerated Mallarmé and Rimbaud as forebears of Ultraism; its experimentation with the space of the page was also indebted to F. T. Marinetti's *parole en libertà*.[35] De Torre celebrated Ultraist poets through comparisons to foreign sources; about Jorge Luis Borges he writes, "Like Marinetti and Cendrars, he has found a way to condense urban sensations with originality."[36] De Torre himself looked to France for innovation, as he explains in the magazine *Alfar* in 1923: "Literarily, we live in a bloated and conformist environment. We lack the love of the modern, the audacious spirit, the taste for adventure, spiritual generosity; and many other things that could make the literary republic habitable. From there the necessity to expatriate. I always write with an eye to France, in whose avant-garde magazines I collaborate."[37] De Torre legitimized his own work, like that of the Ultraists, through his relationships to foreign poets and magazines.

The Ultraists were eager to join an international avant-garde; yet they also hoped to instigate a national movement. The first Ultraist manifesto hails "the necessity for an Ultraism, for which they call on the collaboration of all Spain's literary youth."[38] This declaration emerged from a gathering at the Café Colonial in Madrid at the end of 1918 and was published in the magazine *Grecia* the following March. Although it calls to "affirm our resolve to overcome our precursors," Ultraism's emphasis on youth and rupture seems drawn from "The Founding and Manifesto of Futurism," published in *Le Figaro* in Paris on February 20, 1909, and translated into Spanish by Ramón Gómez de la Serna in the magazine *Prometeo* that April.[39] In 1910 Marinetti wrote another Futurist manifesto aimed at the Spanish, "Proclama futurista a los españoles," which Gómez de la Serna also translated for *Prometeo*.[40] In Argentina "The Founding and Manifesto of Futurism" was summarized, analyzed, and partially translated by Rubén Darío in *La Nación*, and prominent Latin American writers, including José Carlos Mariátegui, César Vallejo, Mário de Andrade, Vicente Huidobro, and Borges, published additional responses to Futurism throughout the 1920s and 1930s.[41]

Many Ultraists met Marinetti or read about his visits to their countries. Marinetti's trip to Buenos Aires in 1926 prompted the tabloid newspaper *Diario Crítica* to publish a questionnaire asking literary luminaries, "What is your opinion of Marinetti, the revolutionary? How will you receive Marinetti here? What influence will Marinetti exert over Argentine literature?" Responses came from Borges, Oliverio Girondo, Ricardo Güiraldes, Victoria Ocampo, and others. By that point, most viewed Futurism as outdated, although Girondo, Güiraldes, Francisco López Merino, and Evar Méndez believed Marinetti's visit would inspire the local avant-garde.[42] The Argentine magazine *Nosotros* reported on Marinetti's visit and *Martín Fierro* published an "Homage to Marinetti," praising his aesthetics while renouncing his politics.[43] Marinetti gave three lectures in Buenos Aires before traveling to Córdoba, La Plata, and Rosario. Thus, Argentines were reading about Marinetti, attending his lectures, being polled about his influence, and writing articles about his legacy, while responding to or refuting his aesthetic platform in their own work.

Marinetti caused a similar uproar in Spain two years later. In February 1928 he traveled to Madrid, where he spoke at the Residencia de Estudiantes, Teatro de Círculo de Bellas Artes, and the Lyceum Club Femenino before heading to Barcelona and Bilbao. Both Gómez de la Serna and De Torre reflected on Marinetti's literary and political contributions in essays for *El Sol* and *La Gaceta Literaria* respectively, even though De Torre was in Buenos Aires at the time of the visit.[44] *La Gaceta Literaria* also featured a conversation between Giménez Caballero and Marinetti, a poem by Marinetti, an overview of Italian literature and magazines, and a short text, "Marinetti and Mussolini: Telegram from One Leader to Another," written by Mussolini in support of Marinetti.[45] Marinetti responded in turn with a poem written about his trip to Spain dedicated to Giménez Caballero, Gómez de la Serna, and De Torre. Titled "España veloz" (Swift Spain), the poem was published in the August 1928 issue of *La Gaceta Literaria*.[46] Although Ultraism had abated by the time of his visits, those who had participated in it remained in active dialogue with Marinetti, responding to him and his movement in person and in print.

Even prior to such contact with Marinetti, his writing had infiltrated Ultraist production, as evidenced by Ultraist manifestos issued on both sides of the Atlantic, which contained traces of Futurism. For instance, Marinetti opens "The Founding and Manifesto of Futurism" with "We had stayed up all night, my friends and I, under hanging mosque lamps with domes of filigreed brass, domes starred like our spirits, shining like them with the prisoned radiance of electric hearts."[47] In their 1921 manifesto, published in the first issue of the Argentine magazine *Prisma*, the Ultraists echo Marinetti: "We have draped the streets with poems, we've lit your way with verbal lamps, we've clung to your walls with vines of verses."[48] The "Manifiesto ultraísta," published in the Spanish magazine *Grecia* in 1919, announces, much like the Futurists, its youthful disregard for the past: "We're young and strong and we represent the evolutionary aspiration of the beyond."[49] However, while the tone of Marinetti's manifesto was aggressive, De Torre describes Ultraism's "reformist intentions" and characterizes its manifestos by "a measured tone."[50] Ultraism skimmed Futurist rhetoric for poetic tactics but adopted a less virulent posture than its Italian predecessor.

Ultraism also demonstrated what De Torre called "a tangential affinity" for Dadaism.[51] Dadaism, born of post–World War I disillusionment by a group of exiled writers and artists in Zurich, developed counterdiscourses to confront accepted versions of morality, progress, and truth through a "principle of contradiction."[52] As Tristan Tzara, the movement's primary manifesto-writer, claims, "the true dadas are against dada."[53] An appetite for Dadaist provocation is legible in Ultraist writings. The "Manifiesto del Ultra" of 1921, for instance, echoes Tzara, by stating: "Our bold and conscious creed is to have no creed."[54] Similarly, the Ultraists declare in 1921, "We advocate for a relentless anti-literature . . . we have already affirmed that literature does not exist: Ultraism has killed it."[55] The Ultraist output that most clearly reveals traces of Dadaist influence are their *boutades*: short, enigmatic phrases included in each issue of the Spanish magazine *Ultra*, such as "Ultraism consists in turning the world upside down" and "after Ultraism, the end of the world."[56] Yet in reflecting on the *boutades* in *Literaturas*, De Torre refers to them as "merely external, epidermal, humorous propaganda," as opposed to "the strict lyrical modules and aesthetic innovations that constitute the authentic face of the program."[57] By dismissing the *boutades* as superficial adornment, De Torre shifts the focus of Ultraism away from provocation—and away from Dadaism—toward poetry.

The Spanish magazine *Grecia* chronicled the rise of Ultraism at its inception, publishing its first manifesto and early articles celebrating the movement and regularly advertising its events.[58] In fact, the term "avant-garde" first appeared in Spain in 1919 in *Grecia*.[59] In 1921, however, the magazine *Ultra* emerged as the primary vehicle for the movement. *Ultra* featured self-reflexive writing such as Rafael Lasso de la Vega's poem "Ballad of Ultra" and Jorge Luis Borges's "Anatomy of My Ultra."[60] Woodcuts by Argentine artist Norah Borges, Uruguayan Rafael Barradas, and Polish Wladyslaw Jahl were featured on *Ultra*'s covers as a way of visually reinforcing the movement's newness. (However, the magazine's covers also foregrounded Ultraism's foreign elements, as none of these artists were Spanish.) "Paisaje de Buenos Aires" (Buenos Aires cityscape) by Norah Borges, which was published after she had returned to Buenos Aires, was printed on the October 1921 cover of *Ultra* (fig. 15). Evoking the cross-hatching technique of the German Expressionists and the perspectival flattening of Cubism, the woodcut features a dynamic, angular stretch of flattened, low-lying buildings with arched windows, repeated balustrades, and tiled rooftops, with the word *almacén* legible on one building and a statue of General José de San Martín placed in the lower left-hand corner.[61] This imagined version of the Palermo neighborhood and its environs reflects what Jorge Luis Borges later describes as an "almost endless city of low buildings with flat roofs, stretching west to the pampa."[62] *Ultra*'s inclusion of this kind of visual art, along with its innovative typography and design, marked a noticeable shift in Spanish publications toward an avant-garde aesthetic.

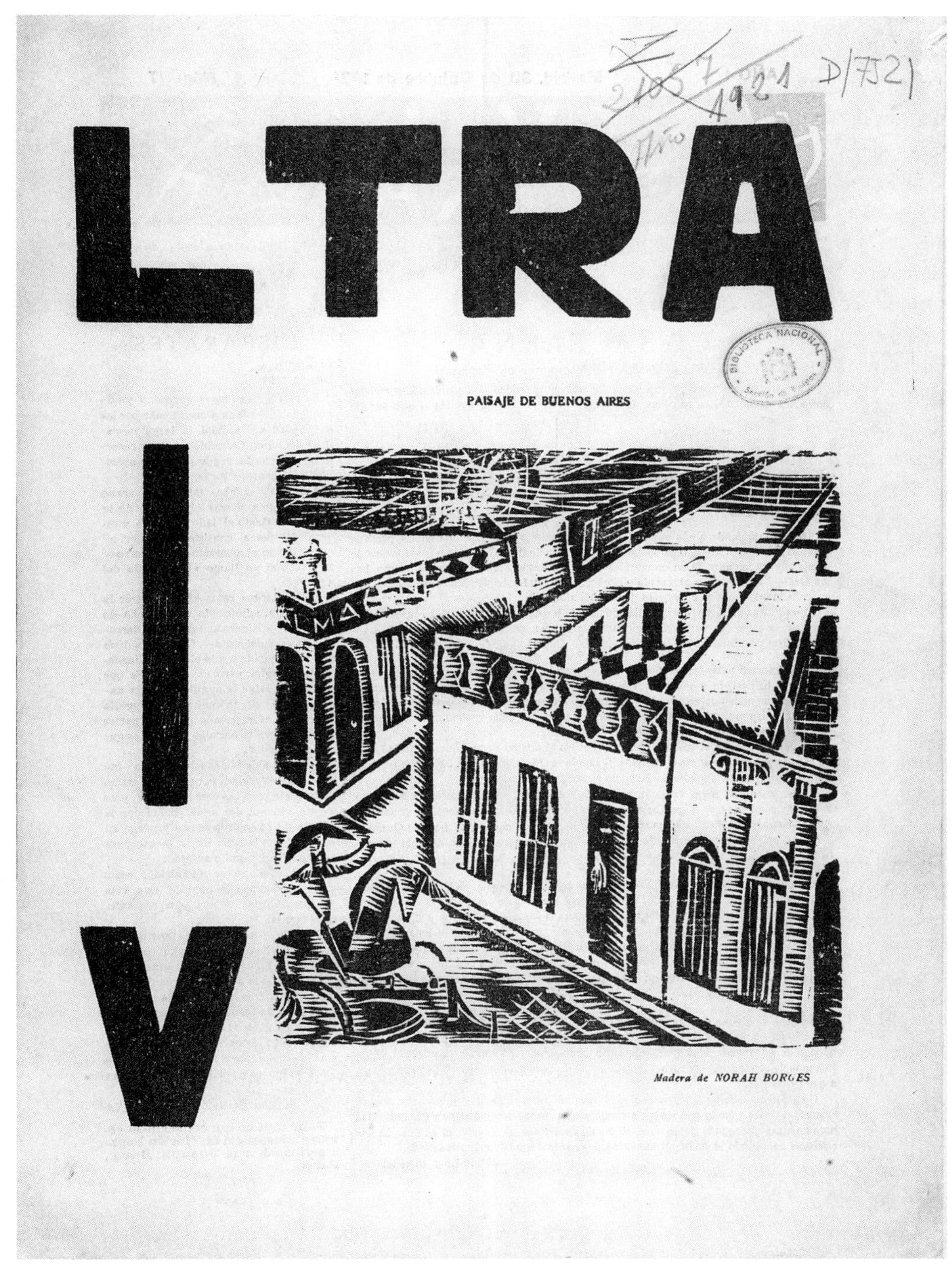

Fig. 15 Norah Borges, "Paisaje de Buenos Aires," cover of *Ultra* (Madrid), no. 17 (October 30, 1921).

Through such choices, as well as by publishing Marinetti, Apollinaire, and Tzara, *Ultra* helped bring Spain into conversation with the international avant-garde.[63] As De Torre announces in *Literaturas*, "We present *Ultra* as the vortex of a powerful fusion where all of the world's battling avant-garde tendencies flow together."[64] Looking back on these developments in Spain in 1930 in their questionnaire responses, the contributors historicized Ultraism, celebrating it for bringing Spain into dialogue with other European movements and for serving as a point of departure for future artistic production, notably the Generation of '27. The group that became known as the Generation of '27 first formally convened in 1927 at the Ateneo de Sevilla, where they had gathered to celebrate the three hundredth anniversary of the death of acclaimed Spanish poet Luis de Góngora. The group included Federico García Lorca, Salvador Dalí, Luis Buñuel, Pedro Salinas, and Rafael Alberti, among others, and their work was featured in *La Gaceta Literaria*. Characterized by poetry, theater, and artwork that synthesized external influences such as Cubism and Surrealism with traditional Spanish music and folklore, this generation's output was at once markedly Spanish and part of an increasingly international avant-garde. Reflecting on Ultraism's accomplishments in his 1925 book, De Torre describes their "essential objective: to mark a clear break with the previous generation."[65] This aspiration was in many ways fulfilled by the artistic outpouring of the Generation of '27. Ultraism, for De Torre, anticipated "an era of artistic internationalism."[66]

Ultraism further advanced its international objectives through two crucial intermediaries who transported the movement from Spain to Argentina: Guillermo de Torre and Jorge Luis Borges. In 1928 De Torre married the artist Norah Borges, sister of Jorge Luis Borges and fellow Ultraist, and eventually settled permanently in Buenos Aires.[67] Norah and Jorge Luis Borges had moved in 1918 from Switzerland to Spain, where they stayed until March 1921, coinciding with the years of the Ultraist movement. They then moved back to Buenos Aires, bringing the movement with them.[68] In the magazines Jorge Luis Borges subsequently launched in Argentina, he sought to clarify and expand what constituted Ultraism while cultivating an audience for his own work. Borges crafted his literary style and drew his subject matter from the Argentine experience, legible even in early work like his poetic compilation *Fervor de Buenos Aires* (1923). Although Borges later dismissed his involvement with Ultraism, this transitional period spurred him and the literary community in Argentina to inaugurate local print institutions and to produce material that eventually broke with Ultraism. Just as Spaniards hailed Ultraism as the point of departure for a more radical national avant-garde, along with the publications to sustain it, so too did Argentine Ultraism serve as a catalyst for autochthonous literary production and print culture in Buenos Aires.

Upon returning to Buenos Aires from Spain in 1921, Jorge Luis Borges founded *Prisma* (1921) and then *Proa* (1922–23; 1924–26), magazines that were aesthetically linked to Ultraism. This connection was made visible through Norah Borges's woodcuts. Like her *Paisaje de Buenos Aires*, printed on the October 1921 cover of the Spanish journal *Ultra, Buenos Aires*, a woodcut she published in the Argentine magazine *Prisma* in December 1921, features the balustrades, potted plants, and arched windows characteristic of Argentine architecture, but the scene is cut into triangular sections, as if the same buildings are refracted through a prism, and the Argentine flag waves in the top left corner. These two woodcuts point to the continuity between Ultraist experiments in Spain and in Buenos Aires; their magazines continued to share contributors as well. As Jorge Luis Borges writes, "When I came back from Europe in 1921, I came bearing the banners of Ultraism."[69] Through *Prisma* and *Proa,* Borges transposed Ultraism from Spain to a new national context, helping to inspire what became known as "the new literary generation" in Argentina. Subsequent questionnaires historicized the place of Ultraism in each country's avant-garde.

Prisma, Proa, and other magazines of the era emerged out of Argentina's rapidly modernizing economy. European immigration doubled the population in Latin America between 1850 and 1900, which led to increased industrialization and social unrest, but also generated a large reading public. As Francine Masiello notes, newspapers flourished in Buenos Aires in the early twentieth century, including *La Nación, La Tribuna, La Prensa*, and *El Tiempo*, thus "guaranteeing the writer an audience."[70] Many young authors published experimental and challenging new literature in the 1920s, including Borges, Oliverio Girondo, Nicolás Olivari, Leopoldo Marechal, Raúl Scalabrini Ortiz, and Roberto Arlt, and much of this work was first printed in magazines.[71] Politically, although Argentina was isolated from many of the effects of World War I, it was plagued by internal turmoil. The implementation of universal (male) suffrage in Argentina in 1912 led to the election of the radical Hipólito Yrigoyen, who was ousted in a coup led by José Félix Uriburu in 1930.[72] The coup coincided with economic struggles resulting from the 1929 stock market crash in the United States; ensuing unrest brought many of the country's rural poor into the country's few metropolises. In the context of these social and political changes, Masiello suggests that the magazine as a form "shows that the writer is part of the public spectacle that appears to be invading the city." She argues that within a magazine's pages, the multiplicity of voices that comprise it "fight for coherence and control."[73] Political and economic instability constituted the backdrop for the rapidly developing network of avant-garde publications in Argentina.

As part of the expanding market for print culture, Borges founded *Prisma: Revista Mural* with his cousin Guillermo Juan and the poet Eduardo González Lanuza in December 1921. Printed on coarse brown paper, it was a large-format broadside (83 × 60 cm), which they wheat-pasted throughout the city.[74] The first issue was comprised of horizontal columns, with the magazine's name in the far left column, followed by a manifesto placed under Norah Borges's woodcut, and several short poems by the magazine's editors and by Spanish Ultraists scattered on the right half of the page, printed with sizable spaces between them. Although the magazine lasted only two issues, it fueled later experiments, particularly the publication of *Proa*. Referring to its unusual size and placement, Masiello explains how *Prisma* "violated traditional stations reserved for political announcements or advertising. Tacked onto the walls or kiosks of the city, like a pamphlet or flyer, *Prisma* competed with other public texts that imposed multiple readings."[75] Through its scale and design, reminiscent also of *Ultra* or the New York–based *291*, the magazine adopted the visual vocabulary of politics or advertising. While it was meant to be provocative, the group was also working with limited resources. As Borges explains, years later,

> Our small Ultraist group was eager to have a magazine of its own, but a real magazine was beyond our means. I had noticed billboard ads, and the thought came to me that we might similarly print a "mural magazine" and paste it up ourselves on the walls of buildings in different parts of town. Each issue was a large single sheet and contained a manifesto and some six or eight short, laconic poems printed with plenty of white space around them and a woodcut by my sister. We sallied forth at night—González Lanuza, Pifiero, my cousin [Guillermo Juan] and I—armed with pastepots and brushes provided by my mother, and, walking miles on end, slapped them up along Santa Fe, Callao, Entre Rios and Mexico streets. Most of our handiwork was torn down by baffled readers, almost at once, but, luckily for us, Alfredo Bianchi, of *Nosotros*, saw one of them and invited us to publish an Ultraist anthology among the pages of his solid magazine.[76]

Here Borges describes the origins and appearance of *Prisma,* as well as the physical work entailed to distribute it. In this reflection he also positions the magazine as a venue for Ultraism and narrates how it established a relationship with *Nosotros*.

Prisma's opening statement emphasized its commitment to Ultraism. Signed by the editors and Guillermo de Torre, it proclaims, "We the Ultraists in this era of hawkers who exhibit dissected hearts and contort their faces in parades of sneers—we would like to de-ossify art."[77] The signatories outline their poetic platform: "We have synthesized poetry in its primordial element: the metaphor, to which we concede the utmost independence, beyond the little games of those who compare similar forms to each other, equating a circus to the moon. . . . Ultraism thus tends to the formation of an emotional and variable mythology."[78] After detailing their approach to poetry, they announce, "We have launched *Prisma* to democratize these norms," and identify the publication as a

vehicle for disseminating Ultraism in Argentina.[79] Further linking *Prisma*
with Ultraism, its first issue featured Spanish writers who had contributed
to Ultraist magazines in Spain, including Pedro Garfias, Adriano del Valle,
and Isaac Vando-Villar. The second issue, from March 1922, featured fewer
Spanish contributors, but it did include work by Del Valle, De Torre, and
Jacobo Sureda, which had previously been published in *Ultra* and *Grecia*,
demonstrating the close relationship between the Spanish and Argentine
groups. Conversely, *Ultra* reproduced *Prisma*'s "Proclama" and some of the
poems it featured.[80] The Spanish magazine *Tableros* also alluded to the first
number of *Prisma*, citing it as a "vibrant Ultraist proclamation" and sending
it a "fraternal greeting."[81]

After printing only two issues of *Prisma*, in July 1922 Borges next founded
the literary review *Proa: Revista de renovación literaria*, a 33 × 21.5 cm cm folio
that continued *Prisma*'s aesthetic project. In its first incarnation it contained
three folded pages that could be read consecutively as six pages, or expanded to
form a kind of poster.[82] As Borges notes years later, "its three sheets could be unfolded like a three-way mirror."[83] *Proa* had two distinct phases. The first, more
explicitly Ultraist phase, consisted of its first three issues, printed from 1922
to 1923 and edited by Borges along with Macedonio Fernández and Ricardo
Güiraldes. In its second phase, lasting from 1924 to 1926, the magazine rejected
Ultraism in favor of the new Argentine literary avant-garde. This decisive shift
occurred after *Nosotros* issued its 1923 questionnaire on the "new literary
generation." As in Spain, a questionnaire enabled contributors to reflect on the
development of a nationally specific avant-garde, first spurred by Ultraism.

In its first issue, *Proa*'s editors offer their own definition of Ultraism:

Ultraism is not an incarcerating sect. While some, in juvenile grandilo-
quence, consider it an open field where there are no hurdles that plague
space, like an insatiable urge for distances; others, simply, define it
as an exultation of the metaphor, that immortal ruse of all literature,
which today, continuing the trend of Shakespeare and Quevedo, we
would like to rejuvenate. From these explanations, the first intuitive and
the second intellectual, choose whichever pleases you most. They are
both superfluous, if our verses do not move you. They are also superfluous if one manages to touch your heart.[84]

Here the editors debunk the elitist nature of Ultraism and urge their readers to
join the movement, while emphasizing its poetic program. The text also playfully encourages its readers to elect whether to have an "intuitive" or "intellectual"
relationship to Ultraism. Inculcating Ultraism in Argentina, the first phase of
Proa clarified the movement, presenting it as international—Shakespeare and
Quevedo are cited as forebears—and timeless, while the editors stake their own
claim to poetic innovation.

Whereas the first iteration of the magazine preceded—and arguably spurred—the development of other avant-garde institutions in Buenos Aires, the second phase of *Proa* emerged alongside the magazine *Martín Fierro* and the establishment of the "new literary generation," the subject of the 1923 *Nosotros* questionnaire. The second incarnation of *Proa* (1924–26) was edited by Borges, Alfredo Brandán Caraffa, Ricardo Güiraldes, and Pablo Rojas Paz. It was produced in a smaller, book-like format (20 × 16 cm) with more pages (approximately sixty-four) and lasted fifteen issues. Each issue was simply and cleanly designed, with different colored covers. Although the magazine contained primarily text, it also featured visual art by Norah Borges, Emilio Pettoruti, Gustav Klimt, and others. In the first issue of *Proa*'s second incarnation, Borges explicitly distinguishes between Spanish and Argentine Ultraism, signaling the magazine's shift in direction: "One must draw a fine and deep distinction between the innermost intentions that motivated Ultraism in Spain and those that flourished here."[85] Borges goes on to distinguish between the Spanish Ultraists' infatuation with novelty and Argentine Ultraism's aspiration to timelessness. He similarly reflects years later, "We came to the conclusion that Spanish Ultraism was overburdened—after the manner of Futurism—with modernity and gadgets. We were unimpressed by railway trains, by propellers, by airplanes, and by electric fans.... What we wanted to write was essential poetry—poems beyond the here and now, free of local color and contemporary circumstances."[86] Unlike in Spain, Borges argues, where Ultraists were responding to Futurism and modern technology, in Argentina Ultraists sought to produce "essential poetry." The second phase of *Proa* soon untethered itself from the Spanish poetic movement entirely and dedicated itself exclusively to Argentina's emerging literary avant-garde.

Proa proudly aligned with "the new literary generation." As Borges later recounts, "One afternoon, Brandán Caraffa, a young poet from Córdoba, came to see me.... He told me that Ricardo Güiraldes and Pablo Rojas Paz had decided to start a magazine that would represent the new literary generation."[87] This stance was made explicit by editorial texts announcing, "*Proa* wants to be the first exponent of the union of youth.... Our young intellectuals do not have a platform to express their thoughts. *Proa* wants to be that platform, capacious and without barriers."[88] However, the new generation was not necessarily young: "We thus declare that the new generation is not limited by temporal and biological fate, that for us an old and fruitful warrior is worth more than ten pessimistic and frivolous youths.... We put *Proa* in the hands of today's young of spirit."[89] This coalition even extended beyond Argentina, as the editors assert: "Manned by the highest-level youth of America and some European countries, *Proa* gives away all of the silence that has surrounded us in our own country to the archives of the foreign press, which early on encouraged our long conversations with the compass."[90] The magazine published writers from Uruguay, Chile, Peru, Mexico, Spain, and France. The editors played with the metaphor of the compass and the ship to describe how *Proa* (Prow) would advance the cause of literature; this mission was visualized by the artist Xul Solar, a friend of Borges who in 1925 designed a poster advertising *Proa* (fig. 16). An imaginative, brightly colored abstraction, the poster features three flattened figures in a boat bearing swords and warding off snakes while waving the Argentine flag and sailing through a perspectiveless space crisscrossed with swaths of clouds and sea, toward a stretch of land called "El Dorado." A fourth figure marked "genio" (which could mean "genius" or "genie") hangs upside down from the top of the page.

Although already different in tone, the new incarnation of *Proa* made an explicit break with Ultraism: "*Proa* reaffirms its blazon of independence from coteries and groups, directed as it is by three writers whose most fitting title is their individualism, conserved against all tactics. And this is the only *-ism* that guides our compass, whose north intensely seeks out eternal paths of art. When certain critics spoke of *Proa*, they spoke of Ultraisms and nostalgic pixies, which we consider excessive."[91] Once again invoking the metaphor of the compass, *Proa* asserted its autonomy, denying any affiliation with Ultraism. To advertise its change in direction, Borges sent an "open letter" on *Proa*'s new course to Alfredo Bianchi, the editor of *Nosotros*, who published it in his magazine in April 1925.[92] While *Nosotros* had previously been the vehicle for Borges's Ultraist tracts, it soon became the barometer for the "new literary generation" that would obviate Ultraism in Argentina.

Nosotros and the New Literary Generation

Borges selected *Nosotros* to publish early Ultraist texts along with the letter announcing *Proa*'s new orientation because it was inclusive and long-standing, what he deemed "a solid magazine" in his reflections on *Prisma*.[93] *Nosotros*, founded in 1907 by Alfredo Bianchi and Roberto Giusti, predated *Prisma*, *Proa*, and *Martín Fierro* (1924–27). *Nosotros* was not affiliated with any specific movement or school, and its long print run (1907–34; 1936–43) is a testament to the soundness of this approach. In its first issue the editors announce, "this magazine will not discriminate. It will not turn away unknown bylines. . . . All that is well conceived and tastefully written that is submitted to its gates will receive a warm welcome."[94] Beatriz Sarlo describes *Nosotros* as "the most universally accepted periodical of the time," and also as "an ideologically and aesthetically eclectic publication."[95] *Nosotros* aimed to showcase an array of Hispanophone developments; the editors write that the magazine "had the objective of establishing ties between the different Latin nations of America and between them and their motherland."[96] In this way, *Nosotros* resembled *La Gaceta Literaria* in Spain, which similarly served to unify a wide range of Spanish voices. As Bianchi and Giusti noted, the third-person plural of *nosotros* intended to include newer and older literary generations alike.[97] With over one hundred pages of literature and criticism per issue, *Nosotros*, Sarlo explains, worked to "organize and

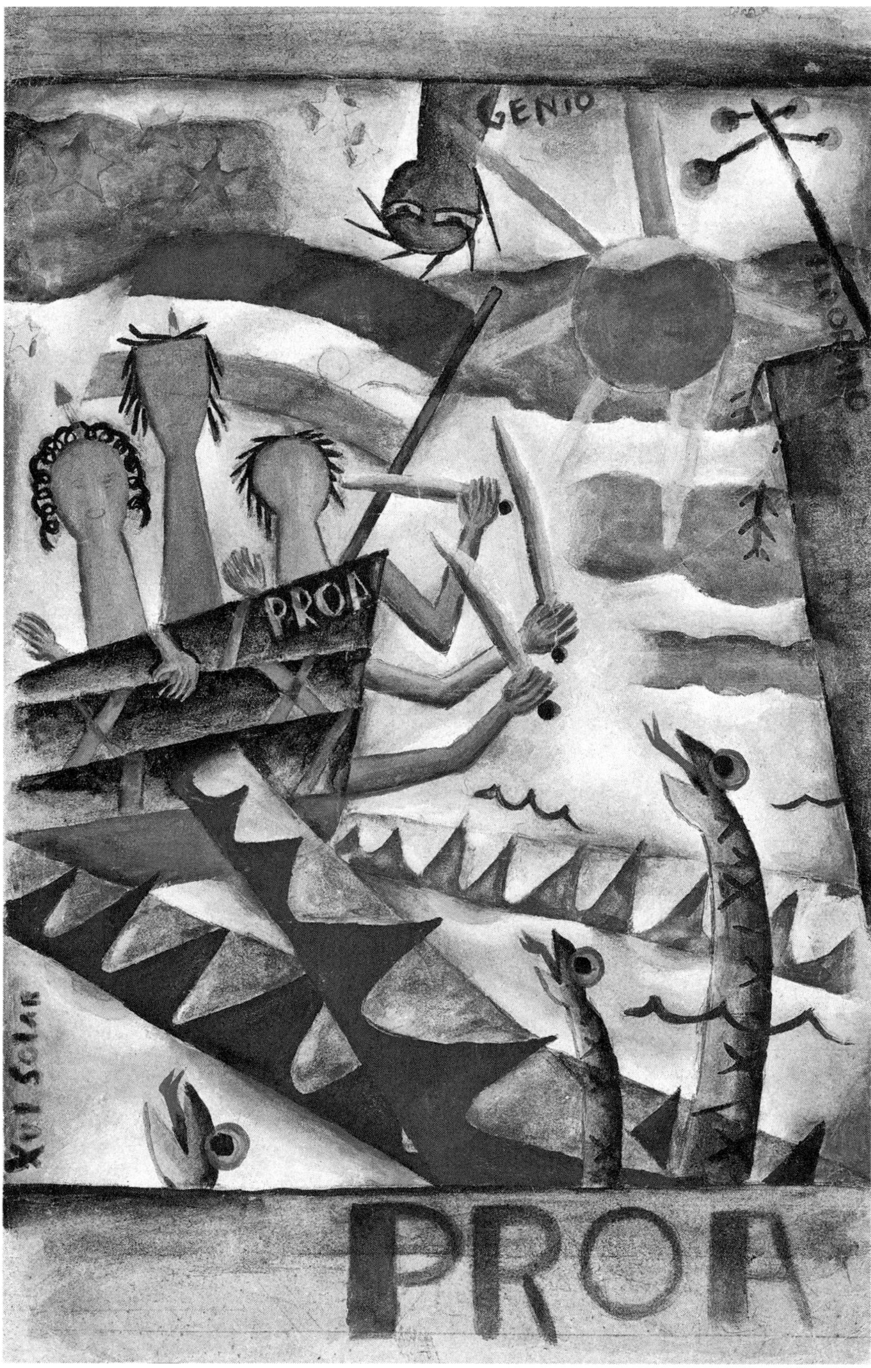

Fig. 16 Xul Solar, poster for advertising the magazine *Proa*, 1925. Watercolor on paper, 21.6 × 13 in.
Collection Museo Nacional de Bellas Artes, Buenos Aires.

disseminate artistic and intellectual production," paving the way for smaller, more divisive publications like *Proa*, *Inicial*, and *Martín Fierro*.[98]

Nosotros reinforced its editorial aspirations throughout its print run by issuing a series of questionnaires, all seeking to map out a national cultural identity.[99] In 1913 the magazine asked, "What is the value of *Martín Fierro?*," centralizing José Hernández's epic poem *El gaucho Martín Fierro* of 1872 and its relevance for Argentine literary culture. The magazine also issued questionnaires on: the consequences of World War I, Argentine folklore, what Spanish writers thought of Latin American literature (which included the question "Do you think that, as a whole, American literature has expressed the new continent?"), the influence of Italian culture on Argentina, and, on the brink of World War II, a survey titled "America and the Destiny of Western Civilization."[100] The critic Noemi Ulla posits that such questionnaires offered "testimonial value" and "signal[ed] . . . the reiterated commitment demonstrated by *Nosotros* to national literature." In regard to the magazine's 1923 questionnaire on the "new literary generation," Ulla describes the editors' "need to respond to questions that had been posed in literary circles since the early moments of Ultraism," and that the survey marked "an effort to clarify the scope of a new aesthetic and a 'new sensibility,' as it was called at that time."[101] "Our Survey on the New Literary Generation" thus shored up a national literary identity through a genre that *Nosotros* often used to reflect on Argentine culture.

As an inclusive forum for Argentine literary developments, *Nosotros* published Borges's essay "Ultraísmo" in December 1921 (just after the first issue of *Prisma* appeared). In this essay Borges expands on the movement's objectives. Ultraism, he writes, calls for the "reduction of poetry to its primordial element: the metaphor" and for the "synthesis of two or more images into one."[102] Beyond its emphasis on metaphor, Borges notes that Ultraism "tends to the prime goal of all poetry, that is, to the transmutation of the palpable reality of the world into an internal and emotional reality," again pointing to the immutability of Argentine Ultraist poetry.[103] Borges then describes a permeable, wandering "I" that "encompasses the plurality of all states of consciousness," a poet who creates work that resembles "an unknown vision of a fragment of life."[104] Masiello observes that "this frequent, ambiguous 'I' becomes the center of the New Generation's literary theory."[105] She argues that magazines in Buenos Aires in the 1920s helped carve out a space for this new artistic self, allowing the writer to feel a sense of political power during a time of social transformation. Read in this context, Borges's expansive poetic subject as outlined in his texts on Ultraism enabled a renewed sense of authorial control, guiding the proliferation of the "new literary generation."

In addition to communicating the foundational tenets of Ultraism and describing the poetic self that it yielded, Borges also historicizes the movement in this text. He writes, "Before we explain the new aesthetic, we should unravel the stitching of the prevailing Rubén Darío–ism and anecdotalism, which we, Ultraist poets, intend to overcome and abolish."[106] After dismissing Darío's influence, Borges also denies that of Futurism: "The exasperated rhetoric and dynamic rubbish of the poets from Milan are as far from us as a verbal buzzing."[107] However, Borges does acknowledge his indebtedness to the French poet Jules Laforgue as well as to Whitman. He also makes special mention of Cansinos-Assens, whom he calls "the great Sevillian prose writer," and hails both his and Vando-Villar's programmatic texts from *Cervantes* and *Grecia*. Borges also publishes several poems that he considers emblematic of the movement, culling his examples from both Argentine and Spanish poets. Enumerating the sources that inform his version of Ultraism, Borges appropriates even those whom he dismisses, like Darío and Marinetti, along with the Spanish poets whom he champions.

In this essay Borges also creates a genealogy of Ultraist print culture, which similarly includes both Spanish and Argentine publications. He writes, "In the field of magazines, the broadsheet *Ultra* currently replaces *Grecia* and radiates Ultraist norms out of Madrid. In Buenos Aires we have just launched *Prisma, revista mural*, founded by González Lanuza, Guillermo Juan, and the signatory. Of real interest is also the astute anthology published in number 23 of *Cosmópolis* by Guillermo de Torre."[108] By listing *Prisma* in the company of *Ultra*, *Grecia*, and *Cosmópolis*, Borges inserts his own work into an Ultraist lineage. Moreover, he makes these claims in *Nosotros*, thus aligning it with the movement as well. Subsequently, in 1922, *Nosotros* published an "anthology" of Ultraist poetry, featuring the work of Argentine poets Borges, Norah Lange, Elena Martínez, Guillermo Juan, and González Lanuza, demonstrating how the magazine served as a vehicle for Argentine Ultraism.[109]

The following year *Nosotros* issued a survey on the "new literary generation," eliciting responses that further ensconced Ultraism in an Argentine literary trajectory. Although Borges had arguably transported Ultraism to Argentina from Spain, the *Nosotros* survey responses worked to establish Argentina's claims to the movement. "Our Survey on the New Literary Generation" was published in May of 1923, and its forty replies were printed in subsequent issues of the magazine, running through December 1923 (fig. 17).[110] In its opening paragraph the editors list some of the questions that inspired the survey, such as "What is the aesthetic orientation of the generation of Argentine writers that has not yet turned thirty? What unrest agitates it? What distinguishes it from its predecessors? Has it been reached by the movement of ideas that across Europe puts young people into disagreement with representative prewar writers?" To assess these concerns, seven questions follow, directed at young writers: "Of writers older than thirty, who are those that deserve your respect? Do you see any of them as your teacher? Who are the three or four poets of ours, older than thirty, whom you most respect? Who are the prose writers?"[111] By addressing the "new literary generation" through the questionnaire, the magazine validated the bur-

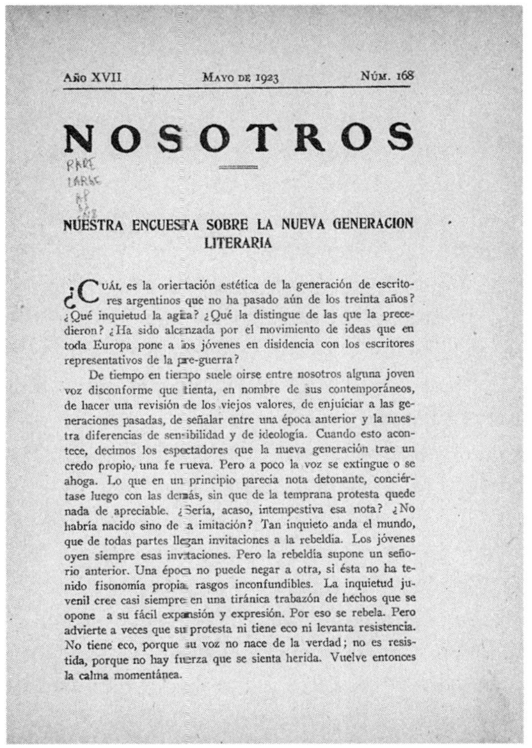

NOSOTROS

NUESTRA ENCUESTA SOBRE LA NUEVA GENERACION LITERARIA

¿Cuál es la orientación estética de la generación de escritores argentinos que no ha pasado aún de los treinta años? ¿Qué inquietud la agita? ¿Qué la distingue de las que la precedieron? ¿Ha sido alcanzada por el movimiento de ideas que en toda Europa pone a los jóvenes en disidencia con los escritores representativos de la pre-guerra?

De tiempo en tiempo suele oirse entre nosotros alguna joven voz disconforme que sienta, en nombre de sus contemporáneos, de hacer una revisión de los viejos valores, de enjuiciar a las generaciones pasadas, de señalar entre una época anterior y la nuestra diferencias de sensibilidad y de ideología. Cuando esto acontece, decimos los espectadores que la nueva generación trae un credo propio, una fe nueva. Pero a poco la voz se extingue o se ahoga. Lo que en un principio parecia nota detonante, conciértase luego con las demás, sin que de la temprana protesta quede nada de apreciable. ¿Sería, acaso, intempestiva esa nota? ¿No habría nacido sino de a imitación? Tan inquieto anda el mundo, que de todas partes llegan invitaciones a la rebeldia. Los jóvenes oyen siempre esas invitaciones. Pero la rebeldía supone un señorio anterior. Una época no puede negar a otra, si ésta no ha tenido fisonomía propia, rasgos inconfundibles. La inquietud juvenil cree casi siempre en una tiránica trabazón de hechos que se opone a su fácil expansión y expresión. Por eso se rebela. Pero advierte a veces que su protesta ni tiene eco ni levanta resistencia. No tiene eco, porque su voz no nace de la verdad; no es resistida, porque no hay fuerza que se sienta herida. Vuelve entonces la calma momentánea.

Fig. 17 "Nuestra encuesta sobre la nueva generación," *Nosotros* (Buenos Aires) 44, no. 168 (May 1923): 5.

geoning local avant-garde, and offered it a platform from which to declare its aesthetic alliances.

As in Spain, Argentina's modern literary culture developed along generational tracks, and the *Nosotros* questionnaire pointed to a significant shift between them. While the Generation of '80 marked the beginning of modernism in Argentina, the centenary celebration of 1910 prompted a search for an authentic Argentine identity, inspiring literary works such as Ricardo Rojas's *La restauración nacionalista* (1910), Leopoldo Lugones's *Odas seculars* (1910), and Manuel Gálvez's *El solar de la raza* (1913).[112] Known as the "Generación del centenario" (Centenary Generation) or the Generation of '10, such authors created a new national literary framework. Intent on promoting *argentinidad*, they recuperated José Sarmiento and José Hernández, as well as the figure of the gaucho, embodied by Martín Fierro, as a symbol of national pride.[113] This generation preceded the Generation of '22 (sometimes called the Generation of '24), which included Borges, and became known as the "new literary generation." *Nosotros* set the stage for the transition from the Generation of '10 to the Generation of

'22 by serving as a venue for Argentine writers of both generations, and by formally conveying the passage between them in its 1923 questionnaire.

Like many questionnaires, the "Survey on the New Literary Generation" enabled writers to solidify positions that they had alluded to in previous publications, establishing what critic Alejandro C. Eujanian calls "a generational movement that has already appeared in the public arena through some magazines in the beginning of the decade."[114] In a canon-building gesture like that of "What Is the Avant-Garde?" in Spain, the Argentine questionnaire worked to establish a "common aesthetic orientation" among writers who were seen as the "most talented youth of their generation."[115] Ultraism was a touchstone for many of the respondents. For instance, in his reply Borges asserts, "In regard to poetry . . . I align with a group of poets of the Ultraist tendency."[116] Similarly, the poet Francisco López Merino claims, "The only young writers in the country that constitute a perfectly defined group are those that call themselves Ultraists." He points to *Nosotros*, *Prisma*, and *Proa* as vehicles for the movement and quotes Borges's essay on Ultraism.[117] Even those who scoffed at Ultraism recognized its influence, as in the contribution of Atilio García y Mellid, who denounces "the sickly pretension of those callow 'Ultraists,' who speak of 'shared aesthetics.'"[118] Taken together, these statements reveal how Borges and his peers at this moment were, according to Jorge Schwartz, "still contaminated by enthusiasm for Ultraist creation, which, in turn, would serve as a catalyst for the formation of an Argentine avant-garde."[119] The *Nosotros* questionnaire marked this transition, highlighting Ultraism's importance as a point of departure for this group of young writers.

In the questionnaire each writer had to determine the "degree of cohesion and identification . . . they experience, in their set, as a group and with respect to Ultraism," Beatriz Sarlo argues.[120] Sarlo claims that it was the group's reflection on Ultraism that created a new sense of community. It was their "self-identification as Ultraists," she writes, "and the design of a common space defined by mutual expectations of a future consecration," that consolidated the group.[121] By articulating their shared generational formation, structured around Ultraism, these young writers voiced their collective literary aspirations. This group consciousness in turn inspired the next phase of the Argentine avant-garde, supported by magazines like *Inicial*, *Proa* in its second iteration, and *Martín Fierro*, which all worked to define and defend *argentinidad*.

Inicial, *Proa*, *Martín Fierro*, and the Argentine Avant-Garde

After the 1923 questionnaire aimed to identify a "common aesthetic orientation" among writers who were the "most talented youth of their generation," an abundance of publications flourished in Buenos Aires that laid claim to this new literary spirit. The magazine *Inicial* (1923–26), for example, called itself the "Magazine of a New Literary Generation." Bianchi, an editor of *Nosotros*, anointed *Inicial* the young writers' official publication, declaring that "the new literary generation had their 'own' outlet in which they could freely express their opinions and new trends, without clashing with the ideas and prejudices of men of other generations."[122] The editors of *Inicial*, in turn, situated themselves as heirs to *Nosotros*: "We would like to fulfill the mission that every youth magazine should achieve, the mission that in our milieu and in our time was realized, for example, by *Nosotros*." [123] *Inicial* hoped to be at once a mouthpiece for youth and the inheritor of a national tradition.

Despite their nod to *Nosotros*, the editors' opening statement contrasts their magazine with past publications: "*Inicial* will be a home for all those scattered youths who wander through publications and magazines more or less faded from our literary culture, without finding where they could elevate the tone of their voices to the level of their convictions."[124] The editors also dismiss earlier publications as insufficiently animated, privileging their "dynamic" periodical over a more staid "anthology" model of magazine: "*Inicial* will not simply be a literary magazine, a feeble and inert anthology of the country's young poets and writers. We want *Inicial* to be a living and dynamic thing, a sensitive register where all the palpitations of youth, even the subtlest, can leave a trace that the future can decipher as the faithful expression of our feelings."[125] This position brings to mind what Ezra Pound later designates an "active periodical," which he contrasts with the belatedness of the anthology.[126] Even its name, "initial," telegraphs newness and temporal rupture, emphasizing what the editors write in 1924: "With this issue, *Inicial* begins a new era."[127] By serving as a vehicle for youthful innovation, *Inicial* hoped to spur a literary awakening at home and abroad. To do so, editor Alfredo Brandán Caraffa brought *Inicial* with him on a trip to Europe, striving to foment "mutual understanding among young Latin Americans and Europeans, united in this historic time, in the same spirit of renewal."[128]

This eagerness to identify as a "new literary generation"—and to transport it abroad—emerged from a range of sources, including an important Spanish source, José Ortega y Gasset's essays on literary generations. "*Inicial* shows a consistent interest in Ortega's generational theories as the ideological basis for understanding the role of intellectuals in modern Argentine society," Masiello writes.[129] This influence stemmed from increased exposure to Ortega's writings on the topic. A year after the *Nosotros* survey, in 1924, Ortega's essay "The Duty of the New Generation in Argentina" was published in *La Nación*, along with his article "Generation Against Generation."[130] In these essays Ortega establishes a dramatically fluctuating hierarchy between the leaders and the masses, in which "each generation has its historic vocation."[131] Ortega argues, "Our time is . . . for youth, initiation, and constructive belligerence," suggesting a dialectical relationship between younger and older generations.[132] Ortega's thinking was adopted by a variety of Argentine publications in the 1920s, and it likely informed the 1923 survey, as *Nosotros* had published a different essay by Ortega on generational distinctions just prior to issuing the questionnaire.[133]

In addition to *Inicial*, other publications sought to weigh in on Ortega's theories, including *Proa* in its second incarnation. In the first issue of the new *Proa*, Borges and the other editors comment, "Ortega y Gasset put forward the problem of generations. But this problem has two different aspects. One is purely biological and the other psychological. We are only interested in the latter. We consider all youths as belonging to the new generation, not because of their youth, but because, generally, the essential patrimony given to youth is restlessness and discontent."[134] At once citing and dismissing Ortega's work, the editors establish themselves as capable of synthesizing outside forces. "Our desire is to give all young people a serene and unbiased platform," the editors declare in the same essay.[135] Yet as part of the proliferation of the Argentine avant-garde, *Proa* had to contend with competing versions of the "new literary generation" and of Argentine culture.

Debates over the nature of *argentinidad* and who would represent it occurred in print throughout Buenos Aires in the 1920s. Starting in 1924, Argentine literary circles were divided, somewhat superficially, into two schools of thought, known as Florida and Boedo, representing an ongoing debate between primarily aesthetic versus socially engaged literature.[136] Florida, named after one of Buenos Aires's central commercial streets, was characterized by formal innovations and an openness to foreign influences. Writers associated with it included Borges, Güiraldes, Oliverio Girondo, and Leopoldo Marechal. Boedo was named after a working-class neighborhood, and those affiliated with it, including Álvaro Yunque, Elías Castelnuovo, Roberto Mariani, and César Tiempo, identified predominantly with social issues, aligning themselves with the Russian Revolution and proletarian literatures. As critic Alfredo Prieto writes, "*Florida* looked to Europe and the aesthetic novelties of the postwar period; *Boedo* looked to Russia and was inflamed with the dream of a worldwide revolution."[137] Magazines such as *Proa*, *Inicial*, and *Martín Fierro* were considered vehicles for Florida writers, while *Claridad*, *Renovación*, and *Los Pensadores* represented the Boedo group. While any distinction between the two camps is highly reductive—authors like Nicolás Olivari switched sides, and many contributed to both groups' publications—the rift played out in Argentine print culture, expanding the literary market through this ostensible rivalry.

Sarlo ascribes the division between Florida and Boedo to Argentina's changing demographics, which produced "two publics and also two literary systems, two systems of translating foreign literature and two groups who accused each other of being cosmopolitan."[138] The debate over the meaning of "cosmopolitan," which had long been an ambivalent designation, intensified for writers of the period, as both the Florida and Boedo groups fought to assert an authentically Argentine identity, while also trying to navigate a new literary economy.[139] To do so, some from Boedo aligned the Florida group with Ultraism, deriding it as derivative of European movements. For instance, the essayist and playwright Leónidas Barletta, writing in defense of the Boedo group in *Crítica* in 1925,

equates Florida with "the new generation—the Ultraists." He further claims
that they have "been led by the hand of 'old and fruitful warriors,' as the saying
goes."[140] Barletta here quotes *Proa*, mocking the magazine's associations with
Ultraism and the "new literary generation." Although Borges was considered
part of the Florida group, he deftly resists this compartmentalization in his
essay "The Useless Discussion of Boedo and Florida," published in *La Prensa*
in 1928 (after the controversy had largely subsided).[141] Borges later called the
divide "partly publicity, partly a boyish prank."[142] Despite the tensions that it
stirred up, the Florida-Boedo rift helped to boost the market for literary magazines in Argentina.

The quintessential Florida magazine—indeed the one that published the
article that triggered the Florida-Boedo polemic—was *Martín Fierro.* Published
from 1924 to 1927 by Evar Méndez, with editorial assistance from Oliverio Girondo, Eduardo J. Bullrich, Sergio Piñero, and Alberto Prebisch, *Martín
Fierro* sought to map out an Argentine sensibility that was young and vibrant,
publishing artists such as Emilio Pettoruti, Xul Solar, and Norah Borges, along
with writers ranging from Borges to Ricardo Molinari. It also featured foreign
poets such as Apollinaire, Cocteau, García Lorca, and Gómez de la Serna and
international artists such as Picasso, Braque, Léger, Chagall, and Dalí.[143]
Committed to aesthetic innovation, *Martín Fierro* published photography along
with cutting-edge art, literature, criticism, and experimental poetry.[144] Through
its title alone, derived from José Hernández's canonical epic poem *El gaucho
Martín Fierro* of 1872, *Martín Fierro* asserted its *argentinidad*. By appropriating
this title, the magazine claimed a patriotic, frontier masculinity while also
promoting itself as an outlet for aesthetic innovation, thereby situating itself
as part of the past and future of Argentine literature. *Martín Fierro* saw
itself as an emblem of "the new literary generation," serving as a vehicle for
youth and a new national identity.[145] The magazine reinforced its alignment
with *argentinidad* and artistic experimentation through a paired manifesto
and questionnaire.

Martín Fierro's manifesto, written by Oliverio Girondo "on behalf of our
twenty fellow founders, collaborators, and shareholders," published in the
fourth issue of the magazine and also as a flyer, situates the magazine firmly
within an avant-garde framework.[146] Girondo reorients the magazine away from
the past, writing that it is "faced with the funeral solemnity of the historian and
the professor, who mummify all that they touch. . . . Faced with the ridiculous
necessity to bolster our intellectual nationalism, swelling up false values that
pop at the first prick like balloons."[147] This gesture of rejecting the "historian
and the professor" hearkens back to Marinetti, who notably opposed the library
and the academy in his Futurist manifesto. Instead, the magazine declares its
intention to define, disseminate, and serve as a mouthpiece for all that is new.
"We find ourselves in the presence of a new sensibility and a new understanding
which, if we align ourselves with it, can lead us to unexpected horizons, new

media, and new forms of expression," Girondo writes, hailing the magazine as a platform for these "new forms of expression."[148]

The manifesto aligns with Latin American culture, announcing that *Martín Fierro* "accepts the consequences and responsibilities of locating itself," and citing "awareness of its ancestors, its anatomy, and the meridian that it walks on." Girondo continues, "*Martín Fierro* believes in the importance of the intellectual contribution of Latin America, after taking a scissors to all umbilical cords."[149] Clearly cutting ties with Spain, the magazine's commitment to Latin American autonomy is also expressed within the legacy of *modernismo*, as the magazine aims "to support and spread to other fields of endeavor the linguistic independence movement that Rubén Darío initiated."[150] Despite its pride in Latin American sources, the magazine positions itself within a global economy emanating from Europe, noting how the magazine's Latin American focus "does not imply for us that we are unaware that we still use every morning our Swedish toothpaste, French towels, and English soap." Playfully acknowledging its transnational dalliances, the magazine declares itself capable of reconciling these various influences: "*Martín Fierro* has faith in our phonetics, our way of seeing, in our habits, in our own ears, in our own ability to digest and assimilate."[151] In this way, the manifesto indicates how the magazine will appropriate and incorporate outside influences. After asserting these aesthetic and geopolitical positions, the text concludes with a plea for its readers to "agree with, collaborate, and subscribe" to the magazine.

Like many manifestos of the era, the one in *Martín Fierro* is bombastic, provocative, and ambitious in scope. Following this proclamation, the subsequent issue of *Martín Fierro* questioned its own bravado by drawing its writers into a conversation about the magazine's goals through a questionnaire. The editors deliberately timed the questionnaire to come out "before the commotion of the polemic provoked by the manifesto dissipates," thereby reinforcing the connection between the two.[152] The questionnaire also inserts the national into the discourse of the manifesto, which was more Latin American and international in focus. While the manifesto had announced "a new sensibility," the questionnaire asked, "Do you believe that there is such a thing as an Argentine sensibility and/or mentality? If so, what are their characteristics?" The respondents, according to the editors, were "a qualified and numerous group of our intellectuals, writers, and artists, from different generations and movements."[153] Note also that the manifesto celebrates youth, while the questionnaire calls on the authority of experience. The boldness of the manifesto was in many ways countered by an invitation for contributors to participate in crafting the magazine's platform, allowing them to voice their own conceptions of the avant-garde through a national lens. However, like many questionnaires, this one was also an exercise in affirmation; by asking if there was an Argentine sensibility, the editors hoped to conjure one into being.

Many responses confirmed the existence of an Argentine sensibility, perhaps even essentializing its characteristics. Ricardo Rojas (who is credited with coining the term *argentinidad*) unsurprisingly validated the existence of an Argentine sensibility, writing, "The soul of the race is felt, not defined. It's useful, nevertheless, to want to define it, because it obliges one to reflect on that great mystery that is the ethnos of a nation."[154] Similarly, Lugones writes, "There are characteristics of the race that we possess and that reveal our Latin temperament."[155] Roberto Mariani, a leftist writer who would go on to spur the Boedo-Florida divide through an article he published in the subsequent issue of *Martín Fierro*, also confirmed the "existence of an Argentine sensibility," and celebrates Argentine tango in particular as being reflective of it.[156] Pablo Rojas Paz lists Sarmiento, Lugones, and Alberdi as evidence of an "Argentine sensibility" and identifies Argentine attributes as "a sharp critical spirit, a great capacity for assimilation, and a spirit of justice free from all prejudice," lofty goals which reiterate some of the language of the manifesto.[157] Even Girondo, the author of the manifesto, responded to the questionnaire, emphatically asserting his belief in a uniquely Argentine outlook despite decrying "the ridiculous necessity to bolster our intellectual nationalism" in the manifesto.[158]

However, the questionnaire fueled dissent as well. The writer Mariano A. Barrenechea flatly denies the questionnaire's premise, stating, "I do not believe in the existence of an Argentine sensibility or mentality." It is foolish to defend "literary nationalism," he argues, since "the differences in sensibility and intelligence among our writers, young or old of today or yesterday, are very profound, and always reveal, almost without exception, foreign influences, European ways of seeing and feeling."[159] The writer Samuel Glusberg dissents on different grounds, arguing for "a *criollo* or American sensibility" instead of an Argentine one, an aspiration to a regional identity that would later be taken up by *Revista de Avance*.[160] The Uruguayan painter Pedro Figari tries to reconcile these positions, arguing that the Argentine mentality is "influenced by two civilizations: the autochthonous and the European, and formed in a supremely rich middle ground, a chimerical territory."[161] However, he continues, "there is no doubt, then, that the '*criollo*' signals our course: autonomy, or better yet, efficiency and dignity."[162] By contrast, Luis María Jordán, another writer for the magazine, argues that the world is simply too globalized to assert any national or regional sensibility: "Thanks to mass media, we're each day more homogenous, which will unfortunately result in the suppression of everything that might be a local characteristic."[163] These diverging responses indicate how the manifesto's claims to Latin American and international identities were up for debate in the context of the questionnaire, as was the questionnaire's positing of a national sensibility. Nevertheless, the terms that both the manifesto and questionnaire propose are reintroduced through the responses, even as they are contested.

In many ways, the *Martín Fierro* questionnaire confronted the same contradictions as the one issued by *Nosotros*; namely, the task of mapping out a new literary sensibility within a national tradition. Schwartz relates the two efforts by describing *Martín Fierro* as "a vehicle for disseminating a *criollo* Ultraism."[164] This claim to a Latin American version of an international movement echoes some of the questionnaire responses. Gloria Videla similarly defines *martínfierrismo* as the "*criollo* version" of Ultraism.[165] The idea of a "*criollo* Ultraism" underscores the magazine's sometimes conflicting aims: to launch an Argentine avant-garde within a Latin American framework that builds on and transcends European artistic experimentation. The questionnaire drew attention to these competing positions, which were constitutive of the magazine. As Sarlo explains, "The *Martinfierrista* discourse is heterogeneous and is based on a system of oppositions and vacillations that were never resolved. . . . On the one hand there was the national subject, the gaucho Martín Fierro, on the other the European and cosmopolitan tenets of aesthetic renovation. . . . [It calls for] an affirmation of the new and an adherence to a preexisting cultural tradition; a revindication of what is 'characteristically Argentine,' and a cosmopolitan point of view . . . [demonstrating] the tension between *criollismo* and modernity or nationalism and cosmopolitanism."[166] This pull between national tradition and aesthetic innovation, characteristic of many avant-gardes, was precisely what motivated questions on "the new literary generation" and an "Argentine sensibility" in *Nosotros* and *Martín Fierro*.

As magazines were polling contributors on their literary and national identities, writers and editors were working to anthologize them. For example, Borges, along with Alberto Hidalgo and Vicente Huidobro, produced the anthology *Índice de la nueva poesía americana* in 1926; the volume included poetry from Argentina, Colombia, Chile, Ecuador, Mexico, Nicaragua, Peru, Uruguay, and Venezuela, thus situating the "new literary generation" in a broader Latin American context. In his prologue Borges mentions Darío and Lugones, only to displace them with the Generation of '22, whose work is most prominently featured in the compilation. He spotlights Ultraism, writing, "The two wings of this poetry (Ultraism, Simplism: the label is unimportant) are free verse and the image. Rhyme is accidental."[167] Julio Noé's 1926 *Antología de la poesía argentina moderna (1900–1925)* similarly affirmed the divisions between Argentine literary generations.[168] Noé positioned the *Nosotros* writers as transitional markers between the older and newer generations, the latter of which was represented by Borges, Brandán Caraffa, Girondo, and Güiraldes. The following year, Pedro Juan Vignale and César Tiempo published *Exposición de la actual poesía argentina*, which they also preface with a generational pivot, declaring, "We present here more than forty poets who appeared after 1922 who constitute the diverse nuclei and peripheries of the new literary generation."[169] These editors all reinforce the impulse to consolidate and canonize a "new literary generation" in Argentina and across Latin America.[170]

Exposición de la actual poesía argentina also included Evar Méndez's essay "The Role of *Martín Fierro* in the Current Poetic Revival," wherein he centralizes the magazine to Argentine literary history. He acknowledges and dismisses the magazine's predecessors, writing, "The result of its activity is not only that *Martín Fierro* left the last vestiges of the school of Rubén Darío and Latin American pseudo-Symbolism far behind; but also it liberated them from the minor influences of figures from our milieu such as Banchs, Fernández Moreno, Capdevila; it definitively shook off the yoke of Lugones, his poetic influence and his pernicious aesthetic ideas based on an archaic and reactionary dogmatism; but also, and above all, the young poets introduced a new concept of poetry, of the poem, and its construction."[171] Méndez sheds Darío, whom the manifesto had cited, and "Latin American pseudo-symbolism," before dismissing the *Nosotros* stable of writers—Banchs, Moreno, and Capdevila—and condemning Lugones. In his response to the *Nosotros* questionnaire, Borges had included this very list among the older writers whom he respected: "My enthusiasms are orthodox. Among the saints of my devotion I count Capdevila, Banchs, and especially our Quevedo, Lugones."[172] Many of the other responses cited Lugones as well. Méndez, however, untethers *Martín Fierro* from the influence of Lugones, denouncing at once his poetics—which focused on the land as fundamental to Argentine identity, presented in a realist style—and his politics, which had turned conservative. (For his part, Lugones contributed an essay to the same anthology criticizing Ultraism and the use of free verse.)[173] The "new concept of poetry" to which Méndez alludes also suggests an affinity with Ultraism and its offshoots. Méndez argues that *Martín Fierro* offered a literary profile that surpassed its antecedents and that "galvanized the innovative spirit of youth."[174] As such polemical essays attest, these anthologies continued the work of the questionnaires issued by *Nosotros* and *Martín Fierro*, as they sought to canonize the "new literary generation" while it was still emerging.

The Intellectual Meridian Debate

Although Ultraism was short-lived in each country, the transportation of the movement across the Atlantic underscored Spain and Argentina's complex and enduring cultural ties. Questionnaires tracked each country's relationship to the movement and to their subsequent avant-gardes, as did parallel print-cultural debates over art and national identity. While Spanish poets were involved in the early days of Ultraism, their influence waned. As *Martín Fierro*'s manifesto and questionnaire attests, forging an autonomous avant-garde was also a means of "taking a scissors to all umbilical cords." Such frictions escalated after Guillermo de Torre published an incendiary article, "Madrid, Intellectual Meridian of Hispanic America," in 1927 in *La Gaceta Literaria,* prompting a series of rebuttals and questionnaires on both sides of the Atlantic, which almost uniformly denied Spanish involvement in Latin America.[175]

De Torre begins the essay with a preamble explaining his distaste for the term *América Latina.* He instead favors *Hispanoamérica,* which helps to distance Latin America from France and reassert Spain's prominence. "Note the care

with which we avoid writing the false and unjustified name 'Latin America,'"
he remarks. "There are not, in our opinion, legitimate and justifiable names . . .
other than Ibero-America, Hispanic America, or Spanish America."[176] While he
acknowledges the region's "autochthonous and indigenous" values, he dismisses any "French, Italian, or Anglo-Saxon" influence and complains that using a
term like *América Latina* means being "unconsciously complicit with the un-
derhanded, annexationist maneuvers that France and Italy have been carrying
out with respect to America." De Torre is distraught at the thought of France's
cultural dominance over Spain, writing, "Enough of passively tolerating our loss
of prestige, that constant diversion of Hispanic American intellectual interests
toward France!" As if imploring his Latin American readers, De Torre argues
that Paris would "annul and neutralize" Latin American ideals, whereas "the
vital atmosphere of Spain . . . does not diminish or annul their personality, but
rather exalts and enhances in its best expressions."[177] De Torre's concern with
nomenclature betrays his deep anxiety over Spain's loss of cultural authority.

To reassert Spanish interests, the article claims Latin American cultural
output for Spain. As De Torre announces, "We have always tended to consider
the American intellectual field an extension of that of Spain. And not for the purpose of reprehensible annexation, but rather for the desire to erase borders, to
not establish distinctions, to group under the same common denominator for
equal consideration all intellectual production in the same language."[178] This
appropriation of the "American intellectual field" demonstrates an investment
in securing not only Spain's cultural prestige but also its literary marketplace.
Declaring Madrid "the most authentic line of intersection between America
and Spain," De Torre touts Spanish influence in Latin America as opposed to
that of France, Italy, and the United States, arguing that "the new generations of
students and intellectuals" in Latin America can receive real attention to their
ideas in Madrid.[179] In this way, De Torre tries to claim Argentina's "new literary generation" for Spain, while eliding French influence. Unsurprisingly, the
provocative essay sparked outrage, inciting intense and protracted debate.

Although De Torre writes that he "implies no political or intellectual
hegemony of any kind," magazines across Latin America mocked, defied,
and undermined his essay and adamantly denied Spanish influence.[180] Nearly
every prominent Latin American journal refuted this article, but the most
vociferous responses came from *Martín Fierro*, which, as Schwartz argues,
had consolidated its *argentinidad* precisely to counteract Spanish influence.[181]
Martín Fierro printed responses to the meridian debate over two issues of the
magazine, including a double-page spread titled "A Reality Check." In these
articles, the magazine's contributors asserted Latin American self-reliance
and denounced De Torre's gesture as imperialist; Pablo Rojas Paz, one of the
editors of *Proa*, even titled his contribution "Barren Imperialism." Yet Rojas Paz
also emphasized Latin America's openness to outside forces, explaining, "We
seek Romanticism from Germany, Impressionism from England, the French

moderns from Baudelaire onward in Poe and Walt Whitman," and concludes that no "intellectual meridian" could encompass the diversity of Latin America.[182]

Many of the responses to the meridian debate published in *Martín Fierro* insist on Latin American autonomy. Ildefonso Pereda Valdés, a Uruguayan writer who also responded to the *Revista de Avance* questionnaire, claims, "The intellectual meridian of America is not Madrid, it's Buenos Aires."[183] Similarly, the Argentine poet Lisardo Zia declares, "America's only aspiration is America itself."[184] Argentine writer Nicolás Olivari takes the debate a step further, pointing to how Latin America had influenced Spain: "Was it not an American, Rubén Darío, who taught them modernism?" Olivari also reports that despite Borges's time in Spain, "he has joined us and brandishes our *criollismo*, robust and forceful."[185] As for Borges, he declares, "Madrid does not understand us," and argues that Buenos Aires is more indebted to Italy than to Spain.[186] Resembling responses to the *Martín Fierro* questionnaire, contributions to the meridian polemic called for autonomy while acknowledging the effects of other cultures on Latin America.

In the last issue of *Martín Fierro*, its director, Méndez, addresses the "meridian debate," reiterating the positions stated in the magazine's manifesto and questionnaire and emphasizing how the periodical had fomented a new literary culture. Méndez argues that its questionnaire on the Argentine mentality "categorically affirmed its existence and defined its characteristics," thereby glossing over any dissenting responses. Yet, after insisting on Argentine cultural independence, Méndez goes on to refute De Torre by paradoxically aligning with North America: "As for the North Americans . . . we feel closer to them, by education, tastes and ways of life, than to Europeans." He further notes the influence of "Poe, Whitman, Emerson," as well as the magazine's indebtedness to Latin American thinkers such as "Martí, Darío, and Rodó" and Argentines such as "Güiraldes, Macedonio Fernández, Victoria Ocampo, Norah Borges, Pettoruti, Xul Solar."[187] Méndez concludes by inverting the terms of the debate, celebrating Argentina's vast influence: "Without waiting for it or suspecting it, in all of America, in Italy, and France, and even among sensible people in Spain, the echo of young Argentine thought has reverberated."[188] In this way, Méndez denies De Torre's claims from every angle: from the stance of Argentine autonomy, from a pan-American point of view, and by positioning Argentina as a model for Europe.

Beyond Argentina, De Torre's contentious article prompted a range of responses in Peru, Cuba, Uruguay, Mexico, Spain, and Italy, many of which cited *Martín Fierro*'s angry rebuttals. The editors of *Revista de Avance* expressed the opinion that both sides had taken the debate too far: "A good lesson to take from this polemic: meridians, even when they are intellectual, cannot be imposed: they fall by spiritual affinity. However, the best thing for the good navigator would be to reorient his ship according to whatever meridian. That way, sometimes it would be Paris, other times London, and many times—why not?—Madrid. One has to be ready for the bypass."[189] By contrast, the Uruguayan magazine *Cruz de Sur* adopted an extreme position, declaring Montevideo the intellectual meridian of the world (thus exceeding even De Torre's bold claim for Madrid).[190] Many writers reacted to the dispute by redoubling their efforts to promote local culture, and called for Latin American solidarity in opposition to Spanish colonialism. For example, Carpentier, writing in the Cuban *Diario de la Marina*, invokes José Martí's formulation "our America" and argues, "The desire to create an autochthonous art conquers all will."[191] In his response, the Peruvian editor and activist José Carlos Mariátegui similarly observes that only by "breaking with the Motherland has our America begun to discover its personality and to forge its destiny," allowing "us to reclaim and revalue the autochthonous as ours."[192] While Mariátegui conceded that Latin American culture was still developing, he asserts, "The ideal of the new generation is, precisely, to give it unity."[193] Mariátegui maintains that in this regard, *Martín Fierro* has a better chance of being the intellectual meridian of Latin America than *La Gaceta Literaria*, thus replacing the cities with the magazines that best represented them.[194]

Many writers said that they wished the polemic had taken the form of a questionnaire, and it did in turn spark further use of the genre. Leopoldo Marechal lamented that the *Gaceta* article did not result from a questionnaire, which he suggested would have more judiciously presented various sides of the debate.[195] Madrid's newspaper *El Sol* referred to the *Martín Fierro* response to the debate *as* a questionnaire, and indeed *Martín Fierro*'s headline rephrases the article's title as a question: "Madrid, Intellectual Meridian of Hispanic America?"[196] In response to an open letter from Pablo Rojas Paz to *La Gaceta Literaria* printed in *Martín Fierro*, *La Gaceta Literaria* issued "A Passionate Debate: A Tournament for the Intellectual Meridian," pitting *La Gaceta Literaria* against *Martín Fierro* in the language of a boxing match. Responses came from Gímenez Caballero, De Torre, Gómez de la Serna, and others who would later participate in the 1930 survey, and were printed in a format resembling a questionnaire.[197] Furthermore, because Italy was drawn into the polemic by comments such as those by Borges in *Martín Fierro*, the Milan-based magazine *La Fiera Letteraria* weighed in on the controversy too.[198] This intervention prompted yet another questionnaire, this time in *Nosotros*. "A Questionnaire About Italian Influence on Our Culture" was issued in 1928 to Lugones, Ricardo Rojas, Alfredo Bianchi, Evar Méndez, and others.[199] The fluidity between questionnaires and polemical essays across the Atlantic demonstrates how such forms were part of a shared repository of print-cultural genres that publications relied on to stake out their national and transnational positions. Moreover, the calls for questionnaires speak to their value at the time as forums for debate, which some writers saw as more democratic than the single-author essay. Questionnaires served as venues in which to construct, refine, or contest national canons in print, particularly in the context of Spain and Argentina, whose literary cultures in the 1920s were entangled through their relationship to Ultraism.

Expanding into the International

Ultraism continued to be a touchstone, even in outraged responses to the "meridian debate." *La Gaceta Literaria*'s role in promoting Ultraism was cited in an editorial in the Uruguayan magazine *La Pluma*, which stated that it was shocked to find such imperialist tendencies "under the Ultraism of *La Gaceta*."[200] The editorial rightly points out that Spain itself received ideas from France, Germany, and the rest of Europe, and that in many ways *La Gaceta Literaria* and the Generation of '27 were responsible for "having opened Spain's borders to the restorative postwar movement and having assimilated the new modes of feeling, thinking, and making of our time."[201] Such a statement suggests that it is precisely receptiveness to the international avant-garde that engenders local innovation, a point underscored in the case of Ultraism. In both Spain and Argentina, Ultraism ignited local literary culture, even though it was itself responding to ideas circulating internationally. In 1932, referring to *Ultra*, the Spanish poet Pedro Garfias claims that Ultraism created "the total and purely literary magazine, [the] immediate predecessor to those of today."[202] Ultraism served as a precursor and model for the Spanish Generation of '27 and the "new literary generation" in Argentina alike, propelling local literary communities and the publications to support them.

The desire to establish a proprietary cultural sensibility was evident in many Argentine questionnaires of the period. Regarding José Hernández's canonical poem, in 1913 *Nosotros* inquired, "What is the value of *Martín Fierro*?"; in 1924 the magazine named for the poem then asked, "Do you believe that there is such a thing as an Argentine sensibility and/or mentality?"[203] While Borges did not respond to these particular questions, he later asserted his position in his 1951 essay "The Argentine Writer and Tradition": "The idea that Argentine poetry must abound in Argentine differential traits and Argentine local color seems to me to be a mistake." Rather, "I believe that our tradition is the whole of Western culture, and I also believe that we have a right to this tradition, a greater right than that which the inhabitants of one Western nation or another might have." He concludes, "We must not be afraid; we must believe that the universe is our birthright."[204] Through such pronouncements he expands on his 1924 assertion in *Proa* that "the high culture that until now has been the exclusive patrimony of Europe and the few Americas that had drunk of it, begins to represent itself, in a miraculous way, as an essential product of our civilization," a position represented by his transposition of Ultraist aesthetics to the Argentine avant-garde.[205] Yet despite his early interest in Ultraism, later in his life Borges surrendered his affiliation with all aesthetic movements, writing, "I regret such participation in literary schools. Today I do not believe in them. They are forms of advertising or conveniences for the history of literature."[206] Borges describes such experiences as "a game, and at times, a game made for advertising, nothing more. Nevertheless, I have good memories of those friends, but not of our arbitrary theories."[207]

In 1964 De Torre revisited Borges's Ultraist period, writing, "I am aware that Jorge Luis Borges condemns, and even scorns, those origins of his work, denouncing Ultraism, and everything connected to it."[208] However, De Torre recognizes Borges as an important link between Spanish and Argentine modernism. He compares the two, asserting, "If Ultraism was defined as a reaction against Rubén Darío-ism in Spain, in Argentina it made Leopoldo Lugones the 'scapegoat' of all modernist poetry, which was considered outdated."[209] In both contexts De Torre saw reactions against earlier influences being used to mark out new poetic territory. While De Torre does not quite manage to insert himself and his poetic movement into Borges's legacy—much as his article in *La Gaceta Literaria* tries but fails to extend Spanish influence over Latin America—he does illustrate how transatlantic exchange was inextricable from both Spain and Argentina's national literary histories.

The ambition of print communities in Spain and Argentina alike was to participate in an international dialogue about what it meant to be modern and to create and reinforce this modernity on a national scale. The year 1930 in particular, when *Gaceta Literaria* issued its survey, was one in which avant-garde groups looked back on the commonalities and differences that had shaped them in the 1920s. While the *Gaceta Literaria* questionnaire proposed a lineage for a national avant-garde, other questionnaires of the period were more international in scope, capitalizing on the genre's ability to bring together writers from around the world to address common concerns. Such is the case for the 1930 questionnaire on "contemporary unrest," which I address in the next chapter. This survey, issued by the French magazine *Cahiers de l'Étoile* to De Torre, Nicolás Olivari, and many other European and Latin American writers, among those from other regions, shifted its focus beyond the national specificity of avant-gardes to reflect on and substantiate a shared experience of the era.

5. EXTENDING INTO THE **CONTEMPORARY**

In 1930 the Parisian magazine *Cahiers de l'Étoile* printed responses to a
questionnaire on "inquiétude contemporaine" (contemporary unrest) that
it had issued two years prior to a wide range of international contributors.[1]
(fig. 18) This questionnaire notably interrogated the "contemporary" as
opposed to "modernism" or the "avant-garde," which had been more
commonly used to periodize at the time and were often called into question in
other inquiries. Moreover, other questionnaires from the 1920s and 1930s
usually focused on national or regional canon-building projects. What distinguished this questionnaire was both its new temporal lens and its broad
geographic reach. It brought together significant literary and artistic figures
from around the world—including many who had participated in other
questionnaires I have analyzed, such as Juan Marinello (*Revista de Avance*),
Guillermo de Torre (*La Gaceta Literaria*), and Nicolás Olivari (*Martín Fierro*),
along with, to name only a few, José Carlos Mariátegui, John Dos Passos, Jean
Toomer, Le Corbusier, Rafael Cansinos-Assens, F. T. Marinetti, Carl Jung, Alfred
Döblin, Ildefonso Pereda Valdés, and Alain Locke—to comment on the
"contemporary," thereby invoking the term to strengthen an international
cultural network.

Despite these significant temporal and geographic shifts, in other ways
the questionnaire's two primary components—"unrest" and "the contemporary"—were emblematic of the era and the genre. First, the notion of disquiet,
anxiety, or unrest—the many meanings of *inquiétude*—fueled a number of
the previous decades' questionnaires, typically issued on specific national
or aesthetic concerns, and would continue to propel the genre forward into
the twenty-first century.[2] Second, questions of periodization were commonly
invoked to define the contours of an era, be it with respect to modernism, the

ORIENTATIONS

Les *Cahiers de l'Etoile* lançaient, il y a environ deux ans, un questionnaire dont voici le texte:

A) — Existe-t-il une inquiétude particulière à notre époque?

B) 1° — La constatez-vous dans votre monde? Quelles formes y prend-elle?

2° — Comment s'exprime cette inquiétude dans et devant la vie sociale?

(L'interdépendance des pays, la condensation de la population dans les grands centres, le machinisme collectif, l'automatisme individuel tendent-ils à anéantir la personnalité humaine?)

3° — Et dans la vie sexuelle?

4° — Et dans la foi?

5° — Quel est son effet sur l'activité créatrice?

C) — L'inquiétude n'est-elle pas la souffrance d'une humanité qui cherche à retrouver son unité en se libérant de ses prisons (temps, espace et solitude individuelle)?

Dans ce cas, une époque de grande inquiétude ne marque-t-elle pas l'éveil d'une nouvelle conscience? Et si nous sommes dans telle époque, pouvons-nous déjà dégager cette nouvelle conscience et ses caractères?

Quelques-unes des personnes auxquelles ce questionnaire fut adressé nous firent les reproches qu'il est d'usage de faire : cette consultation n'était entreprise que dans un but de publicité; nous avions trouvé un prétexte pour interviewer des gens célèbres; ou pour nous procurer sans frais des textes intéressants; et le reproche le plus grave fut celui-ci : notre texte était tendancieux, nos questions étaient

Fig. 18 "Enquête sur l'inquiétude contemporaine," *Cahiers de l'Étoile* (Paris), no. 18
(November–December 1930): 845.

avant-garde, or the contemporary. Indeed, the shifting currency of these terms can be traced by examining questionnaires throughout the century and onward.

The genre persists as a periodizing tool to delineate and assess historical formations into the present, as evidenced by recent surveys such as the "Questionnaire on 'The Contemporary,'" issued by the academic journal *October* in 2009. The questionnaire is a genre in which nearly every critic, artist, author, and movement in the twentieth century across Europe and the Americas has participated—including Clement Greenberg and Harold Rosenberg in the 1940s and Maurice Blanchot and Roland Barthes in the 1960s—and continues to be used by literary magazines, academic journals, and art publications today. The questionnaire has gained surprising traction in the field of contemporary art in particular. Between its role in museum practices, its appropriation by conceptual artists, and its ongoing presence in art magazines, the questionnaire continues to be ubiquitous across Europe and the Americas. This chapter begins with an analysis of the *Cahiers de l'Étoile* survey on "contemporary unrest," and its early invocation of the term "contemporary," and then offers an overview of the questionnaire in the ensuing decades, to demonstrate how the genre has been activated in different contexts, especially in the field of visual culture. At once consistent and evolving, the genre of the questionnaire has managed to remain, essentially, contemporary.

Contemporary Unrest

While many questionnaires from the 1920s and 1930s were national in focus, often seeking to define "America" and its contribution to the international avant-garde, the survey issued by *Cahiers de l'Étoile* on "contemporary unrest" was explicitly international in both the scope of its questions and the geographic range of the contributions it solicited. However, many of the 120 respondents interpreted the questions through a nationally specific lens. This tension between the national and the international reinforced the other anxieties foregrounded in the questionnaire. Unlike other surveys of the time, in which *inquiétude* was an undercurrent, "contemporary unrest" and its manifestations worldwide were the explicit subject of this questionnaire, which asked,

> Does there exist an unrest particular to our era? Do you notice it in
> your world? What forms does it take? How is this unrest expressed
> in social life? (Do the interdependence of countries, the concentration
> of the population in major centers, collective mechanization, and
> individual automation all tend to destroy the human personality?)
> And in sexual life? And in faith? What is its effect on creative activity?
> Is not this unrest the suffering of a humanity that seeks to recover
> its unity by freeing itself from its prisons (time, space, and individual
> solitude)? In this case, does not an era of great unrest mark the
> awakening of a new consciousness? And if we are in such an era,

can we clear the way for this new consciousness and its
characteristics?[3]

An "unrest particular to our era" is positioned here as ever-present and elusive,
registering both on a personal level and on a grand scale. Such anxiety is considered dangerous as it might "destroy the human personality," but also liberating,
potentially marking the "awakening a new consciousness." Clearly the editors
believed that such unrest did exist, and yet they sought collective assistance in
describing it and determining its effects.

This set of leading questions assumes that the magazine's view would be
shared by a diverse set of contributors invested in varied aesthetic projects—
figures ranging from Albert Gleizes to Jane Addams—and hailing from around
the world. Unlike most French questionnaires of the era, this one included
respondents from Asia, Eastern Europe, North America, and Latin America,
as well as from across Europe. Some contributions were reprinted abroad in
other magazines in addition to being published in *Cahiers*, thus transporting
the questions to different national and linguistic contexts and reinforcing the
network established by the magazine's internationalist line of questioning.[4]

Affiliated with the "Star of the Orient" and theosophy, *Cahiers de l'Étoile* was
founded to advance the goals of this esoteric philosophy, which explored the nature of divinity. The magazine was published monthly in Paris from 1928 to 1939
by Carlo Suarès, a French writer and painter interested in kabbalistic mysticism,
along with the French-Russian patron Irma de Manziarly, who was part of the
"Order of the Star," which lent the magazine its name. It frequently published
the work of Jiddu Krishnamurti, a leading theosophist (who also responded to
the questionnaire).[5] Professing to be "based on a new reality," the magazine
emphasized the verb *être* (to be) and focused on releasing the individual's
creative and spiritual potential. Rather than fomenting a movement, the journal
hoped to "trigger awareness." *Cahiers* emphasized its interest in life beyond the
rational through the phrases such as "one reality: dream-reality," which echoed
the Surrealists but worked toward different aesthetic goals.[6]

From its theosophical origins, the magazine turned outward to examine social and political thought, which it believed clarified the life of the individual. In
a 1930 statement the editors assert, "This magazine is studying the symptoms of
renewal offered by modern life in the aspects of political, social, artistic, scientific, and religious problems, [and] in relation to the individual, in search of his
own purpose."[7] Thus, despite its esoteric interests, *Cahiers* also covered political
and social issues, as well as publishing poetry, essays, and prose, including
works by well-regarded figures such as Le Corbusier, Georges Ribemont-Dessaignes, and Benjamin Fondane. International in distribution, the magazine
listed subscription prices for France "and its colonies," along with Greece, Romania, Bulgaria, Belgium, Hungary, Poland, and elsewhere in Eastern Europe
and abroad, demonstrating its international reach.[8]

Likewise, while other surveys of the era examined art and literature as inextricable from national or regional identities, the one issued by *Cahiers de l'Étoile* took as its premise an international horizon. Accordingly, the countries represented by the respondents included Spain, Romania, England, Germany, Italy, the United States, Cuba, Sweden, France, Uruguay, Denmark, Norway, India, Argentina, Japan, Czechoslovakia, and Switzerland.[9] This international representation was important to the editors, who invoked a refrain raised by many concomitant questionnaires, namely, that Europe was in decline. As the editors note, "Today the economic, social, and political situation of the world is such that it becomes almost commonplace to say that Western civilization could very well sink. We will pay for the wars and revolutions that might erase Europe from the map of civilized countries."[10] Thus, part of the questionnaire's internationalism emerged from the fear that Europe had been ruined by war and revolution, as evidenced by the "unrest" that resulted.

Such anxiety was deemed contemporaneous across the world. As cultural and historical phases, modernism and the avant-garde emphasize rupture, newness, and a break with the past, sometimes in an aggressive, militaristic sense. By contrast, the "contemporary" suggests co-presence, a formation that focuses on the present rather than the future.[11] Coupled with the internationalism of the questionnaire, the "contemporary" in this context registers as both temporal and spatial. In this case, the form of the questionnaire reflects its content. Questionnaires on the contemporary fundamentally ask how to belong to the present, that is, how to be simultaneous with one's peers and one's time, much like the questionnaire itself, which models a kind of simultaneity or co-presence in print.

As indicated by the editors' emphasis on war and revolution, many of the countries represented in the survey were united by the legacy of World War I, which created a shared sense of time. War haunts the questionnaire, unknowingly issued a few years prior to the incomprehensible devastation of the Second World War. For the magazine, "contemporary unrest" was a manifestation of various threats to civilization as well as signifying internal malaise, both of which were reactions to the recent war. As the editors note, "war disrupts the rhythm of existence, and external changes have become too fast for individual capacities of internal adjustment," imploding the idea of what the editors call a "'normal,' scheduled, stable, logical life."[12] While such concerns about the pace of modern life were raised at the turn of the century by writers like Georg Simmel and its effects on the mind explored by Freud and those influenced by him, in this context the disruption of daily life was linked directly to the upheaval of war.[13] War, ironically, also served to internationalize the arts; prowar artists such as Marinetti traveled around the world promoting Futurism, while artists fleeing the war gathered in places like Zurich or New York, spawning new art movements.[14] As the editors note, war permeates the questions and answers in the *Cahiers de l'Étoile* inquiry: "War returns as a theme in almost all of the pages of this volume, indicating that the upheaval it produced in consciousness is infinite." "Contemporary unrest," as well as the internationalism that the editors highlight, stemmed from World War I, suggesting that the war's destructive forces generated worldwide anxiety as well as a kind of global cotemporality.[15]

This focus on the war is reflected in the questionnaire's responses. For instance, Marinetti writes about the lead-up to World War I, which coincided with the height of Futurism. He describes the "prewar social anxiety with all its seismographs exasperated by the approach of the conflagration [humanity] had unintentionally prepared."[16] Yet he continues to praise the war, despite the "conflagration" that ensued, writing that "the bloodshed accentuated patriotic instincts and the ancient hope for the fusion of peoples in eternal peace."[17] This rhetoric dovetails with Marinetti's stance in the *Futurist Manifesto*, which announces, "We will glorify war—the world's only hygiene."[18] In *Cahiers de l'Étoile* Marinetti also addresses the aftermath of the war, noting, "the postwar unrest in which we live is a veritable torment that drives some minds to surprise . . . others transform their unrest into patriotic, scientific, innovative, and touristic ambition to conquer and perfect the natural beauties of the earth." Despite addressing the negative effects of war, Marinetti celebrates its potential for transformation.[19]

While Marinetti's Futurist aesthetics in many ways extolled war, most of the other respondents lamented its destruction and the "unrest" that it caused. The wording of the questionnaire intimates a common experience of distress and the desire to alleviate this collective unease. Possible solutions the responses include, as the editors note, "could be provided by social transformations, by new economic systems, policies, which would establish peace, by woman, or by beauty, art, or the search for an ideal." Beyond social or aesthetic reforms, the editors emphasize, change must also happen on the level of the individual: "by recreating themselves, they recreate the universe."[20] This position is in line with the magazine's theosophist bent. Both the questions and the potential solutions catologued by *Cahiers*' editors suggest macro-level thinking about world problems as well as an interest in local and even individual perspectives.

Many of the contributors viewed "contemporary unrest" through a national or regional framework, including several of the North Americans and Latin Americans who responded. John Dos Passos, for example, sees in unrest "the difficulty of thinking effectively and consecutively." He concludes that this is not a result of the war, but rather due to the effects of American capitalism. He supports this position by listing figures who produced creative material before and during wartime: "The great creators of our time such as Lenin, Einstein, Pavlov, and Freud reached their full expression before the anxiety created by the war appeared. It is the same for Picasso, Stravinsky, and Joyce. It remains to be proved whether this particular decade produced agitation or stabilization."[21] Decoupling contemporary unrest from the war, Dos Passos instead reiterates fears about America's increasing economic influence that were voiced in response to *transition*, *Revista de Avance*, and *Imán*'s questionnaires as well.

In contrast to John Dos Passos's answer, an "Anonymous Banker" from the United States who responded to the questionnaire lauds the value of work as a source of pleasure. The banker hails the "acceleration" of daily life, along with the rise of "birth-control and machines that have largely liberated women from their natural occupations as mothers and housewives." He offers "meditation, religion, and work" as ways to combat anxiety, distinguishing what he calls "agitation, irritation, and also a kind of dissatisfaction" from the type of unrest stipulated by the questionnaire. Instead, he calls this kind of unrest "perhaps the driving force of all life and... also the essence of progress and ambition."[22] Meanwhile, H. L. Mencken contests the questionnaire's very premise in his response. He writes, "I do not think there is an unrest particular to our era," cheerfully noting that "nothing prevents, as far as I can see, the activity of creative artists in any field."[23] Dos Passos and Mencken both seem to disassociate creativity from contemporary unrest, while the banker commends such unrest for propelling life forward.

Jean Toomer—known for his groundbreaking prose poem *Cane* (1923) about race in America—critiques America's political and cultural climate in his response to the questionnaire. He argues that "contemporary unrest" emerged alongside "increased class and race consciousness" and "an intensification of negative or destructive forces," including "the preparations for a greater war; the increase of prejudices and antagonisms between races, nations, classes, and smaller groups of people." Such a polarizing political climate, he argues, could yield little creatively. He maintains that the artist "finds comparatively nothing ready for his hand to use; no creative traditions, no energizing symbols, no satisfactory forms. He has no certainty of response from others, for he cannot assume that his forms and values, views and beliefs, are understood and affirmed (or denied) by his audience."[24] Toomer laments his inability to find or create a shared worldview with his readers at a politically volatile moment.

Part of Toomer's despair at the state of political and creative progress stemmed from his view that literature was being treated as a business. Arguing that it hurt the development of an American literary tradition and devalued creative labor, he condemns the literary market: "Never has there been such quantity of cheap, unimportant written matter. Books, magazines, newspapers, pamphlets . . . literature is fast becoming a form of business. A writer is viewed as a natural resource to be exploited for whatever can be gotten out of him." In the face of this industrialization of literature, Toomer declares that writers "need to be able to respond, without over-emphasis, without undervaluation, to the genuine features of our experience. . . . In so far as there is a genuine American literature, this literature experiences the profound unrest involved in all self-creations."[25] By articulating a collective "American literature," Toomer offers hope that writers can build a national canon reflecting the era, one perhaps even driven to greatness by the very forces that threaten it.

Like Dos Passos and Toomer, those responding from Latin America also centralize their nationally or regionally specific experiences in their reflections on "contemporary unrest." For instance, Nicolás Olivari, an Argentine writer involved with *Martín Fierro*, notes, "Yes, uneasiness exists, and I speak of America, the only land I know." He then proceeds to focus on Buenos Aires, observing, "In Buenos Aires work is a curse, one works a lot and earns little." He calls it a "city of the world that deeply despises intellectual values," that instead craves "material wealth, and we pursue it at the price of our intellectual independence."[26] The Argentine writer Manuel Gálvez agrees that "the Argentine only aspires to make money and live well."[27] Olivari laments the state of intellectual life in Buenos Aires, and in particular the recent cessation of *Martín Fierro*: "And when the poet is avant-garde, persecution becomes inconceivable. We, young avant-garde poets who headed the defunct magazine *Martín Fierro* and have made the most profound American intellectual renewal, we are now paying in excess for our courage."[28] In addition to Olivari's intellectual concerns, Gálvez argues that Argentines are confronted by two dangers: "U.S. imperialism and the social revolution." Although these are opposing forces, both threaten economic stability, a common theme in Latin Americans' responses.[29]

Juan Marinello, an editor of *Revista de Avance*, uses the questionnaire as an opportunity to reflect specifically on Cuba, much as Olivari and Gálvez examined Argentina, but he argues that his country lacks the structural conditions necessary for "contemporary unrest" due to imperialist and capitalist forces. His response, printed in French in *Cahiers de l'Étoile* and in Spanish in *Revista de Avance* under the title "Sobre la inquietud cubana," was subsequently published as a book.[30] Marinello translated the questions into Spanish for his audience at home and emphasized the national focus of his answers for readers in both places, steering his responses, as he said, "perhaps excessively, to Cuban reality."[31] He begins by considering Latin America more broadly. Since the questions emanated from France, Marinello addresses the transatlantic pull between Europe and the Americas: "Latin America is still, just as North America is, a European reflection. Neither politically nor intellectually has it said *its word*. Which is not to deny its distinctions or its strong political minds or its world-class artists. Alberdi and Martí. Darío, Diego Rivera, and again, Martí."[32] Despite the contributions of these figures, Marinello maintains, "America has failed to become Europe or essentially different from Europe." Marinello contends, "When we wanted to put down roots we could not find them in our mulatto lands. . . . Spain and Europe have kept us away from America."[33] Reinforcing many of the positions put forth in response to *Revista de Avance*'s questionnaire and to the "meridian debate," Marinello insists that Latin America resist succumbing to a colonialist mindset and instead assert its autonomy from Spain and from Europe.

Part of the problem, according to Marinello, is that Latin Americans historically have not seen their concerns as distinct from those of Europe, and thus "until now solutions have been sought in an old laboratory." Instead, Latin Americans need to arrive collectively at an "American solution . . . a culture/attitude that will succeed one day in giving standards to the old master." Only once Americans recognize their fundamental differences from Europeans, he asserts, will they achieve independence. "Then America—remember what Waldo Frank said—will justify itself before the world." (Notably, Marinello refers to a champion of pan-Americanism in this statement.) By no longer relying on the "old laboratory" of Europe, but rather on its own resources, Latin America, Marinello portends, will enter a world stage.[34]

Despite these lofty aspirations for Latin America, Marinello takes a hard look at the situation in Cuba, suggesting that the country is "still dazed—after only a quarter of a century as a republic." He is most anguished by the protracted presence of the United States, maintaining that "the subordination of our public activities, in more than one essential way, to the action of the Yankee rulers" displaces Cuban interests and expertise while obstructing independence. As a result, he states bluntly, "a legal reality—the Platt Amendment—and a historical reality—economic absorption—make the Government of Cuba the guardian of North American interests."[35] Such subservience hinders intellectual activity; Marinello writes that he and his peers have tried valiantly but in vain to build a public intellectual sphere, which he links with the possibility—or privilege—of having a claim to "contemporary unrest." As he laments, "Without extensive, free, and repeated exposure to these concerns in newspapers, magazines, and books, people cannot be expected to feel them as vital desires. Unrest is, in short, an atmospheric question and the atmosphere could not be built here."[36] Without economic and political independence or a public intellectual sphere, Marinello argues that Cubans are not in a position to participate in an international debate on contemporary unrest.

Moreover, the questionnaire's emphasis on the dehumanizing effects of mechanization signifies differently in Cuba because of its forced subordination to the United States in the labor market. The U.S. domination of the sugar industry in particular, Marinello argues, exemplifies how economic power standardizes and undermines local culture and erodes human dignity. Thus, "the global solution to the problem of industrialization will be the solution to the Cuban problem." He describes how Cuba's economic subjugation has politically paralyzed the populace and neutered intellectuals, while "the people, disoriented, hesitant, stunned by the magnitude of their problems . . . have not been able to incorporate new forms of unrest into their motives for public action."[37] For Marinello, economic liberation is the only way to escape such oppression.

Although Marinello argues that these "delaying, dominant forces extend to the intellectual," stymieing cultural activity, he nevertheless suggests that new

cultural developments can "resonate with vital dissatisfactions" that might lead
to productive change: "Our political reality gives way to despair. Our intellectual, artistic reality gives rise to hope."[38] In both literature and art Marinello
notes that the *vanguardia* "drank from France and Spain," but that "these new
modes have nurtured *criollo* essences: when they were used as tools to capture
their own, rather than as formulas to make fashionable art."[39] Here Marinello
echoes Carpentier's position on utilizing European forms but autochthonous
source material. By way of example, Marinello cites Afro-Cuban music, which,
he writes, "initiated a path to the essentially vernacular, that is, the universal."
While Marinello acknowledges the harsh economic realities that keep Cuba
subject to U.S. interests, he suggests that culturally Cuba might produce work
that is at once local and "universal."

Much like Marinello in his impassioned analysis of Cuba's political and
artistic position, José Carlos Mariátegui—the editor of *Amauta*, who was
committed to the indigenous cause in Peru—responded to the questionnaire
through the lens of Peru's economic and political struggles. He published his
response in Spanish in *Mundial* in Lima only eighteen days before his death.
(Marinello and Mariátegui refer to each other in their responses.) Mariátegui
argues that "one cannot speak of a 'contemporary unrest' as the uniform and
mysterious spiritual preparation for a new world" since the category of "contemporary unrest" could potentially contain every political position, from
Marxism to fascism.[40] Although Mariátegui insists that the questionnaire
cannot result in anything but "a disorienting plurality of propositions" (likely
true of all questionnaires), he does agree that, as in all "ages of transition and
crisis," there is an "unrest specific to our time." However, he notes, just as in
avant-garde art, wherein elements of revolution and decadence can become
confused, "in 'contemporary unrest' the fictional, intellectual, pragmatic faith
of those that encounter their equilibrium in dogmas and in an ancient order is
confused with the impassioned, risky, heroic faith of those dangerously fighting
for the victory of a new order."[41] He warns against this danger and reiterates
that "unrest appears as a great crisis of conscience." It cannot be resolved
with theories of modernity and the new spirit alone, he maintains, but must
be fought in terms of economic and political progress. Regarding *inquiétude*,
Mariátegui suggests that artists and thinkers "refuse, either out of pride or fear,
to see in its instability and anguish the reflection of the crisis of capitalism."[42]
Echoing both Marinello and Dos Passos, Mariátegui argues that any common
experience of unrest stems from capitalist exploitation and thus should not be
sentimentalized.

Other Latin Americans responding to the inquiry consider the effects of
contemporary unrest on creative output. Ildefonso Pereda Valdés, the Uruguayan folklorist who also participated in the *Revista de Avance* questionnaire
and the "meridian debate," writes that each era has its own unrest. In this one,

such unrest is "expressed by great disorientation," which, in poetry, "takes the form of cosmopolitanism. No literature has suffered more from contagion by mechanistic anxiety than the current Frenchified literature."[43] (It is notable that he condemns "Frenchified literature" in a French magazine.) In opposition to such work, Pereda Valdés lauds the development of autochthonous art, which he also attributes to contemporary unrest: "creative activity lives and feeds on contemporary unrest. In all eras something new has been created because creative activity is inexhaustible. Our age has created social ideas and socialist art. . . . Mexico and Peru give very visible examples of this artistic innovation, which absolutely corresponds to the problems of race in these countries."[44] Like Pereda Valdés, Alberto Hidalgo, a Peruvian poet writing from Argentina, acknowledges a certain spiritual dependency on Europe. Yet he too concludes, "We imitate Europe, but we are transforming it," that is, through the invocation of indigenous subject matter.[45]

While writers from across the Americas describe their struggles with the material and political conditions of art-making, the Spanish writer Guillermo de Torre contests the presumption that one can belong to a shared contemporary moment at all. He proposes that *Cahiers* instead reframe its premise as a question and ask, "Is there an era that we can call ours, with its own characteristics and a perfectly differentiated set of features?" To be contemporary, he continues, would mean to distinguish between groups with wildly different intellectual positions, that is, between those who are "adjusting their intellectual conduct to rigorously contemporary laws and postulates and those who, more skeptical and less insightful, fail to distinguish the boundaries specific to the present time, remaining subject to outdated beliefs or dogmas."[46] De Torre argues that a model of copresence is impossible because of such competing, achronic ideas. Such disequilibrium produces variegated forms of dissatisfaction internationally, creating friction rather than any kind of coherent or universal "contemporary unrest."

Perhaps what we can learn from *Cahiers de l'Étoile*'s questionnaire on "contemporary unrest," then, is that, due to varying cultural and political experiences, few can agree on the intellectual texture of their time or its geographic span. Yet every era sees itself in a state of crisis that requires reflection. Whether it be 1930 or today, when unequal economic conditions, dehumanizing technologies, and wars threaten the production of—increasingly commodified—art and literature, many artists and writers are aware of an overarching unrest, an attunement to which might in fact be what constitutes the "contemporary." Questionnaires issued from the 1920s onward create a lineage that tests the limits of terms like the "avant-garde" or the "contemporary." Thereafter, questionnaires explored relationships between artists, art movements, and political causes, and also continued to periodize, even while calling the possibility of periodization into question.

Cahiers de l'Étoile's questionnaire on "contemporary unrest" capped a decade of surveys examining the tension between national and international artistic developments, particularly with respect to the relationship between European culture and a burgeoning art of the Americas. While *Cahiers* focused on the category of the "contemporary," the formations "modern" and "avant-garde" were consistently questioned throughout the 1920s and 1930s. In the context of Latin America, *Lampadario* in Ecuador (later called *Élan*) put out a questionnaire in 1931 asking, "What Is the Avant-Garde?," which included a question on the "importance of nativism in the international avant-garde."[47] In 1932 the Mexican magazine *El Universal Ilustrado* asked, "Is the Avant-Garde Generation in Crisis?"[48] Responses to these questionnaires deliberately resisted the impulse to "Europeanize," as one contributor noted.[49] Similar questions were also being issued internationally, as evidenced by *La Gaceta Literaria*'s 1930 questionnaire asking, "What Is the Avant-Garde?," or the *New York Times Magazine*'s recap of a 1931 survey, "What Is Modern Art?"[50] The simultaneity of these anxieties, crystallized in the form of questions, demonstrates how print communities throughout the Americas and elsewhere sought to define and participate in modernism and the avant-garde. By announcing and articulating their own, locally specific versions of what constituted the avant-garde, these magazines shifted its meaning away from an exclusively European lens—as in the case of *Lampadario*'s insertion of nativism into its questionnaire—thereby allowing regional and national differences to register in the rhetoric of the era.

In the increasingly polarized political climate of the 1930s, questionnaires too became more politically charged. One even remarked on this trend. In 1932 the American Marxist journal *Modern Quarterly* issued a questionnaire asking, "What position should the American writer take in the social crisis that confronts him?" The magazine's editor, V. F. Calverton, notes, "What is apparent from the answers to almost all these questionnaires is that American writers are already beginning to think in different terms from 1928. It is the impact of economic and social change which has made their attitudes alter."[51] Calverton explains that 1928—notably, the year *Revista de Avance* and *transition* issued their questionnaires, and when *Cahiers* first circulated its questions—was the year when he noticed that "politics and literature are no longer viewed as separate and conflicting categories."[52] The rise of a newly politicized literature led to self-reflection on the relationship between nationalism and culture in magazines and their questionnaires at the time.

This conflation of politics and art continued throughout the 1930s. In 1938 the New York–based magazine *Direction* asked, "Should the Nation Support Its Art?"[53] Similarly, *Partisan Review* published numerous surveys on the relationship between American literature and politics. Its 1936 questionnaire asked, "What is your conception of Americanism? Do you think of it as separate and opposed to the cultural tradition of Western Europe?"[54] Such a formulation echoes *transition*'s 1928 questionnaires, but more aggressively pits America against Europe. In 1939 the magazine followed up on this inquiry by asking, "Are you conscious, in your own writing, of the existence of a 'usable past'? Is this mostly American?" Writers were then asked to describe "the political tendency of American writing as a whole since 1930."[55] The magazine issued yet another set of questions in 1948, comparing the 1940s to the 1930s and asking things like "Can the difference between the two postwar periods be defined in relation to the European situation?"[56] These *Partisan Review* questionnaires sought to establish an American tradition distinct from that of Europe, amidst the political instability of the 1930s and 1940s.

Similarly, beyond the North American context, questionnaires from the 1930s problematized the political stakes of aesthetic platforms. For instance, "Should Art Serve a Social Purpose?" was issued by the Argentine magazine *Contra* in 1933 to Borges, Oliverio Girondo, and others. Borges also responded to "America and the Destiny of Western Civilization" issued by *Nosotros* in 1936 on what role Latin America and Argentina would play in the wake of European destruction as a result of World War II.[57] The turmoil of the decade began to divide artists and writers along political lines; in the 1937 survey on the Spanish Civil War issued by the British magazine *Left Review* writers were asked to take sides in support of either the Nationalists or the Spanish Republic.[58] In 1935, in regard to a different political project, the French magazine *Vu* asked, "What would you do if you had to organize the Exposition of 1937?" Additionally, a questionnaire on "war poetry" was issued in Algiers in the magazine *Fontaine* in 1939.[59] Print communities were clearly responding to a range of international concerns—the Spanish Civil War, the rise of communism and fascism, anticolonial independence movements, and World War II—and questionnaires in turn asked artists and writers to stake out positions in these volatile political debates.

Along with rising political anxieties, questions on art and audience persisted during this period, many of which cited and repurposed earlier questions. For instance, the "proletariat regionalist" magazine *New Quarterly* put out a questionnaire in 1934: "For Whom Do You Write? Replies from Forty American Writers."[60] *Commune*, a French communist publication, issued an identical questionnaire earlier the same year asking, "For Whom Do You Write?"[61] Such questions of audience have clear political connotations. Walter Benjamin notably commented on the *Commune* questionnaire and some of its answers in his essay "The Author as Producer."[62] Benjamin used the questionnaire to argue how a writer, despite his bourgeois origins, can express solidarity with the proletariat by reflecting on his position in the process of production. Questionnaires have long become part of the historical record through this kind of citation, that is, both the citation of prior questions by subsequent inquiries and the analysis of questionnaires by historians and critics.

Such repetition indicates the traction of certain shared concerns. In 1935 *Commune* issued another questionnaire asking, "Where Is Painting Going?," polling artists such as Amédee Ozenfant, Antonio Berni, André Derain, Fernand Léger, Marie Laurencin, Gustave Courbet, Yves Tanguy, Valentine Hugo, and Max Ernst.[63] Berni, an Argentine artist who traveled between Latin America and Europe, responded, "Each era and each class has its technical means of artistic expression in accordance with their feelings, concepts, and dominant ideology."[64] Berni then replied to the same question in a different context, this time defending *nuevo realismo* in the face of abstraction in response to "Where Is Painting Going?," issued by the Argentine magazine *Contrapunto* in 1945. The questionnaire was sent to Berni, as well as to Tomás Moldonado, Norah Borges, Emilio Pettoruti, Manuel Espinosa, and Joaquín Torres-García.[65] Such questions traveled between Europe and the Americas, just as many artists and writers did. Questionnaires served as opportunities for such artists to reflect on—as well as to shape—the historical moments and movements in which they participated.

The Persistence of the Genre

The genre expands and persists into the twenty-first century, urging artists and writers toward self- and collective definition in print. As the questionnaire proliferated, the questions that were posed fluctuated according to the political and aesthetic concerns that they tracked. For instance, many artists and writers fled Europe due to World War II, and this move was legible in questionnaires issued in the 1940s. In the Mexico City–based *Dyn*, edited by Wolfgang Paalen, and the New York–based Surrealist magazine *View*, edited by Charles Henri Ford, questionnaires revisited theories underlying Surrealism in the context of the Americas and the politics of World War II. Clement Greenberg, Pierre Mabille, and Philip Rahv responded to a questionnaire on dialectical materialism in *Dyn*, while Harold Rosenberg, Marianne Moore, William Carlos Williams, and Mina Loy replied to an inquiry on the world's drift "Towards the Unknown" in *View*.[66] Other questionnaires from the 1940s were economic in scope. "The Cost of Letters," printed in the British magazine *Horizon* in 1946, asked how much a writer needed to live and if it could be earned by writing; George Orwell, Elizabeth Bowen, and Dylan Thomas responded.[67] Social and economic concerns gave way to questions on emerging art movements in the 1950s. In Argentina a questionnaire was issued on abstraction and neorealism in the magazine *Ver y Estimar* in 1951, and the survey "Abstract Art or Nonfigurative Art?" appeared in 1952 in *Sur*. In 1954 *Letra y Linea* issued a "Questionnaire Among Argentine Painters of the New Generation," in some ways revisiting the 1923 *Nosotros* "Survey of a New Literary Generation."[68]

Questionnaires also remained vital platforms for debate in France in the decades following World War II. In 1959 Maurice Blanchot, along with André Breton and others, issued a "Survey of French Intellectuals" to gauge their resistance to Charles De Gaulle; respondents included Marguerite Duras and Roland Barthes.[69] The following year Barthes responded to a questionnaire on criticism in the journal *Positif* in 1960.[70] *Tel Quel* also printed two surveys in the

1960s; the first asked, "Do you think that you have a gift for writing?" and the second, "Why are you a critic and what are your criteria?"[71] In 1964 the Situationists issued a questionnaire to themselves, in order to respond to questions often posed to them, such as "What does the word 'situationist' mean?," "Are you Marxist?," and "What value can you attribute to a questionnaire?" In regard to this last question, they write that while the questionnaire is a kind of "pseudodialoguge," they can "reply by posing new questions that supersede the old ones."[72] That is, they can reinhabit the form to give it new meaning.

The malleability of the genre allows artists, writers, and critics to position themselves in an avant-garde lineage while superseding those who came before them, much as manifesto writers displace their forebears with bold new declarative platforms. American artists embraced the genre in the 1950s and 1960s, using it to reflect on their work and to insert themselves into an art-historical genealogy. For instance, Mark Rothko, Ad Reinhardt, and Helen Frankenthaler answered Irving Sandler's 1959 questionnaire in *ARTnews* asking, "Is There a New Academy?," affiliating themselves with this "new academy" through their responses. Sandler followed up in 1966, asking artists, "Is there a sensibility of the 60s? How would you characterize it? Is there an avant-garde today?"[73] (Sandler has continued to issue questionnaires, publishing one in 2012 in the *Brooklyn Rail* on the state of art criticism.)[74] These periodizing questions, much like those posed earlier on the "avant-garde" and the "contemporary," essentially invite artists to conceive of new group formations and to situate themselves within them.

For artists in the 1960s and 1970s, the magazine was often seen as an artistic medium itself, as well as a way to make art that circumvented the commercial gallery system and could be distributed on their own terms. Art historian Gwen Allen calls such magazines "oppositional site[s]," wherein artists experimented with the medium's "formal and conceptual possibilities."[75] It is notable that these magazines continued to employ the questionnaire even as they critically reimagined so many other aspects of the medium, including its materiality, ephemerality, seriality, and interactivity. The artist-run magazine *Art-Rite,* for instance, printed in New York from 1973 to 1978, published an "Idea Poll" in many of its issues, including a 1974 questionnaire asking, "Do you think there is a shared female artistic sensibility in the work of female artists?" The questionnaire surveyed artists such as Laurie Anderson, Lynda Benglis, Judy Chicago, Joan Jonas, and Agnes Martin; only Judy Chicago responds in the affirmative that art by women shared a "female sensibility."[76]

Artists' reinvention of the magazine as a medium reflected the rise of new art practices in the 1960s and 1970s, including land art, performance art, and conceptual art, which informed questionnaires of the era. For example, in 1975 *Artforum* issued a survey on the obsolescence of painting to artists such as R. B. Kitaj, Allan McCollum, and Joan Snyder. As if assuming painting's demise, the questionnaire began, "*Artforum* wishes to ask you, as a painter, what you

ARTFORUM

667 MADISON AVENUE   NEW YORK, N.Y. 10021
838-6820

ARTFORUM wishes to ask you, as a painter, what you consider to be the prospects of painting in this decade. It appears that painting has ceased to be the dominant artistic medium at the moment. And we assume that the debates between its two major ideologies, abstract and representational, have outlived their usefulness to the current scene. Our thinking here refers to the fact that neither side has triumphed over the other in a historical verdict to which both had appealed. On the contrary, those understood to be making "the next inevitable step" now work with any material but paint.

1. How do you think this has affected the need to do painting today and the general morale in the field?

2. What possibilities, not found elsewhere, does this medium offer you as an artist?

3. What energies and ideas in painting strike you as worth attention, and why?

PAINTERS REPLY . . .

RUDOLF BARANIK: The media used in making "the next inevitable step" may be anything but paint, you say. I will not argue with that, nor with the nonsubstantiated "those understood to be making"-this-step reasoning, because it all seems to me a needless concern. Do you really believe that the debate between the abstract and the representational ended in a standstill because neither side triumphed, or was it not a sham battle, fought on the periphery, while the best on both sides secretly remained one?
1) You must not parcel out "fields" in such a seigniorial way, *Artforum*. I, for one, while a painter (tubes, brushes, cans of Rustoleum, rollers et al.) do not think of myself as being a fellow painter of, let's say, Fairfield Porter. I do recognize *fellow artists*: late Reinhardt; middle Segal; Robert Morris of *Hearing*; Munch of *Voices*; Ingmar Bergman before he deteriorated; the slow holistic pulsation of an Agnes Martin; the surreal brink of Acconci's defending space. Some others.

How is the morale in the field? In the field of understated expressionist power fused with fine nerve-ends of formal sensibility—splendid.
2) Obviously, painting does offer some possibilities not found in other media, and very specific ones come to mind: subtle value and chromatic relationships find unique hospitality on stable, flat ground. But this is only a route, and as a painter I happen to be most familiar with it. However, what really matters, both formal values and the power to convey feeling, I grant other media without hesitation.
3) The energies and ideas in painting which merit attention may seem technically unique, but they are not autonomous in a significant sense. Medium partisanship is always naive and can be harnessed for both—desperate forced innovation and nostalgic retrograde conservatism. Thus—no hailing of new media and no mourning for Winsor & Newton.

As for the inevitable next step, I know only one: Socialism.

GENE DAVIS: For the past decade or so, it has become increasingly apparent that advanced art must rely, in large measure, on the manipulation of context to achieve its gains. It is an old and, by now, familiar device: simply take another discipline, shift it into the visual art context and you have advanced art. For example, Joseph Kosuth (language and philosophy), Vito Acconci and Chris Burden (theater), Robert Irwin (architecture), Robert Smithson (landscape architecture), Hanne Darboven and Mel Bochner (mathematics), Roy Lichtenstein and Andy Warhol (advertising and comic art) and Joseph Beuys (politics).

Now that the right to utilize context has been decisively won for all artists, perhaps we can look at painting again with some perspective. It is simply one of the numerous available visual arts media in which the artist can, in 1975, work with brilliant or not so brilliant results, depending upon his innate gifts and application. Al Held and a few others are good examples. Like most of the other disciplines, it has its clearly defined limits. It may well be that the best painters today are not worrying so much about the "next inevitable step" as they are about extending the limits of the painting medium itself or, perhaps, working within those limits. As every art student today knows, manipulation of context in the late '60s manner is by now a game anybody can play. However, these comments should in no way be construed as a diatribe against recent advanced art, of which I am an avid and vocal supporter. I simply am somewhat surprised at the assumption implicit in your questionnaire.

After all, the interment of painting is a hardy perennial and *Artforum* is at the bottom of a long and distinguished list of mourners. Wasn't it Malevich's *White Square on White* (c. 1918) that was supposed to have signaled the death of painting shortly after World War I? Before that, in the 19th century, wasn't the introduction of the daguerreotype regarded as the coup de grace to painting? In our own time, didn't Ad Reinhardt characterize his works as "the last paintings that can be painted?"

To paraphrase one of your questions, what do you

Fig. 19 "Painters Reply," *Artforum* (New York) 14, no. 1 (September 1975): 26. © *Artforum*, September 1975, "Painters Reply."

consider to be the prospects of painting in this decade. It appears that painting has ceased to be the dominant artistic medium at the moment," and then included questions such as "What possibilities, not found elsewhere, does this medium offer you as an artist? What energies and ideas in painting strike you as worth attention and why?"[77] (fig. 19). The responses range from Gene Davis's cheeky retort, "What do you consider to be the prospects of *earthworks* in this decade?," to Dona Nelson's defiant comment, "I do not make abstract painting in order to 'triumph' over representational painting; I make it because I would rather paint than do anything else."[78] Although painting was the recurrent subject of anxious questionnaires throughout history—such as the 1935 survey "Where Is Painting Going?," issued by *Commune* in Paris, and a similar one published in 1945 by *Contrapunto* in Buenos Aires—this particular inquiry indicated a shift in both art-making and the use of the questionnaire, which in the 1960s and 1970s was increasingly put in service of the kinds of dematerialized art projects that destabilized the prominence of painting.

Conceptual Art and Museum Questionnaires

While questionnaires continued to be issued in art magazines in the 1960s and 1970s, they were concomitantly seen by a new generation of artists as useful tools for sociological inquiry and institutional critique. Conceptual art, which emerged in the mid-1960s as a critical reflection on the institution of art and the political and economic systems that sustained it, typically minimized or even eliminated the object in favor of language- and idea-based work. As part of this trend toward the "dematerialization" of the art object, questionnaires not only served to poll a community of artists, but also allowed artists to poll the public.[79] Thus, questionnaires such as *Artforum*'s 1975 survey on the obsolescence of painting were being issued just as conceptual artists were themselves using and transforming the genre to challenge the primacy of the material art object. Questionnaires became the basis for many conceptual works of the era, the best known of which is Hans Haacke's *MoMA Poll* (1970; fig. 20). Haacke asked museum visitors to place "yes" and "no" slips into marked boxes in response to the question "Would the fact that Governor Rockefeller has not denounced President Nixon's Indochina Policy be a reason for you not to vote for him in November?" Haacke also issued a visitor poll at Documenta in 1972, and has continued to issue them throughout his career, including at the Reina Sofía in 2012 and the Venice Biennale in 2015.[80] In a different gesture of institutional critique, as part of a larger project on sanitation and labor the artist Mierle Laderman Ukeles issued *The Maintenance Art Questionnaire* (1973–76) to artists and others, asking things like "What is the relationship in your life between maintenance and freedom?"[81] Such questionnaires played on the medium's relationship to social science.[82] For other artists, the questionnaire was itself a compelling subject. Clearly parodying the form, in 1968 the Fluxus artist Benjamin Patterson created a piece that says, "Please answer this question carefully: Yes or No."[83] Artistic practices from this period take the role of the questionnaire seriously, as in the case of Haacke or Laderman Ukeles, and also point to its limits, as in the Fluxus piece, indicating its use at the time for multiple, diverse ends.[84]

The appropriation of the questionnaire by conceptual artists occurred throughout the Americas. Inspired by Haacke, the Chilean artist Alfredo Jaar, as part of a multipronged project called *Studies on Happiness* (1979–81), asked Chileans living under Pinochet's dictatorship "Are you happy?," to which they responded by dropping candies into two different Plexiglas boxes marked "yes" and "no."[85] The Argentine group Tucumán Arde—formed in 1968 to expose a government plan to cover up the weakening economic situation in the Tucumán region of Argentina—also used questionnaires in their work. In *Datos de Tucumán (datos de interés)* (October 1968) the group polled the population of Tucumán about the labor, health, and education conditions in the region. The resulting data became part of an exhibition documenting the economic situation in Tucumán and functioned as an alternative information network,

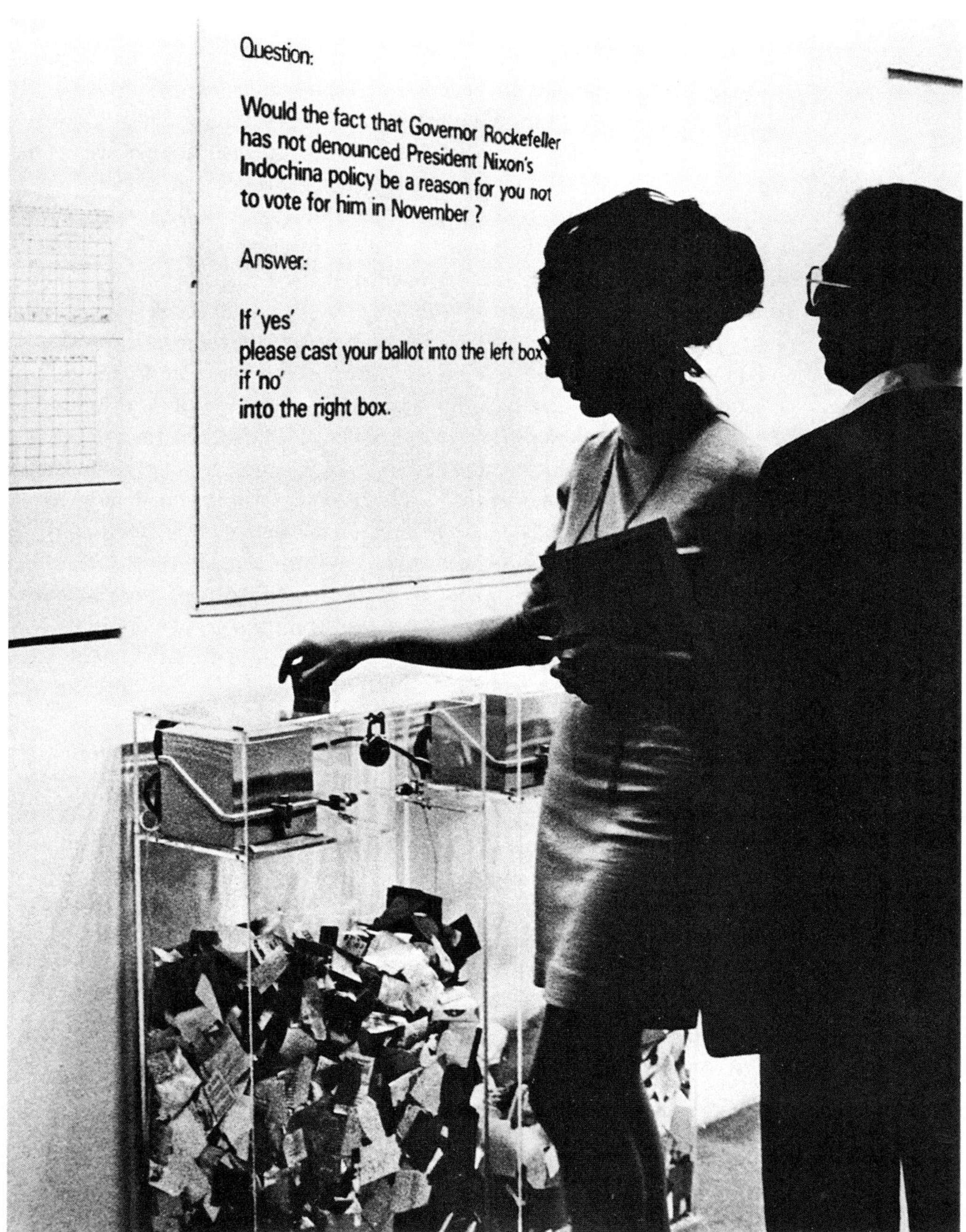

Fig. 20 Hans Haacke, *MOMA-Poll*, 1970. Two transparent ballot boxes with automatic counters, color-coded ballots. Boxes each 40 × 20 × 10 in. (101.6 × 50.8 × 25.4 cm); paper ballot: 3 × 2 ½ in. (7.6 × 6.4 cm). © Hans Haacke / Artists Rights Society (ARS), New York / VG Bild-Kunst, Bonn.

countering that of the dictatorship of General Juan Carlos Onganía. In these examples artists used the tools of bureaucracy, signified by the questionnaire, to elide and resist government oppression.[86]

Other Latin American artists developed questionnaire-based work while in exile. A more playful use of the genre was the project *Minucodes* (1968), produced by the Argentine artist Marta Minujín in New York. She issued questionnaires to participants through local newspapers and gathered the respondents together for cocktail parties, which she then filmed.[87] Similarly tackling the New York art world's social milieu, the Chilean artist Juan Downey created *A Research on the Art World* (1970), which consisted of a series of questionnaires issued to artists, collectors, curators, and critics, whose responses he graphed in a series of drawings. In France, a group of Argentine artists called the Groupe de Recherche d'Art Visuel (GRAV; Visual Art Research Group) printed the pamphlet *Une journée dans la rue* (A day in the street) in 1966, containing a map of interactive activities and a questionnaire asking the public their opinions on art.[88] Such work targeted other artists or the public, demonstrating the whimsical possibilities of the questionnaire as a form.

Curators looking to display conceptual work from the period also deployed questionnaires. For the 1970 exhibition *Information* that he organized at the Museum of Modern Art, curator Kynaston McShine sent out a questionnaire to artists asking, 'How do you want to be represented in the catalogue? Photographs of the piece in the show? Photographs of a previous piece? Any other way?"[89] Under the last question, the Dutch artist Jan Dibbets wrote, "by this paper" and reproduced the questionnaire in full as his catalogue entry.[90] For their contribution to the catalogue, the Argentine collective Grupo Frontera printed sixty-two questions about subjects such as love, suicide, theft, and marriage. The *Information* catalogue also contained a detailed description of Haacke's *MoMA Poll*, which premiered in the show. In sum these entries demonstrated once again the elasticity of the questionnaire and its currency among artists at the time.[91]

The exhibition reflected on and was constituted by different types of information technologies, including the questionnaire. Such media allowed a geographically dispersed group of artists to transmit their work internationally and to engage with a wide audience. Conversely, such forms of communication also enabled the audience to participate in some of the work, orchestrated by artists in ways that McShine describes as "quite often as in a game; at other times it seems almost therapeutic, making us question ourselves and our responses to unfamiliar stimuli." He argues that the artists in the exhibition were "asking that we reassess what we have always taken for granted as our accepted and culturally conditioned aesthetic response to art."[92] Artists used such media, including the questionnaire, to challenge the status of art. Questionnaires made it possible for both artists and audiences to be a part of this new culture of "information;" they drew attention to the institutional apparatus of art and also allowed viewers to question their "culturally conditioned aesthetic response" to it.

Even before questionnaires were adopted by conceptual artists, museums had long considered them part of their practice. For instance, the Museum of Modern Art issues questionnaires to every living artist whose work enters its collection. In 1945 Alfred Barr Jr., the Museum of Modern Art's first director, asked Max Ernst to respond to the museum's questionnaire. Barr explained that "such information would be used by curators in caring for the works, by students, historians and critics for publication in books and articles, by lecturers in schools and colleges, for labels and gallery talks in the museum itself, so that the artist, the student, and the general public may benefit."[93] As Barr predicted, MoMA's questionnaires are cited as art-historical evidence in numerous contexts.[94] Quoted in curatorial texts and analyzed by art historians, artists' responses are viewed as providing unmediated access to an artist's position on their work at the time of its collection.

Questionnaires have also taken on a pedagogical function in an artistic context. Famously, in 1926 Barr devised a questionnaire on modern art as a preliminary exam for his students at Wellesley College, listing fifty artists, writers, and movements and asking, "What is the significance of each of the following in relation to modern artistic expression?" Barr's questionnaire was then recirculated in print when *Vanity Fair* published it in 1927.[95] Such dalliances with pedagogy, museum practices, and art-making suggest the capaciousness of the genre. Nevertheless, the questionnaire has primarily persisted as a means of polling artists and writers through magazines, even in the contemporary period. What unites all of these iterations of the questionnaire is the perception that the genre can help situate an artwork, artist, or tendency within a geographic framework, historical period, or group formation. As such, the questionnaire continues to feverishly mark the passage of time, especially in the context of visual art and in the academy.

The Contemporary Questionnaire

While the manifesto has largely waned in use, the questionnaire remains an active forum for debate, particularly in the sphere of contemporary art. Its co-option by conceptual artists and museums has not deterred magazines—such as *Flash Art*, *frieze*, and the *Brooklyn Rail*—from continuing to issue questionnaires. In recent years *Flash Art* has sent out surveys on the art market, painting, and the status of contemporary art in America, and *frieze* has a section called "questionnaire" at the back of every issue. As an editor of *frieze* explained, the questionnaire section, instituted after a redesign of the magazine in the early 2000s, was intended to be a quick and accessible way to draw in new readers.[96] Beyond practical motivations for issuing questionnaires, sustained interest in the form is telling; even as greater opportunities for communication and collaboration have emerged through mass media and digital culture, the questionnaire remains a powerful means by which to define and delineate a community in print.

Additionally, the questions themselves are revealing, and many of the same kinds of questions that were issued in the 1920s and 1930s continue to surface today. Notably, in 2013 *Flash Art* stoked the persistent anxiety about the status of painting by asking, "Is Painting Still Vital, or Is It a Dead Language?," echoing questions issued by *Artforum*, *Contrapunto*, and *Commune* over the past century.[97] Oscillation between ideas of newness and obsolescence also continues to pervade questionnaires. For instance, in 2012 the *Brooklyn Rail* asked artists such as Matthew Day Jackson and LaToya Ruby Frazier what "newness" means in their work, while in 2002 *October* polled artists such as Luis Camnitzer, Martha Rosler, and Zoe Leonard about the role of obsolescence in theirs.[98] Questions on audience also remain prevalent. The *Brooklyn Rail* issued Irving Sandler's questionnaire on art criticism in 2012, reviving similar questions issued throughout the previous century by asking, "Is there a crisis in criticism? For what audience do you write?"[99] In a related gesture, *frieze* polled critics in 2012, asking, "Who do you write for? What purpose do you think your criticism serves? Do you write with a particular audience in mind?," recalling questionnaires issued by *Tel Quel*, the *New Quarterly*, *Commune,* and the Surrealists before them.[100] Such questions demonstrate both the tenacity of the form and the way that certain concerns endure across geographic and historical contexts.

Today the questionnaire has also been taken up by the academy. For example, Fredric Jameson and Homi Bhabha both responded to a questionnaire on the future of theory issued by the journal *Critical Inquiry* in 2004.[101] The architecture and criticism magazine *Assemblage* also issued a questionnaire on theory in 2000, asking, "What are the possible new formats . . . for the exposition and dissemination of theory?" Much like the poetic or artistic avant-garde, academic journals paradoxically employ a seemingly empirical tool to debate subjects as unwieldy as theory itself. They do so with little attention to the history of the genre. For example, the journal *October* frequently turns to the questionnaire, and has polled its contributors on topics such as visual culture, feminism, the invasion of Iraq, and materialism.[102] One of *October*'s editors, Hal Foster, acknowledges that the journal does not use the questionnaire because of its origins as an avant-garde form, a history that it has not critically examined, but rather, *October* has adopted it to "be polemical in an age that cannot support manifestos." In particular, Foster explains, *October* issues questionnaires "to address a problem that no one person could be tasked with," such as "discursive formations on the rise."[103]

In this vein, *October* published a "Questionnaire on 'The Contemporary'" in 2009 to respond to the idea of contemporary art and its institutionalization.[104] Only one of the questionnaire's respondents explicitly cites the genre's long history. Michelle Kuo, a former editor of *Artforum*, argues that "to glean something about the situation of contemporary art, we might look to the genre of the questionnaire itself." She then offers a provisional genealogy of the form, writing that "it was invented by Sir Francis Galton, that nineteenth-century champion of statistical metrics and visual classification; then deployed in various forms by the Surrealists, Experiments in Art and Technology, and Hans Haacke, to name a few." In addition to offering an abbreviated history of the questionnaire, Kuo also connects the genre to an "eruption of crisis." The questionnaire, she writes, "is a tool of risk management, of damage control. . . . Surveys are part of an attempt to find causality. Yet they often highlight the very absence of it."[105] The impulse, she suggests, is to invoke the reassuring rigidity of the questionnaire form to allay anxieties during historical or aesthetic crises. Her contribution indicates how an interrogation of the contemporary through the questionnaire requires self-reflection on the history of the genre as well.

Embedded in the *October* inquiry is the task of defining what it means to be "contemporary," a question of periodization that echoes the 1930 *Cahiers de l'Étoile* survey on "contemporary unrest." The Italian philosopher Giorgio Agamben similarly sought to define the "contemporary" in a series of lectures in 2008 wherein he asked, "What is the contemporary? . . . Of whom and of what are we contemporaries? . . . What does it mean to be contemporary?" In his lectures Agamben was interested in the notion of being of one's time. He argues that those who are contemporary do not coincide with the time in which they live nor adjust themselves to its demands. Rather, it is this critical distance, this sense of disconnection and anachronism, which enables one to better perceive and grasp one's own time. For Agamben, to be contemporary means to be at once of one's time and out of sync with it.[106] This notion of untimeliness is useful for understanding the logic of the questionnaire as well.

By issuing questionnaires, publications ranging from *Revista de Avance* to *October* are at once of their own time—that is, polling their peers to articulate their shared concerns—and also out of sync with it, inserting themselves back into literary history through the use of a genre with its own conventions and genealogy. The form and function of the questionnaire persist, even as its subject changes. Shifts from the Enlightenment, to modernism, to the avant-garde, to the contemporary are inscribed in the history of the genre, and likewise many related questions explicitly thematize time, periodization, and art's potential obsolescence. Asking whether "Impressionism is finished" in the late nineteenth century or if "art has a female sensibility" in the 1970s, questionnaires all reveal a desire to actively participate in and shape one's historical moment. Both of and outside their own time, questionnaires, their respondents, and the communities that they generate are, in this way, contemporary.

CONCLUSION: INTERROGATING PRINT CULTURE

The questionnaire embodies the tension between individual practice and group affiliation that characterized the avant-garde, in this way resembling the magazine as a medium. Magazines are structured by the juxtaposition of different forms of writing, and by the copresence of diverse contributors, much like responses to questionnaires. As a result of these affinities, magazines themselves are well suited to be interrogated by the questionnaire, a genre that brings together multiple, potentially contradictory, voices to comment on its underlying concerns. The magazine has repeatedly been subject to the scrutiny of the questionnaire, and three surveys issued on magazines at different historical moments—1924, 1976, and 2006—offer insights into how the genre is inextricable from its vehicle.

In 1924 the journal *Belles-Lettres* in Paris issued a questionnaire on "Avant-Garde Magazines: 1870–1914," asking poets, critics, and artists, who were also editors, the following questions: "What were the leanings of (the magazine) of which you were one of the leaders? What motivated you to rally those who collaborated on it? Do you think that (the magazine) has had any influence on the literature of the time, or has contributed to the formation of literature today? What are the ideas that seem to have triumphed and who were, in your group, the main initiators? Among current journals, are there any that seem to perpetuate the tradition that you have pursued?"[1] The magazines in question, according to *Belles-Lettres* editors Maurice Caillard and Charles Forot, "must be consulted to write the literary history of Symbolism, Naturism, Unanimism, and all of the other *isms* that followed, from 1870 to 1914."[2] Many of those that they list—the *Mercure de France*, *La Plume*, *La Revue Blanche*—had also issued questionnaires themselves, underscoring the feedback loop created by the genre.

Like the editors of *Cahiers de l'Étoile* in their 1930 questionnaire on "contemporary unrest," the editors of *Belles-Lettres* cite World War I as indelibly demarcating the era. As a result of the war, the editors observe, "writers are no longer part of a group, an art circle, a school, but [rather] a section, a company, a regiment." Those who survived the war, they continue, "sought, in the tumult of a great era, to create a new literature."[3] Taking the war as a historical and literary marker, the questionnaire reflects on movements that were truncated by it to determine the relationship between those "isms" and the magazines that supported them.

Through the questionnaire, figures such as Jean Cocteau, Paul Valéry, and F. T. Marinetti had a platform from which to advocate for their movements and magazines, and to historicize their contributions to the avant-garde. For instance, in his response Marinetti celebrates Futurism and the magazines that supported it, such as *Poesia*, *Italia Futurista*, and *Roma Futurista*, and he proclaims Futurism's influence "in all of the capitals of Europe and America."[4] The questionnaire culminates with a chronological compendium of French avant-garde magazines published in the period surveyed (1870–1914) and their corresponding editors, after which Caillard and Forot note, "This questionnaire was not like the others, because it was out to prove something. It will therefore be both easier and harder to conclude. We wanted to show that 'little magazines,' that is, avant-garde journals, have a certain usefulness, as the history of literature and ideas is written there daily."[5] The editors make their agenda explicit: to demonstrate that the history of art and literature is written in magazines. As Ezra Pound affirms a few years later, "The history of contemporary letters has, to a very manifest extent, been written in such magazines."[6] The *Belles-Lettres* questionnaire gave those polled a forum in which to map out the era, while foregrounding the centrality of magazines to literary history.

After outlining the history of the avant-garde through its magazines, the editors then emphasize the role of the questionnaire in print culture. They assert that it is "through questionnaires, courteous debates, lively and ever-useful polemics" that magazines reach new solutions to literary questions and thereby propel literature forward.[7] The questionnaire, according to this formulation, reinforces the role of the magazine in literary development; it is a self-referential genre that reflects on the magazine's function within its own pages. The questionnaire enables magazines to at once interrogate and advance the history of literature and art. By invoking the questionnaire, *Belles-Lettres* underscores its own purpose, while acknowledging the pioneering efforts of the magazines that came before it.

In the case of *Belles-Lettres*, these "courteous debates" and "lively polemics" examined the task of producing an art or literary magazine, and questionnaires continued to do so for years to come. In 1976 the British art journal *Studio International* issued "A Survey of Contemporary Art Magazines" to *Avalanche*,

File, *Art in America*, and other art magazines of the time to better understand their practical underpinnings and aesthetic motivations. Richard Cork, *Studio International*'s editor, explains that "art magazines are usually regarded as unapproachable, autocratic monoliths." Cork hopes that "the replies to this questionnaire might help to open up this situation, and make us all more aware of the context in which we operate."[8] Many of the questions address logistics, such as "What are your sources of income? How many members of staff do you employ? How many copies of each issue do you print? What is your scale of payment for writers?" Such transparency was unprecedented, particularly in regard to a magazine's financial backers, its relationship with advertisers, and the amount it paid writers. In this way, the questionnaire reflected its era much as the *Belles-Lettres* questionnaire had; instead of historicizing and centralizing the magazine's contributions to literary culture post–World War I, *Studio International* expressed a commitment to transparency at a time when many artists were frustrated with an increasingly opaque and commercialized art world.

Beyond these practical and financial concerns, the 1976 survey probed magazines' editorial platforms and their relationship to contemporary art, asking, "Do you support a partisan area of art activity, or remain open to every new development? Are you happy about the influence that art magazines exert on the development of contemporary art?" Replies came from Anglo-American magazines such as *Art-Rite*, *Artforum*, and *Flash Art*; *Audio Arts*, a British magazine published as a cassette tape; as well as international magazines such as the Polish *CDN*, the Portuguese *Coloquio/Artes*, and others from Australia, France, Denmark, Italy, West Germany, Switzerland, Yugoslavia, and Israel. Such internationalism highlights the unique capacity of the magazine—and the questionnaire—to cull contributors from across nations.

Many editors were ambivalent about their magazine's relationship to criticism and their potential influence on contemporary art. For instance, Peter Hutton of *Art & Australia* writes, "How much influence *do* the art magazines exert on the development of contemporary art? If in publicizing 'contemporary' art they lead to a rash of derivative work, the answer must be no, we are not happy. If, on the other hand, they stimulate artists to explore previously unexplored territory, the answer must be yes. In the sense that art magazines carry reports, they are merely recording history rather than originating ideas."[9] While Hutton felt uneasy about the role of magazines in promulgating certain forms of art, other editors puzzled over how to determine their effect on the production and reception of art, and on the market. The artist-driven publication *Art-Rite* took a philosophical approach to its relationship to contemporary art: "Perhaps in some way the magazine exists to be a visual and cognitive spectacle as separate as possible from the itinerary of the art and artists it involves," the editors observe, suggesting that the magazine is itself a kind of art project.[10] The questionnaire provided a space for this sort of vacillation, and an opportunity to critically examine one's editorial policies in relation to those of one's peers. Ultimately, it served as a site for self-reflection on the work of putting out a magazine.

Studio International also polled itself. Cork responded on the magazine's behalf, declaring that its central task was "to commission a body of considered opinion from men and women who agree about the crucial need for personal, uncensored and informed art criticism."[11] Similarly, a questionnaire's function is to "commission a body of considered opinion" so as to jointly create "informed criticism," derived from those participating in the field. The range of responses to the "Survey of Contemporary Art Magazines" suggests that much like the magazine, the questionnaire facilitates aesthetic inquiry, showcasing strong, sometimes conflicting positions, which are instrumental to critical debate.

This meditation on the function of the magazine—and by extension, the questionnaire—was revisited when *frieze* reissued *Studio International*'s "Survey of Contemporary Art Magazines" in 2006. *frieze* polled many of the same journals that were included in the 1976 survey, such as *Art in America* and *Flash Art*, as well as newer magazines such as *Cabinet* and *Afterall*. Responses came from thirty-one publications. Like *Studio International*, *frieze* also responded to its own questionnaire. In its version *frieze* asked, "How do art magazines perceive themselves today? Are the questions that were posed thirty years ago still relevant in 2006?" In his introduction to the reissue, Richard Cork ruminates on his impulse to initiate the questionnaire thirty years prior: "Magazines, I believed, needed to question themselves more closely and become more willing to reveal how and why they operated. So I was delighted when so many of them responded to *Studio*'s questionnaire, casting off secrecy and disclosing a great deal about their owners, income sources, conditions of work, overall aims, anxieties and hopes for the future."[12] In the 1970s the magazine as a medium had been consolidated—much like the gallery and museum—as a market-driving apparatus, yet it also offered a space where artists could contest the logic of such institutions. Arguably, such transparency was even more urgently needed in the globalized art world of 2006. The economics of publishing and the production of art had certainly intensified in the intervening years.

Perhaps reflecting the frenzied pace of the art world and its relationship to commerce, many editors responding in 2006 hailed their mission as promoting artists and were quick to disavow their influence. Elizabeth Baker, the editor of *Art in America*, writes in this vein: "We remain skeptical about the influence of art magazines. Artists necessarily take the lead in art's development. This is not to downplay the critic's role. As vehicles for criticism and history, magazines play a crucial part in the exchange of ideas, the transmission of images and the documentation of art activity. . . . As magazines now take their place in this expanded context, they also must examine a changed terrain."[13] While Baker recognizes magazines' "crucial part in the exchange of ideas," she suggests that they must nevertheless follow the lead of artists. Much as in its 1976 iteration, this version of the questionnaire prompted ambivalent reflections on the evolving dynamic between art and magazines.

Baker's answer concludes by noting the "expanded context" and "changed terrain" that art magazines inhabit. Other respondents sought to make sense of their place in this "expanded context" and to determine their magazine's relationship with its readers accordingly. Michal Wolinski, editor of the Polish magazine *Piktogram*, cites Haacke's polls: "There was a questionnaire made by Hans Haacke for one of his exhibitions in the 1970s to analyze the visitors' profile. I have no illusions as to who is interested in reading texts about art. I hope I'm wrong though."[14] By bringing up Haacke's work, Wolinski invokes the multiple uses of the questionnaire, and expresses dissatisfaction with the range of his audience. Other responses also allude to the imbrication of the magazine with the genre of the questionnaire. Christian Höller, editor of the Austrian magazine *Springerin*, argues that "more important than trying to influence art production is trying to start a dialogue and critical exchange with the respective producers, particularly as regards the international institutions and discourses they find themselves in."[15] Echoing Baker, Höller suggests that the magazine is an outlet and impetus for "dialogue and critical exchange." Similarly, the questionnaire enables a community to engage with the ideas that unite or divide them. In these ways, polls issued on magazines reinforce the shared qualities of the questionnaire and the magazine as a medium.

These three questionnaires—from 1924, 1976, and 2006—demonstrate how the genre was continuously reanimated throughout the modern and contemporary periods to assess the magazine itself. Questionnaires have long served as privileged points of entry into a self-reflexive history of art and literature, of which magazines are crucial archival artifacts. By reconciling the philosophical mode of questioning with the magazine's commercial function, questionnaires generate a history of art and literature written by its participants. This is not a singular, dominant discourse, but a polyphonic field of responses, available to be mined for meaning. The genre allows us to pose generative questions that ultimately have no definitive answers, which may be why it continues to have currency today.

It is striking that the questionnaire has remained so viable. The magazine was an integral part of the growth of mass media, a prototype for the kind of transnational collaboration that we now take for granted. Like the magazine, the questionnaire models a form of communication that prefigured our networked, globalized society. Yet in an age of digital media, the questionnaire—whether issued online or in a print magazine—has endured largely unaltered since the height of print culture in the early twentieth century. The genre held great sway during the 1920s and 1930s, a time when magazines were the key tools writers and artists used to work through issues of local significance alongside international models of modernism. So influential was the use of the questionnaire by magazines during this period that the genre has persisted as a means of self-definition in print throughout the twentieth and into the twenty-first century. While manifestos are typically associated with the historical avant-garde, questionnaires continue to structure aesthetic conversations, as evidenced by the innumerable surveys issued by magazines today. This persistence attests to the genre's adaptability, and the sustained appeal of its invitation to debate.

Cumulatively, questionnaires comprise a compendium of anxieties, which we can analyze to better understand concepts of modernism, the avant-garde, the contemporary, and other frameworks for identification. In his reflections on modernism, Raymond Williams argues that we must work to rewrite history from the viewpoint of the future, recuperating those narratives that have been overlooked or reified. He asserts, "We must search out and counterpose an alternative tradition taken from the neglected works left in the wide margin of the century, a tradition which may address itself . . . to a modern future in which community may be imagined again."[16] Williams seeks to recover those works that were not appropriated by the market, so as to build an alternative, *future* history of modernism, one based on the idea of community. Questionnaires offer testimonies that have long been seen as marginal, but that could reorient our understanding of modernism.

This expanded model of modernism could best be summarized by the deceptively simple questionnaire "Do We Have an International Culture?," issued by the French magazine *Créer* in 1925.[17] Responses came from a diverse set of writers, including Thomas Hardy, Pio Baroja, Miguel de Unamuno, Paul Valéry, and Henri Barbusse, and the questionnaire was republished in several magazines. Today, reflecting back on modernism, we must ask this question again: Did we have an international culture? The answer is twofold; while artists and writers of the 1920s responding to questionnaires were clearly positioning themselves in an international field, they also fiercely retained their national and local identities. Such alliances drew upon centralized notions of modernism but could not be wholly assimilated into "an international culture." Rather, as the difficulty in answering this question suggests, these print communities model complex, variegated modernisms, the conflicted allegiances of which are articulated in response to questionnaires.

By reanimating these archives of magazines and their questions, we can reconstruct a history of modernism and the avant-garde as it was in formation, so as to reorient our understanding of the field today. Despite the emergence of new technologies and forms of cultural expression, the questionnaire has remained a meaningful forum for debate. It still provides an opportunity for editors to assert their positions on a public stage and a chance for artists and critics to engage in the aesthetic concerns of their time. The heterogeneous responses to questionnaires can be enigmatic or playful, disappointing or enlightening, but together they constitute an active, lively community in print. Forging an idea of the present, rooted in the past, questionnaires may allow us to imagine a future history of modernism.

APPENDIX

A CENTURY OF QUESTIONNAIRES: A CHRONOLOGICAL INDEX

"¿El arte debe estar al servicio del programa social?," *Contra*, Buenos Aires

"Una encuesta sobre la confusa cuestión de las artes plásticas," *El Ilustrado*, Mexico City

1934 "Pour qui écrivez-vous?," *Commune*, Paris

"For Whom Do You Write? Replies from Forty American Writers," *New Quarterly*, Rock Island, Illinois

1935 "Inquiry About the Malady of Language," *transition*, The Hague

"A Symposium on Communism" and "Will Fascism Come to America?," *Modern Monthly*, New York

"Où va la peinture?," *Commune*, Paris

"Enquête sur l'art d'aujourd'hui," *Cahiers d'Art*, Paris

"Enquête: Que feriez-vous, si vous aviez à organiser l'Exposition de 1937?," *Vu,* Paris

1936 "What Is Americanism? A Symposium on Marxism and the American Tradition," *Partisan Review* and *Anvil*, New York

"América y el destino de la civilización occidental," *Nosotros*, Buenos Aires

1937 "Authors Take Sides on the Spanish War," *Left Review*, London

1938 "Should the Nation Support Its Art?," *Direction*, New York

"Inquiry into the Spirit and Language of Night," *transition*, The Hague

1939 "The Situation in American Writing: Seven Questions," *Partisan Review*, New York

"Enquête sur la poésie de guerre," *Fontaine*, Algiers

1942 "Towards the Unknown," *View*, New York

"Inquiry on Dialectical Materialism," *Dyn*, Mexico City

1945 "¿Adónde va la pintura?," *Contrapunto*, Buenos Aires

1946 "Questionnaire: The Cost of Letters," *Horizon*, London

1948 "The State of American Writing: A Symposium," *Partisan Review*, New York

1950 "Religion and Intellectuals," *Partisan Review*, New York

1951 "Encuesta sobre el arte abstracto y el neorealismo," *Ver y Estimar*, Buenos Aires

1952 "¿Arte abstracto o arte no figurativo?," *Sur*, Buenos Aires

"Our Country and Our Culture: A Symposium," *Partisan Review*, New York

1954 "Encuesta realizada entre pintores argentinos de la nueva generación," *Letra y Línea*, Buenos Aires

1959 "Enquête auprès d'intellectuels français," *Le 14 Juillet*, Paris

"Is There a New Academy?," *ARTnews*, New York

1960 "Enquête: Pensez-vous avoir un don d'écrivain?," *Tel Quel*, Paris

"Enquête sur la critique," *Positif*, Paris

1963 "Enquête sur la critique," *Tel Quel*, Paris

1964 "Le questionnaire," *Internationale Situationniste*, Paris

1965 "¿Arte vivo o arte de vivos?," *Atlántida*, Buenos Aires

"Nuestras encuestas: La pintura en Latinoamérica," *Hoy en la Cultura*, Buenos Aires

1968 "Enquête: Survie et jeunesse des revues littéraires," *Le Monde*, Paris

1974 "Do You Think There Is a Shared Female Artistic Sensibility in the Work of Female Artists?," *Art-Rite*, New York

1975 "Painters Reply," *Artforum*, New York

1976 "How Do Art Magazines Perceive Themselves Today?," *Studio International*, London

1980 "Symposium on the Language Environment," *The Difficulties*, Kent, Ohio

1995 "Questions of Feminism," *October*, New York

1996 "Visual Culture Questionnaire," *October*, New York

2000 "An Inquiry on Architecture and Theory," *Assemblage*, Cambridge, Massachusetts

2002 "Artist Questionnaire," *October*, New York

2004 "Art and Politics: A Survey," *frieze*, London

"The Future of Criticism," *Critical Inquiry*, Chicago

2005 "How Has Art Changed?," *frieze*, London

2006 "What Writing Has Most Influenced the Way You Think About Art?," *frieze*, London

"How do Art Magazines Perceive Themselves Today?," *frieze*, London

2008 "In What Ways Have Artists, Academics, and Cultural Institutions Responded to the U.S.-Led Invasion and Occupation of Iraq?," *October*, New York

2009 "Questionnaire on 'The Contemporary,'" *October*, New York

2012 "Who Do You Write For?," *frieze*, London

"Is Newness Still New?," *Brooklyn Rail*, Brooklyn

"What Should Art Criticism Be Doing?," *Brooklyn Rail*, Brooklyn

2013 "The State of America," *Flash Art*, Milan

"Is Painting Still Vital, or Is It a Dead Language?," *Flash Art*, Milan

2016 "Questionnaire on Matter and Materialisms," *October*, New York

NOTES

LOCATIONS OF FREQUENTLY CITED MAGAZINES

Buenos Aires: *Proa; Martín Fierro; Nosotros*
Havana: *Revista de Avance*
Madrid: *La Gaceta Literaria*
New York: *Camera Work*
Paris (1927–30); The Hague (1932–38): *transition*

INTRODUCTION

1. Jaime Torres Bodet, "Candido o de la estadística," *Contemporáneos* (Mexico City), no. 1 (June 1928): 82. All translations are by the author unless otherwise noted. Note that Torres Bodet responded to the *Revista de Avance* and *Gaceta Literaria* questionnaires that I examine in this book, and was featured in *Imán* as well, thus serving as a protagonist throughout these debates.
2. Ezra Pound, response to a "Complete Handbook of Opinion," *Vanity Fair* (New York) 30, no. 2 (April 1928): 116.
3. "La littérature française jugée par les écrivains anglais d'aujourd'hui," *Le Gaulois du Dimanche* (Paris), February 12, 1899.
4. Torres Bodet, "Candido o de la estadística," 86.
5. The editors, "Algunas Encuestas," *La Gaceta Literaria* 2, no. 27 (February 1, 1928): 5.
6. Gaston Picard, "Grands articles et grandes enquêtes de la saison," in *L'ami du lettré* (Paris: Bernard Grasset, 1927), 61.
7. "Paris, centre mondial des arts," *L'Intransigeant* (Paris) 49, no. 17.948 (December 10, 1928): 5. The editors at *La Gaceta Literaria* took the question and its responses, particularly those of Léger and Braque, as evidence of Paris's demise. See the editors, "Una encuesta," *La Gaceta Literaria* 3, no. 51 (February 1, 1929): 7.
8. Miguel Pérez Ferrero, "Una encuesta sensacional: ¿Qué es la vanguardia?," *La Gaceta Literaria* 4, no. 83 (June 1, 1930): 1.
9. "¿Qué es el modernismo?," *El Nuevo Mercurio* (Barcelona) 1, no. 2 (February 1907): 123–24.
10. Manuel Machado, *La Guerra Literaria 1898–1914* (Madrid: Imprenta Hispano-Alemana, 1913), 31.
11. "Encuesta de vanguardia," *Lampadario* (Quito), no. 2 (April 1931): 8.
12. Eugene Jolas to Maria Jolas, April 21, 1936, letter, Houghton Library, Harvard University. Papers of the Magazine *transition* (MS Am 2068), Series III, Folder 136.

CHAPTER 1

1. "Directrices: Una encuesta," *Revista de Avance* 2, no. 26 (September 15, 1928): 235. All translations are by the author unless otherwise noted.
2. "Inquiry Among European Writers into the Spirit of America," *transition*, no. 13 (Summer 1928): 248; "Why Do Americans Live in Europe?," *transition*, no. 14 (Fall 1928): 97.
3. Although small magazines are arguably more "durable" than the newspapers Benedict Anderson addresses, they still suggest what he calls a "deep horizontal comradeship." Benedict Anderson, *Imagined Communities* (1983), rev. ed. (London: Verso, 1991), 7.
4. Alejo Carpentier, "Música en Cuba" (1946), reproduced in Gilberto Mendonça Teles and Klaus Müller-Bergh, *Vanguardia latinoamericana: Historia, crítica y documentos*, vol. 2, *Caribe, Antillas Mayores y Menores* (Madrid: Iberoamericana, 2002), 23.
5. Charles Allen, "The Advance Guard," *Sewanee Review* 51, no. 3 (July–September 1943): 427.
6. Ezra Pound, "Small Magazines," *English Journal* 19, no. 9 (November 1930): 703.
7. Leah Dickerman, "Inventing Abstraction," in *Inventing Abstraction, 1910–1925: How a Radical Idea Changed Modern Art* (New York: Museum of Modern Art, 2012), 20.
8. Ibid., 19.
9. See Sean Latham and Robert Scholes, "The Rise of Periodical Studies," *PMLA* 121, no. 2 (2006): 521. Scholarship in the field includes Mark Morrisson, *The Public Face of Modernism: Little Magazines, Audiences, and Reception, 1905–1920* (Madison: University of Wisconsin Press, 2001); Ann L. Ardis and Patrick C. Collier, eds., *Transatlantic Print Culture, 1880–1940: Emerging Media, Emerging Modernisms* (New York: Palgrave Macmillan, 2008); Robert Scholes and Clifford Wulfman, *Modernism in the Magazines: An Introduction* (New Haven: Yale University Press, 2010); Peter Brooker, Sascha Bru, Andrew Thacker, and Christian Weikop, eds., *The Oxford Critical and Cultural History of Modernist Magazines*, vols. 1–3 (Oxford: Oxford University Press, 2009–13); and the *Journal of Modern Periodical Studies*, eds. Sean Latham and Mark Morrisson.
10. The Modernist Journals Project, http://dl.lib.brown.edu/mjp/. See also the Blue Mountain Project, http://diglib.princeton.edu/bluemountain/journals; the International Dada Archive, http://sdrc.lib.uiowa.edu/dada/collection.html; and Monoskop's aggregated collection of magazines, http://monoskop.org/Magazines.
11. The Modernist Magazines Project, http://www.modernistmagazines.com/. Note: I contributed the chapter "Madrid: Questioning the Avant-Garde" to Peter Brooker, Sascha Bru, Andrew Thacker, and Christian Weikop, eds., *The Oxford Critical and Cultural History of Modernist Magazines*, vol. 3, *Europe 1880–1940* (Ox-

ford: Oxford University Press, 2013), 369–92. Andrew Thacker, María del Pilar Blanco, and Eric Bulson are currently preparing a fourth volume that expands the geography of the series to cover Latin America and the Caribbean (María del Pilar Blanco, e-mail message to author, September 8, 2015).

12. Peter Brooker and Andrew Thacker, "General Introduction," in *The Oxford Critical and Cultural History of Modernist Magazines*, vol. 1, *Britain and Ireland, 1880–1955*, ed. Peter Brooker and Andrew Thacker (Oxford: Oxford University Press, 2009), 2–3.

13. Spanish-language research on magazines to which I am indebted includes Carlos Ripoll, *La generación del 23 en Cuba y otros apuntes sobre el vanguardismo* (New York: Las Américas, 1968); Héctor René Lafleur, Sergio D. Provenzano, and Fernando Alonso, eds., *Las revistas literarias argentinas, 1893–1967* (Buenos Aires: Ediciones El 8vo. loco, 2006); Boyd G. Carter, *Las revistas literarias de Hispanoamérica: Breve historia y contenido* (Mexico City: Ediciones de Andrea, 1959); Domingo Paniagua, *Revistas culturales contemporáneas II. El ultraísmo en España* (Madrid: Punta Europea, 1970); and Rafael Osuna, *Revistas de la vanguardia española* (Sevilla: Editorial Renacimiento, 2005). English-language material on Hispanophone magazines includes Francine Masiello, "Rethinking Neocolonial Esthetics: Literature, Politics, and Intellectual Community in Cuba's *Revista de Avance*," *Latin American Research Review* 28, no. 2 (1993): 3–31; Gayle Rogers, *Modernism and the New Spain: Britain, Cosmopolitan Europe, and Literary History* (Oxford: Oxford University Press, 2012); Jordana Mendelson, *Revistas y Guerra, 1936–1939 / Magazines and War, 1936–1939* (Madrid: Museo Nacional Centro de Arte Reina Sofía, 2007); Michele Greet, *Beyond National Identity: Pictorial Indigenism as a Modernist Strategy in Andean Art, 1920–1960* (University Park: Penn State University Press, 2009); and Harper Montgomery, *The Mobility of Modernism: Art and Criticism in 1920s Latin America* (Austin: University of Texas Press, 2017). Gwen Allen's book *Artists' Magazines: An Alternative Space for Art* (Cambridge, Mass.: MIT Press, 2011) has expanded the study of magazines for contemporary art historians.

14. Mary Louise Pratt, "Modernity and Periphery: Towards a Global and Relational Analysis," in *Beyond Dichotomies: Histories, Identities, Cultures, and the Challenges of Globalization*, ed. Elizabeth Mudimbe-Boyi (Albany: State University of New York Press, 2002), 22.

15. Laura Doyle and Laura Winkiel, eds., "Introduction: The Global Horizons of Modernism," in *Geomodernisms: Race, Modernism, Modernity* (Bloomington: Indiana University Press, 2005), 3–4. Emphasis in the original.

16. Peter Bürger, *Theory of the Avant-Garde* (1974), trans. Michael Shaw, ed. Jochen Schulte-Sasse (Minneapolis: University of Minnesota Press, 1984).

17. Néstor García Canclini, *Hybrid Cultures: Strategies for Entering and Leaving Modernity* (1995), trans. Christopher L. Chiappari and Silvia L. López, expanded ed. (Minneapolis: University of Minnesota Press, 2005), 41–42.

18. For more see: Ángel Rama, *La ciudad letrada* (Hanover, N.H.: Ediciones del norte, 1984).

19. García Canclini, *Hybrid Cultures*, 41.

20. Alejo Carpentier, "La novela latinoamericana en vísperas de un nuevo siglo" (1979), in *Los pasos recobrados: Ensayos de teoría y crítica literaria*, eds. Alexis Márquez Rodríguez and Araceli García Carranza (Caracas: Biblioteca Ayacucho, 2003), 203. Emphasis in the original.

21. Néstor García Canclini, "Modernity After Postmodernity," in *Beyond the Fantastic: Contemporary Art Criticism from Latin America*, ed. Gerardo Mosquera (London: Institute of International Visual Arts, 1995), 23. Elsewhere he proposes a model of hybridity to describe such uneven development and characterizes Latin American modernization by its "multitemporal heterogeneity." García Canclini, *Hybrid Cultures,* 47.

22. Vicky Unruh, *Latin American Vanguards: The Art of Contentious Encounters* (Berkeley: University of California Press, 1994), 2–4.

23. Ibid., 40.

24. Note: the Brazilian avant-garde in the 1920s is often identified as *modernismo* as well, but is distinct from the *modernismo* of Darío earlier in the century.

25. While *modernismo* drew on aspects of French Symbolism, it was, in turn, circulated by Darío back to Spain during his stays there in 1892 and 1898 and through magazines, instantiating a literary feedback loop between Latin America and Europe. For more on *modernismo*, see Cathy L. Jrade, *Modernismo, Modernity, and the Development of Spanish American Literature* (Austin: University of Texas Press, 1998); Aníbal González, *A Companion to Spanish American Modernismo* (Suffolk, UK: Tamesis, 2007); and Gerard Aching, *By Exquisite Design: The Politics of Spanish American Modernismo* (Cambridge: Cambridge University Press, 1997).

26. Alejandro Mejías-López, *The Inverted Conquest: The Myth of Modernity and the Transatlantic Onset of Modernism* (Nashville: Vanderbilt University Press, 2010), 83–84.

27. It is impossible to generalize about the *vanguardia* across Latin America, as movements were formed in specific political, national, and cultural contexts and were often defined along "generational" lines. However, the term was claimed by artists and writers across the Hispanophone world.

28. Innumerable writers have defined and refined the terms "modernism" and "avant-garde," including: Andreas Huyssen, *After the Great Divide: Modernism, Mass Culture, Postmodernism* (Bloomington: Indiana University Press, 1986); Astradur Eysteinsson, *The*

Concept of Modernism (Ithaca: Cornell University Press, 1990); Renato Poggioli, *The Theory of the Avant-Garde*, trans. Gerald Fitzgerald (Cambridge, Mass.: Harvard University Press, 1968); Peter Nicholls, *Modernisms: A Literary Guide* (London: Macmillan, 1995); Paul Wood, ed., *The Challenge of the Avant-Garde* (New Haven: Yale University Press, 1999); Rosalind Krauss, Yve-Alain Bois, Benjamin Buchloh, and Hal Foster, *Art Since 1900: Modernism, Antimodernism, Postmodernism* (London: Thames and Hudson, 2005); and T. J. Clark, *Farewell to an Idea: Episodes from a History of Modernism* (New Haven: Yale University Press, 2001).

29. In one of the first aesthetic appropriations of the term, the French social theorist Henri de Saint Simon wrote in 1825, "We, the artists, will serve as the avant-garde: for amongst all the arms at our disposal, the power of the Arts is the swiftest and most expeditious." Henri de Saint Simon, "The Artist, the Savant, and the Industrialist" (1825), in *Art in Theory, 1815–1900: An Anthology of Changing Ideas*, ed. Charles Harrison, Paul Wood, and Jason Gaiger (Oxford: Blackwell, 1998), 40.

30. Raymond Williams, *The Politics of Modernism: Against the New Conformists*, ed. Tony Pinkey (New York: Verso, 1989), 51.

31. Matei Calinescu, *Five Faces of Modernity: Modernism, Avant-Garde, Decadence, Kitsch, Postmodernism* (Durham: Duke University Press, 1987), 95.

32. For instance, Clement Greenberg uses the term "avant-garde" to denote a political quality absent from his formal analysis of "modernist painting." Clement Greenberg, "Avant-Garde and Kitsch," *Partisan Review* (New York) 6, no. 5 (Fall 1939): 34–49; Clement Greenberg, "Modernist Painting," in *The Collected Essays and Criticism*, vol. 4, *Modernism with a Vengeance* (Chicago: University of Chicago Press, 1993), 85–94.

33. Miguel Pérez Ferrero, "Una encuesta sensacional: ¿Qué es la vanguardia?," *La Gaceta Literaria* 4, no. 83 (June 1, 1930): 1; "Encuesta de vanguardia," *Lampadario* (Quito), no. 2 (April 1931): 8.

34. Benedetto Varchi, *Due lezzioni di M. Benedetto Varchi, nella prima delle quali si dichiara un sonetto di M. Michelagnolo Buonarroti: Nella seconda si disputa quale sia piu nobile arte la scultura, o la pittura, con una lettera d'esso Michelagnolo, & piu altri eccellentiss: Pittori, et scultori, sopra la quistione sopradetto* (Florence: Lorenzo Torrentino, 1549). I thank Peter Bell for suggesting I analyze *paragoni*.

35. Leatrice Mendelsohn-Martone, *Paragoni: Benedetto Varchi's "Due Lezzioni" and Cinquecento Art Theory* (Ann Arbor: UMI Research Press, 1982), 40–43.

36. Immanuel Kant, "Beantwortung der Frage: Was ist Aufklärung?," *Berlinische Monatsschrift* (December 1784): 484, trans. H. B. Nisbet, in *Kant: Political Writings*, ed. Hans Reiss, 2nd ed. (Cambridge: Cambridge University Press, 1991), 55.

37. Michel Foucault, "What Is Enlightenment?" [Qu'est-ce que les Lumières?], trans. Josué V. Harari, in *The Foucault Reader*, ed. Paul Rabinow (New York: Pantheon Books, 1984), 39.

38. Ibid., 32.

39. Ibid., 38.

40. Proust participated in the game with the daughter of the nineteenth-century French president Félix Faure in both 1886 and 1890–91, writing his answers in "Antoinette Faure's Album" and publishing them as Marcel Proust, "Salon Confidences Écrit par Marcel," *La Revue Illustrée* (Paris) 15 (1892).

41. *Vanity Fair*, which started printing celebrities' responses to Proust's questions in 1993, compiled the results into a book in 2009 and installed it on their website as an interactive feature. Accessed May 4, 2012, http://www.vanityfair.com/culture/features/proust-questionnaire.

42. Jules Huret, *Enquête sur l'évolution littéraire* (Paris: Bibliothèque Charpentier, 1891); Jules Huret, *Enquête sur la question sociale en Europe* (Paris: Librairie académique Perrin et Didier, 1892). Venita Datta argues that the former "was one of the first notable *enquêtes* of the period and served as a model for subsequent inquiries." Venita Datta, *Birth of a Literary Icon: The Literary Avant-Garde and the Origins of the Intellectual in France* (Albany: State University of New York Press, 1999), 21.

43. "Comment définir la poésie?," *La Muse Française* (Paris) 2, nos. 4–6 (April–June 1923); "Une enquête franco-allemande," *Mercure de France* (Paris) 14, no. 64 (April 14, 1895): 1–65.

44. "Enquête sur l'utilité de l'art," *Le Buccin* (Paris) 2, no. 7 (December 1919); Charles Morice, "Enquête sur les tendances actuelles des arts plastiques," *Mercure de France* (Paris) 56, no. 193 (August 1, 1905): 34–49.

45. Datta, *Birth of a Literary Icon*, 21.

46. "The Negro in Art: How Shall He Be Portrayed? A Symposium," *Crisis* (New York) 31, no. 5 (March 1926): 219.

47. "What Should You Most Like to Do, to Know, to Be?," *Little Review* (Paris) 12, no. 2 (May 1929).

48. Craig Calhoun, ed., *Sociology in America* (Chicago: University of Chicago Press, 2007), 42–46. See also Theodore M. Porter and Dorothy Ross, eds., *The Cambridge History of Science: The Modern Social Sciences* (Cambridge: University of Cambridge Press, 2003). These scholars trace sociology as a discipline back to the "moral sciences" introduced in late eighteenth-century France, which were of interest to John Stuart Mill.

49. Martin Bulmer, Kevin Bales, and Kathryn Kish Sklar, eds., *The Social Survey in Historical Perspective, 1880–1940* (Cambridge: Cambridge University Press, 1992), 335.

50. For a history of the social science questionnaire, see Evan Kindley, *questionnaire (Object Lessons)* (New York: Bloomsbury Academic, 2016).

51. Eugene Jolas, Kay Boyle, Whit Burnett, Hart Crane, Caresse Crosby, Harry Crosby, Martha Foley, Stuart Gilbert, A. I. Gillespie, Leigh Hoffman, Elliot Paul, Douglas Rigby, Theo Rutra, Robert Sage, Harold J. Salemson, and Laurence Vail, "Proclamation: Revolution of the Word," *transition*, nos. 16–17 (June 1929): 13.

52. Matthew Josephson, *Life Among the Surrealists* (New York: Holt, Rinehart and Winston, 1962), 335.

53. *La révolution surréaliste* (Paris), no. 1 (December 1, 1924): 1.

54. André Breton and Paul Éluard, "Pouvez-vous dire quelle a été la rencontre capitale de votre vie?," *Minotaure* (Paris), nos. 3–4 (1933): 101.

55. See, for instance, "Le suicide est-il une solution?," *La révolution surréaliste* (Paris), no. 1 (December 1924): 31–32 and "Enquête sur l'amour," *La révolution surréaliste* (Paris), no. 12 (December 1929): 65–76.

56. Harold Monro, "Three Questions Regarding the Necessity, the Function, and the Form of Poetry," *The Chapbook: A Monthly Miscellany* (London), no. 27 (July 1922): 1; W. H. Davies, response to "Three Questions Regarding the Necessity, the Function, and the Form of Poetry," *Chapbook*, 7. I thank James Murphy for this reference.

57. Janet Lyon, *Manifestoes: Provocations of the Modern* (Ithaca: Cornell University Press, 1999), 10.

58. Paul Wood, ed., *The Challenge of the Avant-Garde* (New Haven: Yale University Press, 1999), 35.

59. Karl Marx and Frederick Engels, *Manifesto of the Communist Party* (1848), ed. Frederick Engels (New York: International Publishers, 1994), 3.

60. Martin Puchner, *Poetry of the Revolution: Marx, Manifestos, and the Avant-Gardes* (Princeton: Princeton University Press, 2006), 74.

61. Frederick Karl, *Modern and Modernism: The Sovereignty of the Artist, 1885–1925* (New York: Atheneum, 1985), 121.

62. Samuel Coleridge and William Wordsworth, *Lyrical Ballads: The Text of the 1798 Edition with the Additional 1800 Poems and the Prefaces*, ed. R. L. Brett and A. R. Jones (London: Methuen, 1963), 236.

63. Théophile Gautier, Preface to *Mademoiselle de Maupin* (1835), in *Art in Theory, 1815–1900: An Anthology of Changing Ideas*, ed. Charles Harrison, Paul Wood, and Jason Gaiger (Oxford: Blackwell, 1998), 99.

64. Oscar Wilde, "Preface," in *The Picture of Dorian Gray* (1891;), (New York: Dell, 1967), 6; Walter Pater, "Conclusion to *The Renaissance*" (1868), in Harrison, Wood, and Gaiger, *Art in Theory, 1815–1900*, 830.

65. Jean Moréas, "The Symbolist Manifesto" (1886), trans. Mary Ann Caws, in *Manifesto: A Century of Isms*, ed. Mary Ann Caws (Lincoln: University of Nebraska Press, 2001), 50.

66. Puchner, *Poetry of the Revolution*, 70.

67. Julio Ramos, *Divergent Modernities: Culture and Politics in Nineteenth-Century Latin America*, trans. John D. Blanco (Durham: Duke University Press, 2001), xxxviii.

68. Rubén Darío, "Palabras Liminares" (1896), in *Antología Poética* (Madrid: Edaf, 1981), 27.

69. Ronald Vroon, "The Manifesto as a Literary Genre: Some Preliminary Observations," *International Journal of Slavic Linguistics and Poetics*, no. 38 (1995): 164.

70. Carlo Carrá, "The Painting of Sounds, Noises, and Smells" (1913), trans. Robert Brain, in Caws, *Manifesto,* 202.

71. Kazimir Malevich, "Suprematism" (1927), trans. Howard Dearstyne, in Caws, *Manifesto*, 404.

72. Mikhail Larionov and Natalya Goncharova, "Rayonists and Futurists: A Manifesto" (1913), trans. John E. Bowlt, in Caws, *Manifesto*, 240.

73. Salvador Dalí, Lluís Montanyà, and Sebastià Gasch, "Yellow Manifesto" (1928), trans. John London, in Caws, *Manifesto*, 370–71.

74. I wrote extensively on the origins of the manifesto and its appropriation by avant-garde artists in my undergraduate thesis. See Lori Cole, "Manifesto: Declaring the Political and Aesthetic Intentions of the Avant-Garde" (undergraduate honors thesis, Brown University, 2002).

75. Walter Gropius, "Manifesto of the Bauhaus" (1919), in *Modernism: An Anthology of Sources and Documents*, ed. Vassiliki Kolocotroni, Jane Goldman, and Olga Taxidou (Chicago: University of Chicago Press, 1998), 301.

76. Bürger, *Theory of the Avant-Garde*, 18.

77. Carlo Carrá, "From Cezánne to Us, the Futurists" (1913), in *Theories of Modern Art: A Source Book by Artists and Critics*, ed. Herschel B. Chipp (Berkeley: University of California Press, 1968), 305.

78. Pierre Bourdieu, *The Field of Cultural Production* (New York: Columbia University Press, 1993), 106.

79. Oswald de Andrade, "Manifesto Antropófago," *Revista de Antropofagía* (São Paulo), no. 1 (May 1928), trans. Dawn Ades in *Art in Latin America: The Modern Era, 1820–1980*, ed. Dawn Ades (New Haven: Yale University Press, 1989), 312–13.

80. Oliverio Girondo, "Manifiesto Martín Fierro," *Martín Fierro* 1, no. 4 (May 1924): 25, trans. Patrick Frank in *Readings in Latin American Modern Art*, ed. Patrick Frank (New Haven: Yale University Press: 2004), 12; "¿Cree usted en la existencia de una sensibilidad, de una mentalidad, argentina? En caso afirmativa, ¿cuáles son sus características?," *Martín Fierro* 1, nos. 5–6 (June 15, 1924): 39.

81. Ezra Pound, response to *Authors Take Sides on the Spanish War* (London: Left Review, 1937): 25.

82. Filippo Tommaso Marinetti, *Enquête internationale sur le vers libre et Manifeste du futurisme* (Milan: Éditions de Poesia, 1909).

83. Williams, *The Politics of Modernism*, 33.

84. "¿Cuál es el pintor más grande de México?," *El Universal Ilustrado* (Mexico City) 6, no. 380 (September 1922): 49.

85. One example is René Magritte's photographic compendium of contributors to the Surrealists' questionnaire on love. Photographed with their eyes closed, the male participants' tightly cropped portraits are organized around a central, nude female figure, reflecting some of the movement's problematic gender politics. René Magritte, "Je ne vois pas la (femme) cachée dans la forêt," 1929, photomontage, published alongside "Enquête sur l'amour," *La révolution surréaliste* (Paris), no. 12 (December 1929): 73. The *Little Review* questionnaire also included photographs of many of its participants. "What Should You Most Like to Do, to Know, to Be?," *Little Review* (Paris) 12, no. 2 (May 1929).

86. Gorham Munson, "How to Run a Little Magazine," *Saturday Review of Literature* (New York) (March 27, 1937): 4; Eugene and Maria Jolas Papers, Beinecke Rare Book and Manuscript Library, Yale University, Series XII, Box 60, Folder 1401.

87. "¿Cree usted en la existencia?," 39.

88. Alfred Stieglitz, Opening Statement, *Camera Work*, no. 47 (July 1914): 1.

89. Alberto Giacometti, response to "Où va la peinture?," *Commune* (Paris) 2, no. 22 (June 1935): 1135; Ramón Gómez de la Serna, response to "¿Qué es la vanguardia?," *La Gaceta Literaria*, no. 85 (July 1, 1930): 3.

90. Francisco Ichaso, "Balance de una indagación," *Revista de Avance*, no. 38 (September 15, 1929): 258.

91. Eugene Jolas, response to "Open Letter to the Editor," *transition*, no. 15 (February 1929): 154.

92. Bernard Faÿ, response to "Inquiry Among European Writers into the Spirit of America," *transition*, no. 13 (Summer 1928): 260.

93. Djuna Barnes, response to "What Should You Most Like to Do, to Know, to Be?," *Little Review* (Paris) 12, no. 2 (May 1929): 17.

94. "¿Cuál es, a su juicio, el peor libro del año?," *La Campana de Palo: Periódico Mensual. Bellas Artes y polémica* (Buenos Aires), no. 10 (December 1926).

95. Waverly Louis Root, "Open Letter to the Editor," *transition*, no. 15 (February 1929): 151.

96. Jolas, response to "Open Letter to the Editor," 154.

97. Edward Steichen, response to "What Is 291?," *Camera Work*, no. 47 (July 1914): 65.

98. Ibid., 66.

99. La rédaction, "Orientations," *Cahiers de l'Étoile*, no. 18 (November–December 1930): 845–46.

100. Faith Binckes, *Modernism, Magazines, and the British Avant-Garde: Reading Rhythm, 1910–1914* (New York: Oxford University Press, 2010), 176. I thank Carey Snyder for this reference.

101. "¿Qué somos? Cómo somos?" *Índice* (San Juan) 1, no. 8 (November 1929): 114.

102. For more on modernist collections, see Jeremy Braddock, *Collecting as Modernist Practice* (Baltimore: Johns Hopkins University Press, 2012).

103. Pound, "Small Magazines," 703.

104. Francis Picabia, response to "What Is 291?," *Camera Work*, no. 47 (July 1914): 72.

105. Jonathan Green, "Introduction to *Camera Work*: A Critical Anthology," (1973), in *The Camera Viewed: Writing on Contemporary Photography*, ed. Peninah R. Petruck (New York: Dutton, 1979), 10.

106. *Machine-Age Exposition, May 16–28, 1927*, exh. cat. (New York: Little Review, 1927). Guillermo de Torre, "Modelos de estación," *Síntesis* (Buenos Aires) 2, no. 14 (July 1928): 231.

107. "The Richard Mutt Case," *The Blind Man* (New York), no. 2 (May 1917): 4–5.

108. Guillermo de Torre, "Modelos de estación," *Síntesis* (Buenos Aires) 2, no. 14 (July 1928): 231; García Canclini, *Hybrid Cultures,* 56.

109. "¿Existe una literatura proletaria?," *Amauta* (Lima), no. 18 (October 1928): 1–8. I thank Harper Montgomery for directing me toward this reference.

110. Max Merz wrote in German, Francis Picabia in French, and Torres Palomar in Spanish. Max Merz, response to "What Is 291?," *Camera Work*, no. 47 (July 1914): 39; Francis Picabia, response to "What Is 291?," *Camera Work*, no. 47 (July 1914): 72; Torres Palomar, response to "What Is 291?," *Camera Work*, no. 47 (July 1914): 69.

111. Rubén Darío, "Marinetti y el Futurismo," *La Nación* (Buenos Aires) (April 5, 1909); F. T. Marinetti, "Fundación y Manifiesto del Futurismo," trans. Ramón Gómez de la Serna, *Prometeo* (Madrid) 2, no. 6 (April 1909): 65–73; Gómez de la Serna also translated Marinetti's "Proclama futurista a los españoles," in *Prometeo* (Madrid) 3, no. 20 (1910): 1–2.

112. De Zayas's conversations with Picasso took place in early 1911 and comprised a May 1911 article on the artist that De Zayas wrote for his father's magazine, *América: Revista mensual ilustrada*. De Zayas produced an abridged English translation of this essay for *Camera Work*. Marius de Zayas, "Pablo Picasso," *América: Revista mensual ilustrada* (New York) 6 (May 1911): 363–65; Marius de Zayas, "Pablo Picasso," *Camera Work,* nos. 34–35 (April–July 1911): 65–67.

113. Rafael Arévalo Martínez, "The Man Who Resembled a Horse," trans. William Carlos Williams, *Little Review* (New York) 5, no. 8 (December 1918): 42–53. William Carlos Williams's mother was Puerto Rican and his father English West Indian. His first language was Spanish, but he never mastered it. Jonathan Cohen, "Introduction: Into the American Idiom: Poems from the Spanish," in William Carlos Williams, *By Word of Mouth: Poems from the Spanish, 1916–1959*, ed. Jonathan Cohen (New York: New Directions, 2011), xxi.

114. William Carlos Williams, trans. and quoted in *Revista de Avance* 3, no. 37 (August 15, 1929): 236. *Blues: A Magazine for New Rhythms* (1929–30), edited by Charles Henri Ford, appeared in nine issues from Columbus, Mississippi, featuring work by Gertrude Stein, Ezra Pound, and Eugene Jolas.

115. Simón Bolívar, "Carta de Jamaica (1815)," in *Simón Bolívar: Escritos políticos*, ed. Gabriela Soriano (Madrid: Alianza Editorial, 1990), 61–84; Robert Alexander González, "Introduction: Entering Pan-America," in *Designing Pan-America: U.S. Architectural Visions for the Western Hemisphere* (Austin: University of Texas Press, 2011), 4.

116. Héctor Olea, Mari Carmen Ramírez, and Tomás Ybarra-Frausto, "Resisting Categories," in *Resisting Categories: Latin American and/or Latino?*, ed. Mari Carmen Ramírez, Héctor Olea, and Tomás Ybarra-Frausto, Critical Documents of 20th-Century Latin American Art, vol. 1 (Houston: Museum of Fine Arts, Houston International Center for the Arts of the Americas, 2012), 42. See also Walter D. Mignolo, *The Idea of Latin America* (Oxford: Blackwell, 2005).

117. Pablo Rojas Paz, "Imperialismo baldío" (1927), *Martín Fierro* 4, no. 42 (June 10, 1927): 356, trans. Tony Beckwith in Ramírez, Olea, and Ybarra-Frausto, *Resisting Categories*, 284.

118. Mari Carmen Ramírez, "Introduction to Chapter II: A New Art," in Ramírez, Olea, and Ybarra-Frausto, *Resisting Categories*, 338–39.

119. "Younger American Painters" was on view from March 9–21, 1910 at 291. "Seven Americans" was held at the Anderson Galleries March 9–28, 1925.

120. Francis Picabia, interview with the *New York Times*: "Picabia, Art Rebel, Here to Teach New Movement," *New York Times*, February 16, 1913. The Armory Show included thirteen hundred pieces of American and European modernist art, including works by Cézanne, Duchamp, Picasso, and Gauguin, as well as Americans such as Robert Henri, Charles Sheeler, Marsden Hartley and Stuart Davis. For more, see Milton W. Brown, *The Story of the Armory Show* (New York: Abbeville Press, 1988) and *Documents of the 1913 Armory Show: The Electrifying Moment of Modern Art's American Debut* (Tucson: Hol Art Books, 2009).

121. Marsden Hartley, response to "What Is 291?," *Camera Work*, no. 47 (July 1914): 35.

122. Victoria Ocampo, "Victoria Ocampo on Alfred Stieglitz," *Sur* 1 (1931), Alfred Stieglitz and Georgia O'Keeffe Archive, Yale Collection of American Literature, Beinecke Rare Book and Manuscript Library, Yale University, Series II, Box 100, Folder 2105.

123. Waldo Frank, *Our America* (New York: Boni and Liveright, 1919); Waldo Frank, *The Re-discovery of America: An Introduction to a Philosophy of American Life* (New York: Charles Scribner's Sons, 1929). For more on Frank, see Sebastiaan Faber, "Learning from the Latins: Waldo Franks Progressive Pan-Americanism," *CR: The New Centennial Review* (East Lansing, Mich.) 3, no. 1 (Spring 2003): 257–95. For more on pan-Americanism, see Claire F. Fox, *Making Art Panamerican: Cultural Policy and the Cold War* (Minneapolis: University of Minnesota Press, 2013).

124. It was on this tour that Frank met Ocampo. Michael A. Ogorzaly, *Waldo Frank: Prophet of Hispanic Regeneration* (Lewisburg: Bucknell University Press, 1994), 79.

125. Félix Lizaso, "Waldo Frank y las dos Américas," *Revista de Avance* (1930), translated and quoted in Ogorzaly, *Waldo Frank,* 81.

126. Waldo Frank, *Revista de Avance* (January 15, 1930), quoted in Ogorzaly, *Waldo Frank,* 83.

127. Eugene Jolas and Elliot Paul, "A Review," *transition*, no. 12 (March 1928): 142.

128. Edwin Seaver, response to "Are Artists People?," *New Masses* (New York) 2, no. 3 (January 1927): 5.

129. Diego Rivera and Bertram Wolfe, *Portrait of America* (New York: Covici-Friede, 1934), 19. See also *Vida-Americana*, a magazine issued in 1921 by the Mexican artist David Alfaro Siqueiros which, though published in Barcelona, self-identified as a "North, Central, and South American avant-garde magazine."

130. Rufino Blanco Fombona, response to "¿Qué debe ser el arte americano?," *Revista de Avance* 2, no. 29 (December 15, 1928): 361; Ichaso, "Balance de una indagación," 264.

CHAPTER 2

1. Alejo Carpentier, "El espiritu de equipo," *El Nacional* (Caracas) (November 8, 1953), quoted in Carlos Rincón, "Carpentier, 'extranjero indeseable,'" *Revista de Crítica Literaria Latinoamericana* 34, no. 68 (2008): 196. All translations are by the author unless otherwise noted.

2. Juan A. Martínez, *Cuban Art and National Identity: The Vanguardia Painters, 1927–1950* (Gainesville: University Press of Florida, 1994), 35.

3. José Martí, "Nuestra América," *La Revista ilustrada de Nueva York* (New York) (January 10, 1891) and *El partido liberal* (Mexico City) (January 30 1891), trans. J. A. Sierra, accessed June 17, 2011, http://www.historyofcuba.com/history/marti/America.htm.

4. Ibid.

5. Luis Camnitzer, *New Art Cuba*, 2nd ed. (Austin: University of Texas Press, 2003), 142–43.

6. Antoni Kapcia, "Revolution, the Intellectual, and a Cuban Identity: The Long Tradition," *Bulletin of Latin American Research* 1, no. 2 (May 1982): 66.

7. Ann Wright, "Intellectuals of an Unheroic Period of Cuban History, 1913–1923: The 'Cuba Contemporánea' Group," *Bulletin of Latin American Research* 7, no. 1 (1988): 109.

8. Andrés Valdespino, *Jorge Mañach y su generación de las letras Cubanas* (Miami: Ediciones Universal, 1971), 23.

9. Rubén Martínez Villena et al., "La Protesta de los Trece" (Havana) (March 19, 1923), reprinted in *Vanguardias en su tinta: Documentos de la vanguardia en América Latina*, ed. Celina Manzoni (Buenos Aires: Corregidor, 2007), 109–10.

10. Rubén Martínez Villena et al., "Declaración del grupo minorista," *Carteles* (Havana), no. 21 (May 22, 1927): 16 and 25, *Cuba Literaria: Colección Orígines*, accessed June 24, 2011, http://www.cubaliteraria.cu /monografia/grupo_minorista/declaracion.html. The "Declaration" was also printed in *Social* (Havana) (May 7, 1927) and *Revista de Avance* 1, no. 5 (May 16, 1927): 98 and 102, *Cubanow.net: Cuban Art and Culture*, accessed June 24, 2011, http://www.cubanow .net/pages/loader.php?sec=7&t=2&item=3349.

11. Rubén Martínez Villena et al., "Declaración del Grupo Minorista," *Social* (Havana) (May 7, 1927), reprinted in Manzoni, *Vanguardias en su tinta*, 128. For an alternative translation to my own, see "Manifesto of the Grupo Minorista, May 7, 1927," trans. Patrick Frank, in *Manifestos and Polemics in Latin American Art*, ed. Patrick Frank (Albuquerque: University of New Mexico Press, 2017), 28–30.

12. Both editors of *Social*, Conrado Massaguer and Emilio Roig de Leuchsenring, were part of the Grupo Minorista. María Luisa Lobo Montalvo et al., "The Years of 'Social,'" *Journal of Decorative and Propaganda Arts* 22 (1996): 129.

13. Francisco Ichaso, quoted in Martínez, *Cuban Art and National Identity*, 10.

14. Lobo Montalvo et al., 29n8; Cira Romero, ed., "El Grupo Minorista. Registro en publicacciones periódicas: La Revista Social," *Cuba Literaria: Colección Orígines*, accessed May 8, 2017, http://www.cubaliteraria.cu /monografia/grupo_minorista/social.html.

15. Antonio Benítez-Rojo, *The Repeating Island: The Caribbean and the Postmodern Perspective*, trans. James Maraniss (Raleigh: Duke University Press, 1992), 118.

16. Francine Masiello, "Rethinking Neocolonial Esthetics: Literature, Politics, and Intellectual Community in Cuba's *Revista de Avance*," *Latin American Research Review* 28, no. 2 (1993): 14.

17. Martínez, *Cuban Art and National Identity*, 37 and 43–44.

18. Emilio Roig de Leuchsenring, "Artistas y hombres o titiriteros y malabaristas," *Social* (Havana) (June 1929), quoted in Cira Romero, ed., "Memoria iii: La Falange de Acción Cubana," *Cuba Literaria: Colección Orígines*, accessed June 24, 2011, http://www.cubaliteraria.cu/monografia/grupo_minorista/memoria3. html.

19. Félix Lizaso and José Fernández de Castro, "La moderna poesía en Cuba," *Proa*, no. 7 (1925): 25–38, quoted in Gilberto Mendonça Teles and Klaus Müller-Bergh, *Vanguardia latinoamericana: Historia, crítica y documentos*, vol. 2, *Caribe, Antillas Mayores y Menores* (Madrid: Iberoamericana, 2002), 24.

20. Ibid., 25.

21. Ibid., 32.

22. The magazine was known at the time as 1927, 1928, 1929, or 1930, and "revista de avance" was explicitly lowercase. However, scholars have since referred to the publication as *Revista de Avance*, and thus I adopt that convention. Also, even though each issue of the magazine was approximately thirty pages, the page numbers continue consecutively over multiple issues and years.

23. Alejo Carpentier, Martí Casanovas, Francisco Ichaso, Jorge Mañach, and Juan Marinello ("Los Cinco"), "Al llevar la ancla," *Revista de Avance* 1, no. 1 (March 15, 1927), 1. The editors signed their editorials, in the "Directrices" (Directives) sections as "Los Cinco" (The Five), which consisted of a shifting group of editors.

24. Mendonça Teles and Müller-Bergh, *Vanguardia latinoamericana*, vol. 2, 15.

25. Ángel Rama, "El primer cuento de Alejo Carpentier," *Hispamérica* 3, no. 9 (February 1975): 83. From jail Carpentier wrote the first draft of *¡Ecué-Yamba-O!*, an excerpt of which was published in *Imán*.

26. Upon the arrest of Martí Casanovas in 1927, the magazine announced his detainment for his activities with the Communist Party, asserted its commitment to free and open debate, and declared its solidarity with leftist political struggles. In the same issue the editors expressed their support for Mariátegui, who was also recently imprisoned in Peru, and lauded his political activities as well as his magazine *Amauta*. Los Cinco, "Directrices," *Revista de Avance* 1, no. 8 (June 30, 1927): 181.

27. Los Cinco, "Directrices," *Revista de Avance* 1, no. 3 (April 15, 1927): 41.

28. Los Cinco, "Directrices," *Revista de Avance* 2, no. 26 (September 15, 1928): 236.

29. According to Antoni Kapcia, the publication was inspired by José Ortega y Gasset's *Revista de Occidente*, founded in 1923 and Ortega's pioneering essay "La deshumanización del arte" (1925) served as a point of departure for *Revsita de Avance*'s debate about what constitutes avant-garde art. Kapcia, "Revolution, the Intellectual, and a Cuban Identity," 67.

30. Los Cinco, "Directrices: Sobre un meridiano intelectual," *Revista de Avance* 2, no. 26 (September 15, 1928): 273. I address the "meridian debate" at length in chapter 4.

31. Raúl Roa García, *Revista de Avance* 1, no. 10 (August 30, 1927): 269, quoted in Carlos Ripoll, *La generación del 23 en Cuba y otros apuntes sobre el vanguardismo* (New York: Las Américas, 1968), 85.

32. Félix Lizaso, "Postales de Cuba. El momento: La vanguardia," *La Gaceta Literaria* 1, no. 15 (August 1, 1927): 5.

33. Lino Novas Calvo, "Cuba Literaria II," *La Gaceta Literaria* 5, no. 118 (November 15, 1931): 2.

34. Masiello, "Rethinking Neocolonial Esthetics," 17.

35. "Fragmento de uno de los más recientes frescos de Diego Rivera," *Revista de Avance* 1, no. 9 (August 15, 1927): 227–28.

36. Mendonça Teles and Müller-Bergh, *Vanguardia latino-americana*, vol. 2, 15.

37. "Almanaque," *Revista de Avance* 1, no. 15 (November 15, 1927).

38. For more on Cuban music, see Wilfredo Cancio Isla, *"Revista de Avance,"* in *Encyclopedia of Latin American and Caribbean Literature, 1900–2003*, ed. Daniel Balderston and Mike Gonzalez (London: Routledge, 2004), 484.

39. Martínez, *Cuban Art and National Identity*, 75–76, 78, 81; Michele Greet, "At the Galleries," in *Transatlantic Encounters: Latin American Artists in Paris Between the Wars* (New Haven: Yale University Press, forthcoming). I thank Michele for generously sharing her research with me. For more on *afrocubanismo*, see Robin D. Moore, *Nationalizing Blackness: Afrocubanismo and Artistic Revolution in Havana, 1920–1940* (Pittsburgh: University of Pittsburgh Press, 1997).

40. Both "the most Spanish and most African of Spain's former colonies," according to Martínez, Cuba produced art and literature that reflected this uneasy position. Martínez, *Cuban Art and National Identity*, 93. See also Masiello, "Rethinking Neocolonial Esthetics," 22–23.

41. Juan Marinello, "Sobre la inquietud cubana," *Revista de Avance* 5, no. 43 (February 1930): 52, quoted in Ripoll, *La generación del 23 en Cuba*, 97.

42. Masiello, "Rethinking Neocolonial Esthetics," 20.

43. Los cinco, "Al llevar la ancla," 1.

44. Ibid. For more on the magazine's connection to *Proa*, see Jorge Schwartz, ed., *Las vanguardias latino-americanas: Textos programáticos y críticos* (Madrid: Cátedra, 1991), 311–12.

45. Jorge Mañach, "Vanguardismo," *Revista de Avance* 1, no. 1 (March 15, 1927): 2.

46. Ibid.

47. *Criollo* literally translates as "Creole." While in some cases it means someone of Spanish origin, here it means "native to Latin America" or "autochthonous." Los Cinco, "Letras extranjeras," *Revista de Avance* 1, no. 3 (April 15, 1927): 50.

48. Ibid.

49. Carlos Ripoll, "La *Revista de Avance* (1927–1930): Vocero de vanguardismo y pórtico de revolución," *Revista Iberoamericana* 30, no. 58 (July–December 1964): 265.

50. Cira Romero, ed., "Los Minoristas. Registro en publicacciones periódicas," *Cuba Literaria: Colección Orígines*, accessed May 4, 2012, http://www.cubaliteraria.cu/monografia/grupo_minorista/periodicos.html.

51. Los Cinco, "Directrices," *Revista de Avance* 1, no. 2 (March 30, 1927): 17.

52. Ibid.

53. *Revista de Avance* 1, no. 3 (April 15, 1927): 65.

54. Ibid.

55. The editorial wing of the magazine published Jorge Mañach, *Tiempo muerto* (1928), Juan Marinello, *Juventud y vejez* (1927), Félix Lizaso and José Fernández de Castro, *La poesia moderna en Cuba* (1926), Francisco Ichaso, *Góngora y la nueva poesía* (1927), and additional books by regular contributors to the magazine. Ripoll, "La *Revista de Avance* (1927–1930)," 267.

56. Martha de Castro, *El arte en Cuba* (Miami: Ediciones Universales, 1970), 55.

57. A complete list of artists includes Eduardo Abela, Rafael Blanco, Antonio Gattorno, Gabriel Castaño, José Hurtado de Mendoza, Luis López Méndez, Ramón Loy, Rebeca Peink de Rosado Ávila, Alberto Sobas, José Segura, Marcelo Pogolotti, Carlos Enríquez, Víctor Manuel, Lorenzo Romero Arciaga, Alice Neel, and Adja Madlein Yunkers.

58. Los Cinco, "Exposición de arte nuevo," *Revista de Avance* 1, no. 4 (April 30, 1927): 70, trans. and quoted in Camnitzer, *New Art Cuba*, 103.

59. Néstor García Canclini, "Modernity After Postmodernity," in *Beyond the Fantastic: Contemporary Art Criticism from Latin America*, ed. Gerardo Mosquera (Cambridge, Mass.: MIT Press, 1996), 31. For instance, in the Cuban context, the artist Víctor Manuel García (known as Víctor Manuel) traveled to France in 1925 and returned to Cuba in 1927. Eduardo Abela spent 1921 to 1924 in Spain, and went to Paris from 1927 to 1929 (and again from 1934 to 1937).

60. For a thorough analysis of Latin American artists in Paris, see Greet, *Transatlantic Encounters*.

61. For example, both Víctor Manuel and Antonio Gattorno had one-person shows at the Asociación de Pintores y Escultores.

62. Latin America was home to native populations, and between 1518 and 1870 the Spanish enslaved more than 1.5 million Africans, many of whom were taken to Cuban and Brazilian sugar plantations. The population of Latin America thus included indigenous people, Africans, and Europeans (along with mestizos and mulattos), and this racial composition led to economic hierarchies between races, as well as between those whites born in Europe, known as *peninsulares*, and those born in the New World, often called *criollos*. Thomas E. Skidmore, Peter H. Smith, and James Green, *Modern Latin America*, 7th ed. (New York: Oxford University Press, 2009), 20.

63. For more see Dawn Ades, *Art in Latin America: The Modern Era, 1820–1980* (New Haven: Yale University Press, 1989); Jacqueline Barnitz, *Twentieth-Century Art of Latin America* (Austin: University of Texas Press, 2001); Mari Carmen Ramírez and Hector Olea, eds., *Inverted Utopias: Avant-Garde Art in Latin America* (New Haven: Yale University Press, 2004); and Gerardo

Mosquera, "Africa in the Art of Latin America," *Art Journal* 51, no. 4 (1992): 30–38.

64. As Juan A. Martínez notes, Gattorno and Víctor Manuel likely saw the 1926 retrospective of Paul Gauguin at the Association Paris-Amérique Latine, while Abela seemed drawn to the work of Chagall. Martínez, *Cuban Art and National Identity*, 14. Michele Greet explains that Gaugin was shown at the Association Paris-Amérique Latine because he lived in Peru until he was eight years old. Greet, *Transatlantic Encounters*.

65. Martínez, *Cuban Art and National Identity*, 51.

66. Ibid., 50.

67. "'1927' Exposición de arte nuevo," *Revista de Avance* 1, no. 5 (May 15, 1927).

68. Los cinco, "Directrices," *Revista de Avance* 1, no. 3 (April 15, 1927): 41.

69. Martí Casanovas, "Nuevas Rumbas: La Exposición de 1927," *Revista de Avance* 1, no. 5 (May 15, 1927), trans. and quoted in Martínez, *Cuban Art and National Identity*, 11.

70. Los Cinco, "Directrices: Una encuesta," *Revista de Avance* 2, no. 26 (September 15, 1928): 235.

71. Ibid.

72. "A Survey: What Should American Art Be?," *Revista de Avance* 2, no. 26 (September 15, 1928): 235, trans. in Héctor Olea, Mari Carmen Ramírez, and Tomás Ybarra-Frausto, "Resisting Categories," in *Resisting Categories: Latin American and/or Latino?* Critical Documents of 20th-Century Latin American Art, vol. 1, ed. Héctor Olea, Mari Carmen Ramírez, and Tomás Ybarra-Frausto, María C. Gaztambide, and Melina Kervandjian (Houston: Museum of Fine Arts, Houston International Center for the Arts of the Americas, 2012), 373.

73. Rufino Blanco Fombona, response to "¿Qué debe ser el arte americano?," *Revista de Avance* 2, no. 29 (December 15, 1928): 361.

74. Raúl Roa, response to "¿Qué debe ser el arte americano?," *Revista de Avance* 4, no. 37 (August 15, 1929): 242. (Note: his full name is Raúl Roa García, but he was sometimes called Raúl Roa.)

75. Ibid. Emphasis in the original.

76. Jaime Torres Bodet, response to "¿Qué debe ser el arte americano?," *Revista de Avance* 3, no. 28 (November 15, 1928): 315.

77. Eduardo Áviles Ramírez, response to "¿Qué debe ser el arte americano?," *Revista de Avance* 4, no. 31 (February 15, 1929): 55.

78. Eduardo Abela, response to "¿Qué debe ser el arte americano?," *Revista de Avance* 2, no. 29 (December 15, 1928): 361.

79. Ildefonso Pereda Valdés, response to "¿Qué debe ser el arte americano?," *Revista de Avance* 4, no. 35 (June 15, 1929): 213.

80. Carlos Enríquez, response to "¿Qué debe ser el arte americano?," *Revista de Avance* 4, no. 33 (April 15, 1929): 118.

81. Luis Felipe Rodríguez, response to "¿Qué debe ser el arte americano?," *Revista de Avance* 4, no. 33 (April 15, 1929): 117.

82. José Antonio Ramos, response to "¿Qué debe ser el arte americano?," *Revista de Avance* 4, no. 34 (May 15, 1929): 150–51.

83. Ibid.

84. Francisco Ichaso, "Balance de una indagación," *Revista de Avance* 4, no. 38 (September 15, 1929): 258.

85. Ibid.

86. Ibid., 259.

87. Ibid., 258.

88. Ibid.

89. Ibid., 258–59.

90. Ibid., 260.

91. Ibid.

92. Ibid., 261.

93. Ibid., 262.

94. Vicky Unruh, *Latin American Vanguards: The Art of Contentious Encounters* (Berkeley: University of California Press, 1994), 133.

95. Ichaso, "Balance de una indagación," 261.

96. George Yúdice, "Rethinking the Theory of the Avant-Garde from the Periphery," in *Modernism and Its Margins*, ed. Anthony Geist and José Monleón (New York: Garland, 1999), 54.

97. Ichaso, "Balance de una indagación," 265.

98. Francisco Ichaso, "State of an Investigation" (1929), *Revista de Avance* 4, no. 38 (September 15, 1929): 264, trans. Sonya Montoya in Olea et al., *Resisting Categories*, 373.

99. Ichaso, "Balance de una indagación," 264.

100. Ibid.

101. Ichaso, "State of an Investigation," in *Resisting Categories*, 389.

102. Ichaso, "Balance de una indagación," 264.

103. Valdespino, 32; *Revista de Avance*'s final editorial outlines the dire situation: "Como consecuencia de esta dragonada, un estudiante acaba de morir al escribirse estas líneas. . . . Se rumora que por los sucesos ocurridos se suspenderán las garantías constitucionales, instaurándose la censura previa a la prensa en cuyo caso '1930', para no someterse a esa medida, suspenderá su publicación hasta que el pensamiento pueda emitirse libremente." *Revista de Avance* 5, no. 50 (September 15, 1930): 59.

104. In 1931 Ichaso and Mañach joined the ABC, a group of intellectuals who opposed Machado but did not align with the Communist Party nor student movements, as many of the other editors did. Masiello, "Rethinking Neocolonial Esthetics," 11n16.

105. Juan Marinello, *Literatura Hispanoamérica* (Mexico: Ediciones de la Universidad Nacional de Mexico,

1937), quoted in Ripoll, *La generación del 23 en Cuba,* 110–11.

106. *Orígenes* was initially edited by José Lezama Lima, Mariano Rodríguez, Alfredo Lozano, and José Rodríguez Feo. Kapcia, "Revolution, the Intellectual, and a Cuban Identity," 67. For more on the relationship between the two magazines see: Ben A. Heller, *Assimilation/Generation/Resurrection: Contrapuntal Readings in the Poetry of José Lezama Lima* (Lewisburg, PA: Bucknell University Press, 1997), 26–36.

107. José Antonio Fernández de Castro, who contributed to *Revista de Avance,* edited the literary supplement to Cuba's daily newspaper, *El Diario de la Marina* (1927–30) and worked for *El Fígaro* (1885–1933), while José Z. Tallet, an editor of *Revista de Avance,* worked in multiple capacities for *El Mundo* (1927–33), *Ahora* (1933–35), *El noticiero mercantil* (1936), and *Baraguá* (1937) as well as writing for the foreign newspapers *El País* and *El Mundo.*

108. For more on Carpentier's involvement in Cuban print culture, see Klaus Müller-Bergh, "Corrientes vanguardistas y surrealismo en la obra de Alejo Carpentier," *Revista Hispánica Moderna* 35, no. 4 (October–December 1969): 223–340.

109. "Almanaque," *Revista de Avance* 3, no. 4 (March 15, 1929): 90, quoted in Martínez, *Cuban Art and National Identity,* 12.

110. Camnitzer, *New Art Cuba,* 154–55; Martínez, *Cuban Art and National Identity,* 18.

111. Alfred H. Barr Jr., "Modern Cuban Painters," *Bulletin of the Museum of Modern Art* (New York) 11, no. 5 (April 1944): 2.

112. Jorge Mañach, *Historia y estilo* (Havana, 1944), 200–201, quoted in José Juan Arrom, *Esquema generacional de las letras hispanoamericanas: Ensayo de un método* (Bogotá: Instituto Caro y Cuervo, 1963), 197.

113. Félix Lizaso, "La revista de avance," *Boletín de la Academia Cubana de la Lengua* 10, nos. 3–4 (July–December 1961): 19, quoted in Ripoll, "La *Revista de Avance* (1927–1930)," 261.

114. "Revistas Extranjeras," *Revista de Avance* 4, no. 37 (August 15, 1929): 250–51.

CHAPTER 3

1. "It will be a magazine that will maintain the documentation of its time, interspersing photographs in some numbers and disregarding them in others." Elvira de Alvear, "Imán," *Imán* (Paris), no. 1 (April 1931): 1. All translations are by the author unless otherwise noted.

2. Eugene Jolas, *Man from Babel,* ed. Andreas Kramer and Rainer Rumold (New Haven: Yale University Press, 1998), 2. Jolas's archive contains some of his writing in "Atlantica," his invented language that directly reflected his attempt to create an "Atlantic language."

3. Eugene Jolas et al., "Proclamation: Revolution of the Word," *transition,* nos. 16–17 (June 1929): 13.

4. Alejo Carpentier, "América ante la joven literatura Europea," *Carteles* (Havana) 17, no. 17 (June 28, 1931): 54.

5. Marcy E. Schwartz, *Writing Paris: Urban Topographies of Desire in Contemporary Latin American Fiction* (Albany: State University of New York Press, 1999), 2.

6. Ángel Rama, *Rubén Darío y el modernismo* (1970) (Caracas: Alfadil, 1985), 43; Julio Ramos, *Divergent Modernities: Culture and Politics in Nineteenth-Century Latin America,* trans. John D. Blanco (Durham: Duke University Press, 2001), 82.

7. Michele Greet, "Introduction," in *Transatlantic Encounters: Latin American Artists in Paris Between the Wars* (New Haven: Yale University Press, forthcoming).

8. Darío published a compilation of his chronicles on the 1900 Paris Exposition for *La Nación* as Rubén Darío, *Peregrinaciones* (Paris: Librería de la Viuda de Ch. Bouret, 1901).

9. Jaime Hanneken, "Going Mundial: What It Really Means to Desire Paris," *Modern Language Quarterly* 71, no. 2 (June 2010): 136.

10. Ernest Martinenche, Charles Lesca, and Ventura García Calderón, "Editorial Statement," *La Revue de l'Amérique Latine* (Paris) 1, no. 1 (January 1922): 2. (Note that Ventura García Calderón was the brother of Francisco García Calderón, the editor of *Revista de América,* a Spanish-language magazine in Paris.)

11. The editors, "La 'Revue Sudaméricaine,'" *Nosotros* 15, no. 63 (1914), reprinted in Noemi Ulla, *La Revista "Nosotros"* (Buenos Aires: Editorial Galerna, 1969), 88.

12. For more on *Revue Sud-Américaine,* see Emilio Carilla, "La revista de Lugones: *Revue Sud-Américaine,*" *Thesaurus* 29, no. 3 (September–December 1974): 501–25.

13. Alejo Carpentier, "Abela en la Galerie Zak," *Social* (Havana) 14, no. 1 (January 1929), reprinted in Alejo Carpentier, *Crónicas 2: Arte, literatura, política,* vol. 9 of *Obras completas* (Mexico City: Siglo XXI, 1986), 165–69; Alejo Carpentier, "La obra reciente de Carlos Enríquez," *Social* (Havana) 17, no. 5 (May 1932), reprinted in *Crónicas 2,* 360–63; Alejo Carpentier, "Un pintor cubano con los futuristas italianos: Marcelo Pogolotti," *Social* (Havana) 16, no. 11 (November 1931), reprinted in *Crónicas 2,* 318–21.

14. Michele Greet, "About," *Transatlantic Encounters,* accessed February 20, 2015, http://chnm.gmu.edu/transatlanticencounters/about; see also Michele Greet, "Paris: Capital of Latin America," in *Transatlantic Encounters.*

15. Michele Greet, "Galerie Zak," *Transatlantic Encounters,* accessed February 20, 2015, http://chnm.gmu.edu/transatlanticencounters/items/show/5216. See also Michele Greet, "At the Galleries," in *Transatlantic Encounters.*

16. Schwartz, *Writing Paris,* 18.

17. Pedro Osorio, "La Maison de L'Amérique Latine," *Revue de l'Amérique Latine* (Paris) 7, no. 28 (April 1924)

380, trans. and quoted in Michele Greet, "Paris: Capital of Latin America," in *Transatlantic Encounters*.

18. Pascale Casanova, *The World Republic of Letters*, trans. Malcolm DeBevoise (Cambridge, Mass.: Harvard University Press, 2007).

19. Carmen Vásquez, "Le revue '*Imán*,'" in *Mélusine no. III: Marges Non-frontières*, ed. Henri Behar (Lausanne, Switzerland: Editions l'Age d'Homme, 1982), 115.

20. Robert Desnos et al., *Un cadavre* (Paris: Impremiere Spéciale du Cadavre, January 1930); Alejo Carpentier, "Le musique cubaine," *Documents* (Paris), no. 6 (November 1929): 324–29; Alejo Carpentier, "Lettre des Antilles," *Bifur* (Paris), no. 3 (September 1929): 91–105. James Joyce, William Carlos Williams, and Ramón Gómez de la Serna were listed as "foreign advisors" to *Bifur*. Miguel Ángel Asturias and Vicente Huidobro also contributed to the journal. Vásquez, "Le revue '*Imán*,'" 116.

21. The column ran for about a year, from 1924 to 1925. Through this position Jolas met many writers with whom he would collaborate on *transition*, including Elliot Paul, Robert Sage, Virgil Geddes, and Henry Miller.

22. Eugene Jolas, "Rambles Through Literary Paris," *Chicago Tribune* (Paris), June 8, 1925, 2, Eugene and Maria Jolas Papers, Beinecke Rare Book and Manuscript Library, Yale University, Series II, Box 67, Folder 1579.

23. "The lost generation," a term ostensibly coined by Gertrude Stein, was popularized in the epigraph for Hemingway's *The Sun Also Rises* (1926), to identify the Americans who lived and worked in Paris following the end of World War I. However, as Marc Dolan points out, "The phrase 'lost generation' was first employed by the German Expressionist Franz Pfemfert in *Die Aktion* in 1912 and was used extensively in Britain and France in the first years after the war to describe the literal age cohort that had been severely reduced by the fighting of 1914–18." Marc Dolan, "The History of Their Lives: Mythic Autobiography and 'The Lost Generation,'" *Journal of American Studies* 27, no. 1 (April 1993): 41. For more on American artists abroad, see Wanda Corn, *The Great American Thing: Modern Art and National Identity, 1915–1935* (Berkeley: University of California Press, 1999).

24. Marsden Hartley, quoted by Pierre Loving, "We're in Paris Because," *Chicago Tribune* (Paris), February 1, 1925, in Hugh Ford, ed., *The Left Bank Revisited: Selections from the Paris "Tribune," 1917–1934* (University Park: Penn State University Press, 1972), 46.

25. Jessie Fauset, quoted by Pierre Loving, "We're in Paris Because," *Chicago Tribune* (Paris), February 1, 1925, in Ford, *The Left Bank Revisited,* 47–48.

26. The interest in these responses might have prompted the *Tribune*'s coverage of the 1928 questionnaire in the article "17 Writers and Artists Explain Why They Live Outside of US," *Chicago Tribune* (Paris), October 26, 1928, in Ford, *The Left Bank Revisited,* 49–50.

27. Ford Madox Ford, "Some American Expatriates," *Vanity Fair* 28 (April 1, 1927): 64 and 98, accessed October 10, 2011, http://www.vanityfair.com/culture/features/1927/04/hemingway-192704#gotopage1.

28. Alex Small, "Thirst for Booze and for Liberty Sends Americans Abroad," *Chicago Tribune* (Paris), September 20, 1929, and "Why Americans Leave Home and Settle Down Permanently in Europe," *Chicago Tribune* (Paris), July 10, 1930, in Ford, *The Left Bank Revisited*, 50–51 and 55–57. Note: Small was himself an American abroad.

29. Small, in Ford, *The Left Bank Revisited*, 56.

30. Jolas specifically cites André Gide, who has "expressed the opinion that America will eventually produce the literature for which the present stage of transition is only a preparation." Eugene Jolas, "Rambles Through Literary Paris," *Chicago Tribune* (Paris), June 22, 1924, 4, Eugene and Maria Jolas Papers, Beinecke Rare Book and Manuscript Library, Yale University, Series II, Box 67, Folder 1579.

31. Eugene Jolas, "Rambles Through Literary Paris," *Chicago Tribune* (Paris), August 10, 1924, 2, Eugene and Maria Jolas Papers, Beinecke Rare Book and Manuscript Library, Yale University, Series II, Box 67, Folder 1579.

32. Although Jolas received editorial assistance on *transition* first from Elliot Paul and later from Robert Sage, he signed most of the editorials alone and remains the strongest editorial voice of the magazine. Elliot Paul shifted from associate to contributing editor in 1928; Robert Sage took over in October 1927 as associate editor and remained until late 1929, when Stuart Gilbert filled the position. Maria Jolas assisted with every stage of the publication, although she was not on the masthead.

33. Eugene Jolas and Elliot Paul, "Introduction," *transition*, no. 1 (April 1927): 136–37.

34. Advertisement for *transition*, Eugene and Maria Jolas Papers, Beinecke Rare Book and Manuscript Library, Yale University, Series XII, Box 59, Folder 1372.

35. Eugene Jolas and Elliot Paul, "Introduction," *transition*, no. 1 (April 1927), in Noel Riley Fitch, ed., *In transition: A Paris Anthology. Writing and Art from transition Magazine, 1927–1930* (New York: Doubleday, 1990), 21.

36. The magazine appeared in 1927 as a monthly review. In 1928 it became quarterly, but only three issues were printed in 1928 and 1929. From 1929 to 1938 eight more issues appeared. Starting in 1932 it was published by the Dutch Servire Press in The Hague. For more, see Céline Mansanti, "Between Modernisms: *transition* (1927–38)," in *The Oxford Critical and Cultural History of Modernist Magazines*, vol. 2, *North America, 1894–1960*, ed. Peter Brooker and Andrew Thacker (Oxford: Oxford University Press, 2009), 718–37; Frederick J. Hoffman, Charles Allen, and Carolyn F. Ulrich, *The Little Magazine: A History and a*

Bibliography (Princeton: Princeton University Press, 1946), 175.

37. Mansanti, "Between Modernisms," 730.

38. Jolas, *Man from Babel*, 1–2.

39. Ibid., 2.

40. Eugene Jolas, "*Transition*: An Occidental Workshop, 1927–1938," in *transition workshop* (New York: Viking Press, 1949), 13.

41. Jolas, *Man from Babel*, 85–86.

42. Eugene Jolas, "Rambles Through Literary Paris," *Chicago Tribune* (Paris), October 19, 1924, in Ford, *The Left Bank Revisited*, 98.

43. Eugene Jolas, "Through Paris Bookland," *Chicago Tribune* (Paris), May 25, 1924, 2, Eugene and Maria Jolas Papers, Beinecke Rare Book and Manuscript Library, Yale University, Series II, Box 67, Folder 1579.

44. Eugene Jolas, "Rambles Through Literary Paris," *Chicago Tribune* (Paris), July 13, 1924: 2; Eugene Jolas, "Rambles Through Literary Paris," *Chicago Tribune* (Paris), August 10, 1924, 2, Eugene and Maria Jolas Papers, Beinecke Rare Book and Manuscript Library, Yale University, Series II, Box 67, Folder 1579.

45. Hugh Ford, *Published in Paris: A Literary Chronicle of Paris in the 1920s and 1930s* (New York: MacMillan, 1975), 81. Ezra Pound also launched the *Exile* from Rapallo, Italy, in 1927; however, neither Jolas nor Pound knew that the other had plans to start a magazine. See Ezra Pound, "Small Magazines," *English Journal* 19, no. 9 (November 1930): 702; and Craig Monk, "Exile," in *The Ezra Pound Encyclopedia*, ed. Demetres P. Tryphonopoulos and Stephen J. Adams (Westport, Conn.: Greenwood Press, 2005), 113–14.

46. Jolas and Paul, "Introduction," *transition*, no. 1 (April 1927): 136.

47. Ibid., 137.

48. Ibid.

49. Ibid., 138.

50. "Advertisement," *transition*, no. 7 (October 1927): 171–72; Catherine Turner, *Marketing Modernism Between the Two World Wars* (Boston, Mass.: University of Massachusetts Press, 2003), 89.

51. "Advertisement," *transition*, no. 7 (October 1927): 172.

52. See also Eugene and Maria Jolas Papers, Beinecke Rare Book and Manuscript Library, Yale University, Series XII, Box 60, Folders 1400–1401, *transition* press clippings 1926–52.

53. Jolas, *Man from Babel*, 98.

54. Elliot Paul, "Stuart Davis, American Painter," *transition*, no. 14 (Fall 1928): 146–49.

55. Mansanti, "Between Modernisms," 718n2.

56. Jolas, *Man from Babel*, 88. *transition* can also be read in line with the 1920s group "l'Arc" (the Bridge) and their indebtedness to the Der Brücke (the Bridge) artists, German Expressionists who took their name from Nietzsche's claim that man is a bridge to a higher ideal.

57. Jolas, *Man from Babel*, 88. The precedent for Jolas's choice is the *transatlantic review*, edited by Ford Madox Ford, who had served as the literary columnist for the *Tribune* before Jolas. *transition* was suspended from June 1930 to March 1932, after which it began to use a capital "T," further angering critics. Eugene Jolas, "Introduction," in *transition workshop* (New York: Viking Press, 1949), 14.

58. *transition* paid all of its contributors equally. However, Jolas acknowledged that their payment of twenty (and later thirty) francs a page was a only a gesture, writing, "We realize that our relatively small check in francs, paying all contributors alike at page rates, becomes almost ludicrous when changed into dollars, and compared with the rates which American magazines, subsidized by advertising, are able to pay." Eugene Jolas, "Glossary," *transition*, no. 12 (March 1928): 182.

59. Eugene Jolas, "Glossary," *transition*, no. 4 (July 1927): 179; Eugene and Maria Jolas Papers, Beinecke Rare Book and Manuscript Library, Yale University, Subscribers' list, Series XII, Box 60, Folder 1402 and advertisement for *transition*, Series XII, Box 59, Folder 1372; Hoffman, Allen, and Ulrich, *The Little Magazine*, 175.

60. Since March 1924, when the first installment of "Work in Progress" was printed in the *transatlantic review*, the project had also appeared in three other magazines (the *Criterion*, *Le Navire d'argent,* and *This Quarter*), but Beach and Joyce both sought a permanent outlet for the work. Beach's close friend Adrienne Monnier supplied *transition* with additional contributors from her own publication *Commerce* (1924–32), including Léon-Paul Fargue, Henri Michaux, André Gide, and André Breton. Mansanti, "Between Modernisms," 730.

61. The text's publication in *transition* may have also helped Joyce secure a publisher for *Finnegans Wake*. Stephen John Dilks, "Selling 'Work in Progress,'" *James Joyce Quarterly* 41, no. 4 (Summer 2004): 730. Ezra Pound did not approve of Joyce's serialization of the work in *transition* (perhaps because he wanted to publish it himself). Pound wrote to Joyce, "I think, and always have thought that the 'sample of woik in prog' stunt was bad. The transat. did it because there simply wasn't enough copy to fill the so large review. If I had an encyclopedicly large monthly, the keqestion wd. be different" [*sic*]. Ezra Pound to James Joyce, January 12, 1927, letter, Eugene and Maria Jolas Papers, Beinecke Rare Book and Manuscript Library, Yale University, Series XIV, Box 63, Folder 1486.

62. John Pilling, *Beckett Before Godot* (1997), quoted in Craig Monk, "Beckett Is Vertical: Proselytizing with the Littles," *Canadian Journal of Irish Studies* 27, no. 2 (Fall 2001): 9.

63. Samuel Beckett, "Dante . . . Bruno . . . Vico . . . Joyce," *transition*, nos. 16–17 (June 1929): 242–53.

64. Samuel Putnam, *Paris Was Our Mistress: Memoirs of a Lost and Found Generation* (1947) (Carbondale: Southern Illinois University Press, 1970), 179.

65. Eugene Jolas and Robert Sage, "Notice," *transition*, no. 13 (Summer 1928): 286 in Fitch, *In transition*, 175.

66. "An Elucidation" (1923) was published in *transition* in 1927, *Tender Buttons* (1914) in 1928, and *Four Saints in Three Acts* (1927) in 1929.

67. See for instance, Laura Riding, "The New Barbarism and Gertrude Stein," *transition*, no. 3 (June 1927): 153–68.

68. In the third issue of *transition* the editors contrast the work of Joyce and Stein, stoking Stein's sense of competition. Eugene Jolas and Elliot Paul, "K.O.R.A.A.," *transition*, no. 3 (June 1927): 173–77.

69. In her book Stein centralizes Paul's role in the development of the magazine. Gertrude Stein, *The Autobiography of Alice B. Toklas* (1933) (New York: Vintage Books, 1960), 240.

70. Ibid., 241. This refrain is repeated twice in this section of the *Autobiography*.

71. Georges Braque, contribution to *Testimony Against Gertrude Stein,* supplement to *transition*, no. 23 (February 1935): 13. Maria Jolas accuses Stein of "countless misstatements about practically everybody she had known in France, including Gene and me." Maria Jolas, *Maria Jolas: Woman of Action; A Memoir and Other Writings* ed. Mary Ann Caws (Columbia: University of South Carolina Press, 2004), 90.

72. Craig Monk, *Writing the Lost Generation* (Iowa City: University of Iowa Press, 2008), 15–16.

73. Jolas, *Man from Babel*, 93.

74. Louis Aragon et al., "Hands Off Love," *transition*, no. 6 (September 1927): 155–56. The declaration was a way for the magazine to oppose America's moralizing stance in general, and more specifically, the allegations made by Chaplin's wife during their divorce proceedings.

75. Douglas McMillan, *Transition: The History of a Literary Era, 1927–1938* (London: Calder and Boyars, 1975), 89.

76. Eugene Jolas, "Suggestions for a New Magic," *transition*, no. 3 (June 1927): 179.

77. Malcom Cowley, *Exile's Return: A Literary Odyssey of the 1920s* (1934), ed. Donald W. Faulkner (New York: Penguin, 1994), 275.

78. Eugene Jolas, "Frontierless Decade," *transition* (April–May 1938), quoted in Klaus H. Kiefer and Rainer Rumold, eds., *Eugene Jolas: Critical Writings, 1924–1951* (Evanston: Northwestern University Press, 2009), 118.

79. Eugene Jolas and Elliot Paul, "A Review," *transition*, no. 12 (March 1928): 139.

80. Jason Wilson, *Jorge Luis Borges* (London: Reaktion Books, 2006), 100; Jorge Luis Borges, "Elvira de Alvear," *El hacedor* (Buenos Aires: Emecé, 1960). Elvira de Alvear was, according to some critics, the

81. Jorge Luis Borges, "Prólogo," in *Reposo* (Buenos Aires: M. Gleizer, 1934), 16.

82. Elvira de Alvear, *Reposo* (Buenos Aires: M. Gleizer, 1934).

83. Carmen Vásquez, for instance, is very vague on this front, writing, "Malheureusement ce numéro ne put jamais sortir. En Amérique du Nord et du Sud, autant qu'en Europe, les séquelles du krack de Wall Street se faisaient sentier. Et un jour l'Argentine passa une loi contre l'exportation du capital. Elvira de Alvear connut vite ses conséquences. Elle dut annuler tous ses engagements; quitter son bel appartement parisien, retourner dans son pays natal." Vásquez, "Le revue 'Imán,'" 120. An article in the journal *Criterio* titled "La vida intelectual: Elvira de Alvear" indicates that she was back in Buenos Aires in 1932 but had plans to return to Paris. See: "La vida intelectual: Elvira de Alvear," *Criterio* (Buenos Aires) 5, no. 227 (1932): 262. The National Library of Spain reports that she returned to Buenos Aires in 1937. "Imán," Hemeroteca Digital, Biblioteca Nacional de España, accessed August 3, 2015, http://hemerotecadigital .bne.es/details.vm?q=id:0005350563&lang=en.

84. Jean Cassou, "Poésie: Amités sud-americans," *Les Nouvelles Littéraires* (Paris) (January 30, 1932): 7.

85. Vásquez, "Le revue 'Imán,'" 115; Héctor René Lafleur, Sergio D. Provenzano, and Fernando Alonso, eds., *Las revistas literarias argentinas, 1893–1967* (Buenos Aires: Ediciones El 8vo. loco, 2006), 21n19.

86. Vásquez, "Le revue 'Imán,'" 118.

87. *Imán* (Paris), no. 1 (April 1931): inner cover.

88. Carmen Vásquez, "Alejo Carpentier en París (1928–1939)," *Coloquio 2006 Escritores de América Latina en París* (París, 2006), Centro Virtual Cervantes, 108, accessed December 24, 2016, http://cvc.cervantes.es /Ensenanza/biblioteca_ele/aepe/pdf/coloquio_2006 /coloquio_2006_15.pdf.

89. Carlos Enríquez lived in New York from 1927 to 1930 and in Paris and Madrid from 1930 to 1933 , before returning to Cuba in 1934.

90. Eugene Jolas, "Documento," trans. Manuel Altolaguierre, *Imán* (Paris), no. 1 (April 1931): 123–27; Alejo Carpentier, "Cuban Magic," trans. Frederick M. Murray, *transition*, nos. 19–20 (June 1930): 384–90; Franz Kafka, "The Sentence," trans. Eugene Jolas and Maria Jolas, *transition*, no. 11 (February 1928): 35–47. This story is later translated as "The Judgement" in English. Note that Arqueles Vela translated it as "La Sentencia" for *Imán*, likely because the Mexican writer was working from the Jolases' English translation. Franz Kafka, "La Setencia," trans. Arqueles Vela, *Imán* (Paris), no. 1 (April 1931): 104–115.

91. Carlos Rincón, "Carpentier 'Frances': *Documents, Bifur, Un Cadavre,* y dos cartas a Georges Bataille," *Nuevo Crítico* 22, nos. 42–43 (2009): 101–21; and Alejo Carpentier, *Music in Cuba* (1946), trans. Alan West-Durán, ed. Timothy Brennan (Minneapolis: University of Minnesota Press, 2001), 15.

92. Robert Desnos, introduction to Alejo Carpentier, "Le musique cubaine," *Documents* (Paris), no. 6 (November 1929): 324.

93. "Giacometti in South America," Foundation Alberto et Annette Giacometti, accessed August 3, 2015, http://www.fondation-giacometti.fr/en/art/38 /actualites/180/giacometti-in-south-america/; Cecilia Braschi, "De París a Buenos Aires, relaciones particulares," *La Nación* (Buenos Aires) (October 12, 2012), accessed August 3, 2015, http://www.lanacion.com .ar/1516367-de-paris-a-buenos-aires-relaciones -particulares; and Michel Leiris, "Alberto Giacometti," *Documents* (Paris), no. 4 (September 1929): 209.

94. Gilberto Mendonça Teles and Klaus Müller-Bergh, *Vanguardia latinoamericana: Historia, crítica y documentos,* vol. 5, *Chile y países del Plata: Argentina, Uruguay, Paraguay* (Madrid: Iberoamericana, 2009), 150.

95. Elvira de Alvear, "Imán," *Imán* (Paris), no. 1 (April 1931): 1–3.

96. Ibid., 2.

97. François-René de Chateaubriand, epigraph in Léon-Paul Fargue, "De una pluma a un imán," *Imán* (Paris), no. 1 (April 1931): 6.

98. Léon-Paul Fargue, "De una pluma a un imán," *Imán* (Paris), no. 1 (April 1931): 10.

99. Eugene Jolas and Elliot Paul, Advertisement, *transition*, no. 2 (May 1927): 189.

100. Eugene Jolas, "Glossary," *transition*, no. 12 (March 1928): 182.

101. Eugene Jolas, "Inquiry Among European Writers into the Spirit of America," *transition*, no. 13 (Summer 1928): 248.

102. Jolas, *Man from Babel*, 118.

103. Jolas and Paul, "A Review," 142.

104. Ibid.

105. Ibid., 144.

106. Jolas, "Inquiry Among European Writers into the Spirit of America," 248.

107. Ibid.

108. Ibid.

109. "Number 13 will have as its basic idea an inquiry into modern American literature and ideology. One of the features of this number will be the publication of results of an *enquête* among the writers and artists of Europe about modern America." Jolas, "Glossary," 182.

110. Bernard Faÿ, response to "Inquiry Among European Writers into the Spirit of America," *transition*, no. 13 (Summer 1928): 261.

111. Benjamin Péret, response to "Inquiry," 250.

112. René Lalou, response to "Inquiry," 265; Roger Vitrac, response to "Inquiry," 275.

113. Tristan Tzara, response to "Inquiry," 252.

114. Gottfried Benn, response to "Inquiry," 252; Regis Michaud, response to "Inquiry," 270.

115. Ivan Goll, response to "Inquiry," 256.

116. Marcel Brion, response to "Inquiry," 252.

117. Georges Hugnet, response to "Inquiry," 266.

118. Philippe Soupault, response to "Inquiry," 263.

119. Max Rychner, response to "Inquiry," 256.

120. Vladimir Lindin, response to "Inquiry Among European Writers into the Spirit of America," *transition*, no. 14 (Fall 1928): 275 (Vladimir Lindin's response was submitted from Moscow and printed in the subsequent issue of *transition*); Theo van Doesburg, response to "Inquiry Among European Writers into the Spirit of America," *transition*, no. 13 (Summer 1928): 260.

121. Henry Poulaille, response to "Inquiry," 268.

122. Eugene Jolas, "On the Quest," *transition*, no. 9 (December 1927): 192.

123. Jolas writes in opposition to realism at length in the magazine through statements such as "Realism, as it is still preached in America, is a movement with which we have no sympathy. . . . We are against all methods that believe that the photographic representation of life is the aim of true art." Jolas, "On the Quest," 194. Jolas also writes in an early editorial, "Realism in America has reached its point of saturation. . . . We are not interested in literature that willfully attempts to be of the age." Eugene Jolas, "Suggestions for a New Magic," 178.

124. It is worth noting that *Imán* uses the phrase "América Latina" instead of "América." This is possibly because, unlike *Revista de Avance, Imán* was based in Paris and its readers were familiar with the French "Amérique latine."

125. Carpentier, "América ante la joven literatura Europea," 30.

126. De Alvear, "Imán," 3.

127. Ibid.

128. Michel Leiris, response to "Conocimiento de América Latina," *Imán* (Paris), no. 1 (April 1931): 201; Philippe Soupault, response to "Conocimiento," 207; Roger Vitrac, response to "Conocimiento," 221.

129. Soupault, response to "Conocimiento," 206.

130. Walter Mehring, response to "Conocimiento," 211.

131. Georges Ribemont-Dessaignes, response to "Conocimiento," 189.

132. Ibid., 190.

133. Adapting Mary Louise Pratt's term "industrial reverie," Ericka Beckman coined the term "export reverie" as that which drove modernization in Latin America from roughly 1870–1930, an apt characterization of what Ribemont-Dessaignes describes.

Ericka Beckman, *Capital Fictions: The Literature of Latin America's Export Age* (Minneapolis: University of Minnesota Press, 2013). I thank María del Pilar Blanco for this reference.

134. Robert Desnos, response to "Conocimiento," 196.

135. Leiris, response to "Conocimiento," 201–2.

136. Nino Frank, response to "Conocimiento," 229.

137. Ibid.

138. Alfred Kreymborg, response to "Conocimiento," 213–14.

139. Soupault, response to "Conocimiento," 206.

140. Ibid.

141. Georges Bataille, response to "Conocimiento," 200.

142. Ribemont-Dessaignes, response to "Conocimiento," 190.

143. Ibid., 193.

144. McMillan, *Transition,* 45.

145. Eugene Jolas to Gertrude Stein, August 29, 1928, letter, Gertrude Stein and Alice B. Toklas Papers, Yale Collection of American Literature, Beinecke Rare Book and Manuscript Library, Yale University, Series II, Box 112, Folder 2300.

146. Eugene Jolas and Robert Sage to Gertrude Stein, August 25, 1928, letter, Gertrude Stein and Alice B. Toklas Papers, Yale Collection of American Literature, Beinecke Rare Book and Manuscript Library, Yale University, Series II, Box 112, Folder 2300.

147. "Why Do Americans Live in Europe?," *transition,* no. 14 (Fall 1928): 97.

148. This copyright was implemented starting in *transition,* no. 9 (December 1927).

149. "Why Do Americans Live in Europe?," 97.

150. Kathleen Cannell, response to "Why Do Americans Live in Europe?," *transition,* no. 14 (Fall 1928): 117.

151. Harry Crosby, response to "Why Do Americans Live in Europe?," 114.

152. William Carlos Williams, "The Somnabulists," *transition,* no. 18 (November 1929): 149.

153. H. Wolf Kaufman, response to "Why Do Americans Live in Europe?," 118.

154. Sylvia Beach, *Shakespeare and Company* (New York: Harcourt, Brace, 1959), 23–24.

155. Jolas, "Introduction," *transition workshop* 17.

156. Harold J. Salemson, response to "Why Do Americans Live in Europe?," 116.

157. Robert McAlmon, response to "Why Do Americans Live in Europe?," 98–99.

158. Leigh Hoffman, response to "Why Do Americans Live in Europe?," 101.

159. Gertrude Stein, response to "Why Do Americans Live in Europe?," 97–98.

160. Ibid.

161. Gertrude Stein, *Paris, France* (1940), in J. Gerald Kennedy, *Imagining Paris: Exile, Writing, and American Identity* (New Haven: Yale University Press, 1993), 43.

162. Gertrude Stein, "An American and France," typescript of 1936 lecture, Gertrude Stein and Alice B. Toklas Papers, Yale Collection of American Literature, Beinecke Rare Book and Manuscript Library, in Kennedy, *Imagining Paris,* 40–41.

163. Gertrude Stein, *Paris, France,* in Kennedy, *Imagining Paris,* 43.

164. Berenice Abbott, response to "Why Do Americans Live in Europe?," 111.

165. George Antheil, response to "Why Do Americans Live in Europe?," 101; Ivan Beede, response to "Why Do Americans Live in Europe?," *In transition,* 114.

166. Antheil, response to "Why Do Americans Live in Europe?," 101.

167. Emily Holmes Coleman, response to "Why Do Americans Live in Europe?," 111.

168. Matthew Josephson, "Foreword," to Ford, *The Left Bank Revisited,* xix.

169. Cowley, *Exile's Return,* 83.

170. Ernest Hemingway, *A Moveable Feast* (New York: Macmillan, 1964), 7.

171. Archibald MacLeish, "American Letter" (1929), in *Collected Poems 1917–1982* (Boston: Houghton Mifflin, 1985), 163–65.

172. Walter Lowenfel, response to "Why Do Americans Live in Europe?," 107.

173. Putnam, *Paris Was Our Mistress,* 247.

174. Robert McAlmon with Kay Boyle, *Being Geniuses Together, 1920–1930* (1938) (Baltimore: Johns Hopkins University Press, 1984), 256.

175. Jolas, *Man from Babel,* 2.

176. Kennedy, *Imagining Paris,* 27.

177. Henry Miller, *Tropic of Cancer* (1934) (New York: Grove Press, 1961), 152–53.

178. Edward Said, "Reflections on Exile," in *Out There: Marginalization and Contemporary Cultures,* ed. Russell Ferguson, Martha Gever, Trinh T. Minh-ha, and Cornel West (Cambridge, Mass.: MIT Press, 1990), 362–63.

179. Jolas, "Introduction," 17.

180. Said, "Reflections on Exile," 366.

181. Lansing Warren, response to "Why Do Americans Live in Europe?," 112.

182. Carpentier, "América ante la joven literatura Europea," 30.

183. Ibid.

184. Ibid., 54.

185. Ibid.

186. Ibid.

187. Ibid.

188. Ibid.

189. Ibid.

190. Jolas, *Man from Babel,* 2.

191. Jolas et al., "Proclamation: Revolution of the Word," 13.

192. Ibid.

193. Jolas and Paul, "Introduction," 136.

194. Eugene Jolas, "Transatlantic Letter," *transition,* no. 13 (Summer 1928): 276–77.

195. Eugene Jolas, "Super-Occident," *transition*, no. 15 (November 1929): 15.

196. Eugene Jolas, "The Revolution of Language and James Joyce," *transition*, no. 11 (February 1928): 112.

197. Ibid., 115.

198. Eugene Jolas, "Language of the Night," *transition*, no. 21 (March 1932), in Kiefer and Rumold, *Eugene Jolas*, 142.

199. Jolas, *Man from Babel*, 146–47.

200. Ibid., 146.

201. Jolas, "Documento," 124.

202. Other artists at the time similarly had utopian aspirations for a universal language. The Argentine artist Xul Solar experimented with a language he invented called *neo-criollo* and the Uruguayan artist Joaquín Torres-García pioneered a visual vocabulary that he called "constructive universalism" based on pre-Columbian motifs. For more on Solar, see Patricia M. Artundo, ed., *Xul Solar: Visiones y revelaciones* (Buenos Aires: Malba, 2005). For more on Torres-García, see Mari Carmen Ramírez, "Inversions: The School of the South," in *Inverted Utopias: Avant-Garde Art in Latin America*, ed. Mari Carmen Ramírez and Héctor Olea (New Haven: Yale University Press, 2004); and Luis Pérez-Oramas, ed. *Joaquín Torres-García: The Arcadian Modern* (New York: Museum of Modern Art, 2015).

203. Marjorie Perloff, "'Logocinéma of the Frontiersman': Eugene Jolas' Multilingual Poetics and Its Legacies," in *Differentials: Poetry, Poetics, Pedagogy* (Tuscaloosa: University of Alabama Press, 2004), 101.

204. David Bennett, "Periodical Fragments and Organic Culture: Modernism, the Avant-Garde, and the Little Magazine," *Contemporary Literature* 30, no. 4 (1989): 498.

205. Jolas, *Man from Babel*, xxvii.

206. Eugene Jolas, "Glossary," *transition*, no. 22 (February 1933): 177.

207. Jolas and Paul, "A Review," 144–45.

208. Eugene Jolas, "Glossary," *transition*, no. 18 (November 1929): 287.

209. Ibid. For more, see Craig Monk, "Eugene Jolas and the Translation Policies of *transition*," *Mosaic: A Journal for the Interdisciplinary Study of Literature* (Winnipeg) 32, no. 4 (December 1999): 17–35.

210. Jolas, *Man from Babel*, 107.

211. "*transition*'s Revolution of the Word Dictionary," *transition*, no. 21 (March 1932): 285. There were two more installments published in *transition*, no. 22 (February 1933), and *transition*, no. 23 (July 1935).

212. Eugene Jolas, "What Is the Revolution of Language?," *transition*, no. 22 (February 1933), in Kiefer and Rumold, *Eugene Jolas*, 117.

213. Klaus Müller-Burgh, "Corrientes vanguardiasta y surrealismo en la obra de Alejo Carpentier," in *Asedios a Carpentier: Once ensayos críticos sobre el novelista cubano*, ed. Klaus Müller-Burgh (Santiago de Chile: Editorial Universitaria, 1972), 18.

214. Alejo Carpentier, "Una fuerza musical de América: Héctor Villa-Lobos," *Social* (Havana) 14, no. 6 (June 1929): 26, 77, 92, quoted in Müller-Burgh, *Asedios a Carpentier*, 18.

215. Alejo Carpentier, "Las nuevas ofensivas del cubanismo," *Carteles* (Havana) (December 15, 1929): 533–37, trans. and quoted in Michele Greet, "In the Press," *Transatlantic Encounters*.

216. Amy Fass Emery, *The Anthropological Imagination in Latin American Literature* (Columbia: University of Missouri Press, 1996), 29.

217. Alejo Carpentier, "Les points cardinaux du roman en Amérique latine," *Le Cahier* (Paris), no. 6 (November 1931): 19–28, reproduced in Spanish translation as Alejo Carpentier, "Los puntos cardinales de la novela en América Latina," trans. Andrea Martínez, in Alejo Carpentier, *Los pasos recobrados: Ensayos de teoría y crítica literaria*, ed. Alexis Márquez Rodríguez and Araceli García Carranza (Caracas: Biblioteca Ayacucho, 2003), 107–14. The translations into English are by the author unless otherwise noted.

218. Carpentier, "Los puntos cardinales," 107.

219. Ibid.

220. Ibid.

221. Ibid. Note that Carpentier uses "Amérique Latine" in the essay's title but uses the phrase "sud-Americans" here, toggling between the two throughout the text.

222. Carpentier, "Los puntos cardinales," 108.

223. Ibid.

224. Ibid., 108–9.

225. Ibid., 109–10.

226. Ibid., 110.

227. Ibid.

228. Ibid., 114. Trans. Ramón Urzúa-Navas.

229. Alejo Carpentier, "Homenage a nuestros amigos de Paris," *Carteles* (Havana) (December 24, 1933), reproduced in *La Jiribilla: Revista de Cultural Cubana*, accessed August 5, 2015, http://www.lajiribilla .cu/2010/n453_01/453_01.html.

230. Ibid.

231. Ibid.

232. The group included Etienne Léro, Thélus Léro, René Ménil, Jules-Marcel Monnerot, Michel Pilotin, Maurice-Sabas Quitman, Auguste Thésée, and Pierre Yoyotte. For more, see my essay "*Légitime défense*: From Communism and Surrealism to Caribbean Self-Definition," *Journal of Surrealism and the Americas* 4, no. 1 (2010): 15–30; and Franklin Rosemont and Robin D. G. Kelley, eds., *Black, Brown, and Beige: Surrealist Writings from Africa and the Diaspora* (Austin: University of Texas Press, 2009), 22–24.

233. The Surrealists also wrote two manifestos, which they distributed outside factories and around the Exposition: "Ne visitez pas L'Exposition Coloniale" (Don't visit the Colonial Exposition), and "Premier Bilan de L'Exposition Coloniale" (First assessment of the Colonial Exposition), calling for "the immediate

evacuation of the colonies." Patricia A. Morton, *Hybrid Modernities: Architecture and Representation at the 1931 Colonial Exposition, Paris* (Cambridge, Mass.: MIT Press, 2000), 98–99.

234. Timothy Brennan, "Introduction," in Alejo Carpentier, *Music in Cuba* (1946), trans. Alan West-Durán, ed. Timothy Brennan (Minneapolis: University of Minnesota Press, 2001), 21.

235. Alejo Carpentier, *Entrevistas,* ed. Virgilio López Lemus (Havana: Editorial Letras Cubanas, 1985), 19 trans. and quoted in Brennan, "Introduction," 18.

236. Noel Riley Fitch, *Sylvia Beach and the Lost Generation: A History of Literary Paris in the Twenties and Thirties* (New York: W. W. Norton, 1993), 257.

237. Jolas wrote, "I am now suspending the magazine indefinitely, as I can no longer afford the expenditure of time and labor necessary to its preparation." Eugene Jolas, "Announcement," *transition,* nos. 19–20 (June 1930): 369.

238. Ibid.

239. Jolas, "What Is the Revolution of Language?," in Kiefer and Rumold, *Eugene Jolas,* 116.

240. Jolas, "Frontierless Decade," in Kiefer and Rumold, *Eugene Jolas,* 118.

241. For instance, Buber writes, "Your question is very difficult. I envisage the evolution of individualism, in a collectivistic regime, as revolutionary; and the evolution of metaphysics as partaking of the mood of catacombs." Martin Buber, response to "Metanthropological Crisis: A Manifesto," *transition,* no. 21 (March 1932), quoted in McMillan, *Transition,* 64.

242. Eugene Jolas, "Inquiry About the Malady of Language," *transition,* no. 23 (July 1935): 144, quoted in Michael Finney, "Eugene Jolas, *transition,* and the Revolution of the Word," in *In the Wake of the Wake,* eds. David Hayman and Elliot Anderson (Madison: University of Wisconsin Press, 1978), 51. For more on Jolas's later questionnaires, see my essay "'Do You Believe in Angels?' and Other Inquiries: Eugene Jolas' Questionnaires for *transition* Magazine," *Cabinet,* no. 53 (Spring 2014): 13–20.

243. Eugene Jolas, "Inquiry into the Spirit and Language of the Night," *transition,* no. 27 (April–May 1938): 233, reprinted in Jane Goldman, *Modernism, 1910–1945: Image to Apocalypse* (New York: Palgrave Macmillan, 2004), 220.

244. "Vertical," ca. 1941, Eugene and Maria Jolas Papers, Beinecke Rare Book and Manuscript Library, Yale University, Series XIII, Box 62, Folder 1469. The *Saturday Review of Literature* printed the questions from "Inquiry into the Spirit and Language of Night" in full, while the *New York World Telegram* quoted and summarized the responses. The magazine *Sur* in Buenos Aires translated the questions and answers to "Inquiry into the Spirit and Language of Night" into Spanish. *Saturday Review of Literature* (New York) (April 24, 1937); *New York World Telegram,* June 8,

1938; *Sur* (Buenos Aires), no. 51 (1939): 89–97, Eugene and Maria Jolas Papers, Beinecke Rare Book and Manuscript Library, Yale University, Series XII, Box 60, Folder 1400: *transition* press clippings 1926–52.

245. Putnam, *Paris Was Our Mistress,* 245–46.

246. Matthew Josephson, *Life Among the Surrealists* (New York: Holt, Rinehart and Winston, 1962), 6.

247. Cowley, *Exile's Return,* 9.

248. Ibid., 275.

249. Ibid., 74.

250. Donald Pizer, *American Expatriate Writing and the Paris Moment: Modernism and Place* (Baton Rouge: Louisiana State University Press, 1996), 142.

251. Eugene Jolas, "Suggestions about French enquête." (n.d.), Eugene and Maria Jolas Papers, Beinecke Rare Book and Manuscript Library, Yale University, Series XII, Box 60, Folder 1404. Mansanti cites Betsy Jolas, Eugene and Maria's daughter, as saying that the magazine's archives were stolen from the Jolases' house in Neuilly during the German occupation. Mansanti, "Between Modernisms," 718n3. Elsewhere it is indicated that the original archives were destroyed during World War II. See "Overview," Eugene and Maria Jolas Papers, Beinecke Rare Book and Manuscript Library, Yale University, accessed May 24, 2016, http://drs .library.yale.edu/HLTransformer/HLTransServlet ?stylename=yul.ead2002.xhtml.xsl&pid=beinecke :jolas.

252. William Van O'Connor to Eugene Jolas, July 8, 1948, letter, Eugene and Maria Jolas Papers, Beinecke Rare Book and Manuscript Library, Yale University, Series I, Box 3, Folder 60. I am grateful to Cathryn Setz for this reference.

253. Jolas, *Man from Babel,* 92–93.

254. V. F. Calverton, "The Revolution-in-the-Wordists," *Modern Quarterly* (Baltimore) 3 (Fall 1929): 277. See also "Advertisement," *transition,* no. 18 (November 1929): 7.

255. *Poetry* (Chicago) 54 (September 1939): 350. These included questionnaires in the *Partisan Review,* the London-based *Twentieth Century Verse,* and the Parisian journal *Volontés.* Eugene and Maria Jolas Papers, Beinecke Rare Book and Manuscript Library, Yale University, Series XII, Box 59, Folder 1373.

256. Robert Motherwell to Eugene Jolas, April 2, 1947, letter, Eugene and Maria Jolas Papers, Beinecke Rare Book and Manuscript Library, Yale University, Series XII, Box 59, Folder 1388.

257. Jolas, "Introduction," *transition workshop,* 14.

258. Jorge Luis Borges, "Elvira de Alvear" (1960), trans. Robert Mezey, *American Poetry Review* 23, no. 1 (January–February 1994): 25.

259. Rafael Alberti, *The Lost Grove: Autobiography of a Spanish Poet in Exile* (1959), trans. Gabriel Berns (Berkeley: University of California Press, 1976), 280–81.

260. Pablo Neruda to Héctor Eandi, September 5, 1931, letter, quoted in Edmundo Olivares Briones, *Pablo*

Neruda: Los caminos de oriente, Tras las huellas del poeta itinerante (1927–1933) (Santiago de Chile: LOM Ediciones, 2000), 304.

261. Jason Wilson, *A Companion to Pablo Neruda: Evaluating Neruda's Poetry* (Rochester, N.Y.: Boydell and Brewer, 2008), 95.

262. Vásquez, "Le revue '*Imán*,'" 120.

263. Eugene Jolas, "Preface," in *Transition Stories: Twenty-Three Stories from* "transition" (1929), eds. Eugene Jolas and Robert Sage (Freeport, N.Y.: Books for Libraries Press, 1972), xii.

264. Alexis Márquez Rodríguez, "Prólogo," in Alejo Carpentier, *Los pasos recobrados: Ensayos de teoría y crítica literaria*, eds. Alexis Márquez Rodríguez and Araceli García Carranza (Caracas: Biblioteca Ayacucho, 2003), xv.

265. Ibid.

266. Guillermo de Torre, "Madrid, meridiano intelectual de hispanoamérica," *La Gaceta Literaria* 1, no. 8 (April 15, 1927): 1.

267. Alejo Carpentier, "Carta a Manuel Aznar sobre el meridiano intelectual de Nuestra América," *Diario de la Marina* (Havana) (September 12, 1927), reprinted in Carmen Alemany Bay, *La polémica del meridiano intelectual de Hispanoamérica (1927): Estudio y textos* (Alicante: Universidad de Alicante, 1998), 96–97.

268. Jorge Luis Borges, "The Argentine Writer and Tradition" (1951), trans. Esther Allen, in *The Total Library: Non-Fiction, 1922–1986*, ed. Eliot Weinberger (London: Penguin, 2001), 426.

269. Borges et al., "Proa," *Proa* 1, no. 1 (August 1924): 3.

CHAPTER 4

1. Miguel Pérez Ferrero, "Una encuesta sensacional: ¿Qué es la vanguardia?," *La Gaceta Literaria*, no. 83 (June 1, 1930): 1. I thank Jordana Mendelson for pointing me toward this questionnaire. An earlier version of the section on Madrid was originally published as Lori Cole, "Madrid: Questioning the Avant-Garde," in *The Oxford Critical and Cultural History of Modernist Magazines*, vol. 3, Europe *1880–1940*, ed. Peter Brooker, Sascha Bru, Andrew Thacker, and Christian Weikop (Oxford University Press, 2013), 369–92. A conference paper I gave on the ideas animating the comparative basis of this chapter was published as Lori Cole, "¿Qué es la vanguardia? Ultraism Between Madrid and Buenos Aires," in *Modernidad y vanguardia: Rutas de intercambio entre España y Latinoamérica (1920–1970)*, ed. Paula Barreiro López and Fabiola Martínez Rodríguez (Madrid: Museo Nacional Centro de Arte Reina Sofía, 2015), 127–37. I thank the editors for their permission to include this material. All translations are by the author unless otherwise noted.

2. For more, see Mary Lee Bretz, *Encounters Across Borders: The Changing Visions of Spanish Modernism, 1890–1930* (Lewisburg: Bucknell University Press, 2001); Susan Larson and Eva Woods, eds., *Visualizing Spanish Modernity* (New York: Oxford University Press, 2005); Anthony L. Geist and José B. Monleón, eds., *Modernism and Its Margins: Reinscribing Cultural Modernity from Spain and Latin America* (New York: Garland, 1999); Jordana Mendelson, *Documenting Spain: Artists, Exhibition Culture, and the Modern Nation* (University Park: Penn State University Press, 2005); and Gayle Rogers, *Modernism and the New Spain: Britain, Cosmopolitan Europe, and Literary History* (New York: Oxford University Press, 2012).

3. L. Elena Delgado, Jordana Mendelson, and Oscar Vázquez, "Introduction: Recalcitrant Modernities—Spain, Cultural Difference, and the Location of Modernism," *Journal of Iberian and Latin American Studies* 13, nos. 2–3 (August/December 2007): 107.

4. The designation "Generation of '98" was first coined in 1913 by the Spanish writer José Augusto Trinidad Martínez Ruíz, known as Azorín, in "La generacíon del '98," *Clásicos y Modernos* (Madrid: Renacimiento, 1913), 310–11. Other Generation of '98 authors include Miguel de Unamuno, Antonio Machado, Ramón María del Valle-Inclán, and Pío Baroja. For more on the Generation of '98, see Jesús Torecilla, *La Generación del 98 frente al nuevo fin de siglo* (Amsterdam: Rodopi, 2000); and Joseph Harrison and Alan Hoyle, eds., *Spain's 1898 Crisis: Regenerationism, Modernism, Postcolonialism* (Manchester: Manchester University Press, 2000).

5. José Ortega y Gasset, quoted in Miguel Ángel Hernando, *La Gaceta Literaria (1927–1932): Biografía y valoración* (Valladolid: Universidad de Valladolid, 1974), 13.

6. For more on Ernesto Giménez Caballero, see José-Carlos Mainer, "Ernesto Giménez Caballero o la inoportunidad," in Ernesto Giménez Caballero, *Casticismo, nacionalismo, y vanguardia (Antología 1927–1935)*, ed. José-Carlos Mainer (Santander: Fundación Santander Central Hispano, 2005); D. W. Foard, *The Revolt of the Aesthetes: Ernesto Giménez Caballero and the Origins of Spanish Fascism* (New York: Lang, 1989); and Stanley G. Payne, "The Fascism of the Intellectuals," in *Fascism in Spain, 1923–1977* (Madison: University of Wisconsin Press, 1999).

7. Pérez Ferrero, "Una encuesta sensacional," 1.

8. This questionnaire was cited in the "Foreign Periodicals" section of T. S. Eliot's the *Criterion*: "For the May issue [of *La Gaceta Literaria*], Melchor Fernández Almagro has written an interesting article on the style of José Bergamín, while the June number seems so astir with the launching of a 'sensational enquete' entitled: 'Qué es la Vanguardia,' where prominent 'contemporaries' give their views on 'avant-garde' literature." C. K. Colhoun, "Foreign Periodicals," *Criterion* 10, no. 41 (July 1931): 783–84. I thank Gayle Rogers for this reference.

9. Hernando, *La Gaceta Literaria (1927–1932)*, 59.

10. José Bergamín, response to "¿Qué es la vanguardia?," *La Gaceta Literaria*, no. 83 (June 1, 1930): 1; Melichor Fernández Almagro, response to "¿Qué es la vanguardia?," *La Gaceta Literaria*, no. 84 (June 15, 1930): 3.

11. Ernesto Giménez Caballero, response to "¿Qué es la vanguardia?," *La Gaceta Literaria*, no. 83 (June 1, 1930): 1.

12. Ernestina de Champourcin, response to "¿Qué es la vanguardia?," *La Gaceta Literaria*, no. 84 (June 15, 1930): 4.

13. Esteban Salazar y Chapela, response to "¿Qué es la vanguardia?," *La Gaceta Literaria*, no. 85 (July 1, 1930): 3.

14. Juan Aparicio, response to "¿Qué es la vanguardia?," *La Gaceta Literaria*, no. 86 (July 15, 1930): 4.

15. Enrique Gómez Carrillo, "Una 'enquête' sobre el modernismo: A los escritores de España y de América," *El Nuevo Mercurio* (Barcelona), no. 2 (February 1907): 124.

16. Ibid.

17. Miguel de Unamuno, response to "Una 'enquête' sobre el modernismo," *El Nuevo Mercurio* (Barcelona), no. 5 (May 1907): 505–506..

18. Enrique Gómez Carrillo, "Dos palabras al lector," *El Nuevo Mercurio* (Barcelona), no. 1 (January 1907): 3.

19. Gómez Carrillo, "Una 'enquête' sobre el modernismo," 124.

20. Guillermo Díaz Plaja, response to "¿Qué es la vanguardia?," *La Gaceta Literaria*, no. 86 (July 15, 1930): 4.

21. Ibid.

22. Jaime Torres Bodet, response to "¿Qué es la vanguardia?," *La Gaceta Literaria*, no. 84 (June 15, 1930): 4; Benjamin Jarnés, response to "¿Qué es la vanguardia?," *La Gaceta Literaria*, no. 85 (July 1, 1930): 3.

23. Francisco Vighi, response to "¿Qué es la vanguardia?," *La Gaceta Literaria*, no. 86 (July 15, 1930): 4.

24. Ibid.

25. Valentín Andrés Álvarez, response to "¿Qué es la vanguardia?," *La Gaceta Literaria*, no. 83 (June 1, 1930): 2. De Torre later changed the order and emphasis of his book in its 1965 re-edition. See Guillermo de Torre, *Literaturas europeas de vanguardia* (1925), ed. Jóse María Barerra López, intro. Miguel de Torre Borges (Seville: Renacimiento, 2001) and Guillermo de Torre, *Historia de las literaturas de vanguardia* (1965), vols. 1–3 (Madrid: Guadarrama, 1971).

26. Ramón Gómez de la Serna, response to "¿Qué es la vanguardia?," *La Gaceta Literaria*, no. 85 (July 1, 1930): 3.

27. Guillermo de Torre, response to "¿Qué es la vanguardia?," *La Gaceta Literaria*, no. 94 (November 15, 1930): 3.

28. Xavier Bóveda interviewing Rafael Cansinos-Asséns, "Los intelectuales dicen. Rafael Cansinos-Asséns," *El Parlamentario* (December 1918), quoted in Gloria Videla, *El ultraísmo: Estudios sobre movimientos poéticos de vanguardia en España* (Madrid: Gredos, 1963), 32. Although the word *romántico* was soon dropped, it demonstrated the widespread interest in revitalizing the Romantic project in Spain at this time, as also evidenced by the publication of José Díaz Fernández's book *El nuevo romanticismo* in 1930.

29. Videla, *El ultraísmo*, 36n18.

30. Ibid. For more, see José Ortega y Gasset, "La deshumanización del arte" (1925), in *Obras completas,* vol. 3 (Madrid: Revista de Occidente, 1947), 365.

31. De Torre, *Literaturas europeas de vanguardia*, 75.

32. Ibid., 83.

33. Videla, *El ultraísmo*, 74; Andrew A. Anderson, "Futurism and Spanish Literature in the Context of the Historical Avant-Garde," in *International Futurism in Arts and Literature*, ed. Günter Berghaus (Berlin: Walter de Gruyter, 2000), 157.

34. De Torre, *Literaturas europeas de vanguardia*, 86.

35. Ibid., 88, 86.

36. Ibid., 91–93.

37. Guillermo de Torre, "Visita de 'Interviewer Ignotus' al autor de *Hélices*," *Alfar: Revista de Casa América-Galicia* (La Coruña) 1, no. 28 (April 1923): 5–7.

38. Xavier Bóveda et al., "Ultra. Un manifiesto de la juventud literaria," *Cervantes* (Madrid) 3, no. 1 (January 1919): 2–3, reprinted in *Grecia* (Seville) 2, no. 11 (March 15, 1919): 11.

39. F. T. Marinetti, "Fondation et manifeste du Futurisme," *Le Figaro* (Paris) (February 20, 1909); F. T. Marinetti, "Fundación y manifiesto del Futurismo," trans. Ramón Gómez de la Serna, *Prometeo* (Madrid) 2, no. 6 (April 1909): 65–73.

40. F. T. Marinetti, "Proclama futurista a las españoles," trans. Ramón Gómez de la Serna, *Prometeo* (Madrid) 3, no. 20 (August 1910): 519–31. Note: in 1904 the Catalan writer Gabriel Alomar gave a lecture entitled "El Futurisme," which was published in 1905 in the Catalan journal *L'Avenç*. Although Alomar's version of Futurism was in no way related to Marinetti's, it led some Spaniards to be wary of the Italian version. See Zbigniew Folejewski, *Futurism and Its Place in the Development of Modern Poetry* (Ottawa: Ottawa University Press, 1980), 107.

41. Rubén Darío, "Marinetti y el futurismo," *La Nación* (Buenos Aires) (April 5, 1909). For texts written in reaction to Marinetti by prominent Latin American authors, see the section "Futurismo" in Jorge Schwartz, ed., *Las vanguardias latinoamericanas: Textos programáticos y críticos* (Madrid: Catedra, 1991), 398–425.

42. Sylvia Saítta, "Futurism, Fascism, and Mass-Media: The Case of Marinetti's 1926 Trip to Buenos Aires,"

Stanford Humanities Review 7, no. 1 (1999), accessed July 22, 2015, https://web.stanford.edu/group/SHR /7-1/html/body_saitta.html. For the list of questions along with Borges's response, see "Marinetti fue una medida profiláctica," *Diario Crítica* (Buenos Aires) (May 20, 1926), reprinted in *Textos recobrados, 1919–1929*, ed. Sara Luisa del Carril (Buenos Aires: Emecé, 1997), 391–92.

43. "Homenaje a Marinetti," *Martín Fierro*, nos. 29–30 (June 8, 1926): 209, reprinted in Gilberto Mendonça Teles and Klaus Müller-Bergh, *Vanguardia latino-americana: Historia, crítica y documentos*, vol. 5, *Chile y países del Plata: Argentina, Uruguay, Paraguay* (Madrid: Iberoamericana, 2009), 214. See also "Marinetti," *Nosotros* 23, no. 205 (June 1926): 154–62. Marinetti lectured at the Coliseo Theater, the Aula Magna, the Friends of Art Society, the Círculo Italiano, and the Wagnerian Association in Buenos Aires.

44. Ramón Gómez de la Serna, "Variaciones: El héroe Felipe Marinetti," *El Sol* (Madrid, February 11, 1928): 1; Guillermo de Torre, "Efigie de Marinetti," *La Gaceta Literaria* 2, no. 28 (February 15, 1928): 3.

45. Benito Mussolini, "Marinetti y Mussolini: Telegrama de un duce a otro," *La Gaceta Literaria*, no. 28 (February 15, 1928): 3. For more, see Anderson, "Futurism and Spanish Literature," 144–82.

46. F. T. Marinetti, "España veloz: Poema en palabra libre (fragmento)," *La Gaceta Literaria*, no. 39 (August 1, 1928): 1.

47. F. T. Marinetti, "The Founding and Manifesto of Futurism" (1909), in *Futurist Manifestos*, ed. Umbro Apollonio, trans. Robert Brain (Boston: MFA Publications, 2001), 19.

48. Jorge Luis Borges, Guillermo Juan, Eduardo González Lanuza, and Guillermo de Torre, "Proclama," *Prisma: Revista Mural* (Buenos Aires) 1, no. 1 (December 1921), reprinted in *Vanguardias en su tinta: Documentos de la vanguardia en América Latina*, ed. Celina Manzoni (Buenos Aires: Corregidor, 2007), 27.

49. Isaac del Vando-Villar, "Manifiesto ultraísta," *Grecia* (Seville), no. 20 (June 30, 1919), reprinted in *El ultraísmo: Estudios sobre movimientos poéticos de vanguardia en España*, ed. Gloria Videla (Madrid: Gredos, 1963), 63.

50. De Torre, *Literaturas europeas de vanguardia*, 74.

51. Ibid., 211.

52. Hans Richter, *Dada: Art and Anti-Art*, trans. David Britt (New York: Oxford University Press, 1978), 9.

53. Tristan Tzara, *Seven Dada Manifestos and Lampisteries* (1916–21), trans. Barbara Wright (London: Calder, 1977), 92.

54. Jorge Luis Borges, Jacobo Sureda, Fortunio Bonanova, and Juan Alomar, "Manifiesto del Ultra," *Baleares* (Palma de Mallorca) 5, no. 131 (February 1921), reprinted in Manzoni, *Vanguardias en su tinta*, 24.

55. *Ultra* (Madrid), no. 9 (April 30, 1921): 5.

56. Ibid., 3; *Ultra* (Madrid), no. 8 (April 20, 1921): 3.

57. De Torre, *Literaturas europeas de vanguardia*, 85.

58. Such texts included Isaac del Vando-Villar, "El triunfo del ultraísmo," *Grecia* (Seville) 2, no. 29 (October 1919): 2; "La plenitud del ultraísmo," *Grecia* (Madrid) 3, no. 50 (November 1920): 5; and "Panorama ultraísta," *Grecia* (Madrid) 3, no. 43 (June 1920): 16.

59. *Grecia* (Seville) 2, no. 13 (April 15, 1919): 2; M. Ángeles Vázquez, "Las vanguardias en nuestras revistas, Revista Grecia, España," (June 1, 2005), Cervantes Institute, accessed May 2, 2012, http://cvc.cervantes.es/el _rinconete/anteriores/enero_05/19012005_02.htm.

60. Jorge Luis Borges, "Anatomía de mi 'ULTRA,'" *Ultra* 1, no. 11 (May 1921): 1. Note: *Ultra* published its last issue on March 15, 1922.

61. For more on Norah Borges see Eamon McCarthy, "Flirting with Futurism: Norah Borges and the Avant-Garde," in "Women Futurists and Women Artists Influenced by Futurism," special issue, *International Yearbook of Futurism Studies* 5 (2015), 111–36; Vanessa K. Davidson, "Norah Borges, the Graphic Voice of Ultraísmo in Two Peripheral Centres," *Romance Studies* 27, no. 1 (January 2009): 11–29; Patricia Artundo, *Norah Borges: Obra gráfica 1920–1930* (Buenos Aires: Fondo Nacional de las Artes, 1994); and Harper Montgomery, "Reproduction: Norah Borges Draws Modern Femininity," in *The Mobility of Modernism: Art and Criticism in 1920s Latin America* (Austin: University of Texas Press, 2017), 152–90. I thank these authors for their assistance with my research. For more on German Expressionism, see Jorge Luis Borges, "Acerca del Expresionismo," in *Inquisiciones* (Buenos Aires: Proa, 1925), 6; De Torre, *Literaturas europeas de vanguardia*, 54–55; Carlos García, "Borges y el Expresionismo: Kurt Heynicke," in *Las vanguardias literarias en Argentina, Uruguay, y Paraguay: Bibliografía y antología crítica*, ed. Carlos García and Dieter Reichardt (Madrid: Iberoamericana, 2004), 325–43.

62. Jorge Luis Borges with Norman Thomas di Giovanni, "Autobiographical Notes," *New Yorker* (September 19, 1970): 60.

63. For more, see José María Barrera López, "*Ultra*: Nucleo de las primeras vanguardias," in *Revistas literarias españolas del siglo XX*, vol. 1, *1919–1939*, ed. Manuel José Ramos Ortega (Madrid: Ollero y Ramos, 2006), 122–23.

64. De Torre, *Literaturas europeas de vanguardia*, 75.

65. Ibid., 108.

66. Ibid., 109.

67. Guillermo de Torre traveled to Buenos Aires many times in the 1920s, and married Norah Borges in 1928; they did not settle permanently in Argentina until 1938.

68. By this point Argentine editors were already responding to Spanish Ultraist texts, as evidenced by the publication *Los Raros*, whose one issue, printed in January 1920 by Bartolomé Galíndez, was an amalgam

of Futurism, Symbolism, and Ultraism and featured Spanish Ultraists like Isaac Vando-Villar. However, the critic Carlos García discredits the magazine's command of the movement, writing, "Galíndez attempted the first exegesis of Peninsular Ultraism, without ever comprehending his object of study." Carlos García, "*Prisma* (1921–1922): Entretelones," in *Las vanguardias literarias en Argentina, Uruguay, y Paraguay: Bibliografía y antología crítica*, ed. Carlos García and Dieter Reichardt (Madrid: Iberoamericana, 2004), 243. For more on *Los raros*, see Hanno Ehrlicher, "Bartolomé Galíndez's Magazine, *Los raros*: A 'Symbolist' Fusion of Futurism and Ultraism," *International Yearbook of Futurism Studies* 4 (2014): 360–89.

69. Borges, "Autobiographical Notes," 62.

70. Francine Masiello, *Lenguaje e ideología: Las escuelas argentinas de vanguardia* (Buenos Aires: Hachette, 1986), 31.

71. See Horacio Salas, "El salto a la modernidad," in *Revista Martín Fierro 1924–1927: Edición Facsímilar* (Buenos Aires: Fondo Nacional de las Artes, 1995), ix.

72. Méndez discontinued *Martín Fierro* during the start of Hipólito Yrigoyen's second presidential campaign in 1927, due to political infighting among contributors. For more, see "*Martín Fierro* Versus Irigoyen," *La Pluma* (Montevideo), no. 5 (March 1928): 153, reprinted in Schwartz, *Las vanguardias latinoamericanas,* 511. General José Félix Uriburu's military dictatorship began in 1930.

73. Masiello, *Lenguaje e ideología*, 63.

74. The magazine's second issue was 78 × 56 cm. See C. Jared Loewenstein and Donald L. Shaw, "*Prisma* I and II," *Hispanic Review* 70, no. 1 (Winter 2002): 69–88.

75. Masiello, *Lenguaje e ideología*, 64.

76. Borges, "Autobiographical Notes," 75.

77. Borges et al., "Proclama," in Manzoni, *Vanguardias en su tinta*, 27.

78. Ibid.

79. Ibid.

80. Adriano del Valle, "Naufragio," published in *Prisma* in December 1921, was originally published in *Ultra*, no. 3 (Madrid, February 20, 1921): 5; "Proclama" along with poems from *Prisma* were published in *Ultra*, no. 21 (Madrid, January 1922).

81. *Tableros* (Madrid), no. 3 (January 15, 1922): 11, quoted in García, "*Prisma* (1921–1922)," 244n3.

82. Masiello, *Lenguaje e ideología*, 64.

83. Jorge Luis Borges cited by Daniel E. Nelson, "Norah Borges: On the Margins of the Text," in *A Woman's Gaze: Latin American Women Artists*, ed. Marjorie Agosín (Fredonia, N.Y.: White Pine Press, 1998), 43.

84. Note: *holgar* has many meanings: to rejoice, to go on strike, to exceed, and to be unnecessary. Jorge Luis Borges, et al. "Al oportuno lector," *Proa*, no. 1 (August 1922), quoted in *Las revistas literarias argentinas, 1893–1967*, ed. Héctor René Lafleur, Sergio D. Provenzano, and Fernando Alonso (Buenos Aires:

Ediciones El 8vo. loco, 2006), 95–96. I thank Ramón Urzúa-Navas for his assistance with this translation.

85. Jorge Luis Borges, "Acotaciones," *Proa*, no. 1 (August 1924): 30, quoted in Schwartz, *Las vanguardias latinoamericanas*, 302.

86. Borges, "Autobiographical Notes," 62.

87. Ibid., 76.

88. Jorge Luis Borges, Alfredo Brandán Caraffa, Ricardo Güiraldes, and Pablo Rojas Paz, "Proa," *Proa*, no. 1 (August 1924): 5, reprinted in Patricia M. Artundo, "Punto de convergencia: *Inicial y Proa* en 1924," in *Las vanguardias literarias en Argentina, Uruguay, y Paraguay: Bibliografía y antología crítica*, ed. Carlos García and Dieter Reichardt (Madrid: Iberoamericana, 2004), 270–71.

89. Borges et al., "Proa," no. 7, in Artundo, "Punto de convergencia," 272.

90. Jorge Luis Borges, Alfredo Brandán Caraffa, and Francisco Luis Bernárdez, "Proa," *Proa*, no. 13 (November 1925): 6.

91. Ibid, 5–6.

92. Jorge Luis Borges, "Carta Abierta," *Nosotros* 49, no. 191 (April 1925), in García, "*Prisma* (1921–1922)," 247n14.

93. Borges, "Autobiographical Notes," 75.

94. The editors, "Presentación," *Nosotros* 1, no. 1 (August 1907), in Noemi Ulla, *La Revista "Nosotros"* (Buenos Aires: Editorial Galerna, 1969), 17.

95. Beatriz Sarlo, *Borges, a Writer on the Edge* (1993), Borges Studies Online, J.L. Borges Center for Studies & Documentation, accessed July 12, 2015, http://www.borges.pitt.edu/bsol/bsi7.php.

96. The editors, "Un año de vida," *Nosotros* 2, nos. 13–14 (1908), in Ulla, *La Revista "Nosotros,"* 19.

97. The editors explain how the title *Nosotros* also derived from an unpublished book by Roberto Payró, whose first chapter they serialized in the first three issues of the magazine. The magazine also included Rubén Darío's commentary on the book, originally published in 1896 in *La Nación*, thus inscribing *Nosotros* in a literary lineage traceable back to Darío. It also featured poetry by Evar Méndez, the future editor of *Martín Fierro*, in this first issue. The editors, *Nosotros* 1, no. 1 (August 1907), Cervantes Virtual, accessed March 22, 2011, http://213.0.4.19/servlet/SirveObras/acadLetArg/12826405339062624198624/not0001.htm#N_1_.

98. Sarlo, *Borges, a Writer on the Edge*, accessed July 12, 2015, http://www.borges.pitt.edu/bsol/bsi7.php.

99. According to Mónica Andrea Ogando and Ricardo Ernesto Paramos, *Nosotros* was inspired to issue questionnaires by the French publication *Revue de Deux Mondes*. Mónica Andrea Ogando and Ricardo Ernesto Paramos, "Nosotros," in *Historia de revistas argentinas*, vol. 2 (Buenos Aires: AAER, 1995–99), accessed July 25, 2015, http://www.learevistas.com/notaHistoria.php?nota=19.

100. "¿Cuál es el valor de Martín Fierro?," *Nosotros*, no. 50 (June 1913): 425–33. The other questionnaires that *Nosotros* issued are as follows: "La guerra y sus consecuencias" (1913), "La música y nuestro folklore" (1918), "La literatura hispanoamericana juzgada por los escritores españoles" (1918-19), "Sobre la influencia italiana en nuestra cultura" (1928), and "América y el destino de la civilización occidental" (1936).

101. Noemi Ulla, "Nota preliminar," in *La Revista "Nosotros,"* 12–13.

102. Jorge Luis Borges, "Ultraísmo," *Nosotros* 39, no. 151 (December 1921): 466–71, reprinted in Manzoni, *Vanguardias en su tinta,* 30.

103. Ibid., 35.

104. Ibid., 31.

105. Masiello, *Lenguaje e ideología*, 94.

106. Borges, "Ultraísmo," reprinted in Manzoni, *Vanguardias en su tinta*, 28.

107. Ibid., 34.

108. Ibid.

109. "Poemas ultraístas," *Nosotros* 42, no. 160 (September 1922): 55–62. Beatriz Sarlo, "The Adventure of *Martín Fierro*: The Avant-Garde and *Criollismo*," in *Jorge Luis Borges: A Writer on the Edge*, 2nd ed., ed. John King (1993) (London: Verso, 2006), 96–97.

110. "Nuestra encuesta sobre la nueva generación literaria," *Nosotros* 44, no. 168 (May 1923); its replies were published in subsequent issues through *Nosotros* 45, no. 172 (December 1923).

111. The editors, "Nuestra encuesta sobre la nueva generación literaria," *Nosotros* 44, no. 168 (May 1923), reprinted in Ulla, *La Revista "Nosotros,"* 241.

112. Gloria Videla de Rivero, "La direccion criollista de la vanguardia," in *Las vanguardias literarias en Argentina, Uruguay, y Paraguay: Bibliografía y antología crítica*, ed. Carlos García and Dieter Reichardt (Madrid: Iberoamericana, 2004), 227n30.

113. Masiello, *Lenguaje e ideología*, 35–36.

114. Alejandro C. Eujanian, *Historia de revistas argentinas 1900–1950: La conquista del público* (Buenos Aires: Asociación Argentina de Editores de Revistas, 1999), 67.

115. "Nuestra encuesta sobre la nueva generación literaria," *Nosotros* 44, no. 168 (May 1923): 5–6.

116. Jorge Luis Borges quoted in Beatriz Sarlo, "Vanguardia y criollismo: La aventura de 'Martín Fierro,'" in "Las Vanguardias en América," ed. Nelson Osorio Tejeda, special issue, *Revista de Crítica Literaria Latinoamericana* (Lima) 8, no. 15 (1982): 46.

117. Francisco López Merino, response to "Nuestra encuesta sobre la nueva generación literaria," *Nosotros* 44, no. 168 (May 1923): 17.

118. Atilio García y Mellid, response to "Nuestra encuesta sobre la nueva generación literaria," *Nosotros* 45, no. 172 (December 1923): 104.

119. Schwartz, *Las vanguardias latinoamericanas*, 100.

120. Sarlo, "Vanguardia y criollismo," 44.

121. Ibid., 46.

122. Alfredo Bianchi, "Carta al Director del diario *Crítica*" (1925), published in *Crítica* and reproduced in *Nosotros*, quoted in Artundo, "Punto de convergencia," 256.

123. Roberto A. Ortelli, Alfredo Brandán Caraffa, Homero Guglielmini, and Roberto Smith, "Incial," *Inicial* (Buenos Aires) 1, no. 1 (October 1923): 3–5, reprinted in Schwartz, *Las vanguardias latinoamericanas*, 223–24.

124. Ortelli et al. in Schwartz, *Las vanguardias latinoamericanas*, 223.

125. Ibid.

126. Ezra Pound, "Small Magazines," *English Journal* 19, no. 9 (November 1930): 703.

127. *Inicial* (Buenos Aires) 1, no. 5 (1924): 3–6, reprinted in Artundo, "Punto de convergencia," 267.

128. *Inicial* (Buenos Aires) 1, no. 3 (December 1923): 80, quoted in Artundo, "Punto de convergencia," 257. Note that Brandán Caraffa worked on both *Inicial* and *Proa* in its second phase.

129. Masiello, *Lenguaje e ideología*, 62n24.

130. Ortega y Gasset reformulates the generational theories of August Comte in a work titled *El Tema de Nuestro Tiempo*, which was serialized in magazines from 1922–23 and published in 1923. José Ortega y Gasset, "El deber de la nueva generacion argentina," *La Nación* (Buenos Aires) (April 6, 1924): 2; José Ortega y Gasset, "Generación contra generación," *La Nación* (Buenos Aires), June 28, 1924. These ideas were later systematized by Ortega's disciple Julian Marais in *El método histórico de las generaciones* (Madrid: Revista de Occidente, 1949).

131. José Ortega y Gasset, "El tema de nuestro tiempo" (1923), in *Obras Completas*, vol. 3 (Madrid: Revista de Occidente, 1955), 151. I thank Gayle Rogers for his guidance on Ortega's theories.

132. Ortega y Gasset, "El tema de nuestro tiempo," 149.

133. José Ortega y Gasset, "Las revistas: El tema de nuestro tiempo," *Nosotros* 43, no. 165 (February 1923): 251–58.

134. Borges et al., "Proa," *Proa* 1, no. 1 (August 1924): 7.

135. Ibid., 5.

136. For more, see the selection of readings titled "Boedo vs. Florida," in Schwartz, *Las vanguardias latinoamericanas*, 577–92.

137. Alfredo Prieto, *Estudios de literatura argentina* (Buenos Aires: Galerna 1969), 35, quoted in Schwartz, *Las vanguardias latinoamericanas*, 538.

138. Beatriz Sarlo, *Borges: a Writer on the Edge*, accessed July 29, 2014, http://www.borges.pitt.edu/bsol/bsi7.php.

139. The term "cosmopolitanism," often pitted against "nationalism," has fraught connotations. In the Latin American context it can refer to the multiple racial compositions—Indian, African and European—that comprise the population, but more often the term re-

fers to an international or transnational stance. Many
authors have recently tried to reframe cosmopolitan-
ism in the postcolonial moment, including Walter
Mignolo, who coins the term "critical cosmopolitan-
ism" or James Clifford, who refers to "discrepant cosmopolitanism" so as not to elide national difference
in the name of a Eurocentric universality. See Walter
D. Mignolo, "The Many Faces of Cosmo-polis: Border
Thinking and Critical Cosmopolitanism," *Public
Culture* 12, no. 3 (2000): 721–48; and James Clifford,
"Mixed Feelings," in *Cosmopolitics: Thinking and
Feeling Beyond the Nation*, ed. Pheng Cheah and Bruce
Robbins (Minneapolis: University of Minnesota Press,
1998), 362–69. For more on cosmopolitanism, see
also Mariano Siskind, *Cosmopolitan Desires: Global
Modernity and World Literature in Latin America* (Evan-
ston: Northwestern University Press, 2014); Kwame
Anthony Appiah, *Cosmpolitanism: Ethics in a World
of Strangers* (New York: W. W. Norton, 2007); Timothy
Brennan, *At Home in the World: Cosmopolitanism Now*
(Cambridge, Mass.: Harvard University Press, 1997);
Jessica Berman, *Modernist Fiction, Cosmopolitanism,
and the Politics of Community* (Cambridge: Cambridge
University Press, 2001); and Rebecca L. Walkowitz,
Cosmopolitan Style: Modernism Beyond the Nation
(New York: Columbia University Press, 2006).

140. Leónidas Barletta, "La literatura de la calle Boedo,
contra la literatura de calle Florida," *Crítica* (Buenos
Aires) (June 10, 1925), quoted in Artundo, "Punto de
convergencia," 263.

141. Jorge Luis Borges, "La inutíl discusión de Boedo y
Florida," *La Prensa* (Buenos Aires) (September 30,
1928), reprinted in Jorge Luis Borges, *Textos recobrados 1919–1929*, ed. Sara Luisa del Carril (Buenos Aires:
Emecé, 1997), 365–68.

142. Borges, "Autobiographical Notes," 77.

143. *Martín Fierro* was the name of a magazine that ran for
forty-eight issues from March 1904 to February 1905,
edited by Alberto Ghiraldo. In March 1919 another
group started a magazine called *Martín Fierro* that was
antiyrigoyenista, on which Evar Méndez worked. This
particular iteration is then the third incarnation of the
magazine. Salas, "Prólogo," ix.

144. Masiello, *Lenguaje e ideología*, 60–61.

145. "Editoriales Proa y Martín Fierro," *Martín Fierro* 3, no.
34 (October 1926): 259.

146. *Martín Fierro* 2, no. 7 (July 1925): 54.

147. Oliverio Girondo, "Manifiesto Martín Fierro," *Martín
Fierro* 1, no. 4 (May 1924): 25–26, trans. Patrick Frank
in *Readings in Latin American Modern Art*, ed. Patrick
Frank (New Haven: Yale University Press, 2004), 12.

148. Ibid.

149. Ibid., 12–13. For more on *Martín Fierro* in the context
of the Latin American avant-garde, see Rubén Hitz,
"*Martín Fierro* en la vanguardia argentina," *Revistas
culturales latinoamericanas, 1920–1960*, ed. Lydia

Elizalde (Mexico City: Universidad Iberoamericana,
2008), 65–83.

150. Girondo, "Manifiesto Martín Fierro," in Frank,
Manifestos and Polemics, 13.

151. Ibid.

152. Oliverio Girondo, Evar Méndez, Alberto Prebisch,
and Eduardo J. Bullrich, *El periódico Martín Fierro
1924–1949* (Buenos Aires: Comisión directiva de la
sociedad argentina de escritores, 1949), 19.

153. "¿Cree usted en la existencia de una sensibilidad,
de una mentalidad, argentina? En caso afirmativa,
¿cuáles son sus características?," *Martín Fierro* 1, nos.
5–6 (May–June 1924): 38–39.

154. Ricardo Rojas, "Contestaciones," *Martín Fierro* 1, nos.
5–6 (May–June 1924): 39. Throughout the responses,
Argentine identity is frequently described as a race, a
term used much as "deracination" was in the context
of *transition*'s questionnaires in reference to an ethnic
or national identity, yet still notable in a country that
early on had massacred its indigenous populations.
The "Desert Campaign" of the 1830s, led by Juan
Manuel de Rosas, culminated in the "Conquest of
the Desert" in the 1870s, decimating the indigenous
populations of the pampas.

155. Leopoldo Lugones, "Contestaciones a la encuesta de
Martín Fierro" (1924), in *Martín Fierro (1924–1927):
Antología*, ed. Beatriz Sarlo (Buenos Aires: Carlos
Pérez Editor S.A., 1969), 36.

156. Roberto Mariani, "Contestaciones," *Martín Fierro*
1, nos. 5–6 (May–June 1924): 39. For the article that
sparked the Florida-Boedo debate, see Roberto Mariani, "Martín Fierro y yo," *Martín Fierro* 1, no. 7 (July 25,
1924): 46.

157. Pablo Rojas Paz, "Contestaciones," 39.

158. Oliverio Girondo, "Contestaciones," 39.

159. Mariano A. Barrenechea, "Contestaciones," 39.

160. Samuel Glusberg, "Contestaciones," 39.

161. Pedro Figari, "Contestaciones," 38.

162. Ibid.

163. Luis María Jordán, "Contestaciones," 39.

164. Schwartz, *Las vanguardias latinoamericanas,* 538.

165. Videla de Rivero, "La direccion criollista de la
vanguardia," 220. Rubén Hitz similarly calls the movement an "Ultraísmo porteño." Hitz, "*Martín Fierro* en
la vanguardia argentina," 65.

166. Sarlo, "The Adventure of *Martín Fierro*," accessed July
20, 2015, http://www.borges.pitt.edu/bsol/bsi7.php.

167. Jorge Luis Borges, "Prólogo III," in *Índice de la nueva
poesía americana*, ed. Jorge Luis Borges, Alberto Hidalgo, and Vicente Huidobro (Buenos Aires: Sociedad
de Publicaciones El Inca, 1926), reprinted in Schwartz,
Las vanguardias latinoamericanas, 337.

168. Julio Noé, ed., *Antología de la poesía argentina moderna (1900–1925)* (Buenos Aires: Nosotros, 1926).

169. Pedro Juan Vignale and César Tiempo, "Justificación,"
in *Exposición de la actual poesía Argentina 1922–1927,*

ed. Pedro Juan Vignale and César Tiempo (Buenos Aires: Minerva, 1927), Biblioteca Virtual Miguel de Cervantes, accessed July 15, 2015, http://www.cervantesvirtual.com/obra-visor/exposicion-de-la-actual-poesia-argentina-1922-1927/html/ff3aeef8-82b1-11df-acc7-002185ce6064_2.html.

170. Other anthologies from the period include *La poesía moderna en Cuba* (1926); *Antología de la poesía argentina moderna (1900–1925)* (1926); *Antología de la moderna poesía uruguaya* (1927); *Antología de la poesía mexicana moderna* (1928); and *Antología de poesía chilena nueva* (1935). For excerpts of some of these, see Schwartz, *Las vanguardias latinoamericanas,* 355–97.

171. Evar Méndez, "Rol de 'Martín Fierro' en la renovación poética actual," in *Exposición de la actual poesía argentina (1922–1927)*, ed. Pedro-Juan Vignale and Cesar Tiempo (Buenos Aires: Minerva, 1927), xi–xviii, reprinted in Schwartz, *Las vanguardias latinoamericanas,* 342.

172. Jorge Luis Borges, response to "Nuestra encuesta sobre la nueva generación literaria," *Nosotros* 17, no. 44 (May 1923), reprinted in Ulla, *La Revista "Nosotros,"* 254.

173. Leopoldo Lugones, "Situación del lector: Estética," in Vignale and Tiempo, *Exposición de la actual poesía argentina (1922–1927)*, Biblioteca Virtual Miguel de Cervantes, accessed July 15, 2015, http://www.cervantesvirtual.com/obra-visor/exposicion-de-la-actual-poesia-argentina-1922-1927/html/ff3aeef8-82b1-11df-acc7-002185ce6064_2.html.

174. Méndez, "Rol de 'Martín Fierro,'" in Schwartz, *Las vanguardias latinoamericanas,* 349.

175. The article originally appeared as an anonymous editorial. De Torre claimed authorship in a letter to the Costa Rican magazine *Repertorio Americano* (San José) 15, no. 9 (September 3, 1927): 135. For more, see Juan E. De Castro, "The Intellectual Meridian Debate and Colonialist Nostalgia," in *The Spaces of Latin American Literature: Tradition, Globalization, and Cultural Production* (New York: Palgrave Macmillan, 2008); Marcela Croce, ed., *Polémicas intelectuales en América Latina: Del "meridiano intelectual" al caso Padilla (1927–1971)* (Buenos Aires: Ediciones Simurg, 2006); and Vanessa Fernández, "A Transatlantic Dialogue: Argentina, Mexico, Spain, and the Literary Magazines That Bridged the Atlantic (1920–1930)" (Ph.D. diss., UCLA, 2013).

176. Guillermo de Torre, "Madrid, meridiano intelectual de hispanoamérica," *La Gaceta Literaria* 1, no. 8 (April 15, 1927): 1.

177. Ibid.

178. Ibid.

179. Ibid.

180. Ibid. For more on the responses to the meridian debate, see Carmen Alemany Bay, *La polémica del me-* ridiano intelectual de Hispanoamérica (1927): Estudio y textos (Alicante: Universidad de Alicante, 1998).

181. Schwartz, *Las vanguardias latinoamericanas,* 553.

182. Pablo Rojas Paz, "Carta a los españoles de *La Gaceta Literaria*," *Martín Fierro* 4, nos. 44–45 (August–November 1927): 385.

183. Ildefonso Pereda Valdés, "Madrid, meridiano, etc.," *Martín Fierro* 4, no. 42 (June–July 1927): 356.

184. Lisardo Zia, "Para *Martín Fierro*," *Martín Fierro* 4, no. 42 (June–July 1927): 357.

185. Nicolás Olivari, "Madrid, meridiano intelectual hispano América," *Martín Fierro* 4, no. 42 (June–July 1927): 356.

186. Jorge Luis Borges, "Sobre el meridiano de una gaceta," *Martín Fierro* 4, no. 42 (June–July 1927): 357.

187. Evar Méndez ("El Director"), "Asunto Fundamental," *Martín Fierro* 4, nos. 44–45 (August–November 1927): 375.

188. Ibid.

189. Los cinco, "Directrices: Sobre un meridiano intelectual," *Revista de Avance* 1, no. 11 (September 15, 1927): 1.

190. "Montevideo, meridiano intelectual del mundo," *Cruz de Sur* (Montevideo), no. 18 (July–August 1927), reprinted in Alemany Bay, *La polémica del meridiano intelectual,* 77.

191. Alejo Carpentier, "Carta a Manuel Aznar sobre el meridiano intelectual de Nuestra América," *Diario de la Marina* (Havana) (September 12, 1927), reprinted in Alemany Bay, *La polémica del meridiano intelectual,* 96.

192. José Carlos Mariátegui, "Batalla de *Martín Fierro*," *Variedades* (Lima) (September 24, 1927), reprinted in Schwartz, *Las vanguardias latinoamericanas,* 554.

193. Ibid.

194. Mariátegui also points out that Spain was significantly more conservative under the dictatorship of Primo de Rivera than most Latin American countries were at the time, concluding that "the 'intellectual meridian of Hispanic America' cannot be at the mercy of a reactionary dictatorship." Ibid.

195. Leopoldo Marechal, "A los compañeros de la *Gaceta Literaria*," *Martín Fierro* 4, nos. 44–45 (August–November 1927): 384.

196. "El meridiano de *Martín Fierro*," *El Sol* (Madrid) (August 25, 1927): 1, reprinted in Alemany Bay, *La polémica del meridiano intelectual,* 77–79.

197. Pablo Rojas Paz, "Carta a los españoles de *La Gaceta Literaria*,"; "Un debate apasionado. Campeonato para un meridiano intelectual," *La Gaceta Literaria*, no. 17 (September 1, 1927): 3 and 6.

198. A.R. Ferrarin, "Madrid contra Buenos Aires," *La Fiera Letteraria* (Milan), no. 38 (September 18, 1927), reprinted in Alemany Bay, *La polémica del meridiano intelectual,* 50–51.

199. "Una encuesta sobre la influencia italiana en nuestra cultura," *Nosotros*, no. 227 (April 1928), reprinted in

Alemany Bay, *La polémica del meridiano intelectual*, 160–67.

200. "El meridiano intelectual de América," *La Pluma* (Montevideo) (August 1927): 10–11, reprinted in Schwartz, *Las vanguardias latinoamericanas*, 557–58.

201. Ibid., 558.

202. Pedro Garfias, "Del ultraísmo y VI: Colofón," *Heraldo de Madrid* (Madrid) (June 28, 1934): 6, quoted in José María Barrera López, "Revistas literarias de vanguardia," *La vanguardia en España: Arte y literatura*, ed. Javier Pérez Bazo (Paris: Éditions Ophrys, 1998), 329.

203. ¿Cuál es el valor del Martín Fierro?," *Nosotros*, no. 50 (June 1913): 425–33, *Nosotros*, no. 51, 74–89, and *Nosotros*, no. 52, 186–90.

204. Jorge Luis Borges, "The Argentine Writer and Tradition" (1951), trans. Esther Allen, in *The Total Library: Non-Fiction, 1922–1986*, ed. Eliot Weinberger (London: Penguin, 2001), 426–27.

205. Borges et al., "Proa," *Proa* 1, no. 1 (August 1924): 3.

206. Jorge Luis Borges, quoted in "Borges em São Paulo," *Boletim Bibliográfico Mário de Andrade* 45, nos. 1–4 (São Paulo, December–January 1984): 16, reprinted in Schwartz, *Las vanguardias latinoamericanas*, 50. Borges was not the only Ultraist who distanced himself from the movement. Rafael Cansinos-Assens parodies Ultraism in his 1921 novel *El Movimiento VP*.

207. Ibid.

208. Guillermo de Torre, "Para la prehistoria ultraísta de Borges," *Hispania* 47, no. 3 (September 1964): 457.

209. Ibid., 458.

CHAPTER 5

1. Note: *inquiétude* has no direct translation in English, but can mean unrest, anxiety, concern, uneasiness, or disquiet. "La rédaction," "Orientations," *Cahiers de l'Étoile* (Paris), no. 18 (November–December 1930): 845. All translations are by the author unless otherwise noted.

2. For instance, "¿Qué inquietud la agita?" was one of the questions included in "Nuestra encuesta sobre la nueva generación," *Nosotros* 44, no. 168 (May 1923): 5–6.

3. "La rédaction," "Orientations," 845.

4. Ibid.

5. Jiddu Krishnamurti, response to "Enquête sur l'inquiétude contemporaine," *Cahiers de l'Étoile* (Paris), no. 18 (November–December 1930): 1139–42. For more on Krishnamurti and the Order of the Star, see Mary Lutyens, *The Life and Death of Krishnamurti* (London: John Murray, 1990); Susunaga Weeraperuma, *A Bibliography of the Life and Teachings of Jiddu Krishnamurti* (Leiden: Brill, 1974); Henry Miller, *Mémoires, Plaidoiries et Documents* (New York: New Directions, 1969).

6. *Cahiers de l'Étoile* (Paris), no. 13 (January–February 1930): cover.

7. *Cahiers de l'Étoile* (Paris), no. 14 (March–April 1930): inside front cover.

8. "Conditions de l'Abonnement," *Cahiers de l'Étoile* (Paris), no. 16 (July–August 1930): inside front cover.

9. Table of contents, *Cahiers de l'Étoile* (Paris), no. 18 (November–December 1930): 841–43.

10. "La rédaction," "Orientations," 846.

11. Of course in 1930 the term "contemporary" did not signify the historical formation it does today, typically assumed to be post-1945 (or post-1960 or post-1989) and reflecting the rise of neoliberalism, globalization, and postcolonialism. Terry Smith, for instance, writes in 2008 that the contemporary is characterized by specular culture, the narrowing of media, the spread of the Internet, the rise of protest movements, and "a nearly universal condition of permanent-seeming aftermath." Terry Smith, "Introduction: The Contemporaneity Question," in *Antinomies of Art and Culture: Modernity, Postmodernity, Contemporaneity*, ed. Okwui Enwezor, Nancy Condee, and Terry Smith (Durham: Duke University Press, 2008), 2–3.

12. "La rédaction," "Orientations," 848.

13. Georg Simmel, "The Metropolis and Mental Life" (1903), trans. Kurt Wolff, in *Art in Theory, 1815–1900: An Anthology of Changing Ideas*, ed. Charles Harrison and Paul Wood with Jason Gaiger (Oxford: Blackwell, 1992), 130–35; Sigmund Freud, *The Psychopathology of Everyday Life* (1901) in *The Standard Edition of the Complete Psychological Works of Sigmund Freud*, trans. and ed. James Strachey, vol. 6 (London: Hogarth, 1960), 53–105.

14. Dadaism was founded by a group of exiles fleeing World War I in neutral Switzerland while artists like Duchamp left France for New York, also due to the war. For more on Dadaism, see Robert Motherwell, ed., *The Dada Painters and Poets*, 2nd ed. (Boston: Wittenborn and Schultz, 1951). For more on Duchamp's travels, see T. J. Demos, *The Exiles of Marcel Duchamp* (Cambridge, Mass.: MIT Press, 2007).

15. "La rédaction," "Orientations," 848.

16. F. T. Marinetti, response to "Enquête sur l'inquiétude contemporaine," *Cahiers de l'Étoile* (Paris), no. 18 (November–December 1930): 1063–64.

17. Ibid.

18. F. T. Marinetti, "The Founding and Manifesto of Futurism" (1909), in *Futurist Manifestos*, ed. Umbro Apollonio, trans. Robert Brain (Boston: MFA Publications, 2001), 22.

19. Marinetti, response to "Enquête sur l'inquiétude contemporaine," 1063–64.

20. "La rédaction," "Orientations," 849.

21. John Dos Passos, response to "Enquête sur l'inquiétude contemporaine," 878–79.

22. Banquier Anonyme (USA), response to "Enquête sur l'inquiétude contemporaine," 928–29.

23. H. L. Mencken, response to "Enquête sur l'inquiétude contemporaine," 877.

24. Jean Toomer, response to "Enquête sur l'inquiétude contemporaine," *Cahiers de l'Étoile* (Paris), no. 18 (November–December 1930): 10035–41, reprinted in Jean Toomer, "Opinions on the Questions of *Cahiers de l'Étoile*," trans. Robert B. Jones, quoted in Robert B. Jones, "Introduction," in *Jean Toomer: Selected Essays and Literary Criticism*, ed. Robert B. Jones (Knoxville: University of Tennessee Press, 1996), xxiii.

25. Jean Toomer, "Opinions on the Questions of *Cahiers de l'Étoile*," 89.

26. Nicolás Olivari, response to "Enquête sur l'inquiétude contemporaine," 977.

27. Manuel Gálvez, response to "Enquête sur l'inquiétude contemporaine," 1003–1005.

28. Olivari, response to "Enquête sur l'inquiétude contemporaine," 977.

29. Gálvez, response to "Enquête sur l'inquiétude contemporaine," 1003–1005.

30. His responses were published as Juan Marinello, "Sobre la inquietud cubana," *Revista de Avance* 3, no. 41 (December 15, 1929): 354–57, and "Sobre la inquietud cubana 2," *Revista de Avance* 4, no. 43 (February 15, 1930): 52–54; Juan Marinello, *Sobre la inquietud cubana* (Havana: Revista de Avance, 1930); Juan Marinello, response to "Enquête sur l'inquiétude contemporaine," *Cahiers de l'Étoile* (Paris), no. 18 (November–December 1930): 987–93. My citations are translated from the book.

31. Marinello, *Sobre la inquietud cubana*, 5.

32. Ibid., 5–6. Emphasis in the original.

33. Ibid., 6.

34. Ibid., 8.

35. Ibid., 9–10.

36. Ibid., 12.

37. Ibid., 16–17.

38. Ibid., 18–20.

39. Ibid., 21–23.

40. José Carlos Mariátegui, "¿Existe una inquietud propia de nuestra época?," *Mundial* (Lima) (March 29, 1930): 30, accessed May 21, 2015, https://www.marxists.org /espanol/mariateg/oc/el_artista_y_la_epoca/paginas /existe%20una%20inquietud%20propia.htm.

41. Ibid.

42. Ibid.

43. Ildefonso Pereda Valdés, response to "Enquête sur l'inquiétude contemporaine," 1106–8.

44. Ibid.

45. Alberto Hidalgo, response to "Enquête sur l'inquiétude contemporaine," 993–95.

46. Guillermo de Torre, response to "Enquête sur l'inquiétude contemporaine," 940.

47. "Encuesta de vanguardia," *Lampadario* (Quito), no. 2 (April 1931): 8.

48. Alejandro Núñez Alonso, "¿Está en crisis la generación de vanguardia?," *El Universal Ilustrado* (Mexico City) 15, no. 775 (March 17, 1932): 20–21, 30–31.

49. For instance, José Gorostiza responded to the *Universal Ilustrado* questionnaire by writing, "Yo rectifico mi actitud 'europeizante.'" José Gorostiza, response to "¿Está en crisis la generación de vanguardia?," *El Universal Ilustrado* (Mexico City) 15, no. 775 (March 17, 1932), quoted in Rodolfo Mata, "Contemporáneo, 3. Polémica en torno a la generación de vanguardia, 1932" (May 30, 2001), Centro Virtual Cervantes, accessed August 5, 2015, http://cvc.cervantes.es /el_rinconete/anteriores/mayo_01/30052001_02.htm.

50. Miguel Pérez Ferrero, "Una encuesta sensacional: ¿Qué es la vanguardia?," *La Gaceta Literaria* 4, no. 83 (June 1, 1930): 1; Edward Alden Jewell, "Again a Storm Rages Over 'Modern Art,'" *New York Times Magazine* (February 22, 1931): 12–13, 21.

51. "Whither the American Writer (A Questionnaire)," *Modern Quarterly* (Baltimore) 6, no. 2 (Summer 1932).

52. V. F. Calverton, "The Pulse of Modernity," *Modern Quarterly* (Baltimore) 6, no. 2 (Summer 1932): 5.

53. "Should the Nation Support Its Art?," *Direction* (New York) 1, no. 4 (April 1938).

54. "What Is Americanism? A Symposium on Marxism and the American Tradition," *Partisan Review* (New York) 3, no. 3 (April 1936); "The Situation in American Writing: Seven Questions," *Partisan Review* (New York) 6, no. 4 (Summer 1939). *Partisan Review* continued to issue numerous questionnaires, including one in 1952 called "Our Country and Our Culture," also known as "America and the Intellectuals" sent to Ralph Ellison, Norman Mailer, E. B. White, and Thornton Wilder. "Our Country and Our Culture: A Symposium," *Partisan Review* (New York) 19, no. 3 (May–June 1952).

55. Van Wyck Brooks's idea of a "usable past" was first coined in an essay for the *Dial* in 1918. Van Wyck Brooks, "On Creating a Usable Past," *Dial* (Chicago) 64, no. 7 (April 11, 1918): 337–41.

56. "The State of American Writing, 1948: A Symposium," *Partisan Review* (New York) 15, no. 8 (August 1948).

57. "¿El arte debe estar al servicio del programa social?," *Contra: La revista de los francotiradores* (Buenos Aires) 1, nos. 3–4 (July and August 1933). Jorge Luis Borges, response to "América y el destino de la civilización occidental," Nosotros 1, no. 1 (April 1936): 60–61 in Jorge Luis Borges: Textos Recobrados (1931–1955) Buenos Aires: Eméce, 2001. 350–351.

58. *Authors Take Sides on the Spanish War* (London: Left Review, 1937).

59. "Enquête: Que feriez-vous, si vous aviez à organiser l'Exposition de 1937?," *Vu* (Paris), no. 387 (August 14, 1935); "Enquête sur la poésie de guerre," *Fontaine* (Algiers), no. 3 (April–May 1939).

60. "For Whom Do You Write? Replies from Forty American Writers," *New Quarterly* (Rock Island, Ill.) 1, no. 2 (Summer 1934). Michael Denning refers to the magazine as part of a "proletarian regionalism" in *The*

Cultural Front: The Laboring of American Culture in the Twentieth Century (New York: Verso, 1997), 219.

61. "Pour qui écrivez-vous?," *Commune* (Paris), nos. 5–6 (January–February 1934).

62. Walter Benjamin, "The Author as Producer: Address at the Institute for the Study of Fascism, Paris, April 27, 1934," trans. Edmund Jephcott, in *The Work of Art in the Age of Its Technological Reproducibility and Other Writings on Media*, eds. Michael W. Jennings, Brigid Doherty, and Thomas Y. Levin (Cambridge, Mass.: Harvard University Press, 2008), 79–95.

63. "Où va la peinture?," *Commune* (Paris) 2, nos. 21–22 (May–June 1935).

64. Antonio Berni, response to "Où va la peinture?," *Commune* (Paris) 2, no. 22 (June 1935): 1132.

65. "¿Adónde va la pintura?," *Contrapunto: Literatura-crítica-arte* (Buenos Aires) 1, no. 3 (April 1945). For more on Berni's response, see Daniela Lucena, "La irrupción del arte concreto-invención el el campo artístico de Buenos Aires (1942–1948)," *European Review of Artistic Studies* 2, no. 4 (2011): 78–102.

66. "Inquiry on Dialectical Materialism," *Dyn* (Mexico City), no. 2 (July–August 1942); "Towards the Unknown: Six Points of 'View,'" *View* (New York) 1, nos. 11–12 (February–March 1942).

67. "Questionnaire: The Cost of Letters," *Horizon* (London) 14, no. 81 (September 1946).

68. "Encuesta sobre el arte abstracto y el neorealismo," *Ver y Estimar: Cuadernos de Crítica Artística* (Buenos Aires) 7, no. 26 (November 1951); "¿Arte abstracto o arte no figurativo?," *Sur* (Buenos Aires), nos. 209–10 (March–April 1952); "Encuesta realizada entre pintores argentinos de la nueva generación," *Letra y Línea* (Buenos Aires), no. 4 (July 1954).

69. Maurice Blanchot, André Breton, Dionys Mascolo, and Jean Schuster, "Enquête auprès d intellectuels français," *Le 14 Juillet* (Paris), no. 3 (June 18, 1959).

70. Roland Barthes, response to "Enquête sur la critique," *Positif* (Paris), no. 36 (November 1960): 16–30.

71. "Enquête: Pensez-vous avoir un don d écrivain?," *Tel Quel* (Paris), no. 1 (Spring 1960); "Enquête sur la critique," *Tel Quel* (Paris), no. 14 (Summer 1963).

72. "Questionnaire," *Internationale Situationniste* (Paris), no. 9 (August 1964), accessed May 4, 2012, http://www.cddc.vt.edu/sionline/si/questionnaire.html.

73. Irving Sandler, "Is There a New Academy?," *ARTnews* (New York) 58, no. 4 (Summer 1959): 34–37; 58–60.; Irving Sandler and Barbara Rose, "Is There a Sensibility of the 1960s?," in Robert Smithson *The Writings of Robert Smithson: Essays with Illustrations*, ed. Nancy Holt, intro. Philip Leider (New York: New York University Press, 1979), 216–17.

74. Irving Sandler, "Art Criticism Today," *Brooklyn Rail* (Brooklyn) (December 2012), accessed June 17, 2015, http://www.brooklynrail.org/2012/12/editorsmessage/art-criticism-today.

75. Gwen Allen, *Artists' Magazines: An Alternative Space for Art* (Cambridge, Mass.: MIT Press, 2011), 7.

76. "Unskirting the Issue," *Art-Rite* (New York), no. 5 (Spring 1974): 6–7, quoted in Allen, *Artists' Magazines*, 129.

77. "Painters Reply," *Artforum* (New York) 14, no. 1 (September 1975): 26.

78. Gene Davis, "Painters Reply," *Artforum* (New York) 14, no. 1 (September 1975): 26; Dona Nelson, "Painters Reply," *Artforum* (New York) 14, no. 1 (September 1975): 30.

79. Lucy Lippard and John Chandler, "The Dematerialization of Art," *Art International* (New York) 12, no. 2 (February 1968): 31–36.

80. Hans Haacke, e-mail message to author, April 7, 2015.

81. For more see Patricia C. Phillips, ed., *Mierle Laderman Ukeles: Maintenance Art* (New York: Prestel, 2016).

82. Other scholars are examining the sociological turn in art-making in the 1960s. See Ruth Erickson, "Assembling Social Forms: Sociological Art Practice in Post-1968 Paris" (Ph.D. diss., University of Pennsylvania, 2014).

83. Benjamin Patterson, *Questionnaire* from *Flux Year Box 2*, ca. 1968, *Thing/Thought: Fluxus Editions 1962–1978*, Museum of Modern Art, accessed May 4, 2012, http://www.moma.org/interactives/exhibitions/2011/fluxus_editions/works/questionnaire-from-flux-year-box-2/.

84. More recently, the artist Silvia Kolbowski, who historicized conceptual art in her piece "an inadequate history of conceptual art" (1998–99), suggested that art can model an openness and clarity that is not possible with print questionnaires. Kolbowski issued "Questions of Feminism" in *October* in 1995. That questionnaire, she explains, was "over-determined" and was subject to an aggressive backlash. Silvia Kolbowski, on "The Magazine as Medium 2: The Questionnaire," panelists: Hal Foster and Silvia Kolbowski, moderated by Lori Cole (May 11, 2015). Recording of event available online at http://cabinetmagazine.org/events/conaty_cole_foster_fox_graham_kolbowski_snyder_stein_sussler.php.

85. Shifra M. Goldman, *Dimensions of the Americas: Art and Social Change in Latin America and the United States* (Chicago: University of Chicago Press, 1994), 254; Caille Millner, "Alfredo Jaar and the Happiness of Chile," *Los Angeles Review of Books*, December 8, 2013, accessed June 15, 2015, http://lareviewofbooks.org/article/alfredo-jaar-and-the-happiness-of-chile.

86. See "Datos de Tucumán (datos de interés)," October 1968, personal archive of Graciela Carnevale, Documents of 20th-Century Latin American and Latino Art at the International Center for the Arts of the Americas at the Museum of Fine Arts, Houston, accessed May 4, 2012, http://icaadocs.mfah.org/icaadocs/ELARCHIVO/RegistroCompleto/tabid/99/doc/750902/language/es-MX/Default.aspx.

87. *Minucodes*, first put on at the Center for Inter-American Relations in New York in May 1968, was recreated by the institution (now known as the Americas Society) in the exhibition *Marta Minujín: Minucodes* in 2012.

88. Groupe de Recherche d'Art Visuel, "Une journée dans la rue," April 1966, Julio Le Parc Archive, Documents of 20th-Century Latin American and Latino Art at the International Center for the Arts of the Americas at the Museum of Fine Arts, Houston, accessed May 4, 2012, http://icaadocs.mfah.org/icaadocs /THEARCHIVE/FullRecord/tabid/88/doc/773166 /language/en-US/Default.aspx.

89. "Information," curated by Kynaston McShine, was held at MoMA from July 2 to September 20, 1970.

90. Jan Dibbets, contribution to *Information*, ed. Kynaston McShine (New York: Museum of Modern Art, 1970), 43.

91. Hans Haacke, contribution to *Information*, 57 and Grupo Frontera, contribution to *Information*, 49.

92. Kynaston McShine, "Essay," *Information*, 141.

93. Alfred Barr Jr., to Max Ernst, 1945, letter, quoted in John Elderfield, "Preface," in *Dada in the Collection of the Museum of Modern Art*, ed. Anne Umland and Adrian Sudhalter (New York: Museum of Modern Art, 2008), 9.

94. For instance, Duchamp's questionnaire response on *3 Standard Stoppages*, 1913–14, has become part of the artist's mythology. Duchamp writes in his response that the piece is "a joke about the meter—a humorous application of Riemann's post Euclidean geometry which was devoid of straight lines," and is cited by Linda Henderson, *Duchamp in Context: Science and Technology in the Large Glass and Related Works* (Princeton: Princeton University Press, 1998), 61. His response is also quoted in the work's gallery label, viewable online. Marcel Duchamp, *3 Standard Stoppages*, 1913–14, wall text, Museum of Modern Art, accessed May 4, 2011, http://www.moma.org /collection/object.php?object_id=78990.

95. Alfred Barr Jr., "Modern Art Questionnaire," *Vanity Fair* (New York) 28 (August 1927): 85.

96. Conversation with Dan Fox, coeditor of *frieze*, June 18, 2015.

97. "Is Painting Still Vital, Or Is It a Dead Language?," *Flash Art* (Milan), no. 291 (July–September 2013), accessed June 19, 2015, http://www.flashartonline.com /article/ten-questions-about-painting-2/.

98. "Is Newness Still New?," *Brooklyn Rail* (Brooklyn) (August 1, 2012), accessed June 19, 2015, http://www .brooklynrail.org/2012/08/artseen/is-newness -still-new; "Artist Questionnaire: 21 Responses," *October* (New York), no. 100 (Spring 2002).

99. Irving Sandler, "Art Criticism Today," *Brooklyn Rail* (Brooklyn) (December 10, 2012), accessed June 19, 2015, http://www.brooklynrail.org/2012/12 /editorsmessage/art-criticism-today.

100. "Who Do You Write For?," *frieze* (London), no. 148 (June–August 2012).

101. "*Critical Inquiry* Symposium," *Critical Inquiry* 30, no. 2 (Winter 2004).

102. "Questions of Feminism," *October* (New York), no. 71 (Winter 1995); "Visual Culture Questionnaire," *October* (New York), no. 77 (Summer 1996); "In What Ways Have Artists, Academics, and Cultural Institutions Responded to the U.S.-Led Invasion and Occupation of Iraq?," *October* (New York), no. 23 (Winter 2008); "A Questionnaire on Materialisms," *October* (New York), no. 155 (Winter 2016).

103. Hal Foster, on "The Magazine as Medium 2: The Questionnaire," panelists: Hal Foster and Silvia Kolbowski, moderated by Lori Cole (May 11, 2015). Recording of event available online at http://cabinetmagazine.org /events/conaty_cole_foster_fox_graham _kolbowski_snyder_stein_sussler.php.

104. Hal Foster, for the editors, "Questionnaire on 'The Contemporary,'" *October* (New York), no. 130 (Fall 2009): 3. In short, *October* was asking, "What *is* contemporary art?," a question that philosophers, critics, artists, and market analysts have all been asking and answering in their own ways for years. See Terry Smith, *What Is Contemporary Art?* (Chicago: University of Chicago Press, 2009); and Richard Meyer, *When Was Contemporary Art?* (Cambridge, Mass.: MIT Press, 2013). Note: both Terry Smith and Richard Meyer responded to the *October* questionnaire.

105. Michelle Kuo, response to "Questionnaire on 'The Contemporary,'" *October* (New York), no. 130 (Fall 2009): 28.

106. Giorgio Agamben, "What Is the Contemporary?" (2008), in *What Is an Apparatus? And Other Essays*, trans. David Kishik and Stefan Pedatella (Palo Alto: Stanford University Press, 2009), 41.

CONCLUSION

1. Maurice Caillard and Charles Forot, "Les revues d'avant-garde: 1870–1914; Enquête de *Belles-Lettres*," *Belles-Lettres: Revue Mensuelle des Lettres Françaises* (Paris) 6, nos. 62–66 (December 1924): 105.

2. Ibid., 104.

3. Maurice Caillard and Charles Forot, "Conclusion," *Belles-Lettres: Revue Mensuelle des Lettres Françaises* (Paris) 6, nos. 62–66 (December 1924): 223.

4. F. T. Marinetti, response to "Les revues d'avant-garde: Enquête de *Belles-Lettres*," *Belles-Lettres: Revue Mensuelle des Lettres Françaises* (Paris) 6, nos. 62–66 (December 1924): 160.

5. Caillard and Forot, "Conclusion," 217.

6. Ezra Pound, "Small Magazines," *English Journal* 19, no. 9 (November 1930): 703. Note that *Belles-Lettres* addresses the French literary context, while Pound's article is on Anglo-American magazines.

7. Caillard and Forot, "Conclusion," 224–25.

8. Richard Cork, "A Survey of Contemporary Art Magazines," *Studio International* (London), no. 192 (September 1976): 145.

9. Peter Hutton, response to "A Survey of Contemporary Art Magazines," *Studio International* (London), no. 192 (September 1976): 147.

10. Edit DeAk and Walter Robinson, response to "A Survey of Contemporary Art Magazines," *Studio International* (London), no. 192 (September 1976): 150.

11. Richard Cork, response to "A Survey of Contemporary Art Magazines," *Studio International* (London), no. 192 (September 1976): 182.

12. Richard Cork, "Introduction to Periodical Tables (Parts 1, 2, and 3)," *frieze* (London), no 100 (June–August 2006), accessed June 15, 2015, https://frieze.com/article/periodical-tables-part-1.

13. Elizabeth C. Baker, response to "Periodical Tables," part 1, *frieze* (London), no. 100 (June–August 2006), accessed June 15, 2015, https://frieze.com/article/periodical-tables-part-1.

14. Michal Wolinski, response to "Periodical Tables," part 3, *frieze* (London), no. 100 (June–August 2006), accessed June 15, 2015, https://frieze.com/article/periodical-tables-part-3.

15. Christian Höller, response to "Periodical Tables," *frieze* (London), no. 100 (June–August 2006), accessed June 15, 2015, https://frieze.com/article/periodical-tables-part-3.

16. Raymond Williams, "When Was Modernism?" (1987), in *The Politics of Modernism: Against the New Conformists*, ed. Tony Pinkey (London: Verso, 1989), 35.

17. A series of French magazines reprinted the questionnaire "Avons-nous une culture internationale?," including *Créer* (March 1925), *Les Images de Paris*, nos. 65–66 (February–April 1926), and *Les Chroniques du Jour* 8, no. 2 (March 1927).

Appendix
An earlier version of this index was first published in *Cabinet*, no.53 (Spring 2014): 18–19.

BIBLIOGRAPHY

291 (New York), nos. 1–12 (1915–16).

Aching, Gerard. *By Exquisite Design: The Politics of Spanish American Modernismo.* Cambridge: Cambridge University Press, 1997.

Adams, Julia, Elisabeth S. Clemens, and Shola Orloff, eds. *Remaking Modernity: Politics, History, and Sociology.* Durham: Duke University Press, 2005.

Ades, Dawn. *Art in Latin America: The Modern Era, 1820–1980.* New Haven: Yale University Press, 1989.

"¿Adónde va la pintura?" *Contrapunto: Literatura-crítica-arte* (Buenos Aires) 1, no. 3 (April 1945).

Agamben, Giorgio. "What Is the Contemporary?" 2008. In *What Is an Apparatus? and Other Essays*, translated by David Kishik and Stefan Pedatella, 31–55. Palo Alto: Stanford University Press, 2009.

Alberti, Rafael. *The Lost Grove: Autobiography of a Spanish Poet in Exile.* 1959. Translated by Gabriel Berns. Berkeley: University of California Press, 1976.

Alemany Bay, Carmen. *La polémica del meridiano intelectual de Hispanoamérica (1927): Estudio y textos.* Alicante: Universidad de Alicante, 1998.

"Algunas Encuestas." *La Gaceta Literaria* (Madrid) 2, no. 27 (February 1, 1928): 5.

Allen, Charles. "The Advance Guard." *Sewanee Review* 51, no. 3 (July–September 1943): 410–29.

Allen, Gwen. *Artists' Magazines: An Alternative Space for Art.* Cambridge, Mass.: MIT Press, 2011.

"Almanaque." *Revista de Avance* (Havana) 1, no. 15 (November 15, 1927).

Alonso, Carlos J. *The Burden of Modernity: The Rhetoric of Cultural Discourse in Spanish America.* New York: Oxford University Press, 1998.

Anderson, Andrew A. "Futurism and Spanish Literature in the Context of the Historical Avant-Garde." In *International Futurism in Arts and Literature*, edited by Günter Berghaus, 144–82. Berlin: Walter de Gruyter, 2000.

Anderson, Benedict. *Imagined Communities.* 1983. Rev. ed. London: Verso, 1991.

Antonio Molina, César. *Medio siglo de prensa literaria española (1900–1950).* Madrid: Endymion, 1990.

Appadurai, Arjun. *Modernity at Large: Cultural Dimensions of Globalization.* Minneapolis: University of Minnesota Press, 1996.

Appiah, Kwame Anthony. *Cosmopolitanism: Ethics in a World of Strangers.* New York: W. W. Norton, 2007.

Apter, Emily. *The Translation Zone: A New Comparative Literature.* Princeton: Princeton University Press, 2006.

Aragon, Louis, André Breton, Robert Desnos, Paul Eluard, Max Ernst, Eugene Jolas, Michel Leiris, André Masson, Max Morise, Elliot Paul, Man Ray, Benjamin Péret, and Raymond Queneau. "Hands Off Love." *transition* (Paris), no. 6 (September 1927): 155–56.

Ardis, Ann L. *Modernism and Cultural Conflict, 1880–1922.* Cambridge: Cambridge University Press, 2002.

Ardis, Ann L., and Patrick C. Collier, eds. *Transatlantic Print Culture, 1880–1940: Emerging Media, Emerging Modernisms.* New York: Palgrave Macmillan, 2008.

"Are Artists People?" *New Masses* (New York) 2, no. 3 (January 1927): 5–9.

Arrom, José Juan. *Esquema generacional de las letras hispanoamericanas: Ensayo de un método.* Bogotá: Instituto Caro y Cuervo, 1963.

Arroyo, Anita. *América en su literatura.* 2nd ed. San Juan: Editorial Universitaria Universidad de Puerto Rico, 1978.

"¿Arte abstracto o arte no figurativo?" *Sur* (Buenos Aires), nos. 209–10 (March–April 1952).

"¿El arte debe estar al servicio del programa social?" *Contra: La revista de los francotiradores* (Buenos Aires) 1, nos. 3–4 (July–August 1933).

Arte moderno y revistas españolas 1898–1936. Edited by Eugenio Carmona and Juan José Lahuerta. Madrid: Museo Nacional Centro de Arte Reina Sofía, 1996.

"Artist Questionnaire: 21 Responses." *October* (New York), no. 100 (Spring 2002).

Artundo, Patricia. *Norah Borges: Obra gráfica 1920–1930.* Buenos Aires: Fondo Nacional de las Artes, 1994.

———. "Punto de convergencia: *Inicial y Proa* en 1924." In *Las vanguardias literarias en Argentina, Uruguay, y Paraguay: Bibliografía y antología crítica*, edited by Carlos García and Dieter Reichardt, 253–72. Madrid: Iberoamericana, 2004.

———, ed. *Xul Solar: Visiones y revelaciones.* Buenos Aires: Malba, 2005.

Authors Take Sides on the Spanish War. London: Left Review, 1937.

Barletta, Leónidas. "La literatura de la calle Boedo, contra la literatura de calle Florida." *Crítica* (Buenos Aires) (June 10, 1925).

Barnitz, Jacqueline. *Twentieth-Century Art of Latin America.* Austin: University of Texas Press, 2001.

Barr, Alfred, Jr. "Modern Art Questionnaire." *Vanity Fair* (New York) 28 (August 1927): 85, 96, 98.

———. "Modern Cuban Painters." *Bulletin of the Museum of Modern Art* (New York) 11, no. 5 (April 1944): 2–14.

Barrera López, José. "Revistas literarias de vanguardia." In *La vanguardia en España: Arte y literatura*, edited by Javier Pérez Bazo, 329–49. Paris: Éditions Ophrys, 1998.

———. "*Ultra*: Nucleo de las primeras vanguardias." In *Revistas literarias españolas del siglo XX*, vol. 1, *1919–1939*, edited by Manuel José Ramos Ortega, 117–44. Madrid: Ollero y Ramos, 2006.

———. *El Ultraísmo de Sevilla: Historia y textos.* Seville: Alfar, 1987.

Barthes, Roland. Response to "Enquête sur la critique." *Positif* (Paris), no. 36 (November 1960): 16–30.

———. "Literature Today." 1961. In *Critical Essays*, translated by Richard Howard, 4th ed., 151–61. 1964. Evanston: Northwestern University Press, 2000.

Bassolas, Carmen. *La ideología de los escritores: Literatura y política en La gaceta literaria (1927–1932)*. Barcelona: Fontamara, 1975.

Beach, Sylvia. *Shakespeare and Company*. New York: Harcourt, Brace, 1959.

Beckett, Samuel. "Dante . . . Bruno . . . Vico . . . Joyce." *transition* (Paris), nos. 16–17 (June 1929): 242–53.

Beckman, Ericka. *Capital Fictions: The Literature of Latin America's Export Age*. Minneapolis: University of Minnesota Press, 2013.

Belles-Lettres: Revue Mensuelle des Lettres Françaises (Paris) 6, nos. 62–66 (December 1924).

Benítez Rojo, Antonio. *The Repeating Island: The Caribbean and the Postmodern Perspective*. Translated by James Maraniss. Durham: Duke University Press, 1992.

Benjamin, Walter. "The Author as Producer: Address at the Institute for the Study of Fascism, Paris, April 27, 1934." Translated by Edmund Jephcott. In *The Work of Art in the Age of Its Technological Reproducibility and Other Writings on Media*, edited by Michael W. Jennings, Brigid Doherty, and Thomas Y. Levin, 79–95. Cambridge, Mass.: Harvard University Press, 2008.

Bennett, David. "Periodical Fragments and Organic Culture: Modernism, the Avant-Garde, and the Little Magazine." *Contemporary Literature* 30, no. 4 (1989): 480–502.

Benstock, Shari. *Women of the Left Bank: Paris, 1900–1940*. Austin: University of Texas Press, 1986.

Berghaus, Günter, ed. *International Futurism in Arts and Literature*. Berlin: Walter de Gruyter, 2000.

Berman, Jessica. *Modernist Fiction, Cosmopolitanism, and the Politics of Community*. Cambridge: Cambridge University Press, 2001.

Bernal, José Luis. *El ultraísmo. Historia de un fracaso?* Cáceres: Universidad de Extremadura, 1988.

Binckes, Faith. *Modernism, Magazines, and the British Avant Garde: Reading Rhythm, 1910–1914*. New York: Oxford University Press, 2010.

Bishop, Edward. "Re:Covering Modernism: Format and Function in the Little Magazines." In *Modernist Writers and the Marketplace*, edited by Ian Willison, Warwick Gould, and Warren Chernaik, 287–319. New York: St. Martin's Press, 1996.

Blanchot, Maurice, André Breton, Dionys Mascolo, and Jean Schuster. "Enquête auprès d'intellectuels français." *Le 14 Juillet* (Paris), no. 3 (June 18, 1959).

The Blue Mountain Project. http://diglib.princeton.edu/bluemountain/journals.

Bojórquez, Juan de Dios. "Los minoristas de Cuba." *Social* (Havana) 12, no. 6 (1927): 35.

Bolívar, Simón. "Carta de Jamaica (1815)." In *Simón Bolívar: Escritos políticos*, edited by Gabriela Soriano, 61–84. Madrid: Alianza Editorial, 1990.

Bonet, Juan Manuel. *Diccionario de las vanguardias en España, 1907–1936*. Madrid: Alianza Editorial, 1995.

Borges, Jorges Luis. "Anatomía de mi 'ULTRA.'" *Ultra* (Madrid) 1, no. 11 (May 1921): 1.

———. "The Argentine Writer and Tradition." 1951. Translated by Esther Allen. In *The Total Library: Non-Fiction 1922–1986*, edited by Eliot Weinberger, 420–27. London: Penguin, 2001.

———, with Norman Thomas di Giovanni. "Autobiographical Notes." *New Yorker* (September 19, 1970): 40–99.

———. "Elvira de Alvear." 1960. Translated by Robert Mezey. *American Poetry Review* 23, no. 1 (January–February 1994): 25.

———. Fervor de Buenos Aires. Buenos Aires: Imprenta Serrantes, 1923.

———. Inquisiciones. Buenos Aires: Proa, 1925.

——— et al. "Al oportuno lector." *Proa* (Buenos Aires), no. 1 (August 1922). Reprinted in *Las revistas literarias argentinas, 1893–1967*, edited by Héctor René Lafleur, Sergio D. Provenzano, and Fernando Alonso, 95–96. Buenos Aires: Ediciones El 8vo. loco, 2006.

———. "Prólogo." In Elvira de Alvear, *Reposo*. Buenos Aires: M. Gleizer, 1934.

———. "Prólogo III." In *Índice de la nueva poesía americana*, edited by Jorge Luis Borges, Alberto Hidalgo, and Vicente Huidobro. Buenos Aires: Sociedad de Publicaciones El Inca, 1926.

———. *Textos recobrados, 1919–1929*. Edited by Sara Luisa del Carril. Buenos Aires: Emecé, 1997.

———. "Ultraísmo." *Nosotros* (Buenos Aires) 39, no. 151 (December 1921): 466–71. Reprinted in *Vanguardias en su tinta: Documentos de la vanguardia en América Latina*, edited by Celina Manzoni, 28–36. Buenos Aires: Corregidor, 2007.

Borges, Jorge Luis, Brandán Caraffa, Ricardo Güiraldes, and Pablo Rojas Paz. "Proa." *Proa* (Buenos Aires), no. 1 (August 1924): 3–8.

Borges, Jorge Luis, Brandán Caraffa, and Francisco Luis Bernárdez. "Proa." *Proa* (Buenos Aires), no. 13 (November 1925): 5–6.

Borges, Jorge Luis, Guillermo Juan, Eduardo González Lanuza, and Guillermo de Torre. "Proclama." *Prisma, Revista Mural* 1, no. 1 (Buenos Aires, December 1921). Reprinted in *Vanguardias en su tinta: Documentos de la vanguardia en América Latina*, edited by Celina Manzoni, 25–28. Buenos Aires: Corregidor, 2007.

Borges, Jorge Luis, Jacobo Sureda, Fortunio Bonanova, and Juan Alomar. "Manifiesto del Ultra." *Baleares* (Palma de Mallorca) 5, no. 131 (February 1921). Reprinted in *Vanguardias en su tinta: Documentos de la vanguardia en América Latina*, edited by Celina Manzoni, 23–25. Buenos Aires: Corregidor, 2007.

Bourdieu, Pierre. *The Field of Cultural Production*. New York: Columbia University Press, 1993.

Bóveda, Xavier, César A. Comet, Fernando Iglesias, Guillermo de Torre, Pedro Iglesias Caballero, Pedro Garfias,

J. Rivas Panedas, and J. de Aroca. "Ultra. Un manifiesto de la juventud literaria." *Cervantes* (Madrid) 3, no. 1 (January 1919): 2–3. Reprinted in *Grecia* 2 (Seville), no. 11 (March 15, 1919): 11.

Boyd, Carolyn P. *Historia Patria: Politics, History, and National Identity in Spain. 1875–1975.* Princeton: Princeton University Press, 1997.

Boyle, Kay, and Robert McAlmon. *Being Geniuses Together, 1920–1930.* 1938. Baltimore: Johns Hopkins University Press, 1984.

Braddock, Jeremy. *Collecting as Modernist Practice.* Baltimore: Johns Hopkins University Press, 2012.

Braque, Georges, Eugene Jolas, Maria Jolas, Henri Matisse, André Salmon, and Tristan Tzara. *Testimony Against Gertrude Stein.* Supplement to *transition*, no. 23. The Hague, February 1935.

Braschi, Cecilia. "De París a Buenos Aires, relaciones particulares." *La Nación* (Buenos Aires) (October 12, 2012). Accessed August 3, 2015. http://www.lanacion.com.ar/1516367-de-paris-a-buenos-aires-relaciones-particulares.

Brennan, Timothy. *At Home in the World: Cosmopolitanism Now.* Cambridge, Mass.: Harvard University Press, 1997.

Breton, André, and Paul Éluard. "Pouvez-vous dire quelle a été la rencontre capitale de votre vie?" *Minotaure* (Paris), nos. 3–4 (1933): 101–16.

Bretz, Mary Lee. *Encounters Across Borders: The Changing Visions of Spanish Modernism, 1890–1930.* Lewisburg: Bucknell University Press, 2001.

Brihuega, Jaime, ed. *Arte y política en España (1898–1939).* Seville: Junta de Andalucía, 2002.

———. *Las vanguardias artísticas en España, 1909–1936.* Madrid: Ediciones Istmo, 1981.

Briones, Edmundo Olivares. *Pablo Neruda, los caminos de oriente: Tras las huellas del poeta itinerante (1927–1933).* Santiago de Chile: LOM Ediciones, 2000.

Brooker, Peter, Sascha Bru, Andrew Thacker, and Christian Weikop, eds. *The Oxford Critical and Cultural History of Modernist Magazines.* 3 vols. Oxford: Oxford University Press, 2009–13.

Brooker, Peter, and Andrew Thacker, eds. *Geographies of Modernism: Literatures, Cultures, Spaces.* New York: Taylor and Francis, 2005.

Brooks, Van Wyck. "On Creating a Usable Past." *Dial* (Chicago) 64, no. 7 (April 11, 1918): 337–41.

Brown, Milton W. *The Story of the Armory Show.* New York: Abbeville Press, 1988.

Bulmer, Martin, Kevin Bales, and Kathryn Kish Sklar, eds. *The Social Survey in Historical Perspective, 1880–1940.* Cambridge: Cambridge University Press, 1992.

Bürger, Peter. *Theory of the Avant-Garde.* 1974. Translated by Michael Shaw. Edited by Jochen Schulte-Sasse. Minneapolis: University of Minnesota Press, 1984.

Cahiers de l'Étoile (Paris), nos. 13–18 (January–December 1930).

Caillard, Maurice, and Charles Forot. "Conclusion." *Belles-Lettres: Revue Mensuelle des Lettres Françaises* (Paris) 6, nos. 62–66 (December 1924): 217–25.

———. "Les revues d'avant-garde: 1870–1914: Enquête de *Belles-Lettres.*" *Belles-Lettres: Revue Mensuelle des Lettres Françaises* (Paris) 6, nos. 62–66 (December 1924): 97–217.

Cairo Ballester, Ana. *El grupo minorista y su tiempo.* Havana: Editorial de Ciencias Sociales, 1978.

Calhoun, Craig, ed. *Sociology in America.* Chicago: University of Chicago Press, 2007.

Calinescu, Matei. *Five Faces of Modernity: Modernism, Avant-Garde, Decadence, Kitsch, Postmodernism.* Durham: Duke University Press, 1987.

Calverton, V. F. "The Pulse of Modernity." *Modern Quarterly* (Baltimore) 6, no. 2 (Summer 1932): 1–6.

———. "The Revolution-in-the-Wordists." *Modern Quarterly* (Baltimore) 3 (Fall 1929): 276–77.

Camera Work (New York), nos. 1–53 (1903–17).

Camfield, William A. *Francis Picabia: His Art, Life, and Times.* Princeton: Princeton University Press, 1979.

Camnitzer, Luis. *New Art Cuba.* 2nd ed. Austin: University of Texas Press, 2003.

Cancino Troncoso, Hugo. "José Martí y el paradigma de la modernidad." In *Ideas, cultura e historia en la creacion intelectual latinoamericana siglos XIX y XX*, edited by Hugo Cancino Troncoso and Carmen de Sierra, 301–25. Quito: Ediciones Abya-Yala, 1998.

Cancio Isla, Wilfredo. "*Revista de Avance.*" In *Encyclopedia of Latin American and Caribbean Literature, 1900–2003*, edited by Daniel Balderston and Mike Gonzalez, 484. London: Routledge, 2004.

Canclini, Néstor García. *Hybrid Cultures: Strategies for Entering and Leaving Modernity.* 1995. Translated by Christopher L. Chiappari and Silvia L. López. Expanded ed. Minneapolis: University of Minnesota Press, 2005.

———. "Modernity After Postmodernity." In *Beyond the Fantastic: Contemporary Art Criticism from Latin America*, edited by Gerardo Mosquera, 20–51. London: Institute of International Visual Arts, 1995.

Carilla, Emilio. "La revista de Lugones: *Revue Sud-Américaine.*" *Thesaurus* 29, no. 3 (September–December 1974): 501–25.

Carpentier, Alejo. "América ante la joven literatura Europea." *Carteles* (Havana) 17, no. 17 (June 28, 1931): 30, 51, 54.

———. "Carta a Manuel Aznar sobre el meridiano intelectual de Nuestra América." *Diario de la Marina* (Havana) (September 12, 1927). Reprinted in Carmen Alemany Bay, *La polémica del meridiano intelectual de Hispanoamérica (1927): Estudio y textos*, 95–97. Alicante: Universidad de Alicante, 1998.

———. *Crónicas 2: Arte, literatura, política.* Vol. 9 of *Obras completas.* Mexico City: Siglo XXI, 1986.

———. "Cuban Magic." Translated by Frederick M. Murray. *transition* (Paris), nos. 19–20 (June 1930): 384–90.

———. *Entrevistas*. Edited by Virgilio López Lemus. Havana: Editorial Letras Cubanas, 1985.

———. "Homenage a nuestros amigos de Paris." *Carteles* (Havana) (December 24, 1933). Reproduced in *La Jiribilla: Revista de Cultural Cubana*. Accessed August 5, 2015. http://www.lajiribilla.cu/2010/n453_01/453_01.html.

———. "Lettre des Antilles." *Bifur* (Paris), no. 3 (September 1929): 91–105.

———. *Music in Cuba*. 1946. Translated by Alan West-Durán. Edited by Timothy Brennan. Minneapolis: University of Minnesota Press, 2001.

———. "Le musique cubaine." *Documents* (Paris), no. 6 (November 1929): 324–29.

———. "La novela latinoamericana en vísperas de un nuevo siglo." 1979. In *Los pasos recobrados: Ensayos de teoría y crítica literaria*, edited by Alexis Márquez Rodríguez and Araceli García Carranza, 184–207. Caracas: Biblioteca Ayacucho, 2003.

———. "Les points cardinaux du roman en Amérique latine." *Le Cahier* (Paris), no. 6 (November 1931): 19–28.

———. "Los puntos cardinales de la novela en América Latina." 1931. Translated by Andrea Martínez. In *Los pasos recobrados: ensayos de teoría y crítica literaria*, edited by Alexis Márquez Rodríguez and Araceli García Carranza, 107–15. Caracas: Biblioteca Ayacucho, 2003.

Carter, Boyd G. *Las revistas literarias de Hispanoamérica: Breve historia y contenido*. Mexico City: Ediciones de Andrea, 1959.

Casanova, Pascale. *The World Republic of Letters*. Translated by Malcolm DeBevoise. Cambridge, Mass.: Harvard University Press, 2007.

Casanovas, Martí, ed. *Órbita de la Revista de Avance*. Havanas: Ediciones Unión, 1965.

———. *Revista de Avance*. Coleción Órbita, Havana, 1972.

Cassou, Jean. "Poésie: Amités sud-americans." *Les Nouvelles Littéraires* (Paris) (January 30, 1932): 7.

Caws, Mary Ann, ed. *Manifesto: A Century of Isms*. Lincoln: University of Nebraska Press, 2001.

Chipp, Herschel B., ed. *Theories of Modern Art: A Source Book by Artists and Critics*. Berkeley: University of California Press, 1968.

Los cinco. "Al llevar la ancla." *Revista de Avance* (Havana) 1, no. 1 (March 15, 1927): 1.

———. "Directrices: Una encuesta." *Revista de Avance* (Havana) 2, no. 26 (September 15, 1928): 235.

Cippolini, Rafael. *Manifiestos Argentinos: Políticas de lo visual 1900–2000*. Buenos Aires: Adriana Hidalgo, 2003.

Clark, T. J. *Farewell to an Idea: Episodes from a History of Modernism*. New Haven: Yale University Press, 2001.

Clifford, James. "Mixed Feelings." In *Cosmopolitics: Thinking and Feeling Beyond the Nation*, edited by Pheng Cheah and Bruce Robbins, 362–69. Minneapolis: University of Minnesota Press, 1998.

Cole, Lori. "'Do You Believe in Angels?' and Other Inquiries: Eugene Jolas' Questionnaires for *transition* Magazine." *Cabinet*, no. 53 (Spring 2014): 13–20.

———. "'How Do You Imagine Latin America?' Questioning Latin American Art and Identity in Print." *Global South* 7, no. 2 (2014): 110–33.

———. "*Légitime défense*: From Communism and Surrealism to Caribbean Self-Definition." *Journal of Surrealism and the Americas* 4, no. 1 (2010): 15–30.

———. "Madrid: Questioning the Avant-Garde." In *The Oxford Critical and Cultural History of Modernist Magazines*, vol. 3, Europe *1880–1940*, edited by Peter Brooker, Sascha Bru, Andrew Thacker, and Christian Weikop, 369–92. Oxford: Oxford University Press, 2013.

———. "Manifesto: Declaring the Political and Aesthetic Intentions of the Avant-Garde." Undergraduate honors thesis, Brown University, 2002.

———. "¿Qué es la vanguardia? Ultraism Between Madrid and Buenos Aires." In *Modernidad y vanguardia: Rutas de intercambio entre España y Latinoamérica (1920–1970)*, edited by Paula Barreiro López and Fabiola Martínez Rodríguez, 127–37. Madrid: Museo Nacional Centro de Arte Reina Sofía, 2015.

———. "Reproducing the Avant-Garde: The Art of Modernist Magazines." In *The Aesthetics of Matter. Modernism, the Avant-Garde and Material Exchange*, edited by Sarah Posman, Anne Reverseau, David Ayers, Sascha Bru, and Benedikt Hjartarson, 183–94. European Avant-Garde and Modernism Studies Series 3. Berlin: Walter de Gruyter, 2013.

———. "What Is the Avant-Garde? The Questionnaire as Historiography." *Journal of Art Historiography* (December 2011).

Coleridge, Samuel, and William Wordsworth. *Lyrical Ballads: The Text of the 1798 Edition with the Additional 1800 Poems and the Prefaces*. Edited by R. L. Brett and A. R. Jones. London: Methuen, 1963.

Colhoun, C. K. "Foreign Periodicals." *Criterion* 10, no. 41 (July 1931): 783–84.

Collazos, Óscar. *Los vanguardismos en la América Latina*. Barcelona: Ediciones Península, 1971.

"Comment définir la poésie?" *La Muse Française* (Paris) 2, no. 4–6 (April–June 1923).

"Conocimiento de América Latina." *Imán* (Paris), no. 1 (April 1931): 189–229.

Cork, Richard. "Introduction to Periodical Tables (Parts 1, 2, and 3)." *frieze* (London), no. 100 (June–August 2006). Accessed June 15, 2015. https://frieze.com/article/periodical-tables-part-1.

———. "A Survey of Contemporary Art Magazines." *Studio International* (London), no. 192 (September 1976): 145–87.

Corn, Wanda. *The Great American Thing: Modern Art and National Identity, 1915–1935*. Berkeley: University of California Press, 1999.

Cowley, Malcolm. *Exile's Return: A Literary Odyssey of the 1920s*. 1934. Edited by Donald W. Faulkner. New York: Penguin, 1994.

"*Critical Inquiry* Symposium." *Critical Inquiry* 30, no. 2 (Winter 2004).

Croce, Marcela. *Las revistas literarias argentinas (1893–1967)*. Buenos Aires: El 8vo Loco, 1977.

"¿Cuál es, a su juicio, el peor libro del año?" *La Campana de Palo: Periódico Mensual. Bellas Artes y Polémica* (Buenos Aires), no. 10 (December 1926).

"¿Cuál es el pintor más grande de México?" *El Universal Ilustrado* (Mexico City) 6, no. 380 (September 1922): 49.

"¿Cuál es el valor de Martín Fierro?" *Nosotros* (Buenos Aires), no. 50 (June 1913): 425–33, no. 51, 74–89, and no. 52, 186–90.

Dalí, Salvador, Lluís Montanyà, and Sebastià Gasch. "Yellow Manifesto." 1928. Translated by John London. In *Manifesto: A Century of Isms*, edited by Mary Ann Caws, 367–72. Lincoln: University of Nebraska Press, 2001.

Darío, Rubén. "Marinetti y el Futurismo." *La Nación* (Buenos Aires, April 5, 1909).

———. "Palabras Liminares." 1896. In *Antología Poética*. Madrid: Edaf, 1981.

———. *Peregrinaciones*. Paris: Librería de la Viuda de Ch. Bouret, 1901.

Dash, J. Michael. *The Other America: Caribbean Literature in a New World Context*. Charlottesville: University of Virginia Press, 1998.

"Datos de Tucumán (datos de interés)." October 1968. Personal archive of Graciela Carnevale. Documents of 20th-Century Latin American and Latino Art at the International Center for the Arts of the Americas at the Museum of Fine Arts, Houston. Accessed May 4, 2012. http://icaadocs.mfah.org/icaadocs/ELARCHIVO /RegistroCompleto/tabid/99/doc/750902/language /es-MX/Default.aspx.

Datta, Venita. *Birth of a Literary Icon: The Literary Avant-Garde and the Origins of the Intellectual in France*. Albany: State University of New York Press, 1999.

Davidson, Vanessa K. "Norah Borges, the Graphic Voice of Ultraísmo in Two Peripheral Centres." *Romance Studies* 27, no. 1 (January 2009): 11–29.

De Alvear, Elvira. "Imán." *Imán* (Paris), no. 1 (April 1931): 1–3.

———. *Reposo*. Buenos Aires: M. Gleizer, 1934.

De Andrade, Oswald. "Manifesto Antropófago." *Revista de Antropofagía* (São Paulo), no. 1 (May 1928). Translated by Dawn Ades in *Art in Latin America: The Modern Era, 1820–1980*, edited by Dawn Ades, 312–13. New Haven: Yale University Press, 1989.

"Un debate apasionado. Campeonato para un meridiano intelectual." *La Gaceta Literaria* (Madrid), no. 17 (September 1, 1927): 3, 6.

De Castro, Juan E. *The Spaces of Latin American Literature: Tradition, Globalization, and Cultural Production*. New York: Macmillan, 2008.

De Castro, Martha. *El arte en Cuba*. Miami: Ediciones Universales, 1970.

De Torre, Guillermo. "Efigie de Marinetti." *La Gaceta Literaria* (Madrid) 2, no. 28 (February 15, 1928): 3.

———. *Historia de las literaturas de vanguardia*. 1965. 3 vols. Madrid: Guadarrama, 1971.

———. *Literaturas europeas de vanguardia*. 1925. Edited by Jóse María Barerra López. Introduction by Miguel de Torre Borges. Seville: Renacimiento, 2001.

———. "Madrid, meridiano intelectual de hispanoamérica." *La Gaceta Literaria* (Madrid) 1, no. 8 (April 15, 1927): 1.

———. "Manifiesto Vertical." In *Grecia* (Madrid) 3, no. 50 (November 1920), supplement. Reprinted in *El ultraísmo: Estudios sobre movimientos poéticos de vanguardia en España*, edited by Gloria Videla. Madrid: Gredos, 1963.

———. "Modelos de estación." *Síntesis* (Buenos Aires) 2, no. 14 (July 1928): 231.

———. "Para la prehistoria ultraísta de Borges." *Hispania* 47, no. 3 (September 1964): 457–63.

———. "Visita de 'Interviewer Ignotus' al autor de *Hélices*." *Alfar: Revista de Casa América-Galicia* (La Coruña) 1, no. 28 (1923): 5–7.

Del Vando-Villar, Isaac. "Manifiesto Ultraísta." *Grecia* (Seville), no. 20 (June 30, 1919): 9. Reprinted in *El ultraísmo: Estudios sobre movimientos poéticos de vanguardia en España*, edited by Gloria Videla. Madrid: Gredos, 1963.

———. "El triunfo del ultraísmo." *Grecia* (Seville) 2, no. 29 (October 1919): 2.

Demos, T. J. *The Exiles of Marcel Duchamp*. Cambridge, Mass.: MIT Press, 2007.

Denning, Michael. *The Cultural Front: The Laboring of American Culture in the Twentieth Century*. New York: Verso, 1997.

Desnos, Robert. Introduction to Alejo Carpentier, "Le musique cubaine." *Documents* (Paris), no. 6 (November 1929): 324.

Desnos, Robert, Georges Bataille, Georges Limbour, Raymond Queneau, Michel Leiris, Alejo Carpentier, Jacques Baron, Jacques Prévert, Roger Vitrac, Max Morise, Georges Ribemont-Dessaignes, and Jacques-André Boiffard. *Un cadavre*. Paris: Impremiere Spéciale du Cadavre, January 1930.

De Zayas, Marius. *How, When, and Why Modern Art Came to New York*. Edited by Francis M. Naumann. Cambridge, Mass.: MIT Press, 1996.

———. "Pablo Picasso." *América: Revista mensual ilustrada* (New York), 6 (May 1911): 363–65.

———. "Pablo Picasso." *Camera Work* (New York), nos. 34–35 (April–July 1911): 65–67.

———. Papers, 1814–1948. Columbia University Libraries.

Dickerman, Leah. "Inventing Abstraction." In *Inventing Abstraction, 1910–1925: How a Radical Idea Changed Modern Art*, edited by Leah Dickerman and Matthew Affron, 12–38. New York: MoMA, 2012.

Dilks, Stephen John. "Selling 'Work in Progress.'" *James Joyce Quarterly* 41, no. 4 (Summer 2004): 719–44.

Documents of the 1913 Armory Show: The Electrifying Moment of Modern Art's American Debut. Tucson: Hol Art Books, 2009.

Dolan, Marc. "The (Hi)story of Their Lives: Mythic Autobiography and 'The Lost Generation.'" *Journal of American Studies* 27, no. 1 (April 1993): 35–56.

Doyle, Laura, and Laura Winkiel, eds. *Geomodernisms: Race, Modernism, Modernity.* Bloomington: Indiana University Press, 2005.

Duchamp, Marcel. *3 Standard Stoppages,* 1913–14. Wall text. Museum of Modern Art. Accessed May 4, 2011. http://www.moma.org/collection/object.php?object _id=78990.

"Editoriales Proa y Martín Fierro." *Martín Fierro* (Buenos Aires) 3, no. 34 (October 1926): 259.

Ehrlicher, Hanno. "Bartolomé Galíndez's Magazine, *Los raros*: A 'Symbolist' Fusion of Futurism and Ultraism." *International Yearbook of Futurism Studies* 4 (2014): 360–89.

Elderfield, John. "Preface." In *Dada in the Collection of the Museum of Modern Art*, edited by Anne Umland and Adrian Sudhalter, 8–11. New York: MoMA, 2008.

Emery, Amy Fass. *The Anthropological Imagination in Latin American Literature.* Columbia: University of Missouri Press, 1996.

"Una encuesta." *La Gaceta Literaria* (Madrid) 3, no. 51 (February 1, 1929): 7.

"Encuesta de vanguardia." *Lampadario* (Quito), no. 2 (April 1931): 8.

"Encuesta realizada entre pintores argentinos de la nueva generación." *Letra y Línea* (Buenos Aires), no. 4 (July 1954).

"Encuesta sobre el arte abstracto y el neorealismo." *Ver y Estimar: Cuadernos de Crítica Artística* (Buenos Aires) 7, no. 26 (November 1951).

"Una encuesta sobre la influencia italiana en nuestra cultura." *Nosotros* (Buenos Aires), no. 227 (April 1928).

"Une enquête franco-allemande." *Mercure de France* (Paris) 14, no. 64 (April 14, 1895): 1–65.

"Enquête: Pensez-vous avoir un don d'écrivain?" *Tel Quel* (Paris) 1 (Spring 1960).

"Enquête: Pourquoi écrivez-vous?" *Littérature* (Paris), no. 9 (November 1919).

"Enquête: Que feriez-vous, si vous aviez à organiser l'Exposition de 1937?" *Vu* (Paris), no. 387 (August 14, 1935).

"Enquête sur la critique." *Tel Quel* (Paris), no. 14 (Summer 1963).

"Enquête sur l'amour." *La révolution surréaliste* (Paris), no. 12 (December 1929): 65–76.

"Enquête sur l'inquiétude contemporaine." *Cahiers de l'Étoile* (Paris), no. 18 (November–December 1930).

"Enquête sur la poésie de guerre." *Fontaine* (Algiers), no. 3 (April–May 1939).

"Enquête sur l'utilité de l'art." *Le Buccin* (Paris) 2, no. 7 (December 1919).

Erickson, Ruth. "Assembling Social Forms: Sociological Art Practice in Post-1968 Paris." Ph.D. diss., University of Pennsylvania, 2014.

"¿Está en crisis la generación de vanguardia?" *El Universal Ilustrado* (Mexico City) 15, no. 775 (March 17, 1932) 20–21, 30–31.

Eujanian, Alejandro C. *Historia de revistas argentinas 1900–1950: La conquista del público.* Buenos Aires: Asociación Argentina de Editores de Revistas, 1999.

"¿Existe una literatura proletaria?" *Amauta* (Lima), no. 18 (October 1928): 1–8.

Eysteinsson, Astradur. *The Concept of Modernism.* Ithaca: Cornell University Press, 1990.

Faber, Sebastiaan. "Learning from the Latins: Waldo Frank's Progressive Pan-Americanism." *CR: The New Centennial Review* 3, no. 1 (Spring 2003): 257–95.

Fargue, Léon-Paul. "De una pluma a un imán." *Imán* (Paris), no. 1 (April 1931): 4–11.

Fernández, Vanessa. "A Transatlantic Dialogue: Argentina, Mexico, Spain, and the Literary Magazines That Bridged the Atlantic (1920–1930)." Ph.D. diss., UCLA, 2013.

Finney, Michael. "Eugene Jolas, *transition*, and the Revolution of the Word." In *In the Wake of the Wake*, edited by David Hayman and Elliot Anderson, 39–54. Madison: University of Wisconsin Press, 1978.

Fitch, Noel Riley, ed. *In transition: A Paris Anthology. Writing and Art from transition Magazine, 1927–1930.* New York: Doubleday, 1990.

———. *Sylvia Beach and the Lost Generation: A History of Literary Paris in the Twenties and Thirties.* New York: W. W. Norton, 1993.

Foard, D. W. *The Revolt of the Aesthetes: Ernesto Giménez Caballero and the Origins of Spanish Fascism.* New York: Lang, 1989.

Folejewski, Zbigniew. *Futurism and Its Place in the Development of Modern Poetry.* Ottawa: Ottawa University Press, 1980.

Ford, Ford Madox. "Some American Expatriates." *Vanity Fair* 28 (April 1, 1927): 64 and 98. Accessed October 10, 2011. http://www.vanityfair.com/culture/features /1927/04/hemingway-192704#gotopage1.

Ford, Hugh, ed. *The Left Bank Revisited: Selections from the Paris Tribune, 1917–1934.* University Park: Penn State University Press, 1972.

Ford, Hugh. *Published in Paris: A Literary Chronicle of Paris in the 1920s and 1930s.* New York: MacMillan, 1975.

"For Whom Do You Write? Replies from Forty American Writers." *New Quarterly* (Rock Island, Ill.), no. 2 (Summer 1934).

Foster, Hal. "The Magazine as Medium 2: The Questionnaire." Panelists: Hal Foster and Silvia Kolbowski. Moderated by Lori Cole. May 11, 2015. http ://cabinetmagazine.org/events/conaty_cole _foster_fox_graham_kolbowski_snyder_stein_sussler .php.

————, for the editors. "Questionnaire on 'The Contemporary.'" *October* (New York), no. 130 (Fall 2009): 3.

Foucault, Michel. "What Is Enlightenment?" In *The Foucault Reader*, translated by Josué V. Harari, edited by Paul Rabinow, 32–51. New York: Pantheon Books, 1984.

Fox, Claire F. *Making Art Panamerican: Cultural Policy and the Cold War*. Minneapolis: University of Minnesota Press, 2013.

Frank, Patrick, trans. and ed. *Manifestos and Polemics in Latin American Art*. Albuquerque, NM: University of New Mexico Press, 2017.

————, ed. *Readings in Latin American Modern Art*. New Haven: Yale University Press: 2004.

Frank, Waldo. *Our America*. New York: Boni and Liveright, 1919.

————. *The Re-discovery of America: An Introduction to a Philosophy of American Life*. New York: Charles Scribner's Sons, 1929.

La Gaceta Literaria (Madrid), 1–5, nos. 1–118. (1927–31).

García, Carlos. "Borges y el Expresionismo: Kurt Heynicke." In *Las vanguardias literarias en Argentina, Uruguay, y Paraguay: Bibliografía y antología crítica*, edited by Carlos García and Dieter Reichardt, 325–43. Madrid: Iberoamericana, 2004.

————. "*Prisma* (1921–1922): Entretelones." In *Las vanguardias literarias en Argentina, Uruguay, y Paraguay: Bibliografía y antología crítica*, edited by Carlos García and Dieter Reichardt, 243–52. Madrid: Iberoamericana, 2004.

Geist, Anthony L., and José B. Monleón, eds. *Modernism and Its Margins: Reinscribing Cultural Modernity from Spain and Latin America*. New York: Garland, 1999.

"Giacometti in South America." Foundation Alberto et Annette Giacometti. Accessed August 3, 2015. http://www.fondation-giacometti.fr/en/art/38/actualites/180/giacometti-in-south-america/.

Girondo, Oliverio. "Manifiesto Martín Fierro." *Martín Fierro* (Buenos Aires) 1, no. 4 (May 1924): 25–26. Translated by Patrick Frank in *Readings in Latin American Modern Art*, edited by Patrick Frank, 12–14. New Haven: Yale University Press, 2004.

Girondo, Oliverio, Evar Méndez, Alberto Prebisch, and Eduardo J. Bullrich. *El periódico Martín Fierro 1924–1949*. Buenos Aires: Comisión directiva de la sociedad argentina de escritores, 1949.

Goldman, Arnold. "Elliot Paul's 'Transition' Years: 1926–28." *James Joyce Quarterly* 30, no. 2 (Winter 1993): 241–75.

Goldman, Jane. *Modernism, 1910–1945: Image to Apocalypse*. New York: Palgrave Macmillan, 2004.

Goldman, Shifra M. *Dimensions of the Americas: Art and Social Change in Latin America and the United States*. Chicago: University of Chicago Press, 1994.

Gómez Carrillo, Enrique. "Dos palabras al lector." *El Nuevo Mercurio* (Barcelona), no. 1 (January 1907): 3–4.

————. "Una 'enquête' sobre el modernismo: A los escritores de España y de América." *El Nuevo Mercurio* (Barcelona), no. 2 (February 1907): 123–24.

Gómez de la Serna, Ramón. "Variaciones: El héroe Felipe Marinetti." *El Sol* (Madrid) (February 11, 1928): 1.

González, Aníbal. *A Companion to Spanish American Modernismo*. Suffolk, UK: Tamesis, 2007.

González, Robert Alexander. *Designing Pan-America: U.S. Architectural Visions for the Western Hemisphere*. Austin: University of Texas Press, 2011.

Grecia (Seville and Madrid) 1–3, nos. 1–69 (1918–20).

Green, Jonathan. "Introduction to *Camera Work*: A Critical Anthology." 1973. In *The Camera Viewed: Writing on Contemporary Photography*, edited by Peninah R. Petruck, 1–32. New York: Dutton, 1979.

Greenberg, Clement. "Avant-Garde and Kitsch." *Partisan Review* (New York) 6, no. 5 (Fall 1939): 34–49.

————. "Modernist Painting." In *The Collected Essays and Criticism*, vol. 4, *Modernism with a Vengeance*, 85–94. Chicago: University of Chicago Press, 1993.

Greet, Michele. *Beyond National Identity: Pictorial Indigenism as a Modernist Strategy in Andean Art, 1920–1960*. University Park: Penn State University Press, 2009.

————. "Transatlantic Encounters." Accessed February 20, 2015. http://chnm.gmu.edu/transatlanticencounters.

————. *Transatlantic Encounters: Latin American Artists in Paris Between the Wars*. New Haven: Yale University Press, forthcoming.

Groupe de Recherche d'Art Visuel. "Une journée dans la rue." April 1966. Julio Le Parc Archive. Documents of 20th-Century Latin American and Latino Art at the International Center for the Arts of the Americas at the Museum of Fine Arts, Houston. Accessed May 4, 2012. http://icaadocs.mfah.org/icaadocs/THEARCHIVE/FullRecord/tabid/88/doc/773166/language/en-US/Default.aspx.

Hanneken, Jamie. "Going Mundial: What It Really Means to Desire Paris." *Modern Language Quarterly* 71, no. 2 (June 2010): 129–52.

Harris, Derek, ed. *The Spanish Avant-Garde*. Manchester: Manchester University Press, 1995.

Harrison, Charles, Paul Wood, and Jason Gaiger, eds. *Art in Theory, 1815–1900: An Anthology of Changing Ideas*. Oxford: Blackwell, 1998.

Harrison, Joseph, and Alan Hoyle, eds. *Spain's 1898 Crisis: Regenerationism, Modernism, Postcolonialism*. Manchester: Manchester University Press, 2000.

Heller, Ben A. *Assimilation/Generation/Resurrection: Contrapuntal Readings in the Poetry of José Lezama Lima*. Lewisburg, PA: Bucknell University Press, 1997.

Hemingway, Ernest. *A Moveable Feast*. New York: Macmillan, 1964.

Henderson, Linda. *Duchamp in Context: Science and Technology in the Large Glass and Related Works*. Princeton: Princeton University Press, 1998.

Hernando, Miguel Ángel. *La Gaceta Literaria (1927–1932): Biografía y valoración.* Valladolid: Universidad de Valladolid, 1974.

Hitz, Rubén. "*Martín Fierro* en la vanguardia argentina." In *Revistas culturales latinoamericanas, 1920–1960,* edited by Lydia Elizalde, 65–83. Mexico City: Universidad Iberoamericana, 2008.

Hoffman, Frederick J., Charles Allen, and Carolyn F. Ulrich. *The Little Magazine: A History and a Bibliography.* Princeton: Princeton University Press, 1946.

Hofmann, Irene E. "Documents of Dada and Surrealism: Dada and Surrealist Journals in the Mary Reynolds Collection." Ryerson and Burnham Libraries. The Art Institute of Chicago, 2001, 1–26. Accessed February 1, 2011. http://www.artic.edu/reynolds/essays /hofmann2.php.

Huret, Jules. *Enquête sur la question sociale en Europe.* Paris: Librairie académique Perrin et Didier, 1892.

———. *Enquête sur l'évolution littéraire.* Paris: Bibliothèque Charpentier, 1891.

Huyssen, Andreas. *After the Great Divide: Modernism, Mass Culture, Postmodernism.* Bloomington: Indiana University Press, 1986.

———. "Geographies of Modernism in a Globalizing World." In *Geographies of Modernism: Literatures, Cultures, Spaces,* edited by Peter Brooker and Andrew Thacker, 6–18. New York: Taylor and Francis, 2005.

Ichaso, Francisco. "Balance de una indagación." *Revista de Avance* (Havana) 4, no. 38 (September 15, 1929): 258–65.

Imán (Paris), no. 1 (April 1931).

"Inquiry Among European Writers into the Spirit of America." *transition* (Paris), no. 13 (Summer 1928).

"Inquiry on Dialectical Materialism." *Dyn* (Mexico City), no. 2 (July–August 1942).

The International Dada Archive. http://sdrc.lib.uiowa.edu /dada/collection.html.

"In What Ways Have Artists, Academics, and Cultural Institutions Responded to the U.S.-Led Invasion and Occupation of Iraq?" *October* (New York), no. 23 (Winter 2008).

"Is Newness Still New?" *Brooklyn Rail* (Brooklyn) (August 1, 2012). Accessed June 19, 2015. http://www.brooklynrail .org/2012/08/artseen/is-newness-still-new.

"Is Painting Still Vital, or Is It a Dead Language?" *Flash Art* (Milan), no. 291 (July–September 2013). Accessed June 19, 2015. http://www.flashartonline.com/article/ten-questions-about-painting-2/.

Jewell, Edward Alden. "Again a Storm Rages Over 'Modern Art.'" New York Times Magazine (February 22, 1931): 12–13, 21.

Jolas, Eugene. "Documento." Trans. Manuel Altolaguierre. *Imán* (Paris), no. 1 (April 1931): 123–27.

———. *Eugene Jolas: Critical Writings, 1924–1951.* Edited by Klaus H. Kiefer and Rainer Rumold. Evanston: Northwestern University Press, 2009.

———. Glossary (column). *transition,* nos. 4–22 (1927–33).

———. *Man from Babel.* Edited by Andreas Kramer and Rainer Rumold. New Haven: Yale University Press, 1998.

———. "On the Quest." *transition* (Paris), no. 9 (December 1927): 190–95.

———. Rambles Through Literary Paris. *Chicago Tribune* (Paris), nos. 17–26 (1924–25).

———. Response to "Open Letter to the Editor." *transition* (Paris), no. 15 (February 1929): 154–56.

———. "The Revolution of Language and James Joyce." *transition* (Paris), no. 11 (February 1928): 112–15.

———. "Suggestions for a New Magic." *transition* (Paris), no. 3 (June 1927): 178–79.

———. "Super-Occident." *transition* (Paris), no. 15 (November 1929): 11–16.

———. "Transatlantic Letter." *transition* (Paris), no. 13 (Summer 1928): 276–77.

———, ed. *transition workshop.* New York: Viking Press, 1949.

Jolas, Eugene, Kay Boyle, Whit Burnett, Hart Crane, Caresse Crosby, Harry Crosby, Martha Foley, Stuart Gilbert, A. I. Gillespie, Leigh Hoffman, Elliot Paul, Douglas Rigby, Theo Rutra, Robert Sage, Harold J. Salemson, and Laurence Vail. "Proclamation: Revolution of the Word." *transition,* nos. 16–17 (Paris, June 1929): 13.

Jolas, Eugene, and Elliot Paul. "Introduction." *transition* (Paris), no. 1 (April 1927): 135–38.

———. "K.O.R.A.A." *transition* (Paris), no. 3 (June 1927): 173–77.

———. "A Review." *transition,* no. 12 (March 1928): 139–47.

Jolas, Eugene, and Maria Jolas Papers. General Collection, Beinecke Rare Book and Manuscript Library, Yale University.

Jolas, Eugene, and Robert Sage, eds. *Transition Stories: Twenty-Three Stories from "transition."* 1929. Freeport, N.Y.: Books for Libraries Press, 1972.

Jolas, Maria. *Maria Jolas, Woman of Action: A Memoir and Other Writings.* Edited by Mary Ann Caws. Columbia: University of South Carolina Press, 2004.

Josephson, Matthew. *Life Among the Surrealists.* New York: Holt, Rinehart and Winston, 1962.

Joyce, James. *Finnegans Wake.* 1939. New York: Penguin, 1976.

Jrade, Cathy L. *Modernismo, Modernity, and the Development of Spanish American Literature.* Austin: University of Texas Press, 1998.

Kafka, Franz. "The Sentence." Translated by Eugene and Maria Jolas. *transition,* no. 11 (February 1928): 35–47.

Kant, Immanuel. "Beantwortung der Frage: Was ist Aufklärung?" *Berlinische Monatsschrift* (December 1784): 481–94. Translated by H. B. Nisbet. In *Kant: Political Writings,* edited by Hans Reiss, 2nd ed., 54–60. Cambridge: Cambridge University Press, 1991.

Kapcia, Antoni. *Havana: The Making of Cuban Culture.* Oxford: Berg, 2005.

———. "Revolution, the Intellectual, and a Cuban Identity: The Long Tradition." *Bulletin of Latin American Research* 1, no. 2 (May 1982): 63–78.

Karl, Frederick R. *Modern and Modernism: The Sovereignty of the Artist, 1885–1925.* New York: Atheneum, 1985.

Kennedy, Gerald. *Imagining Paris: Exile, Writing, and American Identity.* New Haven: Yale University Press, 1993.

Kindley, Evan. *questionnaire (Object Lessons).* New York: Bloomsbury Academic, 2016.

Kolbowski, Silvia. "The Magazine as Medium 2: The Questionnaire." Panelists: Hal Foster and Silvia Kolbowski. Moderated by Lori Cole. May 11, 2015. http ://cabinetmagazine.org/events/conaty_cole_foster _fox_graham_kolbowski_snyder_stein_sussler.php.

Kolocotroni, Vassiliki, Jane Goldman, and Olga Taxidou, eds. *Modernism: An Anthology of Sources and Documents.* Chicago: University of Chicago Press, 1998.

Krauss, Rosalind, Yve-Alain Bois, Benjamin Buchloh, and Hal Foster. *Art Since 1900: Modernism, Antimodernism, Postmodernism.* London: Thames and Hudson, 2005.

Kroiz, Lauren. *Creative Composites: Modernism, Race, and the Stieglitz Circle.* Berkeley: University of California Press, 2012.

Kuo, Michelle. Response to "Questionnaire on 'The Contemporary.'" *October* (New York), no. 130 (Fall 2009): 28–29.

Lafleur, Héctor René, and Sergio D. Provenzano, and Fernando Alonso, eds. *Las revistas literarias argentinas, 1893–1967.* Buenos Aires: Ediciones El 8vo. loco, 2006.

Larionov, Mikhail, and Natalya Goncharova. "Rayonists and Futurists: A Manifesto." 1913. Translated by John E. Bowlt. In *Manifesto: A Century of Isms,* edited by Mary Ann Caws, 240–44. Lincoln: University of Nebraska Press, 2001.

Larson, Susan, and Eva Woods, eds. *Visualizing Spanish Modernity.* New York: Oxford, 2005.

Latham, Sean, and Robert Scholes. "The Rise of Periodical Studies." *PMLA* 121, no. 2 (March 2006): 517–31.

Leiris, Michel. "Alberto Giacometti." *Documents* (Paris), no. 4 (September 1929): 209–14.

"Letras extranjeras." *Revista de Avance* (Havana) 1, no. 3 (April 15, 1927): 50.

Lippard, Lucy, and John Chandler. "The Dematerialization of Art." *Art International* (New York) 12, no. 2 (February 1968): 31–36.

"La littérature française jugée par les écrivains anglais d'aujourd'hui." *Le Gaulois du Dimanche* (Paris) (February 12, 1899).

Lizaso, Félix. "Postales de Cuba. El momento: La vanguardia." *La Gaceta Literaria* (Madrid) 1, no. 15 (August 1, 1927): 5.

Lobo Montalvo, María Luisa, Zoila Lapique Becali, Narciso G. Menocal, and Edward Shaw. "The Years of 'Social.'" *Journal of Decorative and Propaganda Arts* 22 (1996): 104–31.

Loewenstein, C. Jared, and Donald L. Shaw. "*Prisma* I and II." *Hispanic Review* 70, no. 1 (2002): 69–88.

Lucena, Daniela. "La irrupción del arte concreto-invención el el campo artístico de Buenos Aires (1942–1948)." *European Review of Artistic Studies* 2, no. 4 (2011): 78–102.

Lugones, Leopoldo. "Situación del lector: Estética." *Exposición de la actual poesía argentina (1922–1927).* Edited by Pedro-Juan Vignale and César Tiempo. Buenos Aires: Minerva, 1927. Biblioteca Virtual Miguel de Cervantes. Accessed July 15, 2015. http://www .cervantesvirtual.com/obra-visor/exposicion-de-la -actual-poesia-argentina-1922-1927/html/ff3aeef8 -82b1-11df-acc7-002185ce6064_2.html.

Lutyens, Mary. *The Life and Death of Krishnamurti.* London: John Murray, 1990.

Lyon, Janet. *Manifestoes: Provocations of the Modern.* Ithaca: Cornell University Press, 1999.

Machado, Manuel. *La Guerra Literaria 1898–1914.* Madrid: Imprenta Hispano-Alemana, 1913.

Machine-Age Exposition, May 16–28, 1927. Exhibition catalogue. New York: Little Review, 1927.

MacLeish, Archibald. *Collected Poems, 1917–1982.* Boston: Houghton Mifflin, 1985.

Mainer, José-Carlos. "Ernesto Giménez Caballero o la inoportunidad." In Ernesto Giménez Caballero, *Casticismo, nacionalismo, y vanguardia (Antología 1927–1935),* edited by José-Carlos Mainer, xi–lxviii. Santander: Fundación Santander Central Hispano, 2005.

Malevich, Kazimir. "Suprematism." 1927. Translated by Howard Dearstyne. In *Manifesto: A Century of Isms,* edited by Mary Ann Caws, 404. Lincoln: University of Nebraska Press, 2001.

Mañach, Jorge. "Vanguardismo." *Revista de Avance* (Havana) 1, no. 1 (March 15, 1927): 2.

Manrique, Jorge A. "¿Identidad o modernidad?" In *América Latina en sus Artes,* edited by Damián Bayón, 19–33. Mexico: Siglo XXI Editores, 1974.

Mansanti, Celine. "Between Modernisms: *transition* (1927–38)." In *The Oxford Critical and Cultural History of Modernist Magazines,* vol. 2, *North America, 1894–1960,* edited by Peter Brooker and Andrew Thacker, 718–37. Oxford: Oxford University Press, 2009.

Manzoni, Celina, ed. *Vanguardistas en su tinta: Documentos de la vanguardia en América Latina.* Buenos Aires: Ediciones Corregidor, 2007.

Marais, Julian. *El método histórico de las generaciones.* Madrid: Revista de Occidente, 1949.

Mariani, Roberto. "Martín Fierro y yo." *Martín Fierro* (Buenos Aires) 1, no. 7 (July 25, 1924): 46.

Mariátegui, José Carlos. "¿Existe una inquietud propia de nuestra época?" *Mundial* (Lima) (March 29, 1930): 30. Accessed May 21, 2015. https://www.marxists.org /espanol/mariateg/oc/el_artista_y_la_epoca/paginas /existe%20una%20inquietud%20propia.htm.

Marinello, Juan. *Sobre la inquietud cubana.* Havana: Revista de Avance, 1930.

Marinello, Juan, Jorge Mañach, Martí Casanovas, Francisco Ichaso, and Alejo Carpentier. "Notas sobre Revista de Avance." In *Índice de Revistas Cubanas,* vol. 2. Havana: Biblioteca Nacional José Martí, 1969.

"Marinetti." *Nosotros* (Buenos Aires) 23, no. 205 (June 1926): 154–62.

Marinetti, Filippo Tommaso. *Enquête internationale sur le vers libre et Manifeste du futurism.* Milan: Éditions de Poesia, 1909.

———. "España veloz: Poema en palabra libre (fragmento)." *La Gaceta Literaria* (Madrid), no. 39 (August 1, 1928): 1.

———. "Fondation et manifeste du Futurisme." *Le Figaro* (Paris) (February 20, 1909).

———. "The Founding and Manifesto of Futurism." 1909. In *Futurist Manifestos*, edited by Umbro Apollonio, translated by Robert Brain, 19–24. 1973. Boston: MFA Publications, 2001.

———. "Fundación y Manifiesto del Futurismo." Translated by Ramón Gómez de la Serna. *Prometeo* (Madrid) 2, no. 6 (April 1909): 65–73.

———. "Proclama futurista a los españoles." Translated by Ramón Gómez de la Serna. *Prometeo* (Madrid) 3, no. 20 (1910): 1–2.

Martí, José. "Nuestra América." *La Revista Ilustrada de Nueva York* (New York) (January 10, 1891) and *El Partido Liberal* (Mexico City) (January 30, 1891). Translated by J. A. Sierra. Accessed June 17, 2011. http://www.historyofcuba.com/history/marti/America.htm.

Martinenche, Ernest, Charles Lesca, and Ventura García Calderón. "Editorial statement." *La Revue de l'Amérique Latine* (Paris) 1, no. 1 (January 1922): 2.

Martínez, Juan A. *Cuban Art and National Identity: The Vanguardia Painters, 1927–1950.* Gainesville: University Press of Florida, 1994.

Mártinez, Rafael Arévalo. "The Man Who Resembled a Horse." Translated by William Carlos Williams. *Little Review* (New York) 5, no. 8 (December 1918): 42–53.

Martínez Ruíz, José Augusto Trinidad ("Azorín"). "La generación del '98." In *Clásicos y Modernos*, 310–11. Madrid: Renacimiento, 1913.

Martínez Villena, Rubén, José Antonio Fernández de Castro, Calixto Masó, Félix Lizaso, Francisco Ichaso, Luis Gómez Wanguemert, Juan Marinello Vidaurreta, José Z. Tallet, José Manuel Acosta, Jorge Mañach, Enrique Serpa, Agustín Acosta, Emilio Roig de Leuchsenring, María Villar Buceta, Mariblanca Sabas Alomá, Antonio Gattorno, José Hyrtado de Mendoza, Otto Blumhe, Alejo Carpentier, Orosmán Viamantes, Juan Antiga, Arturo Alfonso Roselló, Juan José Sicre, Diego Bonilla, Conrado W. Massaguer, Eduardo Abela, Luis López Méndez, Armando Maribona, Guillermo Martínez Márquez, A. T. Quílez, F. de Ibarzábal, Juan Luis Martín, Martí Casanovas, Luis A. Baralt, and Felipe Pichardo Moya. "Declaración del grupo minorista." *Carteles* (Havana), no. 21 (May 22, 1927): 16, 25. Accessed June 24, 2011. http://www.cubaliteraria.cu/monografia/grupo_minorista/declaracion.html.

Martínez Villena, Rubén, José Antonio Fernández de Castro, Calixto Masó, Félix Lizaso, Alberto Lamar Schweyer, Francisco Ichaso, Luis Gómez Wanguemert, Juan Marinello Vidaurreta, José Z. Tallet, José Manuel Acosta, Primitivo Cordero Leyva, Jorge Mañach, and J. L.

García Pedrosa. "La Protesta de los Trece," (Havana) (March 1, 1923). In *Vanguardias en su tinta: Documentos de la vanguardia en América Latina*, edited by Celina Manzoni, 109–10. Buenos Aires: Corregidor, 2007.

Marx, Karl, and Frederick Engels. *Manifesto of the Communist Party.* 1848. Edited by Frederick Engels. New York: International Publishers, 1994.

Masiello, Francine. "Argentine Literary Journalism: The Production of a Critical Discourse." *Latin American Research Review* 20, no. 1 (1985): 27–60.

———. *Lenguaje e ideología: Las escuelas de vanguardia en Argentina.* Buenos Aires: Hachette, 1986.

———. "Rethinking Neocolonial Esthetics: Literature, Politics, and Intellectual Community in Cuba's *Revista de Avance.*" *Latin American Research Review* 28, no. 2 (1993): 3–31.

Mata, Rodolfo. "Contemporáneo, 3. Polémica en torno a la generación de vanguardia, 1932." May 30, 2001. Centro Virtual Cervantes. Accessed August 5, 2015. http://cvc.cervantes.es/el_rinconete/anteriores/mayo_01/30052001_02.htm.

McCarthy, Eamon. "Flirting with Futurism: Norah Borges and the Avant-Garde." In "Women Futurists and Women Artists Influenced by Futurism," special issue, *International Yearbook of Futurism Studies* 5 (2015): 111–36.

McMillan, Douglas. *Transition: The History of a Literary Era, 1927–1938.* New York: George Braziller, 1976.

McShine, Kynaston, ed. *Information.* New York: Museum of Modern Art, 1970.

Mejías-López, Alejandro. *The Inverted Conquest: The Myth of Modernity and the Transatlantic Onset of Modernism.* Nashville: Vanderbilt University Press, 2010.

Mendelsohn-Martone, Leatrice. *Paragoni: Benedetto Varchi's "Due lezzioni" and Cinquecento Art Theory.* Ann Arbor: UMI Research Press, 1982.

Mendelson, Jordana. *Documenting Spain: Artists, Exhibition Culture, and the Modern Nation.* University Park: Penn State University Press, 2005.

——— *Revistas y Guerra, 1936–1939 / Magazines and War, 1936–1939.* Madrid: Museo Nacional Centro de Arte Reina Sofia, 2007.

Mendelson, Jordana, L. Elena Delgado, and Oscar Vázquez. "Introduction: Recalcitrant Modernities—Spain, Cultural Difference, and the Location of Modernism." *Journal of Iberian and Latin American Studies* 13, nos. 2–3 (August/December 2007): 105–19.

Mendelson, Jordana, and Estrella de Diego. "Political Practice and the Arts in Spain, 1927–1936." In *Art and Journals on the Political Front, 1910–1940*, edited by Virginia Hagelstein Marquardt, 183–214. Gainesville: University Press of Florida, 1997.

Méndez, Evar. "Rol de 'Martín Fierro' en la renovación poética actual." In *Exposición de la actual poesía argentina (1922–1927)*, xi–xviii. Buenos Aires: Minerva, 1927.

Meyer, Richard. *When Was Contemporary Art?* Cambridge, Mass.: MIT Press, 2013.

Mignolo, Walter D. *The Idea of Latin America*. Oxford: Blackwell, 2005.

———. "The Many Faces of Cosmo-polis: Border Thinking and Critical Cosmopolitanism." *Public Culture* 12, no. 3 (2000): 721–48.

Miller, Henry. *Mémoires, Plaidoiries et Documents*. New York: New Directions, 1969.

———. *Tropic of Cancer*. 1934. New York: Grove Press, 1961.

Millner, Caille. "Alfredo Jaar and the Happiness of Chile." *Los Angeles Review of Books* (December 8, 2013). Accessed June 15, 2015. http://lareviewofbooks.org /essay/alfredo-jaar-and-the-happiness-of-chile.

The Modernist Journals Project. http://dl.lib.brown.edu /mjp/.

The Modernist Magazines Project. http://www .modernistmagazines.com/.

Monk, Craig. "Beckett Is Vertical: Proselytizing with the Littles." *Canadian Journal of Irish Studies* 27, no. 2 (Fall 2001): 8–19.

———. "Eugene Jolas and the Translation Policies of Transition." *Mosaic* (Winnipeg) 32, no. 4 (December 1999): 17–34.

———. "Exile." In *The Ezra Pound Encyclopedia*, edited by Demetres P. Tryphonopoulos and Stephen J. Adams, 113–14. Westport, Conn.: Greenwood Press, 2005.

———. *Writing the Lost Generation*. Iowa City: University of Iowa Press, 2008.

Monro, Harold. "Three Questions Regarding the Necessity, the Function, and the Form of Poetry." *Chapbook* (London), no. 27 (July 1922).

Montgomery, Harper. *The Mobility of Modernism: Art and Criticism in 1920s Latin America*. Austin: University of Texas Press, 2017.

Moore, Robin D. *Nationalizing Blackness: Afrocubanismo and Artistic Revolution in Havana, 1920–1940*. Pittsburgh: University of Pittsburgh Press, 1997.

Moréas, Jean. "The Symbolist Manifesto." 1886. Translated by Mary Ann Caws. In *Manifesto: A Century of Isms*, edited by Mary Ann Caws, 50. Lincoln: University of Nebraska Press, 2001.

Morice, Charles. "Enquête sur les tendances actuelles des arts plastiques." *Mercure de France* (Paris) 56, no. 193 (August 1, 1905): 34–49.

Morrisson, Mark. *The Public Face of Modernism: Little Magazines, Audiences, and Reception, 1905–1920*. Madison: University of Wisconsin Press, 2001.

Morton, Patricia A. *Hybrid Modernities: Architecture and Representation at the 1931 Colonial Exposition, Paris*. Cambridge, Mass.: MIT Press, 2000.

Monoskop's collection of magazines. http://monoskop.org /Magazines.

Mosquera, Gerardo. "Africa in the Art of Latin America." *Art Journal* 51, no. 4 (1992): 30–38.

Motherwell, Robert, ed. *The Dada Painters and Poets*. 2nd ed. Boston: Wittenborn and Schultz, 1951.

Müller-Bergh, Klaus. "Corrientes vanguardistas y surrealismo en la obra de Alejo Carpentier." *Revista Hispánica Moderna* 35, no. 4 (October–December, 1969): 223–340.

———. "Indagación del vanguardismo de las Antillas: Cuba, Puerto Rico, Santo Domingo, Haiti." In *Prosa Hispánica de vanguardia*, edited by Fernando Burgo, 55–76. Madrid: Orígines, 1986.

Müller-Bergh, Klaus, and Gilberto Mendonça Teles, eds. *Vanguardia latinoamericana: Historia, crítica, y documentos*. Vol. 2, *Caribe, Antillas Mayores y Menores*. Madrid: Iberoamericana, 2002.

———. *Vanguardia latinoamericana: Historia, crítica, y documentos*. Vol. 5, *Chile y países del Plata: Argentina, Uruguay, Paraguay*. Madrid: Iberoamericana, 2009.

Mussolini, Benito. "Marinetti y Mussolini: Telegrama de un duce a otro." *La Gaceta Literaria* (Madrid), no. 28 (February 15, 1928): 3.

"The Negro in Art: How Shall He Be Portrayed? A Symposium." *Crisis* (New York) 31, no. 5 (March 1926).

Nelson, Daniel E. "Norah Borges: On the Margins of the Text." In *A Woman's Gaze: Latin American Women Artists*, edited by Marjorie Agosín, 29–54. Fredonia, N.Y.: White Pine Press, 1998.

Nicholls, Peter. *Modernisms: A Literary Guide*. 2nd ed. 1995. New York: Palgrave Macmillan, 2009.

Noé, Julio, ed. *Antología de la poesía argentina moderna (1900–1925)*. Buenos Aires: Nosotros, 1926.

Nosotros. (Buenos Aires), 1907–34; 1936–43.

Novas Calvo, Lino. "Cuba Literaria II." *La Gaceta Literaria* (Madrid) 5, no. 118 (November 15, 1931): 2.

"Nuestra encuesta sobre la nueva generación literaria." *Nosotros* (Buenos Aires) 44, no. 168 (May 1923)–45, no. 172 (December 1923).

El Nuevo Mercurio (Barcelona) 1, nos. 1–6 (1907).

Ogando, Mónica Andrea, and Ricardo Ernesto Paramos. "Nosotros." In *Historia de Revistas Argentinas*, vol. 2. Buenos Aires: AAER, 1995–99. Accessed July 25, 2015. http://www.learevistas.com/notaHistoria.php?nota=19.

Ogorzaly, Michael A. *Waldo Frank: Prophet of Hispanic Regeneration*. Lewisburg: Bucknell University Press, 1994.

Ortega y Gasset, José. "El deber de la nueva generación argentina." *La Nación* (Buenos Aires) (April 6, 1924): 2.

———. "La deshumanización del arte." In *Obras Completas*, vol. 3, 353–86. Madrid: Revista de Occidente, 1947.

———. "Generación contra generación." *La Nación* (Buenos Aires) (June 28, 1924).

———. "Las revistas: el tema de nuestro tiempo." *Nosotros* (Buenos Aires) 43, no. 165 (February 1923): 251–58.

———. "El tema de nuestro tiempo." 1923. In *Obras Completas*, vol. 3, 143–242. Madrid: Revista de Occidente, 1955.

Ortelli, Roberto A., Alfredo Brandán Caraffa, Homero Guglielmini, and Roberto Smith. "Incial." *Inicial* (Buenos Aires) 1, no. 1 (October 1923): 3–5.

Osuna, Rafael. *Revistas de la vanguardia española*. Sevilla: Editorial Renacimiento, 2005.

———. *Las revistas españolas entre dos dictaduras: 1931–1939.* Valencia: Pre-textos, 1986.

"Our Country and Our Culture: A Symposium." *Partisan Review* (New York) 19, no. 3 (May–June 1952).

"Où va la peinture" *Commune* (Paris) 2, nos. 21–22 (May and June 1935).

"Painters Reply." *Artforum* (New York) 14, no. 1 (September 1975): 26–37.

Paniagua, Domingo. *Revistas culturales contemporáneas I. De "Germinal" a "Prometeo."* Madrid: Punta Europea, 1964.

———. *Revistas culturales contemporáneas II. El ultraísmo en España.* Madrid: Punta Europea, 1970.

"Paris, centre mondial des arts." *L'Intransigeant* (Paris) 49, no. 17.948 (December 10, 1928): 5.

Patterson, Benjamin. *Questionnaire* from *Flux Year Box 2*, ca. 1968. In *Thing/Thought: Fluxus Editions, 1962–1978.* New York: Museum of Modern Art. Accessed May 4, 2012. http://www.moma.org/interactives /exhibitions/2011/fluxus_editions/works /questionnaire-from-flux-year-box-2/.

Paul, Elliot. "Stuart Davis, American Painter." *transition* (Paris), no. 14 (Fall 1928): 146–49.

Payne, Stanley G. *Fascism in Spain, 1923–1977.* Madison: University of Wisconsin Press, 1999.

Pérez Ferrero, Miguel. "Una encuesta sensacional: ¿Qué es la vanguardia?" *La Gaceta Literaria* (Madrid) 4, no. 83 (June 1930): 1.

Pérez-Oramas, Luis, ed. *Joaquín Torres-García: The Arcadian Modern.* New York: Museum of Modern Art, 2015.

"Periodical Tables (Parts 1, 2, and 3)." *frieze* (London), no. 100 (June–August 2006). Accessed June 15, 2015. https://frieze.com/article/periodical-tables-part-1, https://frieze.com/article/periodical-tables-part-2, and https://frieze.com/article/periodical-tables-part-3.

Perloff, Marjorie. *Differentials: Poetry, Poetics, Pedagogy.* Tuscaloosa: University of Alabama Press, 2004.

Phillips, Patricia C., ed. *Mierle Laderman Ukeles: Maintenance Art.* New York: Prestel, 2016.

Picabia, Francis. "Picabia, Art Rebel, Here to Teach New Movement." Interview. *New York Times,* February 16, 1913.

Picard, Gaston. "Grands Articles et grandes enquêtes de la saison." In *L'ami du lettré,* 56–66. Paris: Bernard Grasset, 1927.

Pini, Ivonne. "Aproximación a la idea de 'Lo propio' en el arte latinoamericano a fines del siglo XIX y comienzos del siglo XX." *Historica crítica,* no. 13 (December 1997): 5–15.

Pizer, Donald. *American Expatriate Writing and the Paris Moment: Modernism and Place.* Baton Rouge: Louisiana State University Press, 1996.

"Poemas ultraístas." *Nosotros* (Buenos Aires) 42, no. 160 (September 1922): 55–62.

Poggioli, Renato. *The Theory of the Avant-Garde.* Translated by Gerald Fitzgerald. Cambridge, Mass.: Harvard University Press, 1968.

Porter, Theodore M., and Dorothy Ross, eds. *The Cambridge History of Science: The Modern Social Sciences.* Cambridge: University of Cambridge Press, 2003.

Poulaille, Henri. "Avons-nous une culture internationale? Enquête d'Henri Poulaille." *Les images de Paris,* nos. 65–66 (February–April 1926).

Pound, Ezra. Response to *Authors Take Sides on the Spanish War,* 25–26.

———. "Small Magazines." *English Journal* 19, no. 9 (November 1930): 689–704.

"Pour qui écrivez-vous?" *Commune* (Paris), nos. 5–6 (January–February 1934).

Pratt, Mary Louise. "Modernity and Periphery: Towards a Global and Relational Analysis." In *Beyond Dichotomies: Histories, Identities, Cultures, and the Challenges of Globalization,* edited by Elizabeth Mudimbe-Boyi, 21–49. Albany: State University of New York Press, 2002.

Prieto, Adolfo, ed. *El periódico Martín Fierro.* Buenos Aires: Ediciones Galerna, 1968.

Prisma: Revista Mural (Buenos Aires) 1, nos. 1–2 (November 1921–March 1922).

Proa (Buenos Aires) 1, nos. 1–3 (August 1922–July 1923).

Proa (Buenos Aires) 1–2, nos. 1–15 (August 1924–December 1925).

Proust, Marcel. "Salon Confidences Écrit par Marcel." *La Revue Illustrée* 15 (1892).

"Proust Questionnaire." *Vanity Fair.* Accessed May 4, 2012. http://www.vanityfair.com/culture/features /proust-questionnaire.

Puchner, Martin. *Poetry of the Revolution: Marx, Manifestos, and the Avant-Gardes.* Princeton: Princeton University Press, 2006.

Putnam, Samuel. *Paris Was Our Mistress: Memoirs of a Lost and Found Generation.* 1947. Carbondale: Southern Illinois University Press, 1970.

"¿Qué es el modernismo?" *El Nuevo Mercurio* (Barcelona) 1, no. 2 (February 1907): 123–24.

"¿Qué es la vanguardia?" *La Gaceta Literaria* (Madrid), nos. 83–86 (June–July 1930) and no. 94 (November 1930).

"¿Qué somos? Cómo somos?" *Índice* (San Juan) 1, no. 8 (November 1929): 114.

"Questionnaire." *Internationale Situationniste* (Paris), no. 9 (August 1964). Accessed May 4, 2012. http://www.cddc .vt.edu/sionline/si/questionnaire.html.

"Questionnaire: The Cost of Letters." *Horizon* (London) 14, no. 81 (September 1946).

"A Questionnaire on Materialisms." *October* (New York), no. 155 (Winter 2016).

"Questions of Feminism." *October* (New York), no. 71 (Winter 1995).

Rama, Ángel. *Ciudad Letrada.* Hanover, N.H.: Ediciones del norte, 1984.

———. "El primer cuento de Alejo Carpentier." *Hispamérica* 3, no. 9 (February 1975): 83–86.

———. *Rubén Darío y el modernismo.* 1970. Caracas: Alfadil, 1985.

Ramírez, Mari Carmen, and Héctor Olea, eds. *Inverted Utopias: Avant-Garde Art in Latin America.* Houston: Museum of Fine Arts Houston, 2004.

Ramírez, Mari Carmen, Héctor Olea, Tomás Ybarra-Frausto, María C. Gaztambide, and Melina Kervandjian, eds. *Resisting Categories: Latin American and/or Latino?* Critical Documents of 20th-Century Latin American Art, vol. 1. Houston: Museum of Fine Arts, Houston International Center for the Arts of the Americas, 2012.

Ramos, Julio. *Divergent Modernities: Culture and Politics in Nineteenth-Century Latin America.* Translated by John D. Blanco. Durham: Duke University Press, 2001.

Revista de Avance (Havana) 1–4, nos. 1–45 (March 1927–January 1930).

Revista Martín Fierro 1924–1927: Edición Facsímilar. Buenos Aires: Fondo Nacional de las Artes, 1995.

"Revistas Extranjeras." *Revista de Avance* (Havana) 4, no. 37 (August 15, 1929): 250–51.

"The Richard Mutt Case." *The Blind Man* (New York), no. 2 (May 1917): 4–5.

Richter, Hans. *Dada: Art and Anti-Art.* Translated by David Britt. New York: Oxford University Press, 1978.

Riding, Laura. "The New Barbarism and Gertrude Stein." *transition* (Paris), no. 3 (June 1927): 153–68.

Rincón, Carlos. "Carpentier, 'extranjero indeseable.'" *Revista de Crítica Literaria Latinoamericana* 34, no. 68 (2008): 185–200.

———. "Carpentier 'Frances,': *Documents, Bifur, Un Cadavre,* y dos cartas a Georges Bataille." *Nuevo Crítico* 22, nos. 42–43 (2009): 101–21.

Ripoll, Carlos. *La generación del 23 en Cuba y otros apuntes sobre el vanguardismo.* New York: Las Américas, 1968.

———. *Índice de la Revista de Avance: Cuba 1927–1930.* New York: Las Américas, 1969.

———. "*La Revista de Avance* (1927–1930): Vocero de vanguardismo y pórtico de revolución." *Revista Iberoamericana* 30, no. 58 (July–December 1964): 261–82.

Rivera, Diego, and Bertram Wolfe. *Portrait of America.* New York: Covici-Friede, 1934.

Rogers, Gayle. *Modernism and the New Spain: Britain, Cosmopolitan Europe, and Literary History.* New York: Oxford University Press, 2012.

Rojas Paz, Pablo. "Carta a los Españoles de la Gaceta Literaria." *Martín Fierro* (Buenos Aires) 4, nos. 44–45 (August–November 1927): 385.

Romero, Cira, ed. "El Grupo Minorista. Registro en publicacciones periódicas: La Revista *Social.*" In *Cuba Literaria: Colección Orígines.* Accessed May 8, 2017. http://www.cubaliteraria.cu/monografia/grupo_minorista/social.html.

———, ed. "Memoria iii: La Falange de Acción Cubana." In *Cuba Literaria: Colección Orígines.* Accessed June 24, 2011. http://www.cubaliteraria.cu/monografia/grupo_minorista/memoria3.html.

———, ed. "Los Minoristas. Registro en publicacciones periódicas." In *Cuba Literaria: Colección Orígines.* Accessed May 4, 2012. http://www.cubaliteraria.cu/monografia/grupo_minorista/periodicos.html.

Root, Waverly Louis. "Open Letter to the Editor." *transition* (Paris), no. 15 (February 1929): 151–52.

Rosemont, Franklin, and Robin D. G. Kelley, eds. *Black, Brown, and Beige: Surrealist Writings from Africa and the Diaspora.* Austin: University of Texas Press, 2009.

Said, Edward. "Reflections on Exile." In *Out There: Marginalization and Contemporary Cultures,* edited by Russell Ferguson, Martha Gever, Trinh T. Minh-ha, and Cornel West, 357–67. Cambridge, Mass.: MIT Press, 1990.

Saint Simon, Henri de. "The Artist, the Savant, and the Industrialist." 1825. In *Art in Theory, 1815–1900: An Anthology of Changing Ideas,* edited by Charles Harrison, Paul Wood, and Jason Gaiger, 37–41. Oxford: Blackwell, 1998.

Saítta, Sylvia. "Futurism, Fascism, and Mass-Media: The Case of Marinetti's 1926 Trip to Buenos Aires." *Stanford Humanities Review* 7, no. 1 (1999). Accessed June 12, 2017. https://web.stanford.edu/group/SHR/7-1/html/saitta.html.

Salas, Horacio. "El salto a la modernidad." In *Revista Martín Fierro 1924–1927: Edición Facsímilar,* viii–xv. Buenos Aires: Fondo Nacional de las Artes, 1995.

Sandler, Irving. "Art Criticism Today." *Brooklyn Rail* (Brooklyn) (December 2012). Accessed June 17, 2015. http://www.brooklynrail.org/2012/12/editorsmessage/art-criticism-today.

———. "Is There a New Academy?" *ARTnews* (New York) 58, no. 4 (Summer 1959): 34–37; 58–60.

Sandler, Irving, and Barbara Rose. "Is There a Sensibility of the 1960s?" Cited in Robert Smithson, *The Writings of Robert Smithson: Essays with Illustrations,* edited by Nancy Holt, introduction by Philip Leider, 216–17. New York: New York University Press, 1979.

Sarlo, Beatriz. *Borges, a Writer on the Edge.* 1993. Borges Studies Online. J.L. Borges Center for Studies & Documentation.

———. *Jorge Luis Borges: A Writer on the Edge.* 1993. 2nd ed. Edited by John King. London: Verso, 2006.

———. *Martín Fierro (1924–1927): Antología.* Buenos Aires: Carlos Pérez Editor S.A., 1969.

———. *Una Modernidad Periférica: Buenos Aires 1920 y 1930.* Buenos Aires: Ediciones Nueva Vision, 1988.

———. "Vanguardia y criollismo: La aventura de 'Martín Fierro.'" In "Las Vanguardias en América Latina," edited by Nelson Osorio Tejeda, special issue, *Revista de Crítica Literaria Latinoamericana* (Lima) 8, no. 15 (1982): 39–69.

Sarmiento, José Antonio. "Ultra Tenía Razón." In *Ultra.* Madrid: Visor Libros, 1993.

Sebreli, Juan José. *Cuadernos.* Buenos Aires: Sudamérica, 2010.

Scholes, Robert, and Clifford Wulfman. *Modernism in the Magazines: An Introduction.* New Haven: Yale University Press, 2010.

Schwartz, Jorge, ed. *Las vanguardias latinoamericanas: Textos programáticos y críticos*. Madrid: Cátedra, 1991.

Schwartz, Marcy E. *Writing Paris: Urban Topographies of Desire in Contemporary Latin American Fiction*. Albany: State University of New York Press, 1999.

Serrano, Carlos, and Serge Salaün, eds. *Los felices años veinte: España, crisis y modernidad*. Madrid: Marcial Pons, 2006.

Silverman, Renée M. "Questioning the Territory of Modernism: *Ultraísmo* and the Aesthetic of the First Spanish Avant-Garde." *Romanic Review* 97, no. 1 (January 2006): 51–71.

Siskind, Mariano. *Cosmopolitan Desires: Global Modernity and World Literature in Latin America*. Evanston: Northwestern University Press, 2014.

"The Situation in American Writing: Seven Questions." *Partisan Review* (New York) 6, no. 4 (Summer 1939).

Skidmore, Thomas E., Peter H. Smith, and James Green. *Modern Latin America*. 7th ed. New York: Oxford University Press, 2009.

———. *What Is Contemporary Art?* Chicago: University of Chicago Press, 2009.

Smith, Terry. "Introduction: The Contemporaneity Question." In *Antinomies of Art and Culture: Modernity, Postmodernity, Contemporaneity*, eds. Okwui Enwezor, Nancy Condee, and Terry Smith, 1–23. Durham: Duke University Press, 2008.

"The State of American Writing, 1948: A Symposium," *Partisan Review* (New York) 15, no. 8 (August 1948).

Stein, Gertrude. *The Autobiography of Alice B. Toklas*. 1933. New York: Vintage, 1990.

Stein, Gertrude, and Alice B. Toklas Papers. Yale Collection of American Literature. Beinecke Rare Book and Manuscript Library, Yale University.

Stieglitz, Alfred, and Georgia O'Keeffe Archive. Yale Collection of American Literature. Beinecke Rare Book and Manuscript Library, Yale University.

Studio International (London), no. 192 (September 1976).

Toomer, Jean. "Opinions on the Questions of *Cahiers de l'Étoile*." Translated by Robert B. Jones. In *Jean Toomer: Selected Essays and Literary Criticism*, edited by Robert B. Jones, 86–91. Knoxville: University of Tennessee Press, 1996.

Torecilla, Jesús. *La Generación del 98 frente al nuevo fin de siglo*. Amsterdam: Rodopi, 2000.

Torres Bodet, Jaime. "Candido o de la estadística." *Contemporáneos* (Mexico City), no. 1 (June 1928): 82–86.

"Towards the Unknown: Six Points of 'View.'" *View* (New York) 1, nos. 11–12 (February–March 1942).

transition (Paris and The Hague), nos. 1–27 (1927–38).

transition. Papers of the Magazine Transition. Houghton Library, Harvard University.

Turner, Catherine. *Marketing Modernism Between the Two World Wars*. Boston: University of Massachusetts Press, 2003.

Tzara, Tristan. *Seven Dada Manifestos and Lampisteries*. 1916–21. Translated by Barbara Wright. London: Calder, 1977.

Ulla, Noemi. *La Revista "Nosotros."* Buenos Aires: Editorial Galerna, 1969.

Ultra (Madrid, 1919–21). Edición facsímil. Edited by José Antonio Sarmiento and José María Barrera. Madrid: Visor libros, 1993.

Unamuno, Miguel de. Response to "Una 'enquête' sobre el modernismo." *El Nuevo Mercurio* (Barcelona), no. 5 (May 1907): 504–506.

Unruh, Vicky. *Latin American Vanguards: The Art of Contentious Encounters*. Berkeley: University of California Press, 1994.

"Unskirting the Issue." *Art-Rite* (New York), no. 5 (Spring 1974): 6–7.

Valdespino, Andres. *Jorge Mañach y su generación de las letras Cubanas*. Miami: Ediciones Universal, 1971.

Varchi, Benedetto. *Due lezzioni di M. Benedetto Varchi, nella prima delle quali si dichiara un sonetto di M. Michelagnolo Buonarroti: Nella seconda si disputa quale sia piu nobile arte la scultura, o la pittura, con una lettera d'esso Michelagnolo, & piu altri eccellentiss: pittori, et scultori, sopra la quistione sopradetto*. Florence: Lorenzo Torrentino, 1549.

Vásquez, Carmen. "Alejo Carpentier en Paris (1928–1939)." In *Coloquio 2006 Escritores de América Latina en París* (París, 2006). Centro Virtual Cervantes, 101–15. Accessed December 24, 2016. http://cvc.cervantes.es /Ensenanza/biblioteca_ele/aepe/pdf/coloquio_2006 /coloquio_2006_15.pdf.

———. "Le revue '*Imán*.'" In *Mélusine no. III: Marges Non-frontières*, edited by Henri Behar. Lausanne, Switzerland: Editions l'Age d'Homme, 1982.

Vázquez, M. Ángeles. "Las vanguardias en nuestras revistas, Revista Grecia, España." June 1, 2005. Cervantes Institute Accessed May 2, 2012. http://cvc.cervantes.es /el_rinconete/anteriores/enero_05/19012005_02.htm.

Vázquez Pérez, Marléne. "The *Revista de Avance* in Cuban Culture." *Cubanow.net: Cuban Art and Culture*. Accessed December 4, 2010. http://www.cubanow.net/pages /loader.php?sec=7&t=2&item=3349.

Videla, Gloria. "La direccion criollista de la vanguardia." In *Las vanguardias literarias en Argentina, Uruguay, y Paraguay: Bibliografía y antología crítica*, edited by Carlos García and Dieter Reichardt, 217–31. Madrid: Iberoamericana, 2004.

———. *El ultraísmo: Estudios sobre movimientos poéticos de vanguardia en España*. Madrid: Gredos, 1963.

Vignale, Pedro Juan, and César Tiempo. "Justificación." In *Exposición de la actual poesía Argentina 1922–1927*, edited by Pedro Juan Vignale and César Tiempo. Buenos Aires: Minerva, 1927. Biblioteca Virtual Miguel de Cervantes. Accessed July 15, 2015. http://www .cervantesvirtual.com/obra-visor/exposicion-de-la -actual-poesia-argentina-1922-1927/html/ff3aeef8- 82b1-11df-acc7-002185ce6064_2.html.

"Visual Culture Questionnaire." *October* (New York), no. 77 (Summer 1996).

Vroon, Ronald. "The Manifesto as a Literary Genre: Some Preliminary Observations." *International Journal of Slavic Linguistics and Poetics*, no. 38 (1995): 163–73.

Walkowitz, Rebecca. *Cosmopolitan Style: Modernism Beyond the Nation*. New York: Columbia University Press, 2006.

Walkowitz, Rebecca, and Douglas Mao. "New Modernist Studies." *PMLA* 123, no. 3 (May 2008): 737–48.

Weeraperuma, Susunaga. *A Bibliography of the Life and Teachings of Jiddu Krishnamurti*. Leiden: Brill, 1974.

"What Is Americanism? A Symposium on Marxism and the American Tradition." *Partisan Review* (New York) 3 no. 3 (April 1936).

"What Should You Most Like to Do, to Know, to Be?" *Little Review* (Chicago) 12, no. 2 (May 1929).

"Whither the American Writer (A Questionnaire)." *Modern Quarterly* (Baltimore) 6, no. 2 (Summer 1932).

"Who Do You Write For?" *frieze*, no. 148 (June–August 2012).

"Why Do Americans Live in Europe?" *transition* (Paris), no. 14 (Fall 1928).

Wilde, Oscar. Preface to the *The Picture of Dorian Gray*. 1891. New York: Dell, 1967.

Williams, Raymond. *The Politics of Modernism: Against the New Conformists*. Edited by Tony Pinkey. New York: Verso, 1989.

Williams, William Carlos. *By Word of Mouth: Poems from the Spanish, 1916–1959*. Edited by Jonathan Cohen. New York: New Directions, 2011.

———. "The Somnabulists." *transition* (Paris), no. 18 (November 1929): 147–51.

Wilson, Jason. *A Companion to Pablo Neruda: Evaluating Neruda's Poetry*. Rochester, N.Y.: Boydell and Brewer, 2008.

———. *Jorge Luis Borges*. London: Reaktion Books, 2006.

Wood, Paul, ed. *The Challenge of the Avant-Garde*. New Haven: Yale University Press, 1999.

Wright, Ann. "Intellectuals of an Unheroic Period of Cuban History, 1913–1923: The 'Cuba Contemporánea' Group." *Bulletin of Latin American Research* 7, no. 1 (1988): 109–22.

Yúdice, George. "Rethinking the Theory of the Avant-Garde from the Periphery." In *Modernism and Its Margins*, edited by Anthony Geist and José Monleón, 52–80. New York: Garland, 1999.

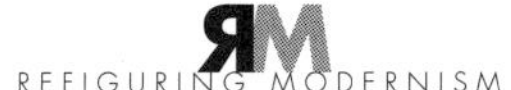

(A SERIES EDITED BY)

Jonathan Eburne

Refiguring Modernism features cutting-edge interdisciplinary approaches to the study of art, literature, science, and cultural history. With an eye to the different modernisms emerging throughout the world during the twentieth century and beyond, we seek to publish scholarship that engages creatively with canonical and eccentric works alike, bringing fresh concepts and original research to bear on modernist cultural production, whether aesthetic, social, or epistemological. What does it mean to study modernism in a global context characterized at once by decolonization and nation-building; international cooperation and conflict; changing ideas about subjectivity and identity; new understandings of language, religion, poetics, and myth; and new paradigms for science, politics, and religion? What did modernism offer artists, writers, and intellectuals? How do we theorize and historicize modernism? How do we rethink its forms, its past, and its futures?

(OTHER BOOKS IN THE SERIES)

David Peters Corbett *The World in Paint: Modern Art and Visuality in England, 1848–1914*

Jordana Mendelson *Documenting Spain: Artists, Exhibition Culture, and the Modern Nation, 1929–1939*

Barbara Larson *The Dark Side of Nature: Science, Society, and the Fantastic in the Work of Odilon Redon*

Alejandro Anreus, Diana L. Linden, and Jonathan Weinberg, eds. *The Social and the Real: Political Art of the 1930s in the Western Hemisphere*

Margaret Iversen *Beyond Pleasure: Freud, Lacan, Barthes*

Stephen Bann, ed. *The Coral Mind: Adrian Stokes's Engagement with Architecture, Art History, Criticism, and Psychoanalysis*

Charles Palermo *Fixed Ecstasy: Joan Miró in the 1920s*

Marius Roux *The Substance and the Shadow*

Aruna D'Souza *Cézanne's Bathers: Biography and the Erotics of Paint*

Abigail Gillman *Viennese Jewish Modernism: Freud, Hofmannsthal, Beer-Hofmann, and Schnitzler*

Stephen Petersen *Space-Age Aesthetics: Lucio Fontana, Yves Klein, and the Postwar European Avant-Garde*

Stefanie Harris *Mediating Modernity: Literature and the "New" Media, 1895–1930*

Michele Greet *Beyond National Identity: Pictorial Indigenism as a Modernist Strategy for Andean Art, 1920–1960*

Paul Smith, ed. *Seurat Re-viewed*

David Prochaska and Jordana Mendelson, eds. *Postcards: Ephemeral Histories of Modernity*

David Getsy *From Diversion to Subversion: Games, Play, and Twentieth-Century Art*

Jessica Burstein *Cold Modernism: Literature, Fashion, Art*

Adam Jolles *The Curatorial Avant-Garde:* Surrealism and Exhibition Practice in France, 1925–1941

Juli Highfill *Modernism and Its Merchandise: The Spanish Avant-Garde and Material Culture, 1920–1930*

Damien Keane *Ireland and the Problem of Information: Irish Writing, Radio, Late Modernist Communication*

Allison Morehead *Nature's Experiments and the Search for Symbolist Form*

Laura Kalba *Color in the Age of Impressionism: Commerce, Technology, and Art*

Catherine Walworth *Soviet Salvage: Imperial Debris, Revolutionary Reuse, and Russian Constructivism*

Jo Applin, Catherine Spencer, and Amy Tobin, eds. *London Art Worlds: Mobile, Contingent, and Ephemeral Networks, 1960–1980*

Erik M. Bachman *Literary Obscenities: U.S. Case Law and Naturalism after Modernism*